ESSENTIAL SCHOOL ATLAS

Map Reading 1
Scale and Direction 2–3
Latitude and Longitude 4–5
Map Reading from Aerial Photographs 6–7
Map Reading from Satellite Imagery 8–9
Earth Observation Satellites 10–11

UNITED KINGDOM AND IRELAND 12–27

United Kingdom and Ireland from Space 12
United Kingdom and Ireland Relief of Land 13
United Kingdom and Ireland Towns and Cities 14
United Kingdom and Ireland Counties and Regions 15
England and Wales 16–17
Scotland 18
Ireland 19
United Kingdom and Ireland Climate 20
United Kingdom and Ireland Geology and Water 21
United Kingdom and Ireland Food 22
United Kingdom and Ireland Energy 23
United Kingdom and Ireland Work 24
United Kingdom and Ireland People 25
United Kingdom and Ireland Travel 26
United Kingdom and Ireland Conservation 27

THE WORLD 28–89

Europe 28–30
Northern Europe 31
Western Europe 32–33
Southern Europe 34–35
Italy 36–37
Asia 38–39
Russia and Northern Asia 40–41
China and the Far East 42–43
China 44
Japan 45
Southern Asia 46–47
Middle East 48–49
Africa 50–51
Nigeria and Ghana 52
Kenya 53
Australia and Oceania 54–55
North America 56–57
United States of America 58–60
Caribbean Hurricanes 61
Mexico, Central America and the Caribbean 62–63
South America 64–65
Brazil 66
The Arctic nd Antarctica 67
World Relief of Land 68–69
World Countries 70–71
World Climate 72–73
World Climate Change 74–75
World Biomes 76–77
World Volcanoes and Earthquakes 78–79
World People 80–81
World Energy 82
World Food 83
World Globalization 84
World Tourism 85
World Statistics 86–89

INDEX 90–97

SUBJECT LIST

Aerial photography 6, 7
Agriculture 22, 83
Airports 26
Antarctic ice 11, 74
Biomes 76, 77
Carbon dioxide emissions 74
Climate change 74, 75
Climate graphs 20, 72
Climate regions 72
Coal 23, 82
Conservation 27, 53
Continental drift 78
Deforestation 77
Desertification 76
Earthquakes 45, 79
Electricity generation 23, 82
Employment 24, 44
Energy production and consumption 23, 49, 82
European Union 30
Fishing 22, 83
Flood risk 21
Food 22, 83
Fuels 23, 49, 52, 82
Geology 21
Global warming 74, 75
Globalization 84
Great Rift Valley 53
Greenhouse effect 74
Hurricanes 11, 61
Hydro-electric power 23, 44
Income 24, 30, 37, 81
Indian Ocean tsunami 79
Industry 24, 44
International aid 84
Irrigation 60
Land use 22
Latitude and longitude 4, 5
Life expectancy 81
Manufacturing 24
Mining 21, 82
Montserrat volcano 78
Motorways 26
National parks 27, 53, 60
Nationality 25
Natural disasters 45, 61, 78, 79
Natural gas 23, 49, 52, 82
Natural vegetation 53, 76, 77
New York 60
Nuclear power 23, 82
Oil 23, 49, 52, 82
Plate tectonics 78, 79
Population change 25, 80
Population density 25, 37, 45, 53, 66, 80
Railways 26
Rainfall 20, 73, 75
Renewable energy 23
Satellite imagery 8–12, 36, 37, 45, 49, 52, 60, 61, 74, 79
Scale 2, 3
Seaports 26
Service industry 24
Sunshine hours 20
Temperature 20, 73, 75
Time Zones 85
Three Gorges Dam 44
Tokyo 45
Tourism 27, 30, 60, 85
Trade 24, 84
Travel 26
Unemployment 24, 37
Urban population 80
Volcanoes 36, 78
Water supply 21, 49, 60, 83
Wealth 24, 30, 37, 66, 81
Windfarms 23
Young and old 25

Published in Great Britain in 2021 by Philip's,
a division of Octopus Publishing Group Limited
(www.octopusbooks.co.uk)
Carmelite House, 50 Victoria Embankment
London EC4Y 0DZ
An Hachette UK Company
(www.hachette.co.uk)

Printed in Dubai

Cartography by Philip's
Previously published as
Philip's Student Atlas

Hardback Edition
ISBN 978-1-84907-585-5
Paperback Edition
ISBN 978-1-84907-586-2

Details of other Philip's titles and services can be found on our website at:
www.philips-maps.co.uk

MAP SYMBOLS

- Sea
- Coastline
- Airport
- Cape name
- Colours showing the height of the land
- Country name
- River
- National boundary (international boundaries are shown as ▭▭▭▭)
- Lake
- Line of longitude
- High point, with height in metres
- River name
- Name of mountain range
- Regional name
- Main railway
- Main road
- Sea feature name
- Line of latitude
- Symbols indicating towns: the larger the population of the town, the larger the symbol

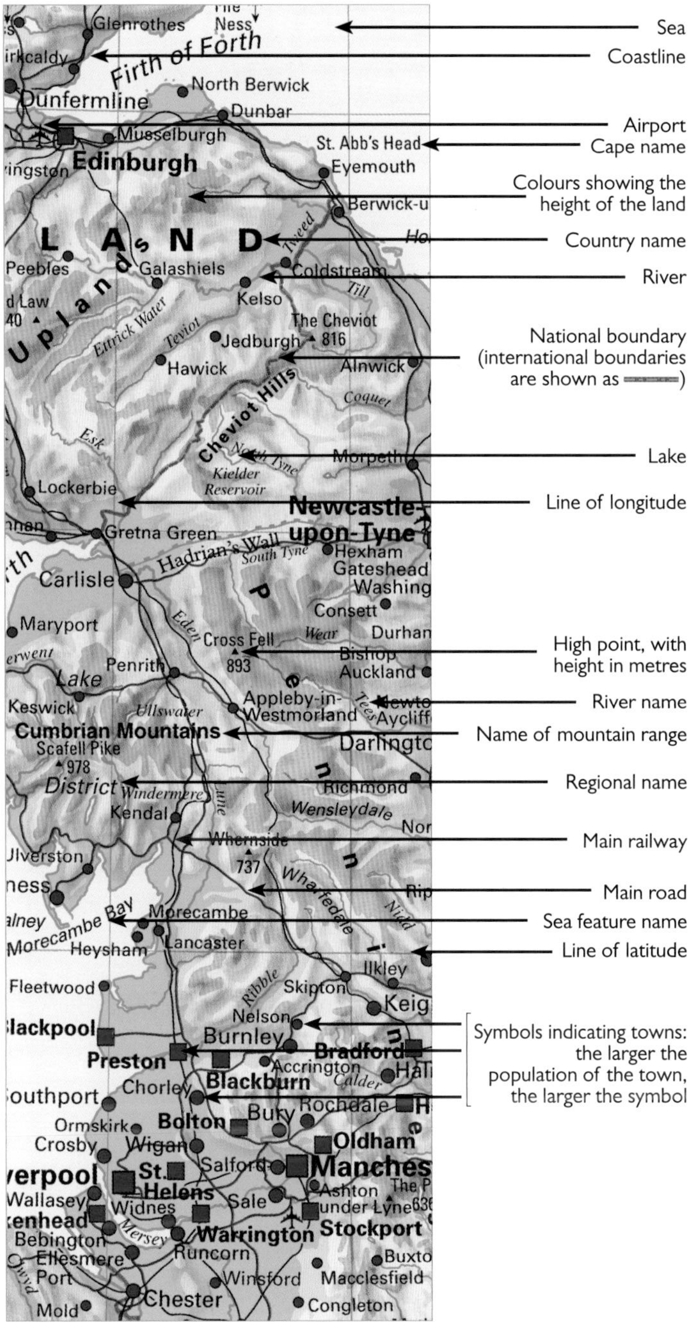

HEIGHT OF LAND

There is an explanation like this one on every page where different colours are used to show the height of the land above sea level.

The highest point in a region is shown with the symbol ▲ plus the height in metres.

Height of the land (metres)
- Over 4000
- 3000 – 4000
- 2000 – 3000
- 1500 – 2000
- 1000 – 1500
- 750 – 1000
- Under 750
- Sea level
- Below sea level

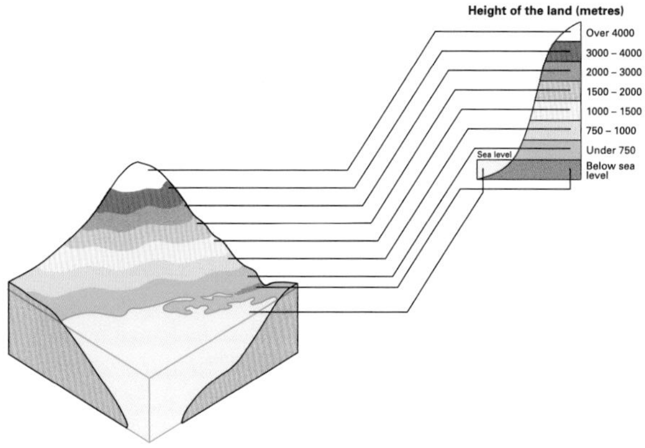

SCALE BAR

Every map has a scale statement, scale bar and ruler accompanying it. For a full explanation of scale and how to use the scale bar, see page 2.

Scale 1:48 000 000   1 cm on the map = 480 km on the ground

0   960km   1920km   2880km

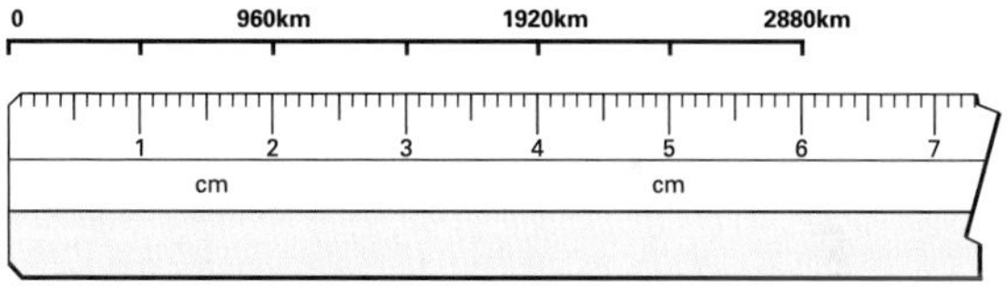

SCALE COMPARISON MAP

This map, or one of the U.K. and Ireland, appears on most of the maps of the continents at the same scale as the main map. They give an idea of the size of that continent.

ENGLAND & WALES
on same scale

LOCATOR MAP

There is a small map such as this on every map page. The bright green area shows how the main map fits into its larger region.

Royal Geographical Society
with IBG

Advancing geography and geographical learning

Philip's World Atlases are published in association with The Royal Geographical Society (with The Institute of British Geographers).

The Society was founded in 1830 and given a Royal Charter in 1859 for 'the advancement of geographical science'. Today it is a leading world centre for geographical learning – supporting education, teaching, research and expeditions, and promoting public understanding of the subject.

Further information about the Society and how to join may be found on its website at: **www.rgs.org**

PHOTOGRAPHIC ACKNOWLEDGEMENTS

Alamy /Roger Bamber p. 24 (centre), / Ian Dagnall p.26, /Robert Evans p.24 (top), /Kevin Schafer p.61, /Stocktrek Images, Inc. p. 36; **Corbis** /Tim Graham p. 24 (bottom), /Reuters p. 44, /Royalty Free p. 73; **Crown Copyright** p. 7 (map extract); **Fotolia.co.uk** p.76; **NPA Satellite Mapping, CGG Services (UK) Ltd** pp. 8, 9, 10, 12, 26, 27, 37, 49, 60, 74, 78, 79; **Patricia and Angus Macdonald** p. 7; **NASA** front cover (top right), p.11; **Precision Terrain Surveys Ltd** p. 6.

Map data

Page 6: The Edinburgh city plan is based on mapping data licensed from Ordnance Survey® with the permission of the Controller of Her Majesty's Stationery Office. © Crown copyright 2020. All rights reserved. Licence number 100011710.

Scale and Direction

TYPES OF SCALE

In this atlas the scale of the map is shown in three ways:

WRITTEN STATEMENT

This tells you how many kilometres on the Earth are represented by one centimetre on the map.

1 cm on the map = 20 km on the ground

SCALE RATIO

This tells you that one unit on the map represents two million of the same unit on the ground.

Scale 1:2 000 000

SCALE BAR

This shows you the scale as a line or bar with a section of ruler beneath it.

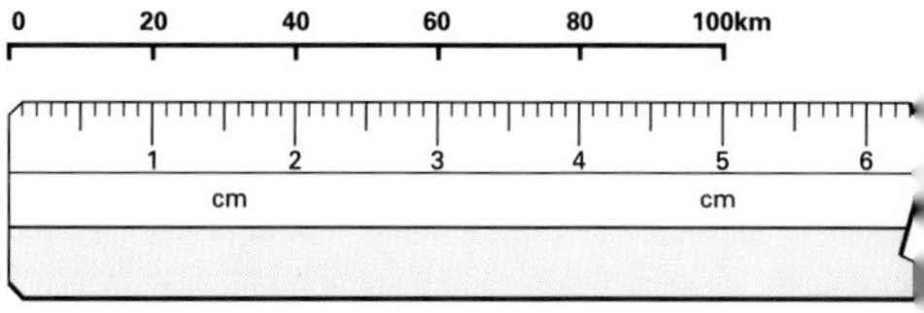

HOW TO MEASURE DISTANCE

The map on the right is a small part of the map of Southern Europe, which is on page 34 in the World section of the atlas.

The scale of the map extract is shown below:

Scale 1:10 000 000 1 cm on the map = 100 km on the ground

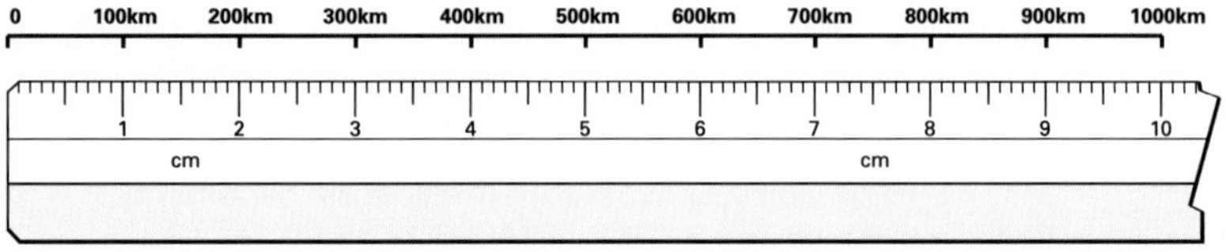

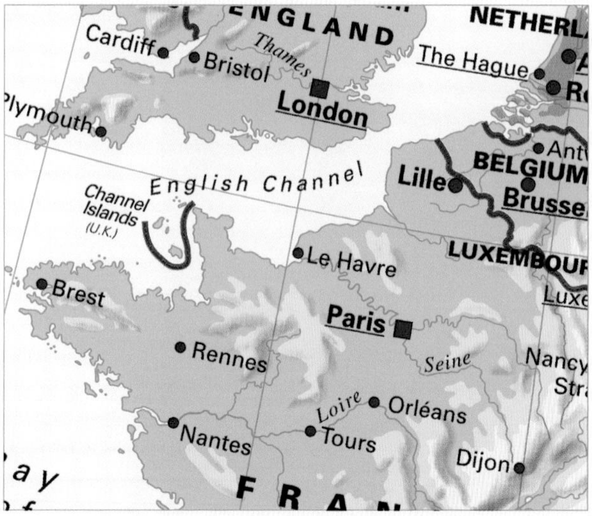

To measure the distance from London to Paris you can use any of the three methods described above.

For example:

USING THE WRITTEN STATEMENT

Using the scale above, you can see that 1 centimetre on the map represents 100 kilometres on the ground.

Measure the distance on the map between London and Paris. You will see that this is about 3.5 centimetres.

If 1 cm = 100 km

then 3.5 cm = 350 km (3.5 x 100)

USING THE SCALE RATIO

Using the scale above, you can see that the ratio is 1:10 000 000.

We know that the distance on the map between the cities is 3.5 cm and we know from the ratio that 1 cm on the map = 10 000 000 cm on the ground.

We multiply the map distance by the ratio.

= 3.5 x 10 000 000 cm
= 35 000 000 cm
= 350 000 m
= 350 km

USING THE SCALE BAR

We know that the distance on the map between the cities is 3.5 centimetres.

Measure 3.5 cm along the scale bar (or use the ruler as a guide) and read off the distance in kilometres.

Using these three methods, now work out the distance between London and Cardiff on the map above.

The map on the left is an extract from the map of Asia on page 39 in the World section of the atlas. Below, you can see the scale of this map. See if you can calculate the distance between Kolkata and Bangkok.

Scale 1:48 000 000 1 cm on the map = 480 km on the ground

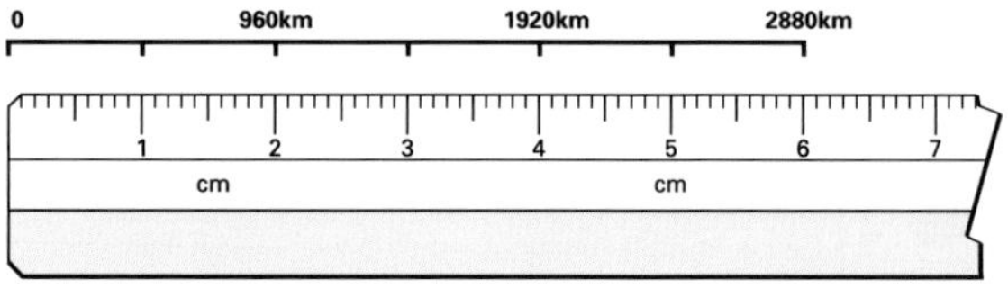

DIFFERENT SIZES OF SCALE

The table on the right shows the distances from London to Paris and Bangkok to Kolkata on the maps on page 2. The map distances are both 3.5 centimetres, but the distances on the ground are very different. This is because the maps are at different scales.

	Map Distance	Map Scale	Distance on the Ground
London – Paris	3.5 centimetres	1:10 000 000	350 kilometres
Bangkok – Kolkata	3.5 centimetres	1:48 000 000	1,680 kilometres

Included on most of the continent maps, in the World section of this atlas, are **scale comparison maps**. These show you the size of the UK and Ireland, or England and Wales, drawn at the same scale as the main map on that page. This is to give you an idea of the size of that continent.

Below are three maps which appear in this atlas:

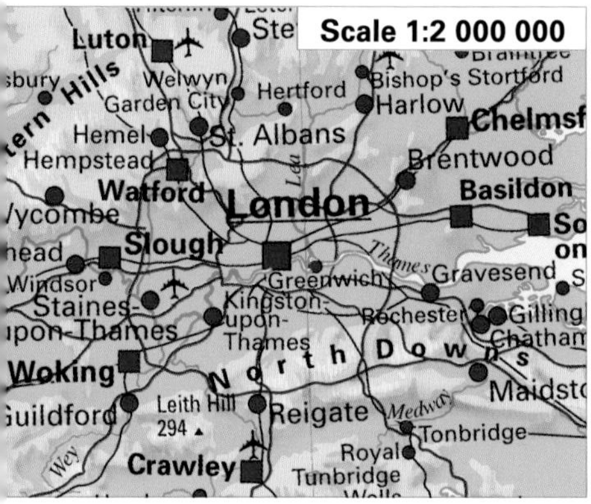

These maps all show London, but the map above shows much more detail than the maps on the right. The map above is a larger-scale map than the maps on the right.

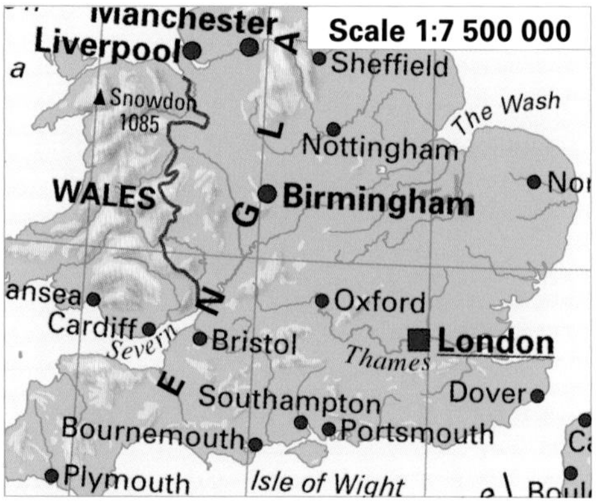

A **large-scale** map shows more detail of a **small** area.

A **small-scale** map shows less detail of a **large** area.

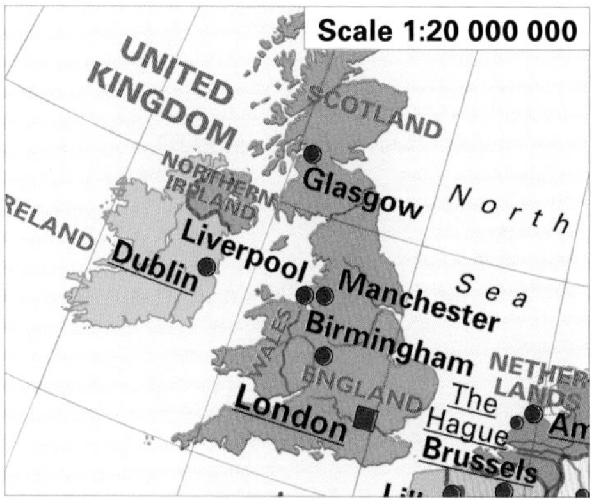

Notice how the scale ratios at the top right of each map are getting larger as the scale of the map gets smaller.

DIRECTION ON THE MAPS

On most of the atlas maps, north is at the top of the page. Lines of latitude cross the maps from east to west. Longitude lines run from south to north. These usually curve a little because the Earth is a globe and not a flat shape.

POINTS OF THE COMPASS

Below is a drawing of the points of a compass. North, east, south and west are called **cardinal points**. Direction is sometimes given in degrees. This is measured clockwise from north. To help you remember the order of the compass points, try to learn this sentence:

Naughty **E**lephants **S**quirt **W**ater

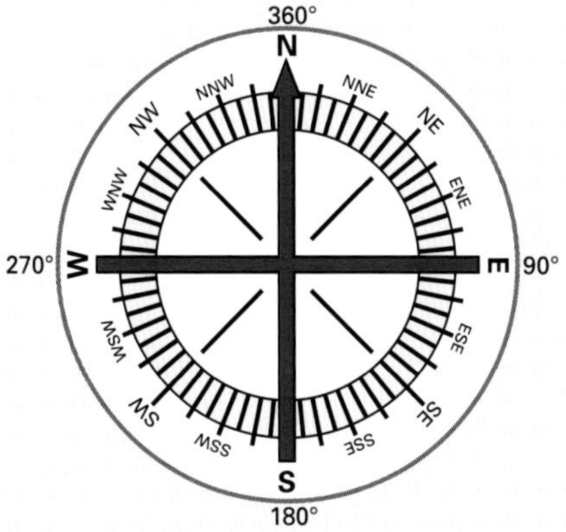

USING A COMPASS

Compasses have a needle with a magnetic tip. The tip is attracted towards the Magnetic North Pole, which is close to the Geographical North Pole. The compass tells you where north is. You can see the Magnetic North Pole on the diagram below.

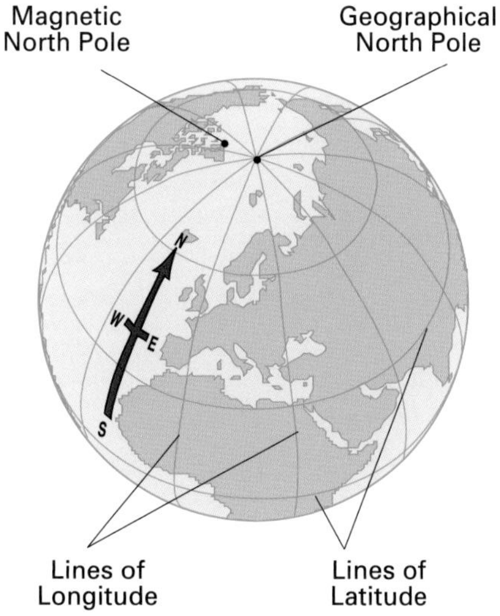

ACTIVITIES

Look at the map below.
If Ambleside is east of Belfast then:

- Valencia is ______________ of Belfast;
- Renfrew is ______________ of Ambleside;
- Oxford is ______________ of Plymouth;
- Belfast is ______________ of Oxford;
- Plymouth is ______________ of Renfrew.

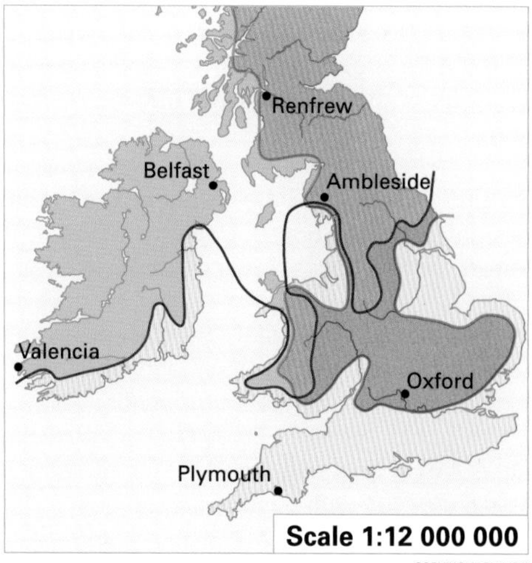

Latitude and Longitude

LATITUDE

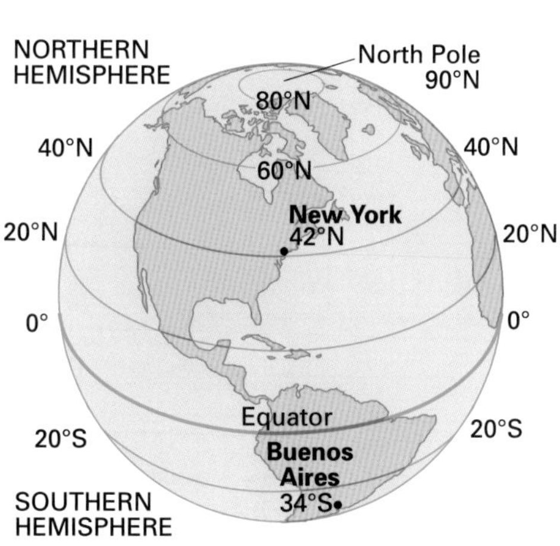

Lines of latitude cross the atlas maps from east to west. The **Equator** is at 0°. All other lines of latitude are either north of the Equator, or south of the Equator. Line 40°N is almost halfway towards the North Pole. The North Pole is at 90°N. At the Equator, a degree of longitude measures about 110 km.

LONGITUDE

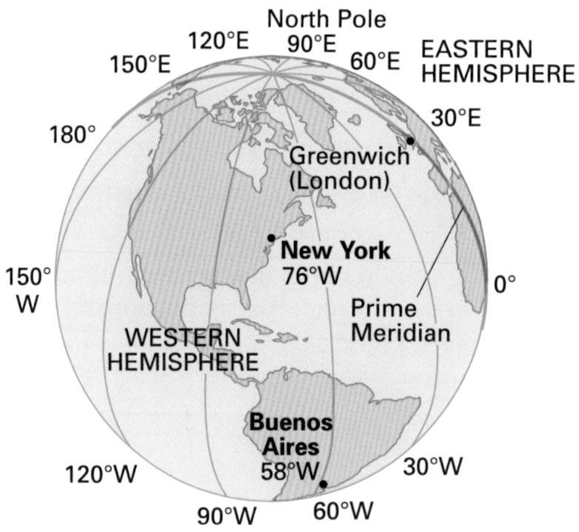

Lines of longitude run from north to south. These lines meet at the North Pole and the South Pole. Longitude 0° passes through Greenwich. This line is also called the Prime Meridian. Lines of longitude are either east of 0° or west of 0°. There are 180 degrees of longitude both east and west of 0°.

USING LATITUDE & LONGITUDE

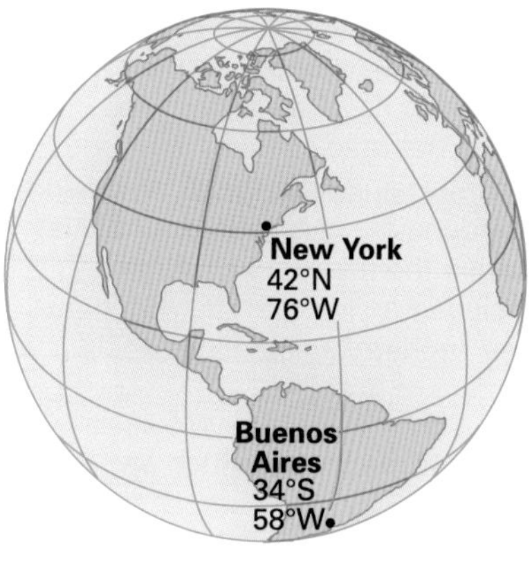

There are 60 minutes in a degree. Latitude and longitude lines make a grid. You can find a place if you know its latitude and longitude number. The latitude number is either north or south of the Equator. The longitude number is either east or west of the Greenwich Meridian.

SPECIAL LATITUDE LINES

The Earth's axis is tilted at an angle of approximately 23½°. In June, the northern hemisphere is tilted towards the Sun. On 21 June the Sun is directly overhead at the **Tropic of Cancer**, 23°26′N, and this is midsummer in the northern hemisphere. Midsummer in the southern hemisphere occurs on 21 December, when the Sun is overhead at the **Tropic of Capricorn**, 23°26′S. On the maps in this atlas these are shown as blue dotted lines.

In the North and South Polar regions there are places where the Sun does not rise or set above the horizon at certain times of the year. These places are also shown by a blue dotted line on the maps. The **Arctic Circle** is at 66°34′N and the **Antarctic Circle** is at 66°34′S.

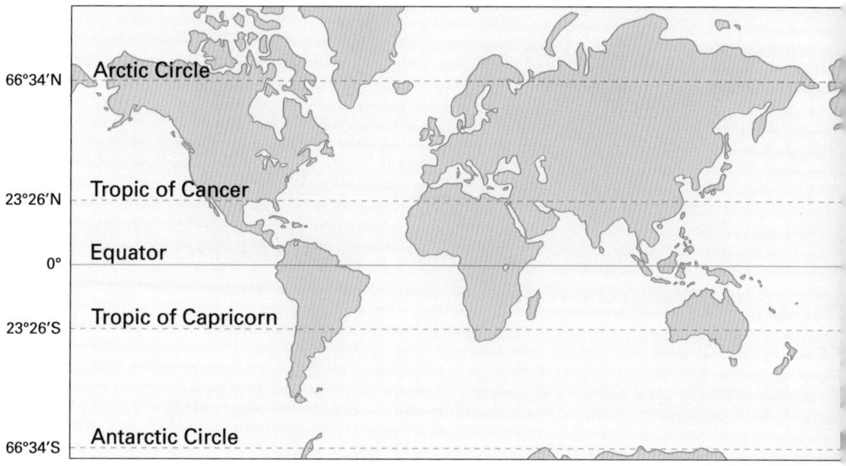

LATITUDE AND LONGITUDE IN THIS ATLAS

In this atlas lines of latitude and longitude are coloured blue.

On large-scale maps, such as those of England and Wales on pages 16–17, there is a line for every degree. On smaller-scale maps only every other, every fifth or even tenth line is shown.

The map on the right shows the UK and Ireland. The latitude and longitude lines are numbered at the edges of the map. The bottom of the map shows whether a place is east or west of Greenwich. The side of the map tells you how far north from the Equator the line is.

Around the edges of the map are small yellow pointers with letters or figures in their boxes. Columns made by longitude lines have letters in their boxes; rows made by latitude lines have figures.

In the index at the end of the atlas, places have figure-letter references as well as latitude and longitude numbers to help you locate the place names on the maps.

On the map opposite, London is in rectangle **8M** (this is where row 8 crosses with column M). Edinburgh is in **4J** and Dublin is in **6F**.

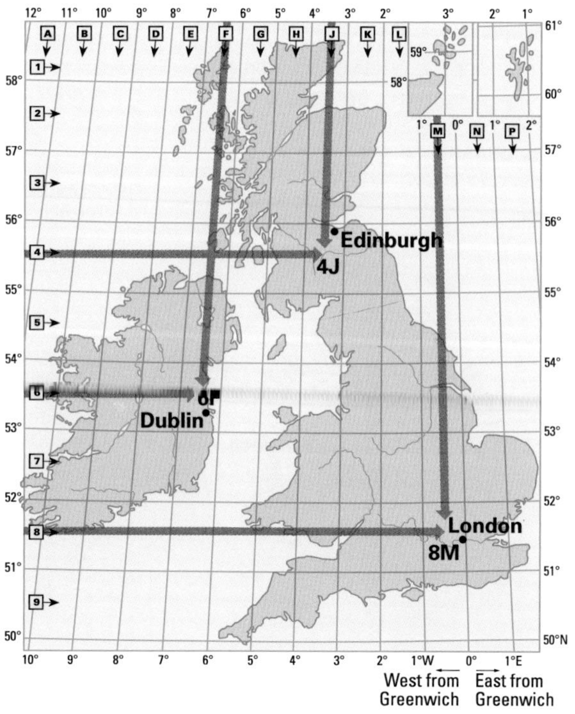

HOW TO FIND A PLACE

The map on the right is an extract from the map of Scotland on page 18. If you want to find Stornoway in the atlas, you must look in the index. Places are listed alphabetically. You will find the following entry:

Stornoway .... 58° 13'N 6° 23'W **18 1B**

The first number in **bold** type is the page number where the map appears. The figure and letter which follow the page number give the grid rectangle on the map in which the feature appears. Here we can see that Stornoway is on page 18 in the rectangle where row 1 crosses column B.

The latitude and longitude number corresponds with the numbered lines on the map. The first set of figures represent the latitude and the second set represent the longitude. The unit of measurement for latitude and longitude is the degree (°) which is divided into minutes (').

Latitude and longitude can be used to locate places more accurately on smaller-scale maps such as those in the World section. A more detailed explanation of how to estimate the minutes can be found on page 90.

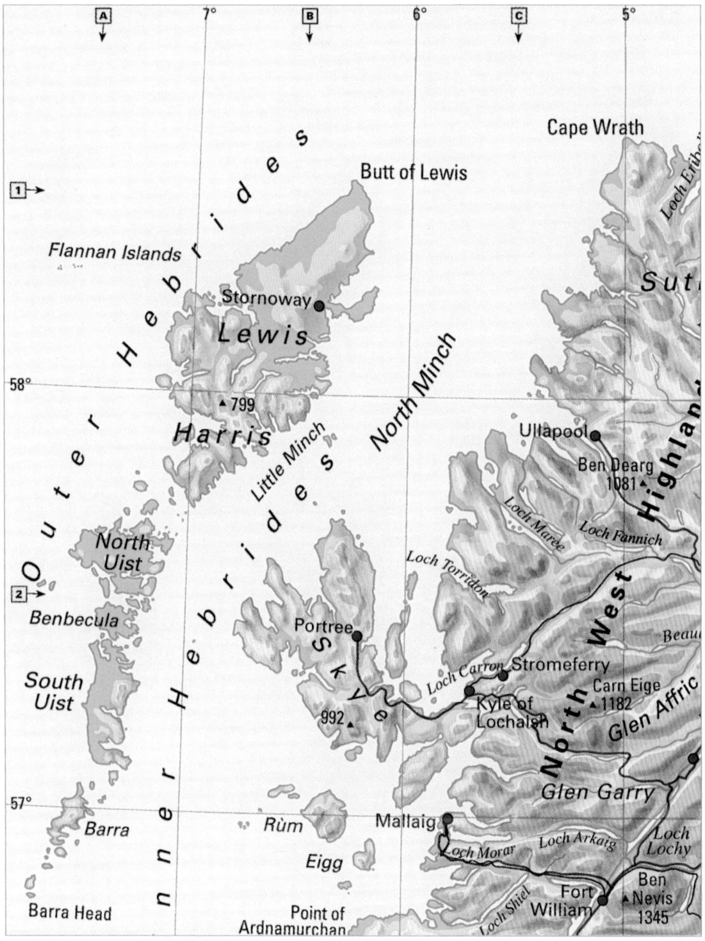

MAKING MAPS

One of the greatest problems in making maps is how to draw the curved surface of the globe on a flat piece of paper. As a globe is three dimensional, it is not possible to show its surface on a flat map without some form of distortion.

This map (right) shows one way of putting the globe on to paper, but because it splits up the land and sea it is not very useful.

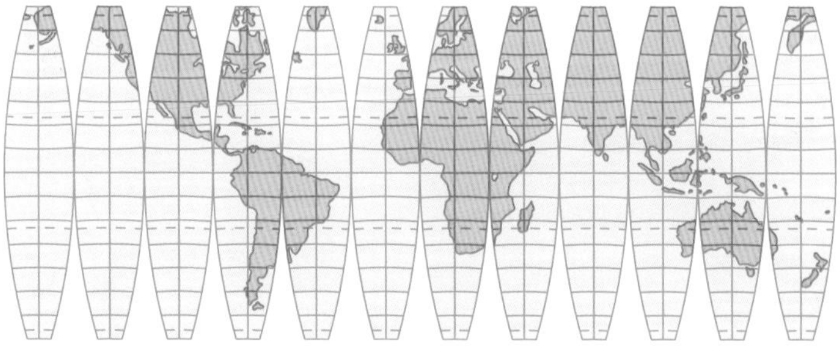

The map below is better because it shows the correct size of places. It is an **equal-area map**. For example, Australia is the correct size in relation to North America, and Europe is the correct size in relation to Africa. Comparing certain areas is a useful way to check the accuracy of maps. Comparing Greenland (2.2 million km²) with Australia (7.7 million km²) is a good 'area test'.

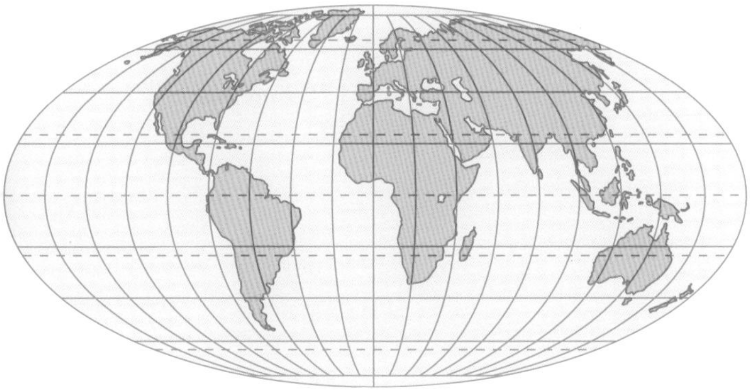

The map below is called **Mercator**. It has been used since the 16th century. The area scale is not equal area, but many sea and air routes are drawn on this type of map because direction is accurate. The scale of distances is difficult to put on a world map. On the Mercator map, scale is correct along the Equator but is less correct towards the Poles.

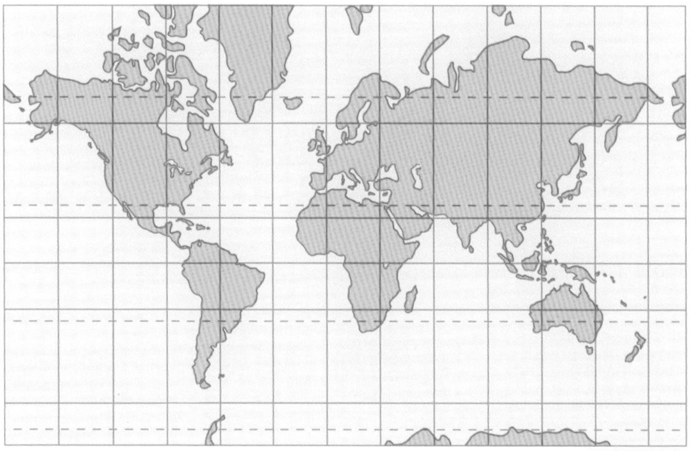

Map Reading from Aerial Photographs

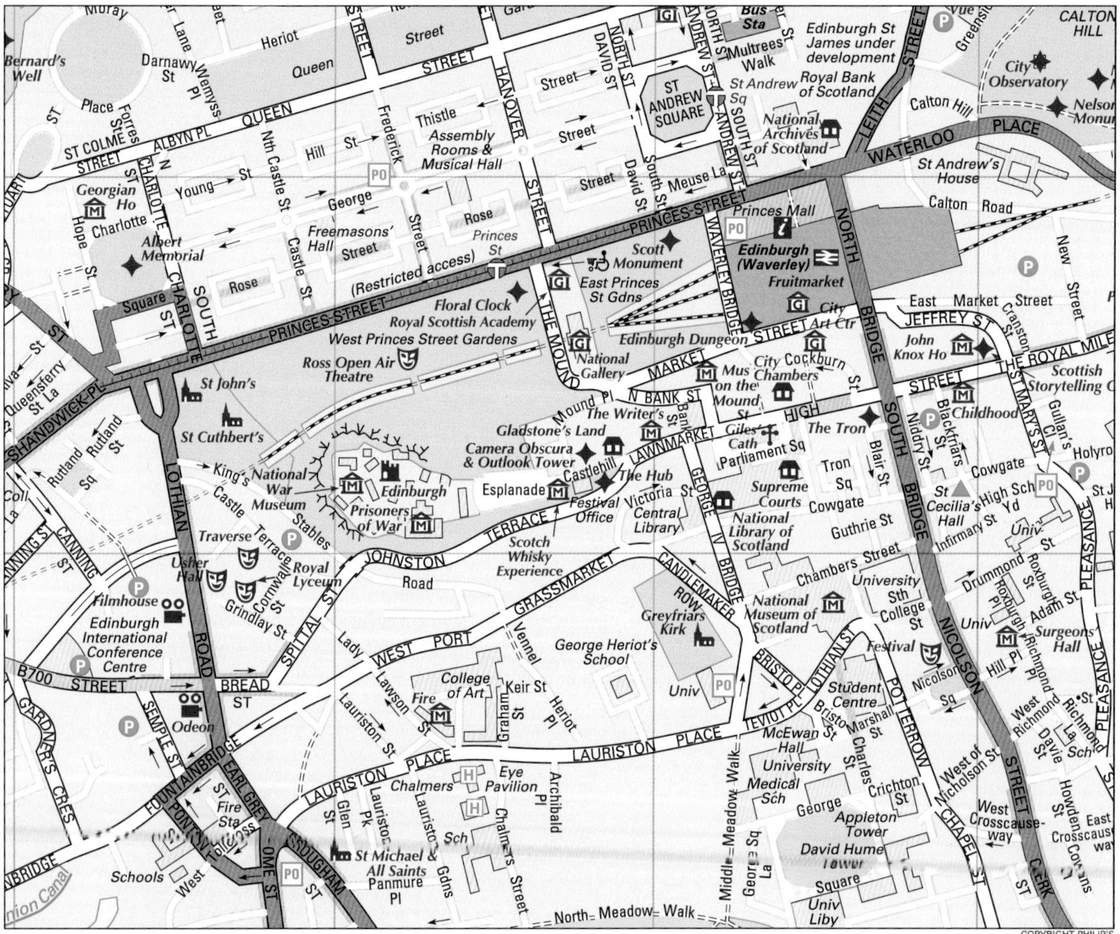

KEY TO MAP SYMBOLS

- Main Road Dual
- Secondary Road Single
- Minor Road
- One Way Street
- Pedestrian Roads
- Abbey/Cathedral
- Art Gallery
- Building of Public Interest
- Castle
- Church of interest
- Cinema
- Museum
- Railway Station
- Shopping Street
- Tram Route with Station
- Railway
- Railway/Bus Station
- Shopping Precinct/Retail Park
- Park
- Theatre
- Tourist Information Centre
- Other Place of Interest
- Hospital
- Parking
- Post Office
- Youth Hostel

Scale 1:10 000 1 centimetre on the map and aerial photograph = 100 metres on the ground

0 500 metres 1 kilometre

1 2 3 4 5 6 7 8 9 10
cm cm

Locator map

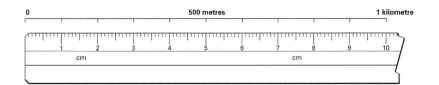

KEY TO MAP SYMBOLS

Main road | Other road, drive or track, fenced and unfenced
Secondary road | Path
Road generally more than 4m wide | Footpath
Road generally less than 4m wide | National Trail/ Long Distance Route; Recreation Route
Single track | Cutting; tunnel; embankment
Road over; Road under; Level crossing; | Station, open to passengers; siding

Coniferous trees | Scrub
non-coniferous trees | Bracken, heath or rough grassland
Coppice | Slopes

Place of worship

r former worship { with tower / with spire, minaret or dome

CH Clubhouse

FB Footbridge

Building; important building

PO Post office

Lighthouse, disused lighthouse; beacon

Sch School

Triangulation pillar; mast

W; Spr Well; spring

Ground survey height

Air survey height

Surface heights are to the nearest metre above mean sea level. Where two heights are shown, the first height is to the base of the triangulation pillar and the second (in brackets) to the highest natural point of the hill

Vertical face/cliff

75 60 50 Contours may be at 5 or 10 metres vertical interval

Parking/Park & Ride, all year/seasonal | Camp site/caravan site
Information centre, all year/seasonal | Recreation/leisure/ sports centre
Museum | Golf course or links

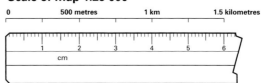

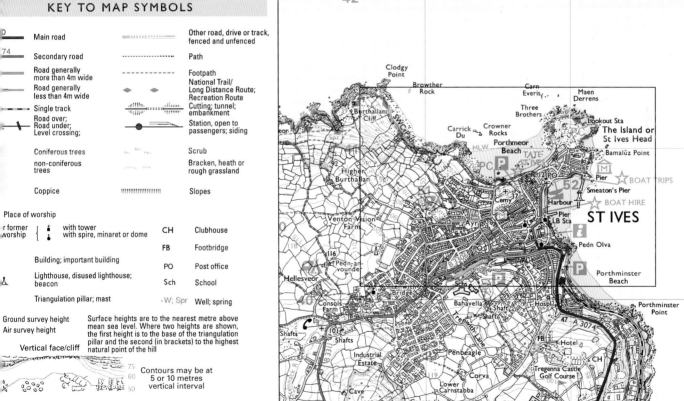

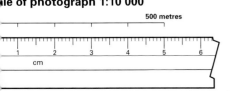

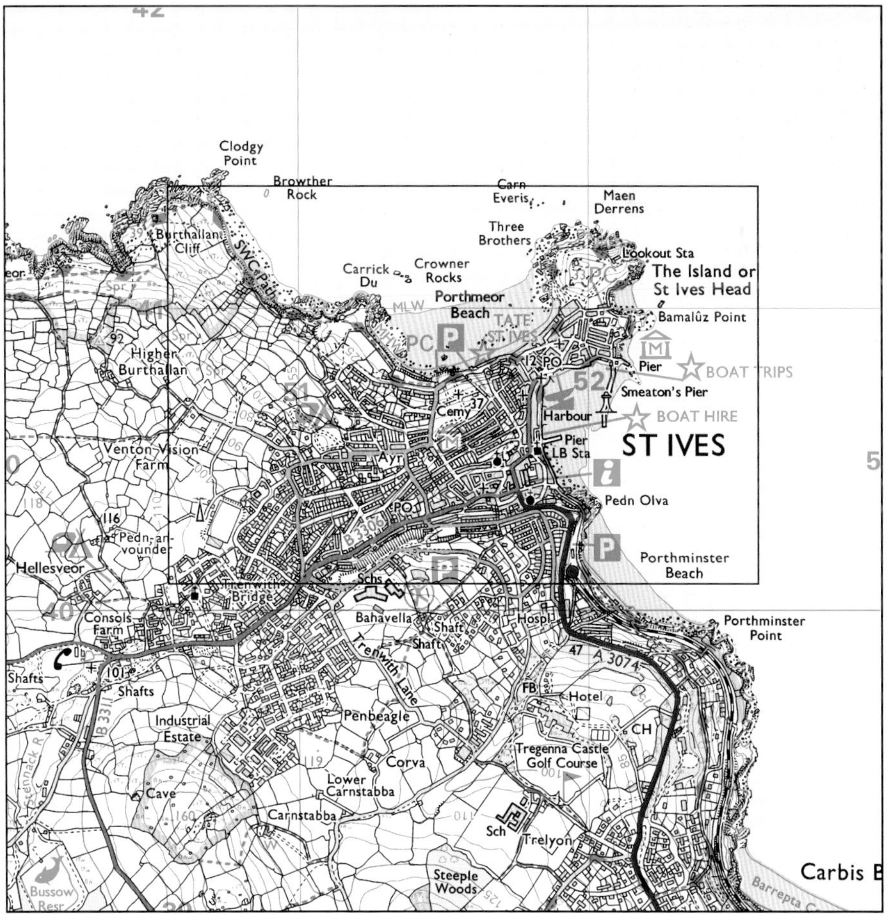

Reproduced from the 2008 Ordnance Survey 1:25,000 Explorer Map with permission of the controller of Her Majesty's Stationery office © Crown Copyright

…le of photograph 1:10 000

500 metres

1 2 3 4 5 6 cm

…ntimetre on the photograph = 100 metres on the ground

Scale of map 1:25 000

0 500 metres 1 km 1.5 kilometres

1 2 3 4 5 6 cm

1 centimetre on the map = 250 metres on the ground

Map Reading from Satellite Imagery

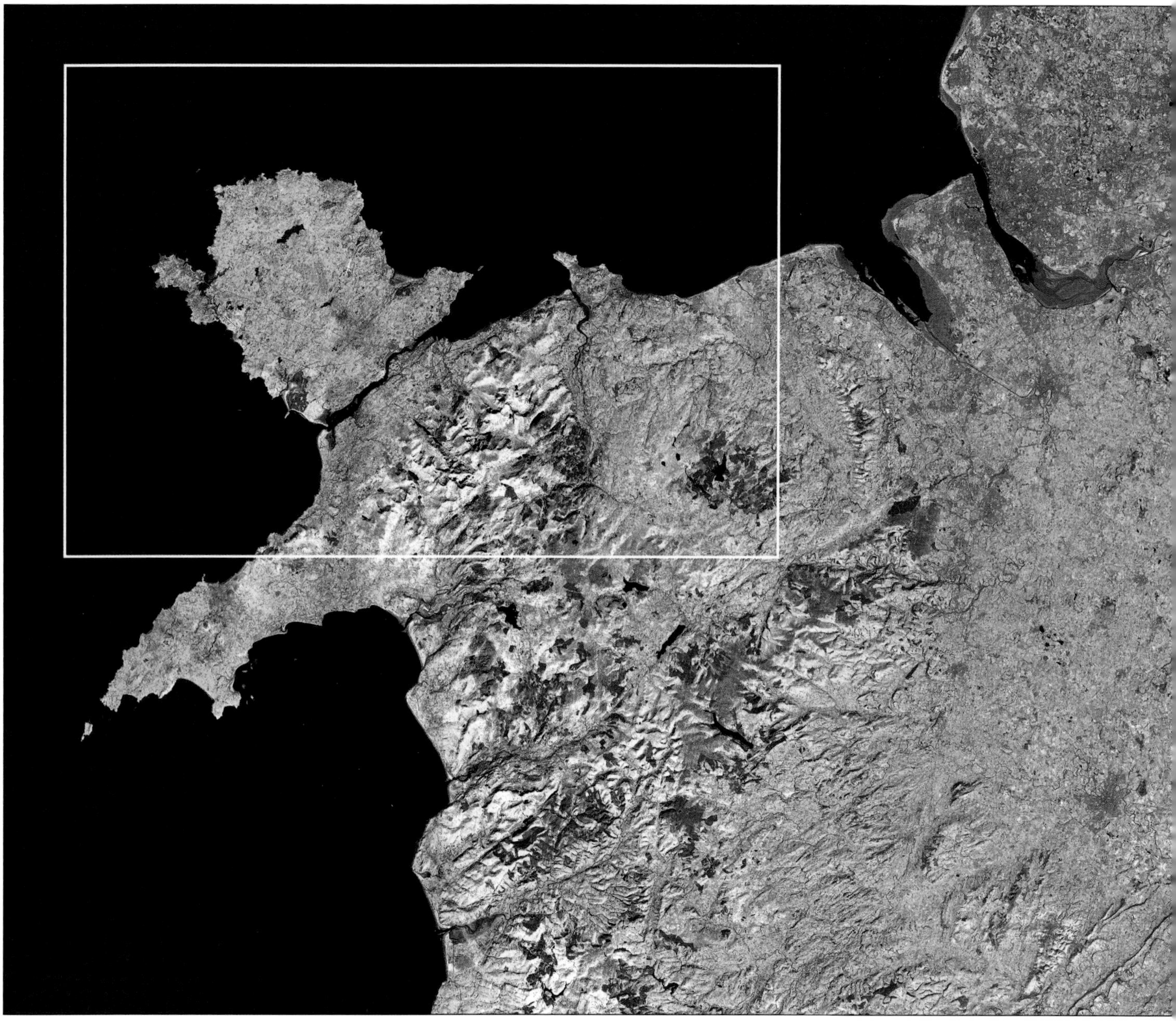

KEY TO MAP SYMBOLS

Symbol	Meaning	Symbol	Meaning
	Town symbols		
	Built-up areas		Main passenger railways
CONWY	Administrative area names		Other passenger railways
SNOWDONIA	National park names		Major airports
	Motorways		Rivers
	Major roads		Lakes or reservoirs
	Other important roads	1085	Elevation in metres
	Administrative boundaries		Place of interest

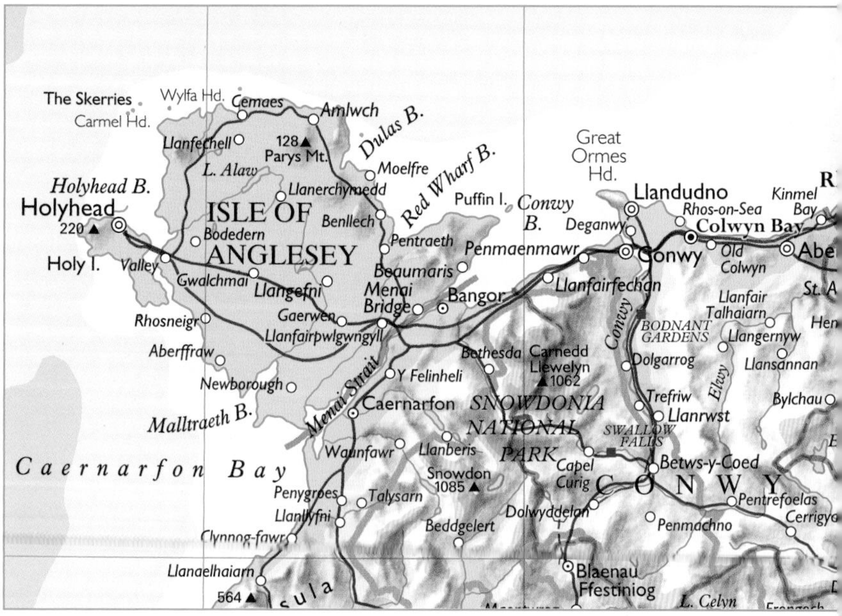

Locator map

Scale 1:760 000 1 cm on the map and satellite image = 7.6km on the ground

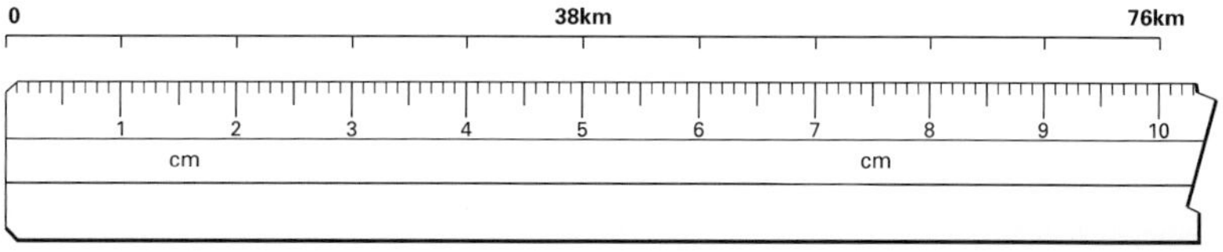

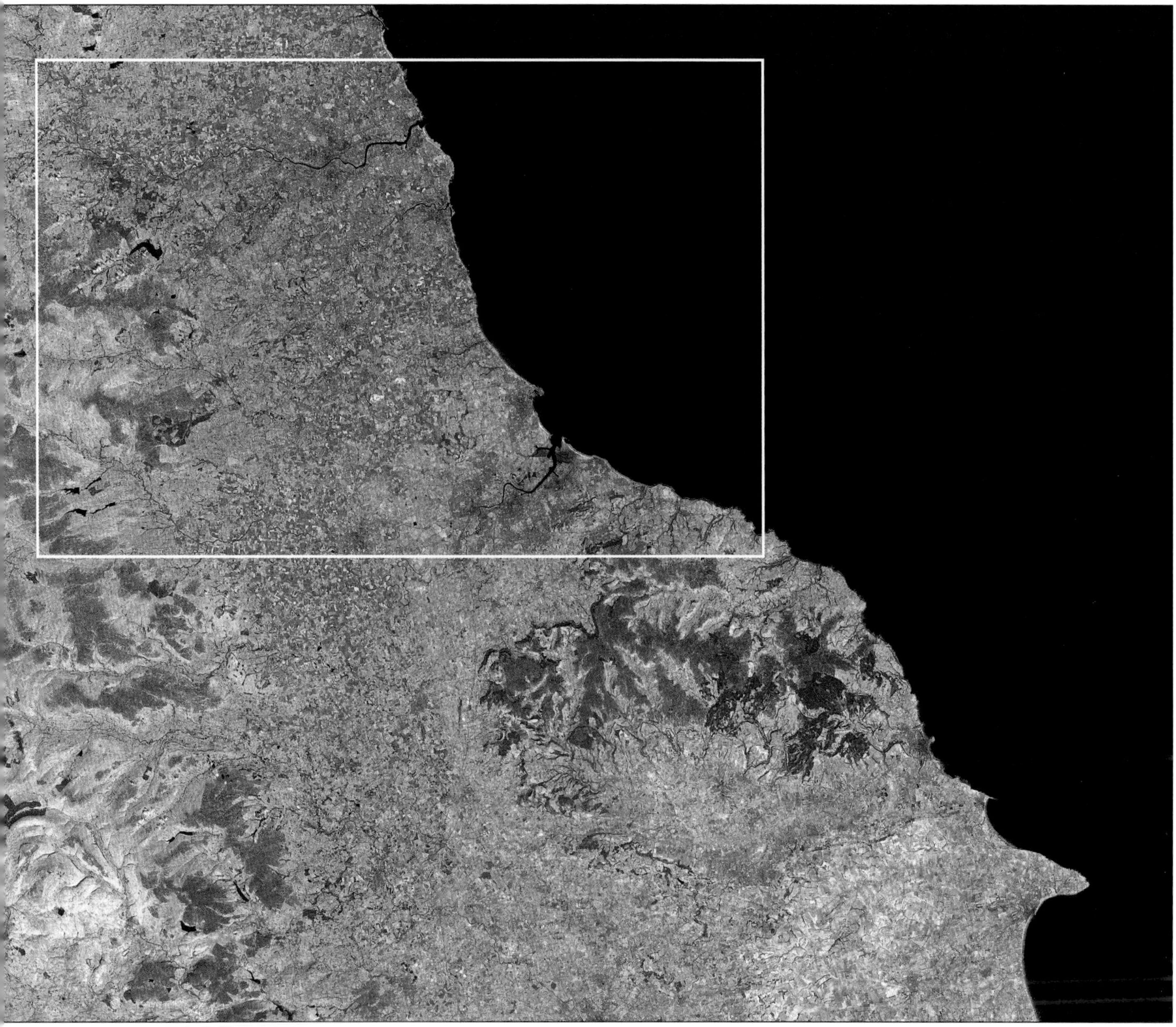

SATELLITE IMAGERY

ıages on these pages were produced by the
ıt 7 satellite, launched by NASA in 1999.
ıls around the Earth at a height of over
ı. It is able to scan every part of the Earth's
e once every 16 days. The data is
ıitted back to Earth where it is printed in
olours to make certain features stand out.
hese pages grass and crops appear light
soils and exposed rock light grey, woodland
reen, moorland brown, water black and
p areas dark grey. The image on this page
North-east England and the image on page
vs North Wales. Both images were
ed in late March. Comparing the maps,
are taken from *Philip's Modern School Atlas,*
ıe images helps identify specific features on
ages.

Scale 1:760 000 1 cm on the map and satellite image = 7.6km on the ground

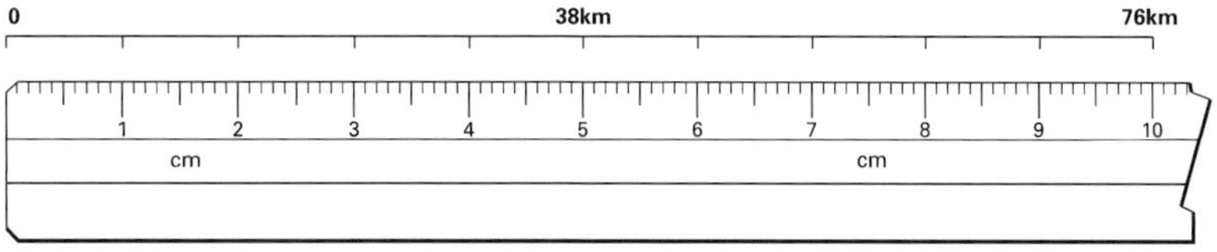

Earth Observation Satellites

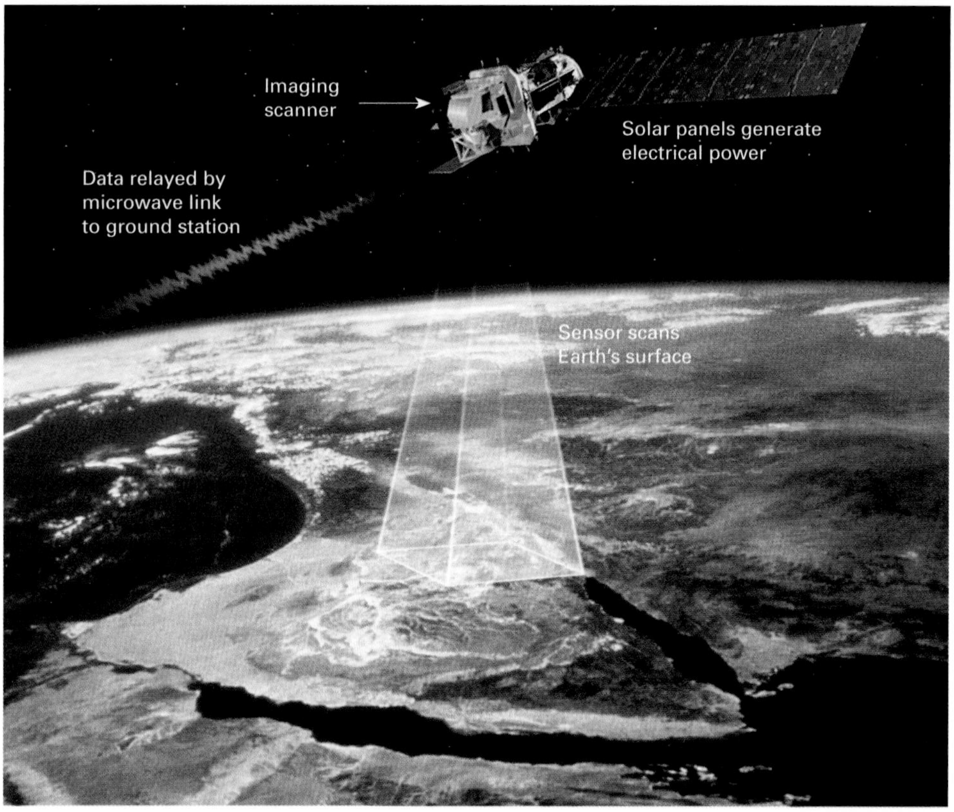

◀ Earth Observation Satellites
Powered by outstretched solar panels, Earth Observation Satellites, such as the one shown here, can collect and relay back to Earth huge volumes of geographical data which is then processed and stored on computers.

Depending on the sensors fitted, the choice of orbit and altitude, these satellites can provide detailed imagery of the Earth's surface at close range or monitor environmental issues covering the entire world. Objects less than 1 metre across can now be seen from space as well as the entire surface of our planet, allowing us to monitor issues such as the atmosphere, land and sea temperature, vegetation, rainfall and ice cover.

The importance of recording this information over time is that it enables us to see long-term changes and increases our understanding of the processes involved. Some satellites have been collecting data for over 25 years. A few of their uses are shown on this page and the page opposite.

▲ The River Thames, London
This image shows central London from St Paul's Cathedral, in the upper left-hand corner, across to the Tower of London and Tower Bridge on the right-hand side. The image was captured from a satellite 680 km above the Earth and travelling at 6 km per second. It was captured at about midday in late October, the low sun showing clearly the shadows of the Shard and the chimney of Tate Modern. *(Image © EUSI, Inc. All Rights Reserved/NPA Satellite Mapping)*

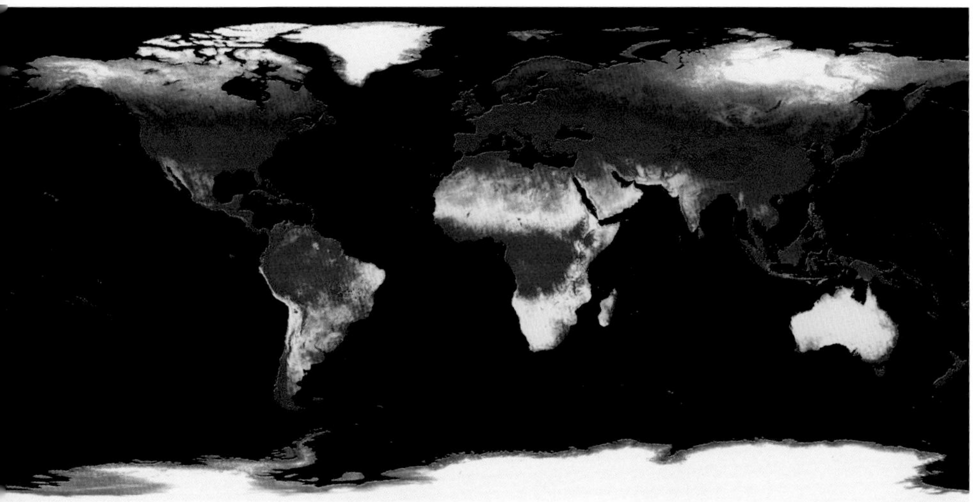

◄ **World Land Surface Temperature, November**
The satellite which captured this data uses another set of sensors that enable it to capture different data and over a much wider area. The colours range from light blue, indicating –25°C, through reds and oranges up to yellow, indicating +45°C. The land surface temperature thus shows the beginning of winter north of the Equator and summer south of the Equator.

▲ **Ice Cover, Alexander Island, Antarctica**
An important use for satellites is to monitor inaccessible areas of the world that are environmentally sensitive, such as the ice caps surrounding the North and South Poles. This image shows the Hampton Glacier, which is at the foot of the image, flowing towards the sea. The ice then breaks off into a series of icebergs, which can be seen at the top. Because satellites revisit these areas regularly, changes to the extent of the ice can be monitored.

▲ **Weather**
Weather satellites travel at the same speed as the Earth's rotation and stay in daylight to allow them to monitor the same area for major storms and other events. In order to capture as much of the Earth's surface as possible, they orbit farther out in space, about 35,000 km above the Earth's surface. This image clearly shows a hurricane approaching the coast of central America and the Gulf of Mexico.

United Kingdom and Ireland from Space

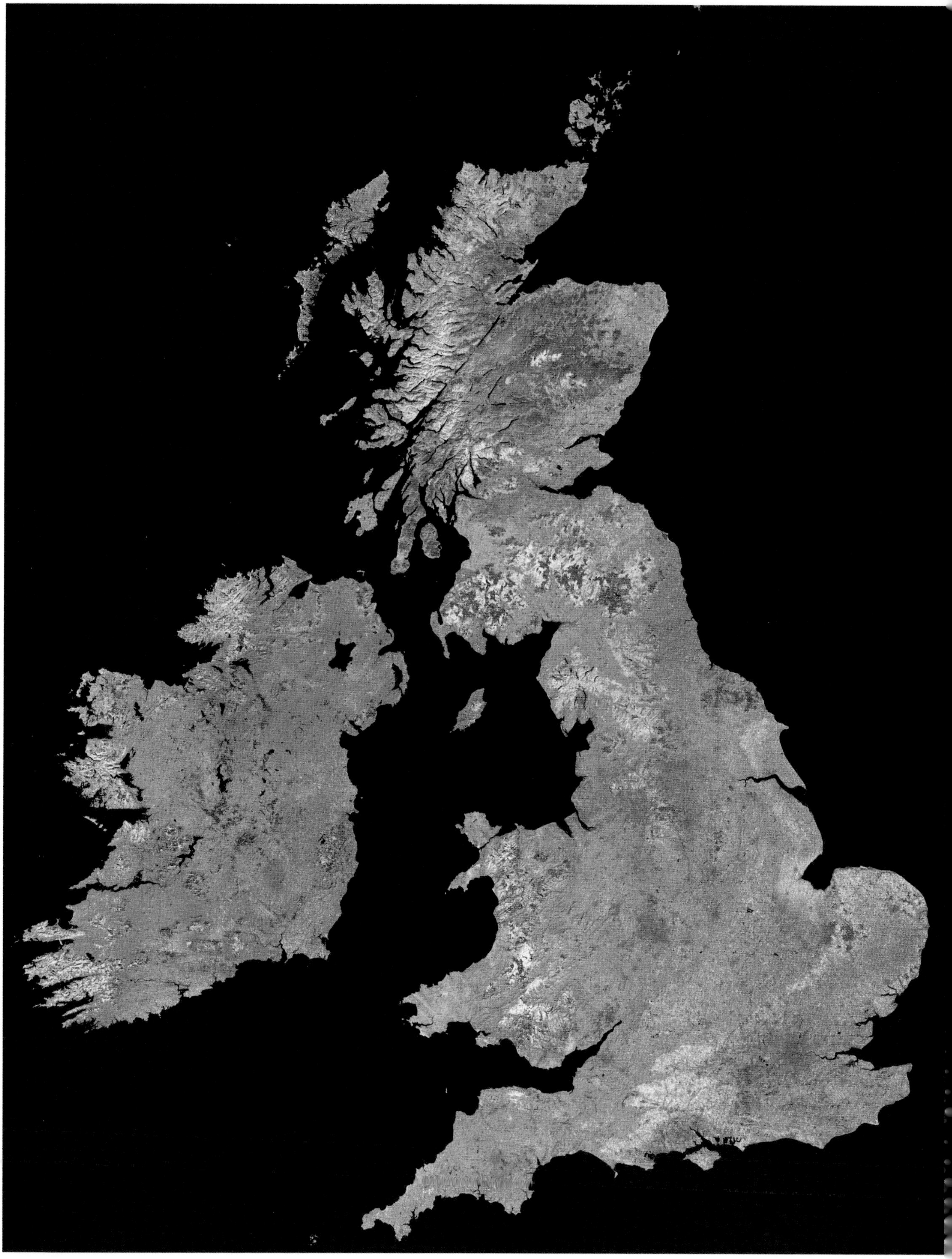

▲ The United Kingdom and Ireland, seen from Space
The colours on this image have been processed to match the natural tone of the landscape. The large amount of agricultural land in the UK is reflected by the extensive green on the image. In Scotland, the snow-covered Cairngorm Mountains can be seen, with brownish-green coniferous forests below the snow line. Most of Ireland has a mid-green colour, which indicates the presence of rich pasture. In the west, the lighter colour indicates moorland or bare rock and is also visible in the Cambrian Mountains in Wales, the Pennines and the Lake District in England, and the Scottish Highlands. Urban areas are shown as dark grey in colour.

Scale 1:4 600 000
1 cm on the map = 46 km on the ground
0
100km
200km
300km
400km
cm
Height of the land (metres)
over 1000
400-1000
200-400
100-200
0-100
sea level
below sea level
Highest mountains
Largest lakes
Longest rivers
England
Scafell Pike 978m
Windermere 15km²
Thames 346km
Severn 354km
Wales
Snowdon 1085m
Bala Lake 5km²
Tywi 109km
Severn 354km
Scotland
Ben Nevis 1345m
Loch Lomond 70km²
Tay 188km
Northern Ireland
Slieve Donard 852m
Lough Neagh 396km²
Bann 128.7km
Ireland
Carrauntoohill 1041m
Lough Corrib 176km²
Shannon 370km
Shetland Islands
Unst
Yell
Mainland
Foula
Fair Isle
Orkney Islands
Westray
Sanday
Mainland
Hoy
Pentland Firth
Duncansby Head
North Rona
Cape Wrath
Outer Hebrides
Lewis
Harris
799
St. Kilda
North Uist
Benbecula
South Uist
Barra
Inner Hebrides
Skye
Rùm
Eigg
Coll
Tiree
Mull
Colonsay
Jura
Islay
North West Highlands
1182
Dornoch Firth
Moray Firth
Kinnairds Head
Spey
Loch Ness
Ben Macdhui
1309
Don
Dee
Grampian Mountains
Ben Nevis
1345
1214
Tay
Loch Lomond
Firth of Forth
St. Abb's Head
Holy Island
Clyde
Tweed
The Cheviot
816
Southern Uplands
840
843
Arran
Firth of Clyde
North Channel
Rathlin Island
Malin Head
ATLANTIC OCEAN
North Sea
Great Britain
Arranmore
752
554
Bann
Mourne
683
Lough Neagh
Lower Lough Erne
Donegal Bay
644
Erris Head
852
Slieve Donard
Mull of Galloway
620
Isle of Man
Solway Firth
Lake District
Scafell Pike
978
Windermere
Pennines
893
Tyne
Tees
North York Moors
454
Flamborough Head
Achill Island
819
Ireland
Lough Mask
Lough Corrib
Lough Ree
Boyne
Liffey
Irish Sea
Morecambe Bay
Aire
Ouse
Spurn Head
Humber
Liverpool Bay
Mersey
The Peak
636
Galway Bay
Aran Islands
Shannon
Wicklow
926
Mountains
Lough Derg
Barrow
Anglesey
Snowdon
1085
Bala Lake
Cambrian Mountains
Dee
Trent
The Wash
The Fens
Great Ouse
Yare
Lowestoft Ness
Nene
Severn
315
Shannon
953
920
Suir
Blackwater
St. George's Channel
Cardigan Bay
Dingle Bay
1041
Carrauntoohill
Lee
Avon
Wye
330
Cotswold Hills
Chiltern Hills
St. David's Head
Tywi
Brecon
886
Beacons
Bantry Bay
Fastnet Rock
Cape Clear
Carmarthen Bay
Severn
Thames
North Foreland
Bristol Channel
297
Salisbury Plain
North Downs
Lundy
Exmoor
Hartland Point
South Downs
Strait of Dover
Celtic Sea
Tamar
621
Dartmoor
Lyme Bay
Portland Bill
Isle of Wight
Beachy Head
English Channel
Start Point
Land's End
Isles of Scilly
Lizard
Channel Islands
Guernsey
Jersey
France
West from Greenwich 0° East from Greenwich

Scale 1:4 600 000
1 cm on the map = 46 km on the ground
0 100km 200km 300km 400km
cm
Height of the land (metres)
Over 1000
400 – 1000
200 – 400
Under 200
sea level
Key to map symbols
978 Height in metres
International boundaries
LONDON Over 1,000,000 inhabitants
Leeds 500,000 – 1,000,000 inhabitants
Plymouth 200,000 – 500,000 inhabitants
Oxford 100,000 – 200,000 inhabitants
Guildford 50,000 – 100,000 inhabitants
Dover Under 50,000 inhabitants
ATLANTIC OCEAN
North Sea
Irish Sea
Celtic Sea
English Channel
St. George's Channel
Bristol Channel
North Channel
Firth of Clyde
Pentland Firth
Moray Firth
The Wash
Str. of Dover
Cardigan Bay
Galway B.
Shetland Islands
Unst
Yell
Mainland
Lerwick
Foula
Fair Isle
Orkney Islands
Westray
Sanday
Mainland
Kirkwall
Hoy
North Rona
Cape Wrath
Thurso
Wick
Outer Hebrides
Lewis
Stornoway
Harris
St. Kilda
North Uist
Benbecula
South Uist
Barra
Inner Hebrides
Skye
Portree
Rùm
Eigg
Mallaig
Coll
Tiree
Tobermory
Mull
Iona
Oban
Colonsay
Jura
Islay
Arran
Campbeltown
North West Highlands
Grampian Mts.
Southern Uplands
Cheviot Hills
SCOTLAND
Helmsdale
Lairg
Golspie
Ullapool
Tain
Invergordon
Dingwall
Nairn
Inverness
Elgin
Buckie
Banff
Fraserburgh
Peterhead
Huntly
Inverurie
Aberdeen
L. Ness
Spey
Aviemore
Don
Dee
Ballater
Stonehaven
Ben Nevis
Fort William
Montrose
Arbroath
Forfar
Tay
Dundee
Perth
St. Andrews
L. Lomond
Stirling
Glenrothes
Kirkcaldy
Dunfermline
Dunbar
Dumbarton
Greenock
GLASGOW
Paisley
Motherwell
Edinburgh
East Kilbride
Hamilton
Irvine
Clyde
Kilmarnock
Ayr
Galashiels
Jedburgh
Hawick
Berwick-upon-Tweed
Alnwick
Girvan
Dumfries
Stranraer
Kirkcudbright
Annan
Mull of Galloway
Malin Head
Arranmore
Buncrana
Coleraine
Letterkenny
Derry/Londonderry
Ballymena
Larne
Lifford
NORTHERN IRELAND
Antrim
Bangor
Donegal
Lough Neagh
Omagh
Belfast
Lisburn
Bundoran
Lower L. Erne
Portadown
Lurgan
Enniskillen
Armagh
Sligo
Clones
Newry
Ballina
L. Conn
Leitrim
Cavan
Castleblaney
Achill I.
Castlebar
Dundalk
Westport
Lough Mask
Roscommon
Longford
Kells
Drogheda
Boyne
Lough Ree
Mullingar
Lough Corrib
Athlone
Galway
Ballinasloe
Tullamore
Liffey
Dublin
Dun Laoghaire
Bray
Aran Is.
IRELAND
Birr
Portlaoise
Athy
Lough Derg
Carlow
Wicklow Mts.
Ennis
Nenagh
Arklow
Kilrush
Limerick
Thurles
Kilkenny
Shannon
Listowel
Tipperary
Tralee
Clonmel
Carrick-on-Suir
Wexford
Dingle
Rosslare
Waterford
Carrauntoohill
Killarney
Mallow
Blackwater
Dungarvan
Macgillycuddy's Reeks
Valencia I.
Cork
Youghal
Bantry
Bandon
Cóbh
Kinsale
Cape Clear
UNITED KINGDOM
Douglas
Isle of Man
Cumbrian Mts.
Pennines
Workington
Whitehaven
Carlisle
Hexham
Newcastle-upon-Tyne
South Shields
Gateshead
Sunderland
Durham
Hartlepool
Redcar
Darlington
Middlesbrough
Stockton-on-Tees
Barrow-in-Furness
Scarborough
Bridlington
Lancaster
Harrogate
York
Beverley
Keighley
Leeds
Kingston upon Hull
Blackpool
Burnley
Preston
Bradford
Blackburn
Halifax
Huddersfield
Scunthorpe
Humber
Bolton
Barnsley
Doncaster
Grimsby
MANCHESTER
Oldham
Rotherham
Liverpool
Salford
Stockport
Sheffield
Lincoln
Louth
Warrington
Chesterfield
Skegness
Anglesey
Holyhead
Bangor
Colwyn Bay
Chester
Crewe
Mansfield
Boston
Snowdon
Wrexham
Stoke-on-Trent
Derby
Nottingham
Trent
Grantham
Cromer
Pwllheli
Stafford
King's Lynn
Cambrian Mts.
Shrewsbury
Telford
ENGLAND
Norwich
Great Yarmouth
Welshpool
Wolverhampton
Nuneaton
Leicester
Great Ouse
Peterborough
Thetford
Lowestoft
BIRMINGHAM
Coventry
Corby
Aberystwyth
Redditch
Rugby
Ely
Bury St. Edmunds
Worcester
Royal Leamington Spa
Northampton
Cambridge
Ipswich
Felixstowe
WALES
Hereford
Severn
Bedford
Milton Keynes
Stevenage
Harwich
Colchester
Fishguard
Carmarthen
Brecon
Cheltenham
Cotswold Hills
Luton
Hemel Hempstead
Harlow
Chelmsford
Haverfordwest
Milford Haven
Pembroke
Merthyr Tydfil
Neath
Gloucester
Oxford
Watford
Basildon
Llanelli
Swansea
Port Talbot
Rhondda
Cwmbran
Newport
High Wycombe
Slough
Southend-on-Sea
Cardiff
Bristol
Swindon
Thames
LONDON
Margate
Barry
Newbury
Reading
Chatham
Canterbury
Bath
Basingstoke
Reigate
Maidstone
Weston-super-Mare
Guildford
Ashford
Dover
Barnstaple
Exmoor
Salisbury
Winchester
Crawley
Folkestone
Calais
Taunton
Yeovil
Southampton
Fareham
Havant
Hastings
Bude
Exeter
Bournemouth
Brighton
Worthing
Eastbourne
Boulogne-sur-Mer
Dartmoor
Poole
Newport
Portsmouth
Exmouth
Weymouth
Isle of Wight
Newquay
Torbay
Plymouth
Truro
St. Austell
Falmouth
Land's End
Penzance
Isles of Scilly
Dieppe
FRANCE
Alderney
Cherbourg
St. Peter Port
Guernsey
Sark
Jersey
St. Helier
West from Greenwich
East from Greenwich

COUNTRY FACTS

Country Name	Area (square kilometres)	Inhabitants (thousands 2019)	Capital City or Town
UNITED KINGDOM	**240,883**	**66,797**	**LONDON**
of which England	129,652	56,287	London
Wales	20,628	3,153	Cardiff
Scotland	77,097	5,463	Edinburgh
Northern Ireland	13,532	1,894	Belfast
*Isle of Man	572	85	Douglas
* Jersey	116	108	St. Helier
*Guernsey	63	63	St. Peter Port
IRELAND	**68,896**	**4,904**	**DUBLIN**

** Crown Dependencies which are not part of the U.K.*

Scale 1:4 600 000

SCOTLAND
1. ABERDEEN CITY
2. DUNDEE CITY
3. WEST DUNBARTONSHIRE
4. EAST DUNBARTONSHIRE
5. CITY OF GLASGOW
6. INVERCLYDE
7. RENFREWSHIRE
8. EAST RENFREWSHIRE
9. NORTH LANARKSHIRE
10. FALKIRK
11. CLACKMANNANSHIRE
12. WEST LOTHIAN
13. CITY OF EDINBURGH
14. MIDLOTHIAN

WALES
15. SWANSEA
16. NEATH PORT TALBOT
17. BRIDGEND
18. RHONDDA CYNON TAFF
19. MERTHYR TYDFIL
20. CAERPHILLY
21. BLAENAU GWENT
22. TORFAEN
23. CARDIFF
24. NEWPORT

ENGLAND
25. HARTLEPOOL
26. DARLINGTON
27. STOCKTON-ON-TEES
28. MIDDLESBROUGH
29. REDCAR AND CLEVELAND
30. BLACKPOOL
31. BLACKBURN WITH DARWEN
32. HALTON
33. WARRINGTON
34. KINGSTON UPON HULL
35. NORTH EAST LINCOLNSHIRE
36. STOKE-ON-TRENT
37. TELFORD AND WREKIN
38. DERBY CITY
39. CITY OF NOTTINGHAM
40. LEICESTER CITY
41. RUTLAND
42. PETERBOROUGH
43. MILTON KEYNES
44. LUTON
45. NORTH SOMERSET
46. CITY OF BRISTOL
47. BATH AND N. E. SOMERSET
48. SWINDON
49. READING
50. WOKINGHAM
51. WINDSOR AND MAIDENHEAD
52. SLOUGH
53. BRACKNELL FOREST
54. THURROCK
55. SOUTHEND-ON-SEA
56. MEDWAY
57. PLYMOUTH
58. TORBAY
59. BOURNEMOUTH, CHRISTCHURCH & POOLE
60. SOUTHAMPTON
61. PORTSMOUTH
62. BRIGHTON AND HOVE
63. BEDFORD
64. CENTRAL BEDFORDSHIRE

The map shows the 11 districts in Northern Ireland, the 32 unitary authorities in Wales and the 55 unitary authorities in England. Authorities which are too small to name on the map are numbered and listed separately.

Greater London and the 6 English metropolitan counties are coloured white on the map.

Greater London is divided into 32 borough councils and the City of London.

The 6 English metropolitan counties have 36 district councils.

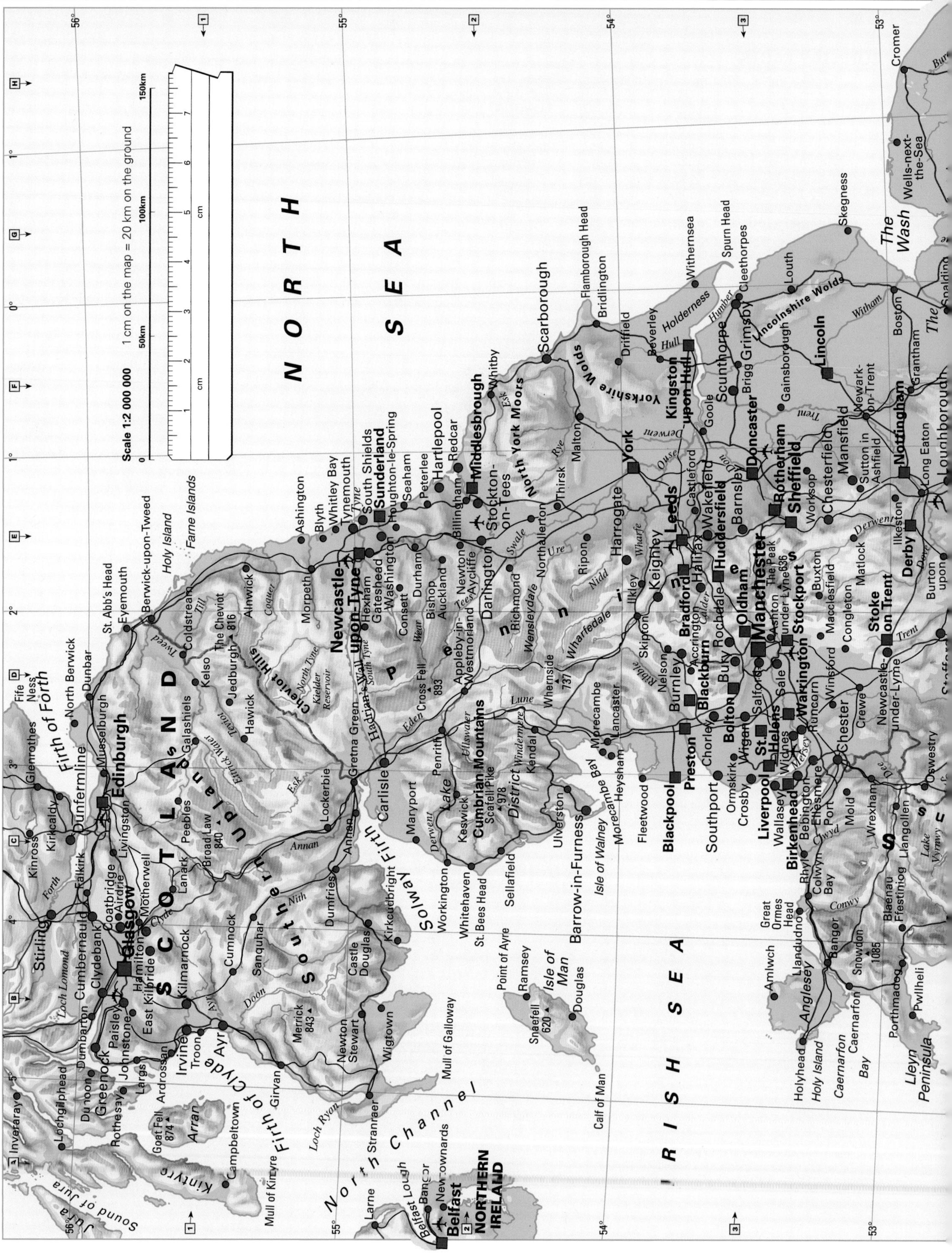
Scale 1:2 000 000
1 cm on the map = 20 km on the ground
0
50km
100km
150km
NORTH SEA
IRISH SEA
North Channel
Solway Firth
Firth of Forth
Firth of Clyde
Sound of Jura
SCOTLAND
NORTHERN IRELAND
Southern Uplands
Pennines
Cumbrian Mountains
Lake District
Cheviot Hills
North York Moors
Yorkshire Wolds
Lincolnshire Wolds
The Wash
Isle of Man
Isle of Walney
Anglesey
Holy Island
Lleyn Peninsula
Caernarfon Bay
Arran
Kintyre
Farne Islands
Edinburgh
Glasgow
Newcastle-upon-Tyne
Sunderland
Middlesbrough
Leeds
Bradford
Manchester
Liverpool
Sheffield
York
Kingston upon Hull
Lincoln
Nottingham
Derby
Stoke on Trent
Carlisle
Blackpool
Preston
Belfast
Stirling
Dunfermline
Scarborough
Whitby
Hartlepool
Darlington
Durham
Doncaster
Huddersfield
Oldham
Stockport
Bolton
Blackburn
Burnley
Wigan
Warrington
Chester
Wrexham
Lancaster
Kendal
Barrow-in-Furness
Dumfries
Kilmarnock
Ayr
Douglas
Grimsby
Scunthorpe
Skegness
Boston
Cromer
Wells-next-the-Sea
Snowdon 1085
Scafell Pike 978
The Cheviot 816
Merrick 843
Goat Fell 874
Snaefell 620
Cross Fell 893
Broad Law 840
Whernside 737
The Peak 636

Height of the land (metres)

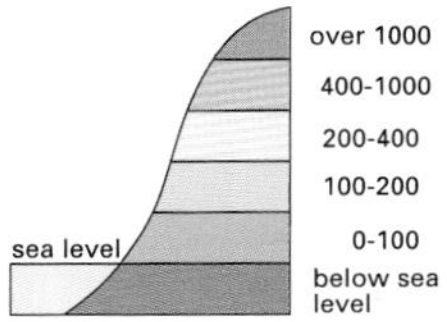

Key to map symbols

- ■ Over 1,000,000 inhabitants
- ▪ 100,000 - 1,000,000 inhabitants
- ● 50,000 - 100,000 inhabitants
- • Under 50,000 inhabitants
- **London** Capital cities underlined
- Main roads
- Railways
- International airports
- Historical sites
- Country boundaries

See page 15 for counties and regions

Locator map

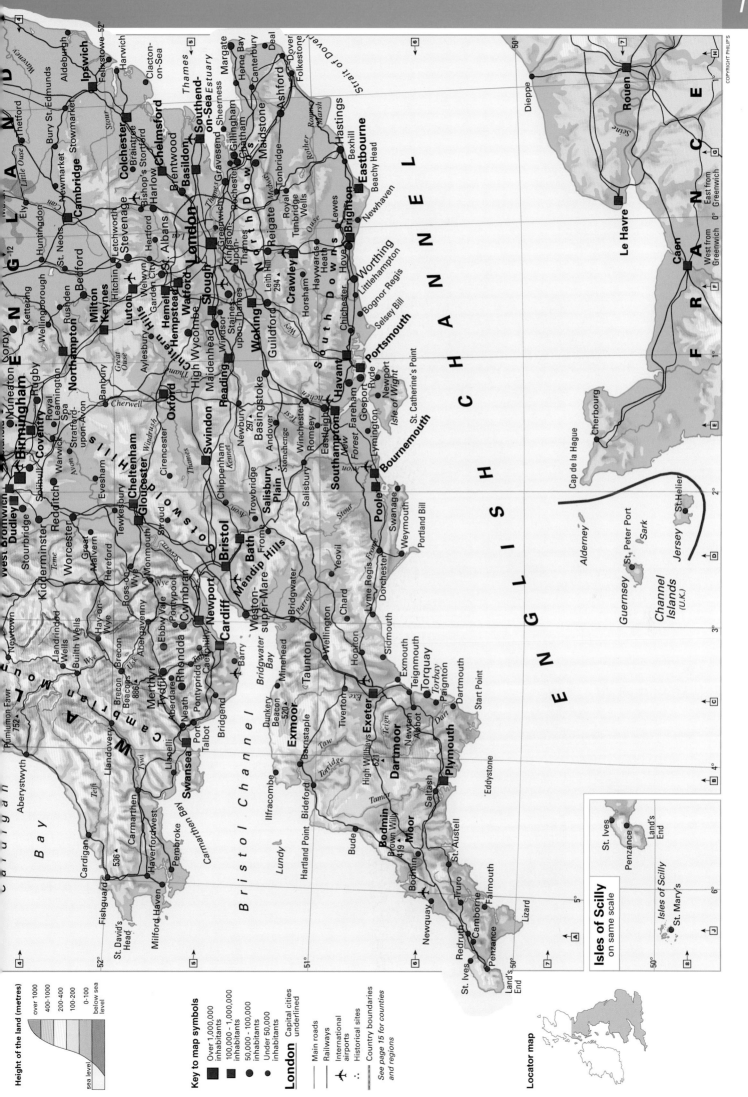

Scotland

Locator map

Scale 1:2 000 000 1 cm on the map = 20 km on the ground

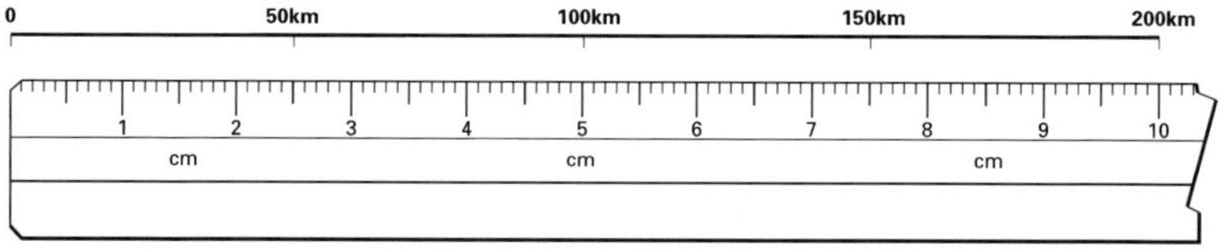

Height of the land (metres)

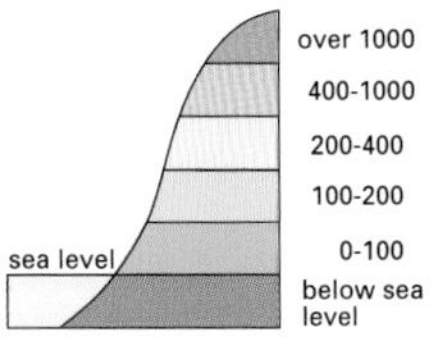

Key to map symbols

- Over 1,000,000 inhabitants
- 100,000 - 1,000,000 inhabitants
- 50,000 - 100,000 inhabitants
- Under 50,000 inhabitants
- **Dublin** Capital cities underlined

Scale 1:2 000 000

- Main roads
- Railways
- International airports
- Country boundaries

See page 15 for counties and regions

See page 15 for counties and regions

Locator map

Weather is measured in terms of rainfall, temperature, cloudiness, sunshine and wind over a short period of time, usually less than a day. Climate is the average of the weather over a longer period, usually 30 years.

RENFREW

°C Temperature
Rainfall 1109mm

AMBLESIDE

°C Temperature
Rainfall 1851mm

CLIMATE MAP

- Cool summer, cold winter
- Cool summer, mild winter
- Warm summer, cool winter
- Warm summer, mild winter

15°C in July
4°C in January

Renfrew
Belfast
Ambleside
Cromer
Valencia
Oxford
Plymouth

BELFAST

°C Temperature
Rainfall 845mm

CROMER

°C Temperature
Rainfall 618mm

CLIMATE GRAPHS

Colour of climate region on map
Name of town — **OXFORD**
Average monthly daily maximum temperature
Average monthly temperature
Average monthly daily minimum temperature
Average annual rainfall
Average monthly rainfall
Months of the year

VALENCIA

°C Temperature
Rainfall 1400mm

PLYMOUTH

°C Temperature
Rainfall 950mm

OXFORD

°C Temperature
Rainfall 660mm

COPYRIGHT PHILIP'S

Average annual rainfall — **ANNUAL RAINFALL**

- 2000 millimetres
- 1000 millimetres
- 750 millimetres
- Prevailing

Average hours per day — **DAILY SUNSHINE**

- 4.5 hours
- 4 hours
- 3.5 hours
- 3 hours

Average monthly temperature — **JANUARY TEMPERATURE**

- 6°C†
- 4°C
- 2°C
- 0°C*

* Freezing point
† Minimum temperature for plant growth

Oban 408 — Average number of hours of sunshine November–April

Braemar 383
Oban 408
Edinburgh 509
Belfast 426
Ambleside 424
Scarborough 518
Blackpool 526
Dublin 497
Shannon 493
Birmingham 502
Cardiff 527
Kew 551
Newquay 615
Bournemouth 598

Average monthly temperature — **JULY TEMPERATURE**

- 16°C
- 14°C
- 12°C
- 10°C

Oban 811 — Average number of hours of sunshine May–October

Braemar 834
Oban 811
Edinburgh 918
Belfast 821
Ambleside 771
Scarborough 1035
Blackpool 1041
Dublin 889
Shannon 893
Birmingham 977
Cardiff 1023
Kew 1107
Newquay 1128
Bournemouth 1169

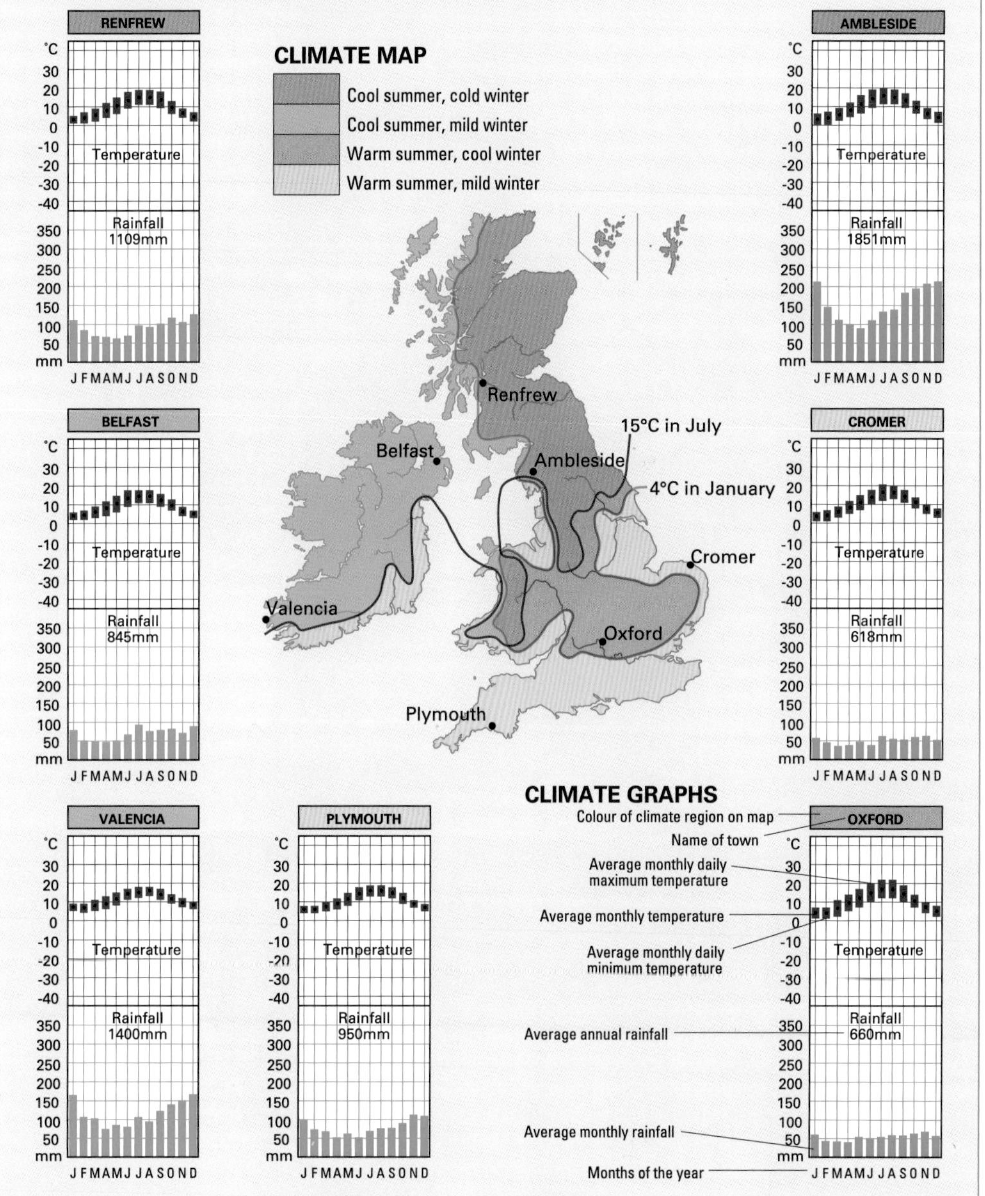

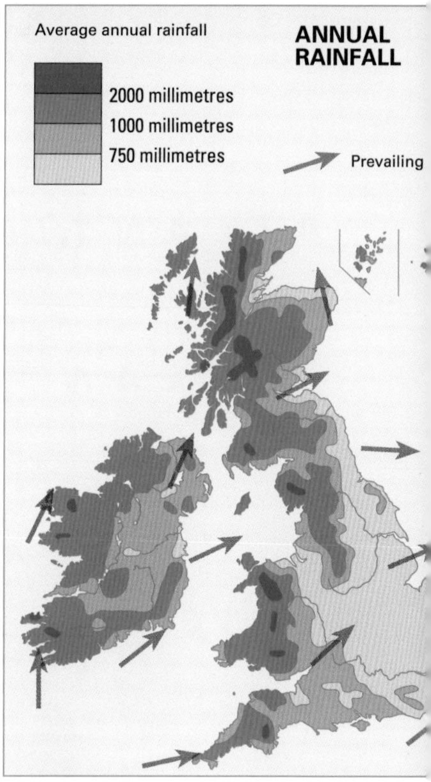

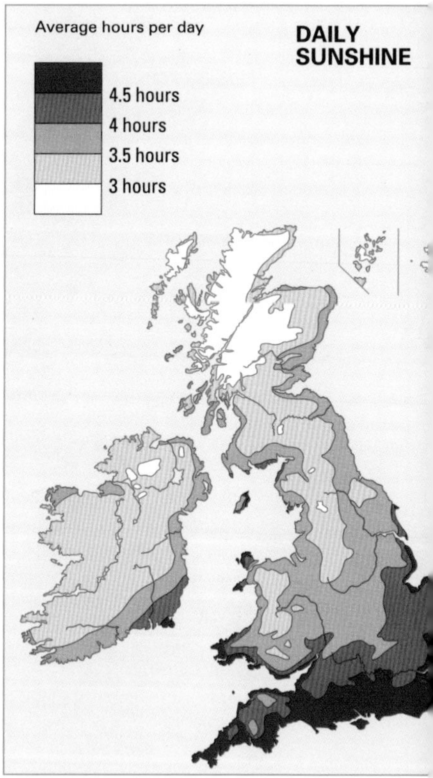

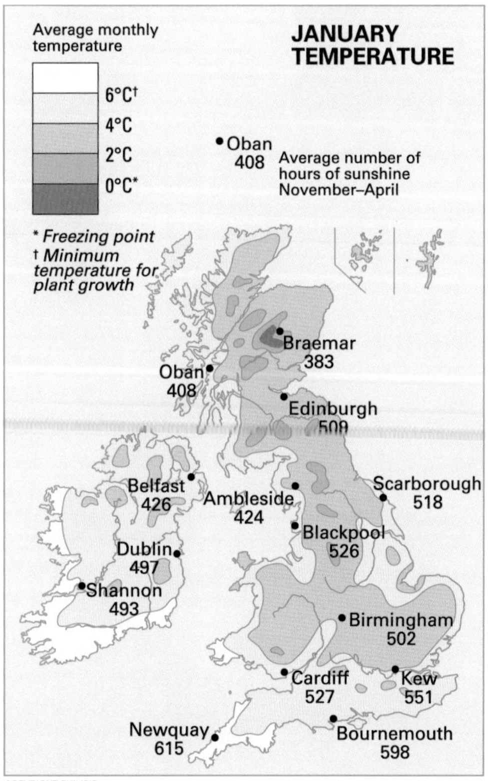

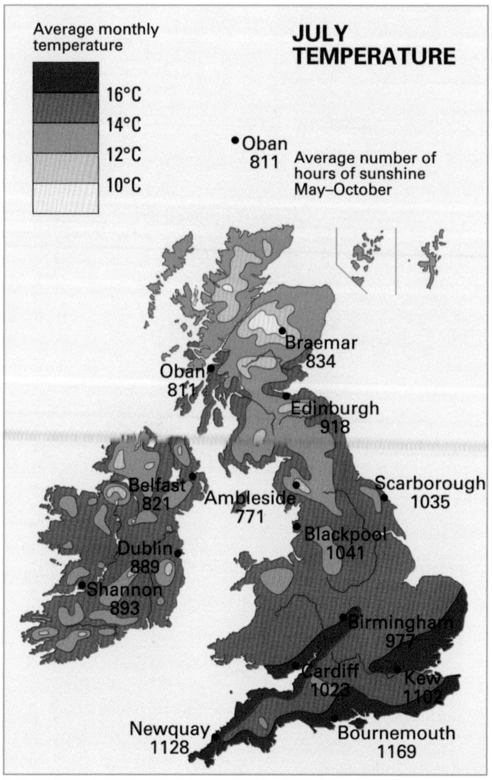

Temperature Records

Highest
38.7°C Cambridge Botanic Garden, 25 July 2019
Lowest
-27.2°C Braemar, Aberdeenshire, 10 January 1982 and 11 February 1895, Altnaharra, Highland, 30 December 19

Rainfall Records

Highest 24 hour total
279 mm Martinstown, near Dorchester, Dorset, 18 July
The highest total for any 24 hour period is 316mm at Seathwaite, Cumbria on 19 November 2009.

Sunshine Records

Highest monthly total
390 hours Eastbourne and Hastings, Sussex, July 1911
Lowest monthly total
0 hours Westminster, Greater London, December 1890

Winds (highest gusts)
150 knots Cairngorm, 20 March 1986

GEOLOGY

MINING

Minerals are rocks that are used as resources. A selection of places where minerals are mined are shown on the map. There is a separate map for energy sources on page 23. Rocks such as limestone, granite and sandstone which are used in the building industry as well as sand and gravel are quarried widely.

Rock type	Geological Era
Sands and clays	TERTIARY (0–65 million years old)
Chalk	SECONDARY (65–230 million years old)
Clays, sands, sandstone	
Limestone	
Coal measures	PRIMARY (230–570 million years old)
Limestone, millstone grit	
Sandstone	
Shales and slates	
Gneiss, quartzite, schists	Various ages
Basalt and granite	

Cleveland (potash)

Navan (lead and zinc)

Winsford (salt)

southern limit of glaciation

St. Austell (china clay)

FLOOD RISK IN ENGLAND AND WALES

■ Areas at greatest risk from flooding

WATER SUPPLY

Spey
33 Loch Ness Dee
Blackwater 34
Tay
Loch Lomond 30 31 Loch Katrine
Carron Valley 36
SCOTTISH WATER
Clyde Tweed
Daer 35 32 Megget
1 Kielder
Derwent 15 Tyne NORTHUMBRIAN WATER
Thirlmere 6 3 5 Cow Green
NORTHERN IRELAND WATER
Haweswater 19 Balderhead
YORKSHIRE WATER
IRISH WATER (UISCE ÉIREANN)
16 Grimwith
UNITED UTILITIES
Longendale
Mersey 22 11 Ladybower
Bann
Erne
Boyne
Poulaphouca 37
Brenig
Celyn 24 26 Carsington 7
Vyrnwy 27 Rutland Water
Shannon
Barrow
Clywedog SEVERN-TRENT WATER 2 Nene ANGLIAN WATER
Elan 28
DŴR CYMRU Valley 23 14 4 Grafham Water
(WELSH WATER) Wye Draycote Water
Suir
Brianne 25 13 Abberton
Blackwater
Carrigadrohid 39 38 Llandegfedd 29 THAMES 21 12 Hanningfield
Inishcarra WATER Lea Valley Thames
18 Chew Valley 20 Thames Valley 9 Bewl Water
17 Wimbleball
SOUTH WEST WATER Roadford
In Ireland each county and London borough is responsible for its own water supply.
8 Colliford
WESSEX WATER SOUTHERN WATER

MAJOR RESERVOIRS
(with capacity in million m³)

England

1	Kielder Reservoir	198
2	Rutland Water	123
3	Haweswater	85
4	Grafham Water	59
5	Cow Green Reservoir	41
6	Thirlmere	41
7	Carsington Reservoir	36
8	Roadford Reservoir	35
9	Bewl Water Reservoir	31
10	Colliford Lake	29
11	Ladybower Reservoir	28
12	Hanningfield Reservoir	27
13	Abberton Reservoir	25
14	Draycote Water	23
15	Derwent Reservoir	22
16	Grimwith Reservoir	22
17	Wimbleball Lake	21
18	Chew Valley Lake	20
19	Balderhead Reservoir	20
20	Thames Valley (linked reservoirs)	
21	Lea Valley (linked reservoirs)	
22	Longendale (linked reservoirs)	

Wales

23	Elan Valley	99
24	Llyn Celyn	74
25	Llyn Brianne	62
26	Llyn Brenig	60
27	Llyn Vyrnwy	60
28	Llyn Clywedog	48
29	Llandegfedd Reservoir	22

Scotland

30	Loch Lomond	86
31	Loch Katrine	64
32	Megget Reservoir	64
33	Loch Ness	26
34	Blackwater Reservoir	25
35	Daer Reservoir	23
36	Carron Valley Reservoir	21

Ireland

37	Poulaphouca Reservoir	168
38	Inishcarra Reservoir	57
39	Carrigadrohid Reservoir	33

WATER SUPPLY

——	Boundaries of water and sewerage service companies in the U.K.
	Regions of reliably high rainfall
③	Major reservoirs
→	Direction of water supply (by pipeline and river)
→	Proposed pipeline
□	Proposed estuary storage site
▽	Proposed groundwater storage site
	Principal sources of groundwater

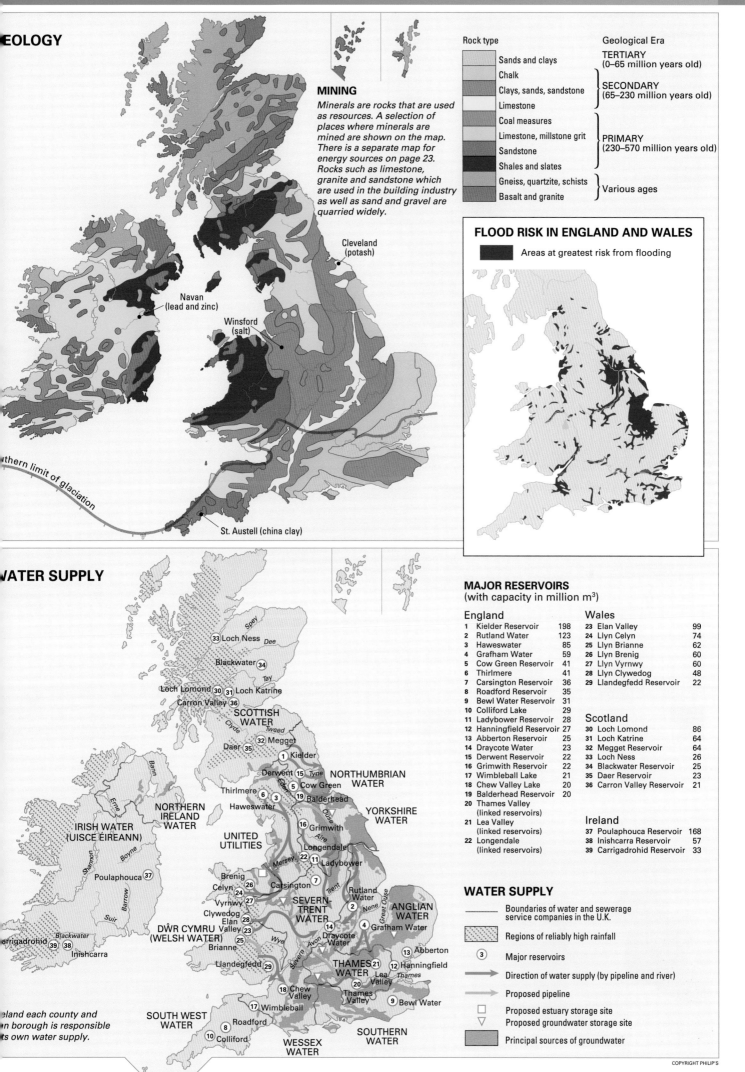

COPYRIGHT PHILIP'S

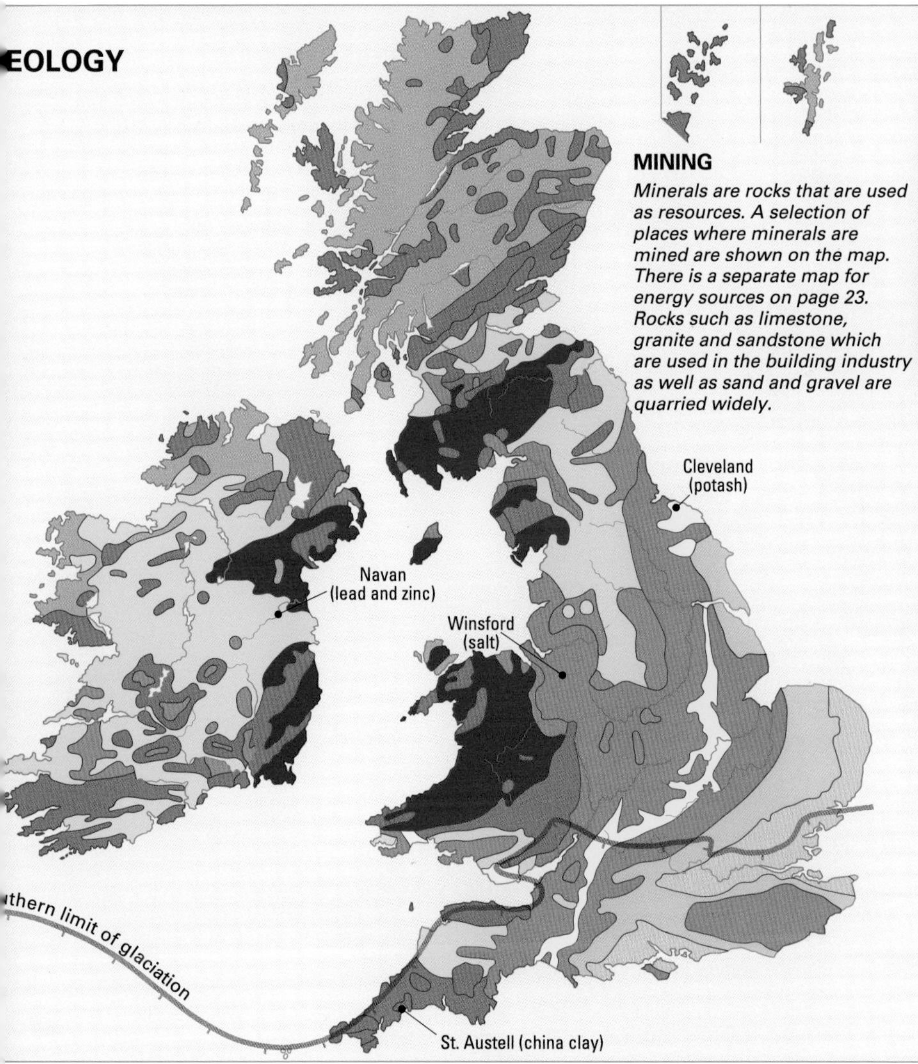

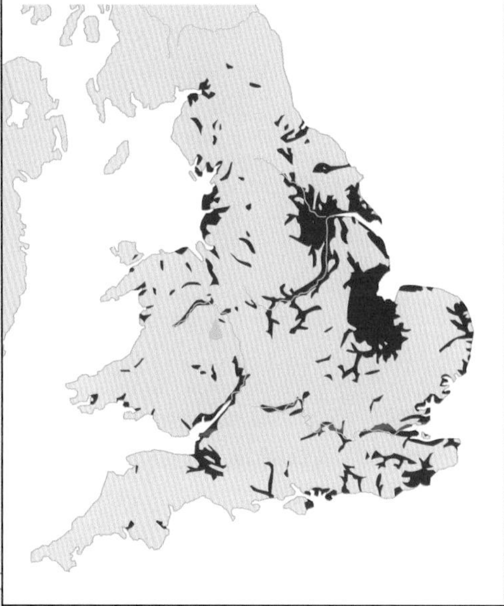

TYPES OF FARM

- Dairy cattle
- Beef cattle
- Sheep
- ● Pigs and/or poultry
- Mixed farming
- Market gardening (fruit and vegetables)
- Cereals
- Other crops (mainly potatoes, sugar beet)
- Northern limit of 9 month growing season
- Forests
- Built-up areas

UPLAND BRITAIN

LOWLAND BRITAIN

Over 9 months growing season south of this line

Areas with over 1000 mm rainfall per year

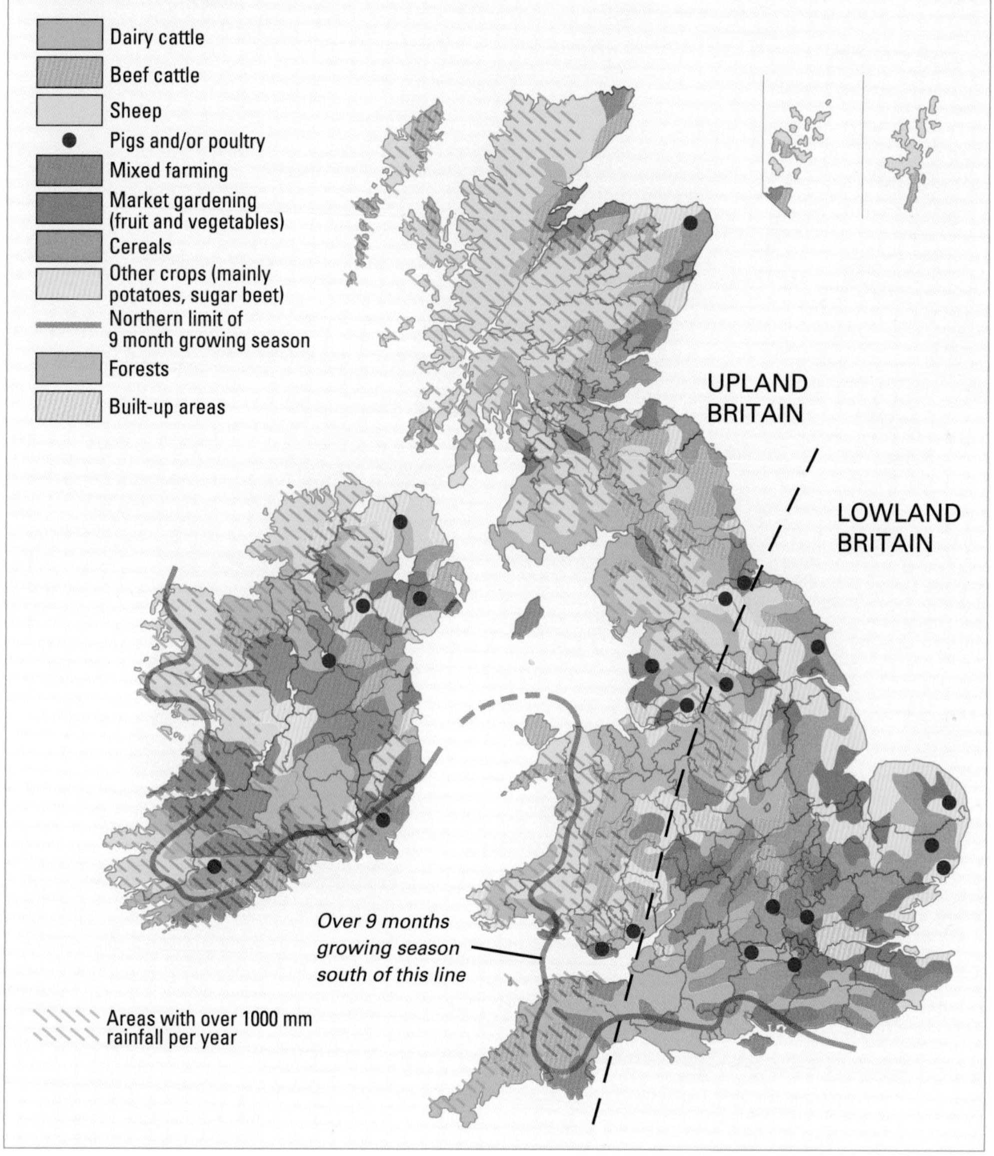

CEREAL FARMING

The percentage of the total farmland used for growing cereals in 2018

- Over 40%
- 25 – 40%
- 10 – 25%
- 5 – 10%
- 0 – 5%

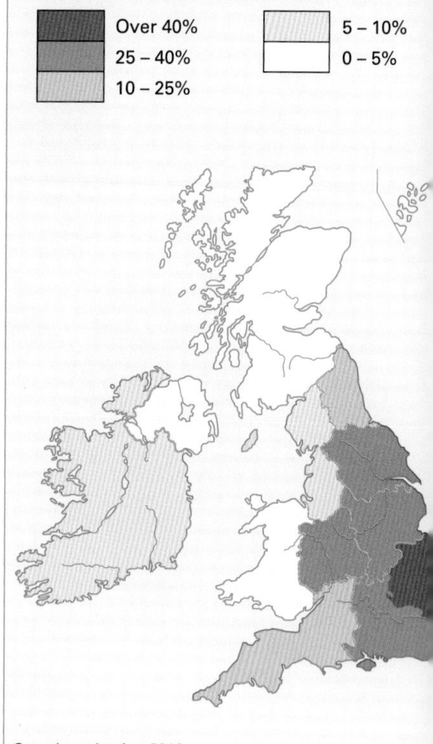

Cereal production 2018
UK 21.1 million tonnes
Ireland 1.9 million tonnes

DAIRY FARMING

The number of dairy cows per 100 hectares of farmland in 2018

- Over 30
- 20 – 30
- 10 – 20
- 0 – 10

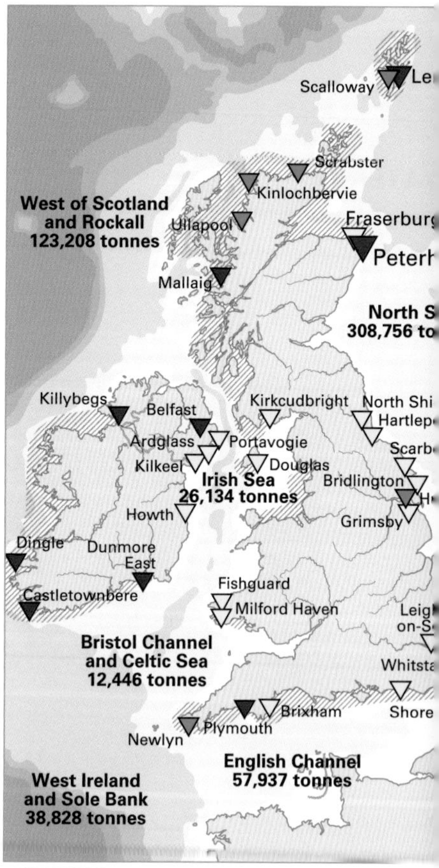

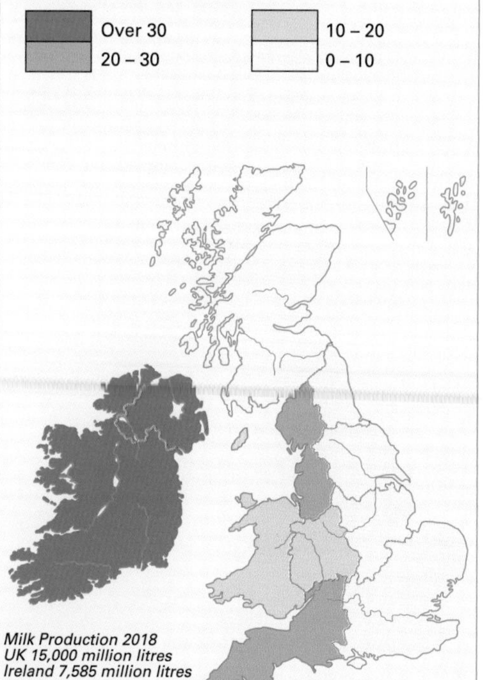

Milk Production 2018
UK 15,000 million litres
Ireland 7,585 million litres

LIVESTOCK FARMING

The number of beef cattle, sheep and pigs per 100 hectares of farmland in 2018

- Over 400
- 300 – 400
- 200 – 300
- 100 – 200
- Under 100

Scalloway   Le

West of Scotland and Rockall
123,208 tonnes   Ullapool   Scrabster
Kinlochbervie   Fraserburg
Peterh
Mallaig

North S
308,756 to

Killybegs   Belfast   Kirkcudbright   North Shi
Ardglass   Portavogie   Hartlep
Kilkeel   Douglas   Scarb
Irish Sea   Bridlington
26,134 tonnes   H
Howth   Grimsby

Dingle   Dunmore
East   Fishguard
Castletownbere   Milford Haven   Leig
on-S

Bristol Channel and Celtic Sea
12,446 tonnes   Whitsta

Brixham   Shore
Newlyn   Plymouth

West Ireland and Sole Bank
38,828 tonnes   English Channel
57,937 tonnes

FISHING

Major fishing ports by size of catch landed

The most import
inshore fishing g

- ▼ Mainly deep sea fish (e.g. cod)
- ▼ Mainly shallow sea fish (e.g. mackerel)
- ▽ Mainly shellfish e.g. lobster

North Sea
308,756 tonnes

Total amount landed
each fishing region 2

1000 500 200 100 50 m   Depth of sea in metres

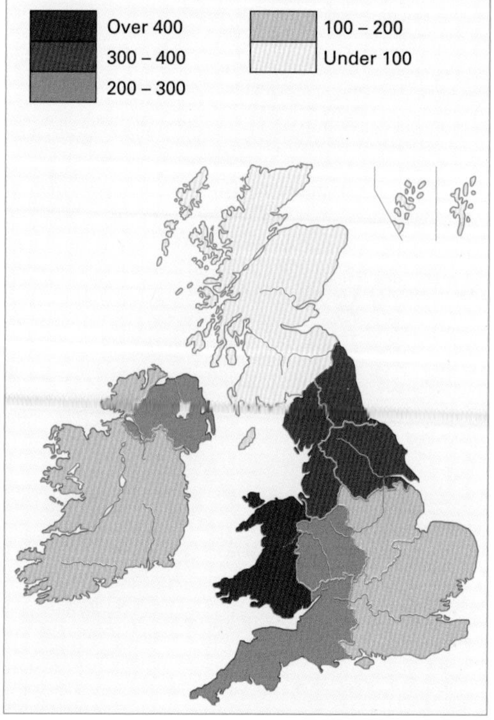

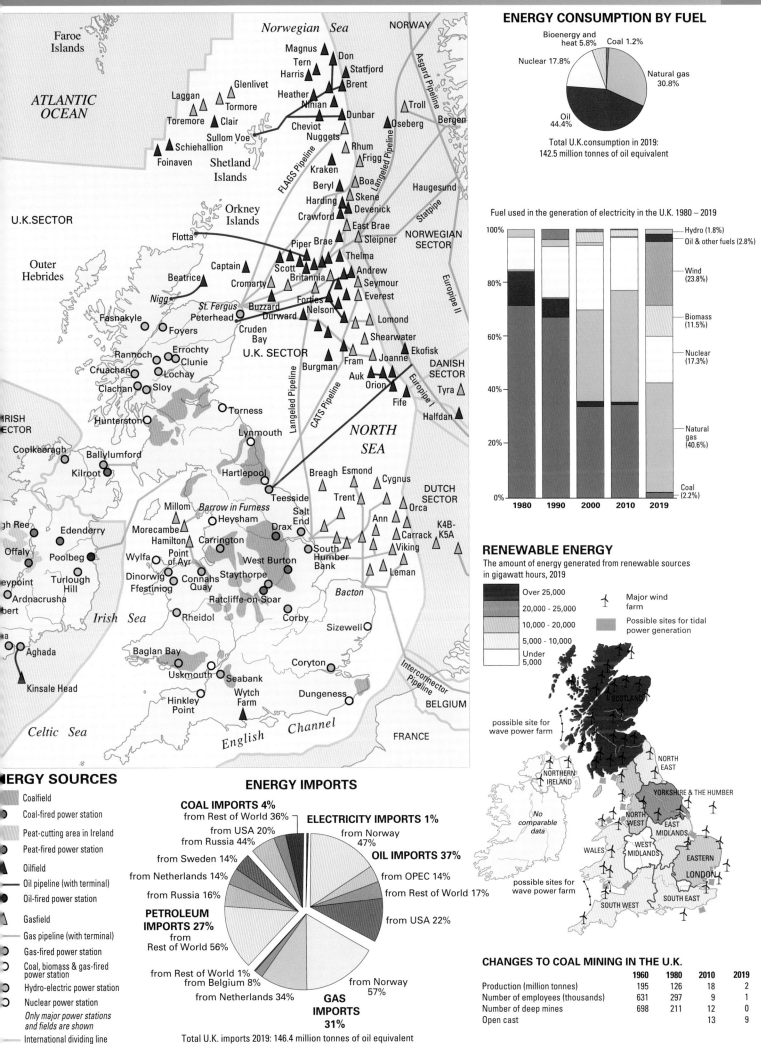

ENERGY CONSUMPTION BY FUEL

- Bioenergy and heat 5.8%
- Coal 1.2%
- Nuclear 17.8%
- Natural gas 30.8%
- Oil 44.4%

Total U.K. consumption in 2019: 142.5 million tonnes of oil equivalent

Fuel used in the generation of electricity in the U.K. 1980 – 2019

(Bar chart 1980, 1990, 2000, 2010, 2019; scale 0%–100%)

- Hydro (1.8%)
- Oil & other fuels (2.8%)
- Wind (23.8%)
- Biomass (11.5%)
- Nuclear (17.3%)
- Natural gas (40.6%)
- Coal (2.2%)

RENEWABLE ENERGY

The amount of energy generated from renewable sources in gigawatt hours, 2019

- Over 25,000
- 20,000 – 25,000
- 10,000 – 20,000
- 5,000 – 10,000
- Under 5,000
- ✦ Major wind farm
- Possible sites for tidal power generation

SCOTLAND
NORTHERN IRELAND
No comparable data
possible site for wave power farm
NORTH EAST
YORKSHIRE & THE HUMBER
NORTH WEST
EAST MIDLANDS
WALES
WEST MIDLANDS
EASTERN
LONDON
possible sites for wave power farm
SOUTH WEST
SOUTH EAST

ENERGY SOURCES

- Coalfield
- Coal-fired power station
- Peat-cutting area in Ireland
- Peat-fired power station
- Oilfield
- Oil pipeline (with terminal)
- Oil-fired power station
- Gasfield
- Gas pipeline (with terminal)
- Gas-fired power station
- Coal, biomass & gas-fired power station
- Hydro-electric power station
- Nuclear power station

Only major power stations and fields are shown

- International dividing line

ENERGY IMPORTS

COAL IMPORTS 4%
- from Rest of World 36%
- from USA 20%
- from Russia 44%

ELECTRICITY IMPORTS 1%
- from Norway 47%

OIL IMPORTS 37%
- from OPEC 14%
- from Rest of World 17%
- from USA 22%
- from Norway 57%

PETROLEUM IMPORTS 27%
- from Rest of World 56%
- from Sweden 14%
- from Netherlands 14%
- from Russia 16%

GAS IMPORTS 31%
- from Rest of World 1%
- from Belgium 8%
- from Netherlands 34%

Total U.K. imports 2019: 146.4 million tonnes of oil equivalent

CHANGES TO COAL MINING IN THE U.K.

	1960	1980	2010	2019
Production (million tonnes)	195	126	18	2
Number of employees (thousands)	631	297	9	1
Number of deep mines	698	211	12	0
Open cast			13	9

COPYRIGHT PHILIP'S

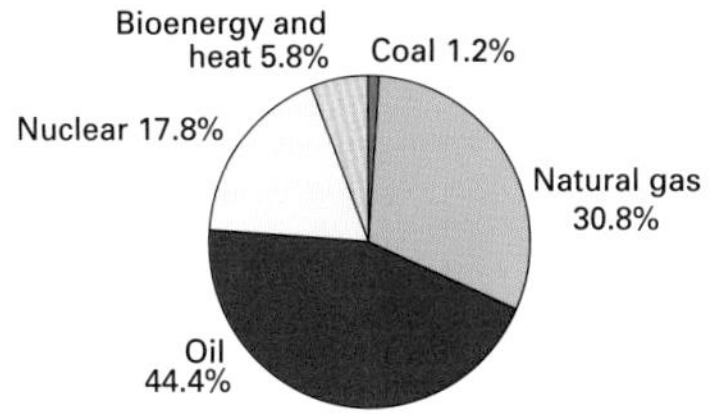

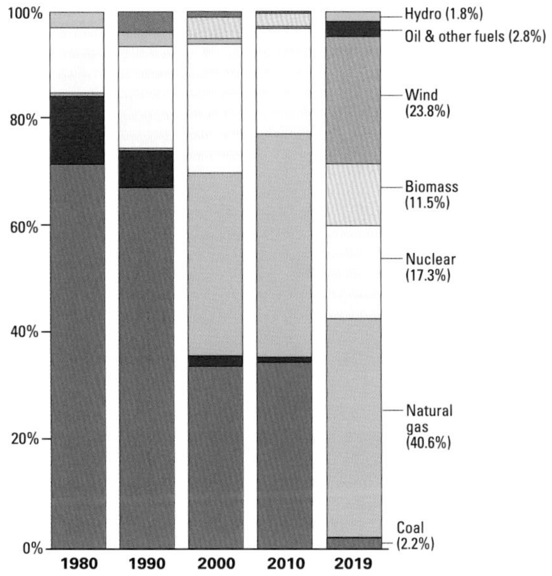

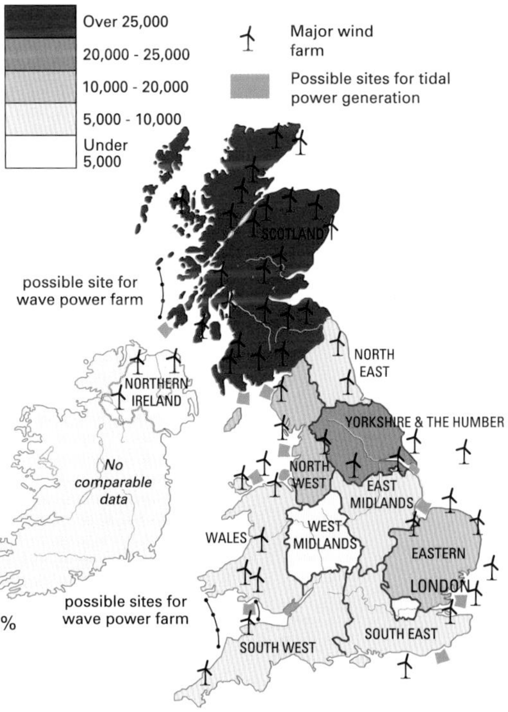

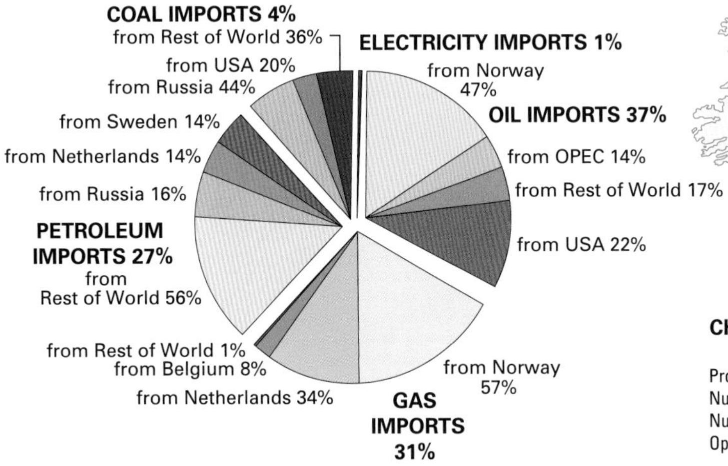

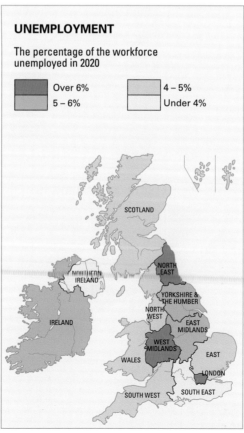

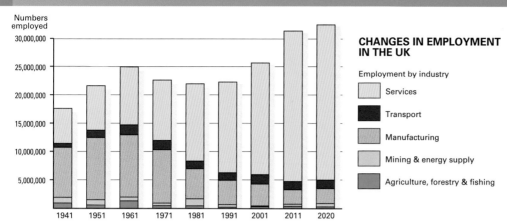

CHANGES IN EMPLOYMENT IN THE UK

Numbers employed

Employment by industry
- Services
- Transport
- Manufacturing
- Mining & energy supply
- Agriculture, forestry & fishing

1941 1951 1961 1971 1981 1991 2001 2011 2020

▲ Canary Wharf, London, is a centre of ba – an important part of the service industry

▲ These Mini Clubman cars are being manufactured at the BMW factory, Oxford.

▲ An engineer is shown working on a jet engine in the Rolls-Royce factory, Derby.

INCOME

The average gross weekly earnings of males and females in full employment in 2020

- Over £800
- £700 – £800
- £625 – £700
- £600 – £625
- £550 – £600

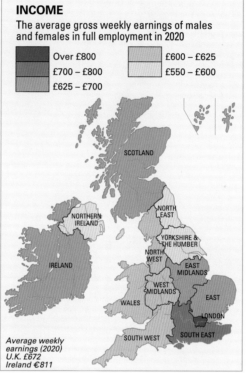

Average weekly earnings (2020)
U.K. £672
Ireland €811

EMPLOYMENT IN SERVICES

The percentage of the workforce employed in the service industry in 2020

- Over 90%
- 85 – 90%
- 82.5 – 85%
- 80 – 82.5%
- Under 80%

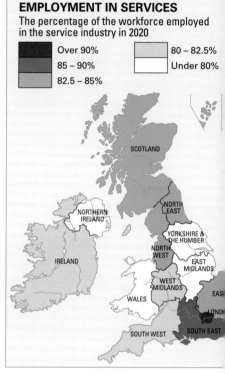

EMPLOYMENT IN MANUFACTURING INDUSTRY

The percentage of the workforce employed in manufacturing in 2020

- Over 11%
- 10 – 11%
- 9 – 10%
- 7 – 9%
- 5 – 7%
- Under 5%

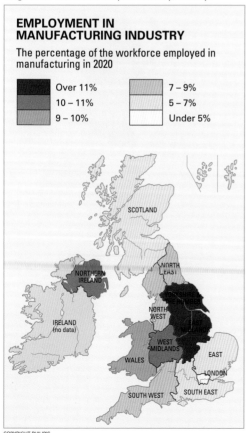

UNEMPLOYMENT

The percentage of the workforce unemployed in 2020

- Over 6%
- 5 – 6%
- 4 – 5%
- Under 4%

U.K. TRADE

Trade is balanced by money coming in for servic such as banking and insurance.

Total Imports 2020 £427.5 billion

- Machinery & transport 22%
- Miscellaneous goods 26%
- Electronics 12%
- Oil & other fuels 4%
- Medicines & pharmaceuticals 5%
- Chemicals 7%
- Food & drink
- Clothing & textiles 7%
- Metals 8%

Total Exports 2020 £311.5 billion

- Machinery & transport 30%
- Miscellaneous goods 20%
- Clothing & textiles 3%
- Oil & other fuels 4%
- Food & drink 7%
- Medicines & pharmaceuticals 7%
- Electronics 8%
- Metals 11
- Chemicals 9%

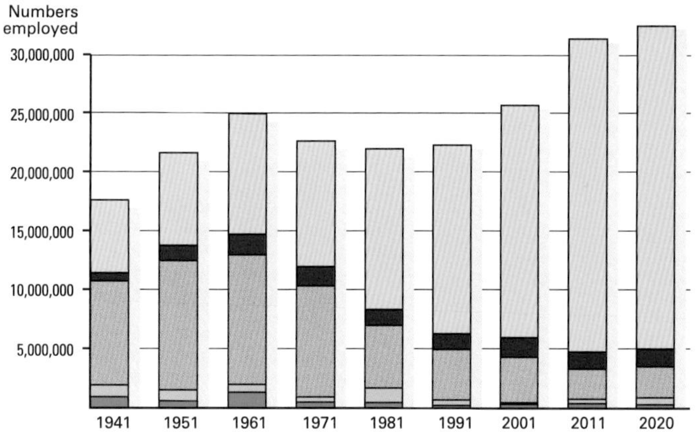

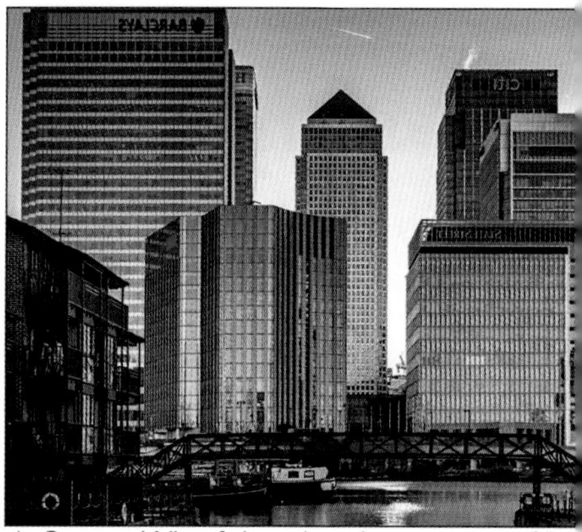

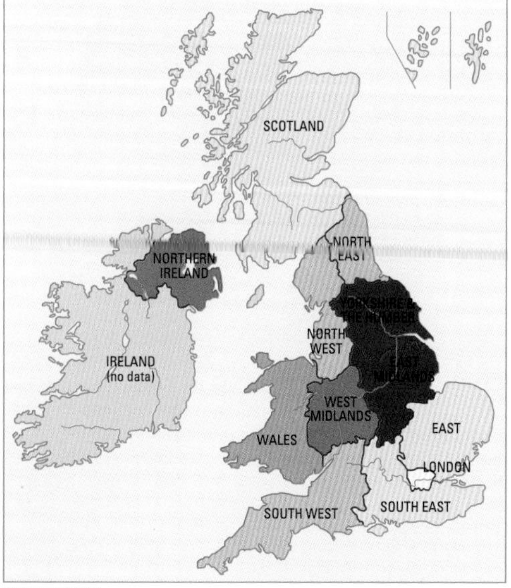

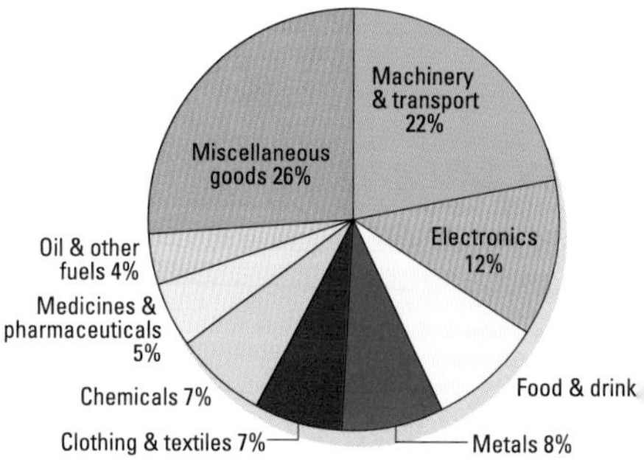

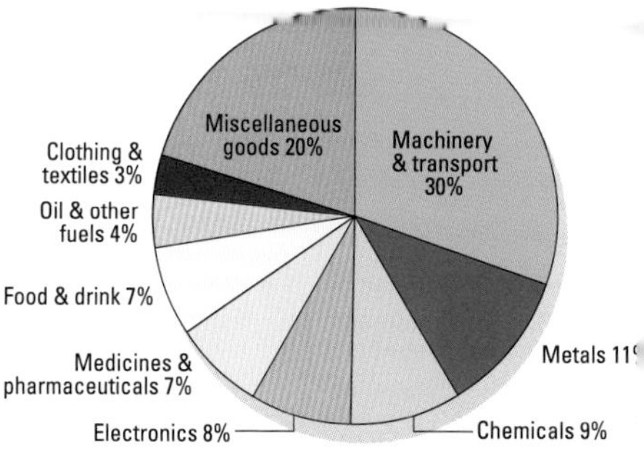

POPULATION FACTS

U.K. Population 2019	**66,796,807**
of which England	56,286,961
Scotland	5,463,300
Wales	3,152,879
Northern Ireland	1,893,667
Ireland Population 2019	**4,904,000**

AGE STRUCTURE OF THE U.K. IN 1901 AND 2019

age structure shows how old people are and the
entage in each age group that is male and female.
diagram is called a population pyramid. For example,
01, 20% of the female population was aged between
9. In 2019, about 11% were in this group.

POPULATION DENSITY

Number of people per square kilometre in 2019

- Over 1000
- 500 – 1000
- 200 – 500
- 100 – 200
- 50 – 100
- 25 – 50
- Under 25

The average density for the U.K. is 275 people per km².

The average density for Ireland is 70 people per km².

Population of major cities

- ■ Over 5,000,000
- ● 1,000,000 – 5,000,000
- ■ 400,000 – 1,000,000
- ● 200,000 – 400,000
- • 100,000 – 200,000

ATIONALITY

n-British as a percentage of total
ulation in 2020

- Over 10%
- 7.5 – 10%
- 5 – 7.5%
- 0 – 5%

00 Total number of
non-British
people in each
region

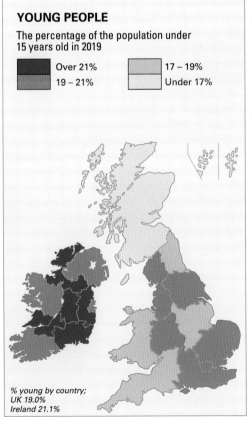

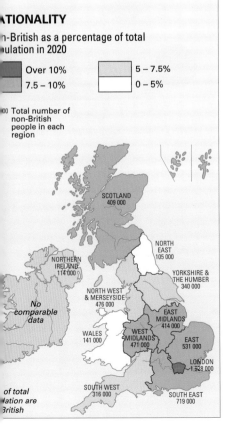

SCOTLAND
409 000

NORTH EAST
105 000

NORTHERN IRELAND
114 000

YORKSHIRE & THE HUMBER
340 000

No comparable data

NORTH WEST & MERSEYSIDE
476 000

EAST MIDLANDS
414 000

WALES
141 000

WEST MIDLANDS
471 000

EAST
531 000

LONDON
1 928 000

SOUTH WEST
316 000

SOUTH EAST
719 000

of total
ation are
British

YOUNG PEOPLE

The percentage of the population under
15 years old in 2019

- Over 21%
- 19 – 21%
- 17 – 19%
- Under 17%

% young by country;
UK 19.0%
Ireland 21.1%

OLDER PEOPLE

The percentage of the population aged 65 and
over in 2019

- Over 22%
- 20 – 22%
- 18 – 20%
- 16 – 18%
- 14 – 16%
- Under 14%

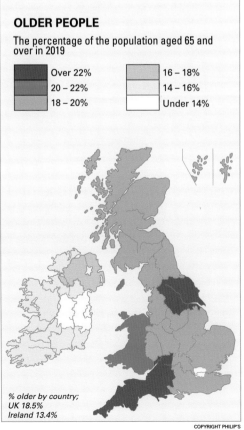

% older by country;
UK 18.5%
Ireland 13.4%

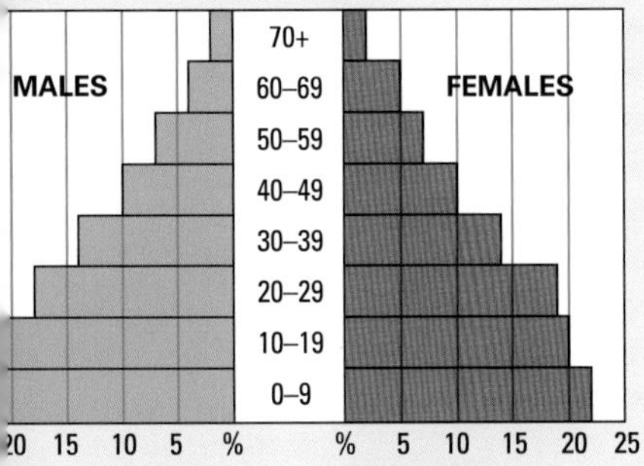

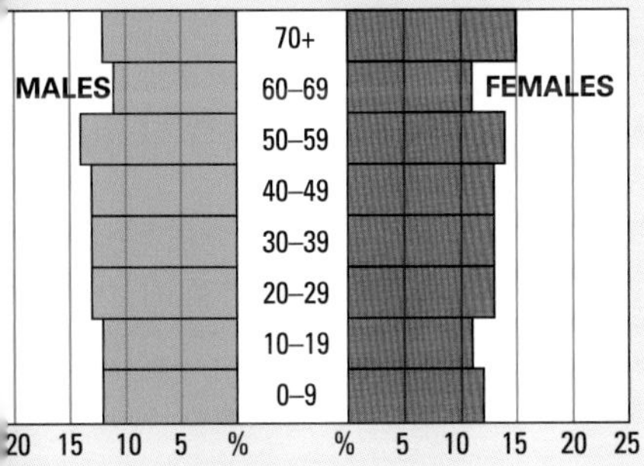

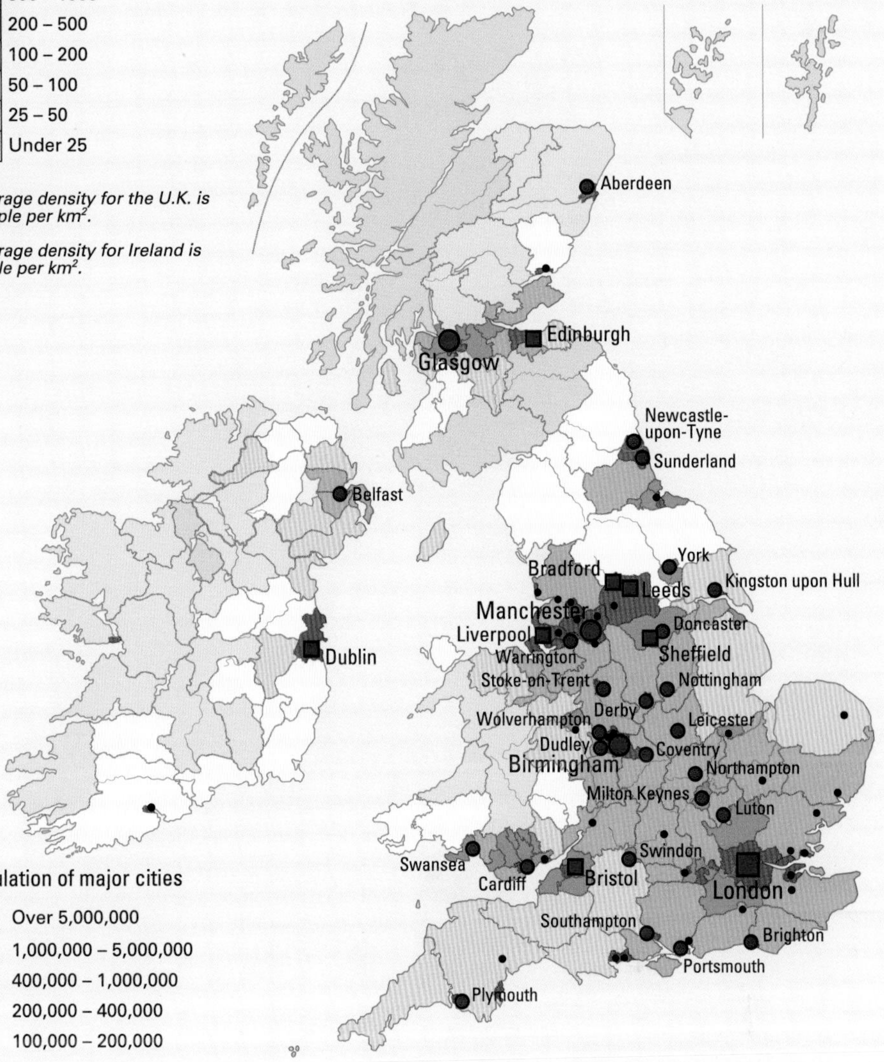

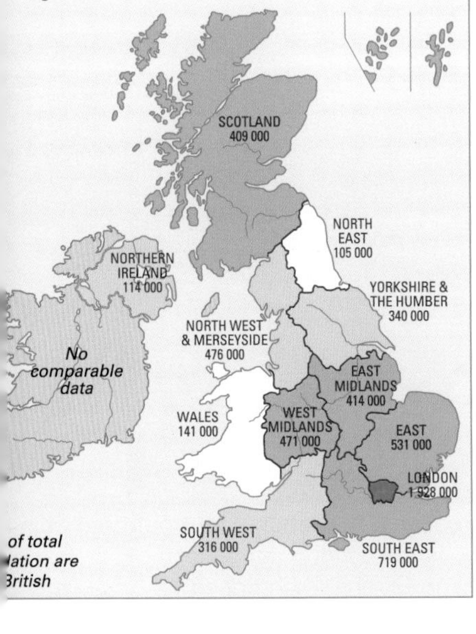

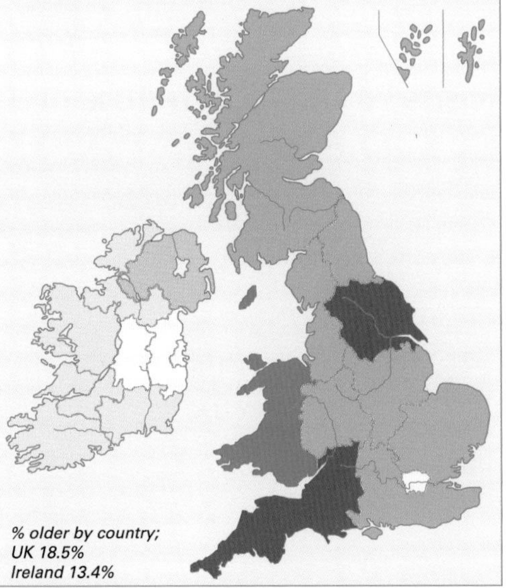

ROADS AND FERRIES

- M6 Motorways
- Other main roads
- Principal car ferry routes
- Channel Tunnel

RAILWAYS

- Electrified lines
- Other main lines
- High-speed rail link London to Lille, Brussels and Paris
- High Speed 2 (HS2) rail link (under con.) London to Birmingham, Leeds and Manchester

AIRPORTS

Passenger traffic in millions (2019)

70,000
35,000
10,000
5,000
1,000

SEAPORTS

Goods traffic by port in million tonnes (2019)

60,000
30,000
10,000
5,000

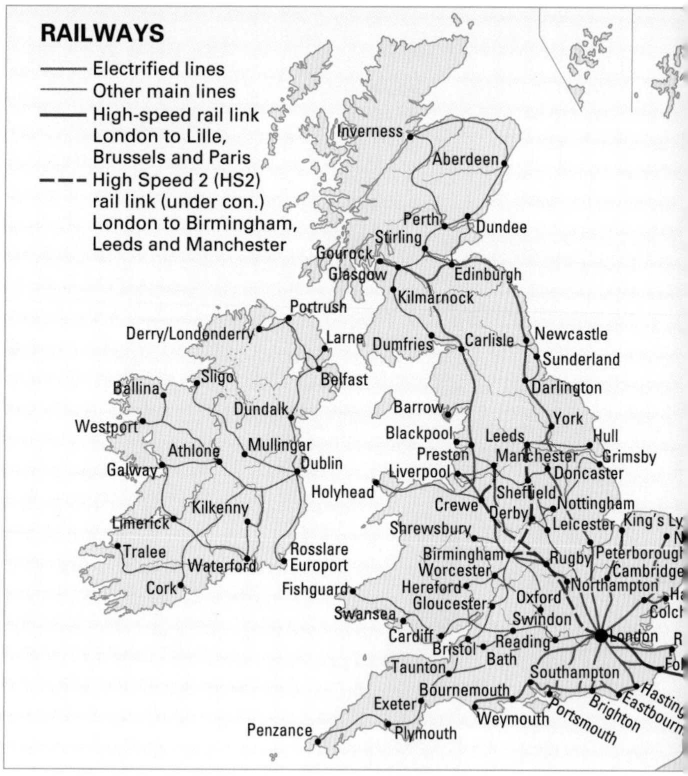

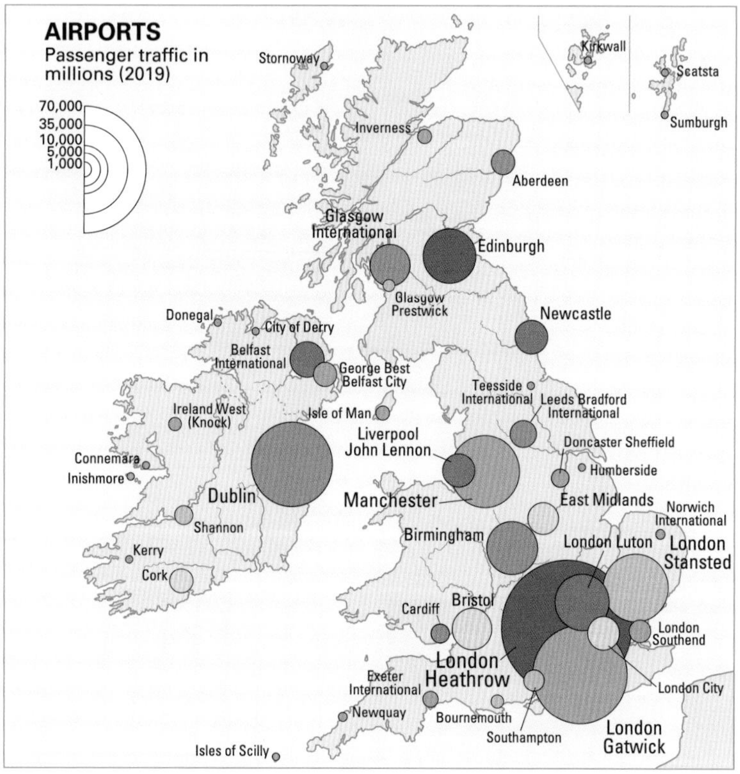

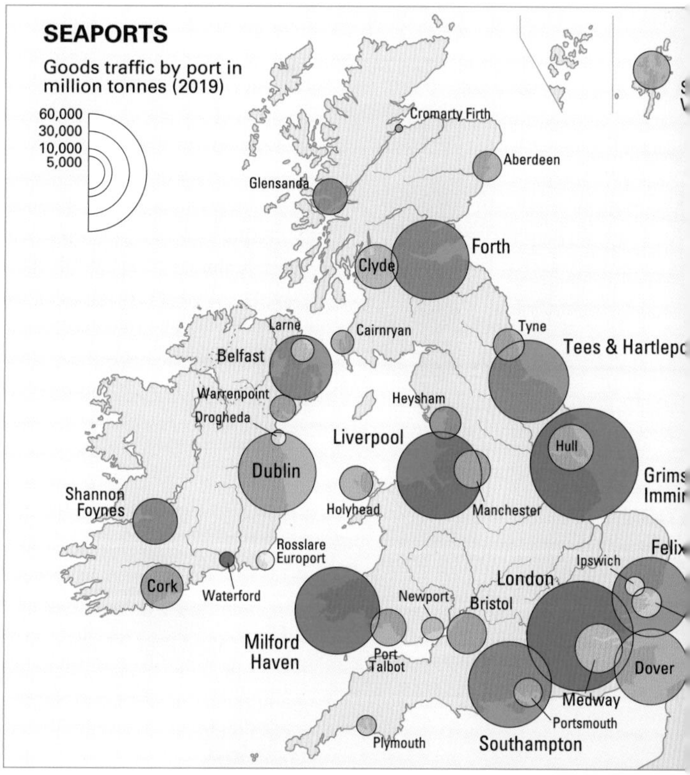

VISITS TO AND FROM THE U.K.

Millions of visitors from U.K. (2019)

0 1 2 3 4 5 6 7 8 9 10 11 12 13 14 15 16 17 18

- Spain
- France
- Italy
- U.S.A.
- Rep. of Ireland
- Netherlands
- Greece
- Germany
- Portugal
- Poland

VISITS ABROAD BY U.K. RESIDENTS

VISITS TO U.K. BY FOREIGN VISITORS

- Netherlands
- Italy
- Spain
- Rep. of Ireland
- Germany
- France
- U.S.A.

5 4 3 2 1 0
Millions of visitors to the U.K. (2019)

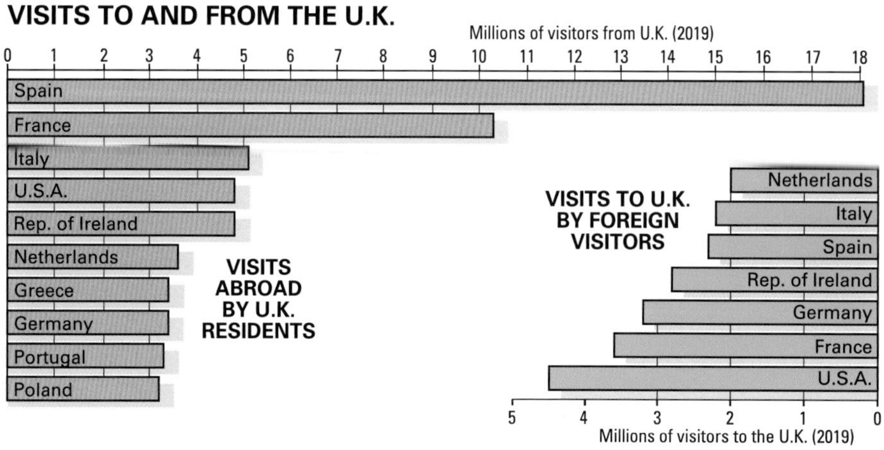

▲ Eurostar at St. Pancras International. This station is the London terminus of the high-speed rail link to Europe, High Speed 1.

LEISURE

- National Parks
- Areas of Outstanding Natural Beauty
- National Scenic Areas
- Built-up areas
- - - - Long distance footpaths
- ● Main tourist resorts
- ◆ Other tourist attractions

TRAVEL

- Motorways
- Other important roads
- Main railways
- Main ferry routes
- - - - Channel Tunnel
- ⊕ Main airports
- ○ Ports and other towns

TOP UK TOURIST ATTRACTIONS

- ● Museum or gallery   ● Historic Property
- ○ Other attraction

		Visitors in millions (2019)
1.	British Museum, London	● 6.2
2.	Tate Modern, London	● 6.1
3.	National Gallery, London	● 6.0
4.	Natural History Museum, London	● 5.4
5.	Southbank Centre, London	○ 4.4
6.	Victoria & Albert Museum, London	● 4.0
7.	Science Museum, London	● 3.3
8.	Tower of London	● 3.0
9.	Royal Museums, Greenwich	● 2.9
10.	Somerset House, London	● 2.8
11.	Royal Botanic Gardens, Kew	○ 2.3
12.	National Museum of Scotland, Edinburgh	● 2.2
13.	Edinburgh Castle	● 2.2
14.	Chester Zoo	○ 2.1
15.	Kelvingrove Art Gallery & Museum, Glasgow	● 1.8
16.	Tate Britain, London	● 1.8
17.	Royal Albert Hall, London	○ 1.7
18.	St Paul's Cathedral, London	● 1.7
19.	National Portrait Gallery, London	● 1.6
20.	Stonehenge, Wiltshire	● 1.6

TOP IRELAND TOURIST ATTRACTIONS

- ● Museum or gallery   ● Historic Property
- ○ Other attraction

		Visitors in millions (2019)
1.	Guinness Storehouse, Dublin	○ 1.7
2.	Cliffs of Moher Visitor Experience, Clare	○ 1.6
3.	Dublin Zoo	○ 1.3
4.	Book of Kells, Dublin	○ 1.1
5.	Castletown House Parklands, Kildare	● 1.0
6.	Kilkenny Castle Parklands	● 0.9
7.	National Gallery of Ireland, Dublin	● 0.8
8.	Glendalough Site, Wicklow	● 0.7
9.	Tayto Park, Meath	○ 0.7
10.	National Botanic Gardens, Dublin	○ 0.7

COPYRIGHT PHILIP'S

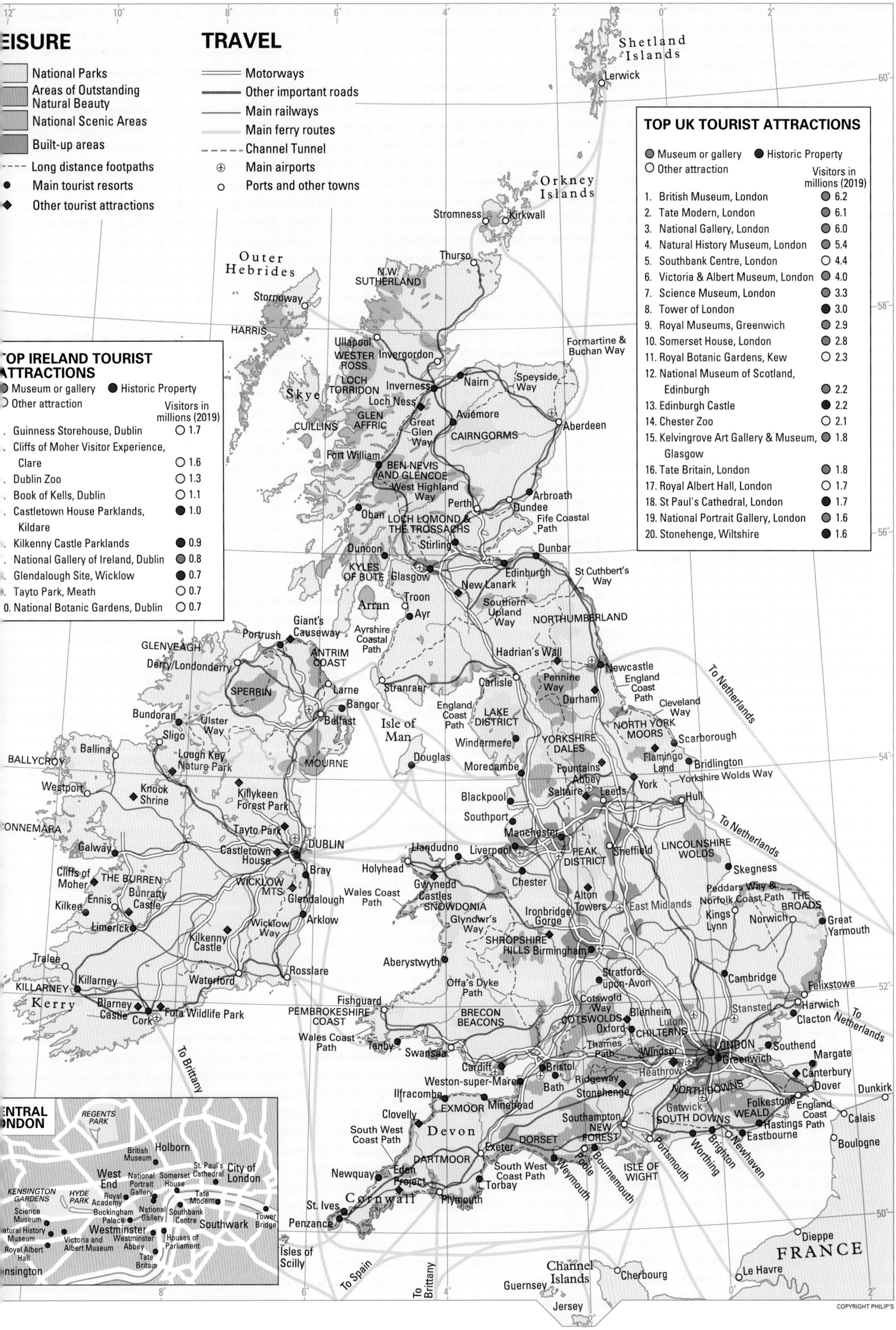

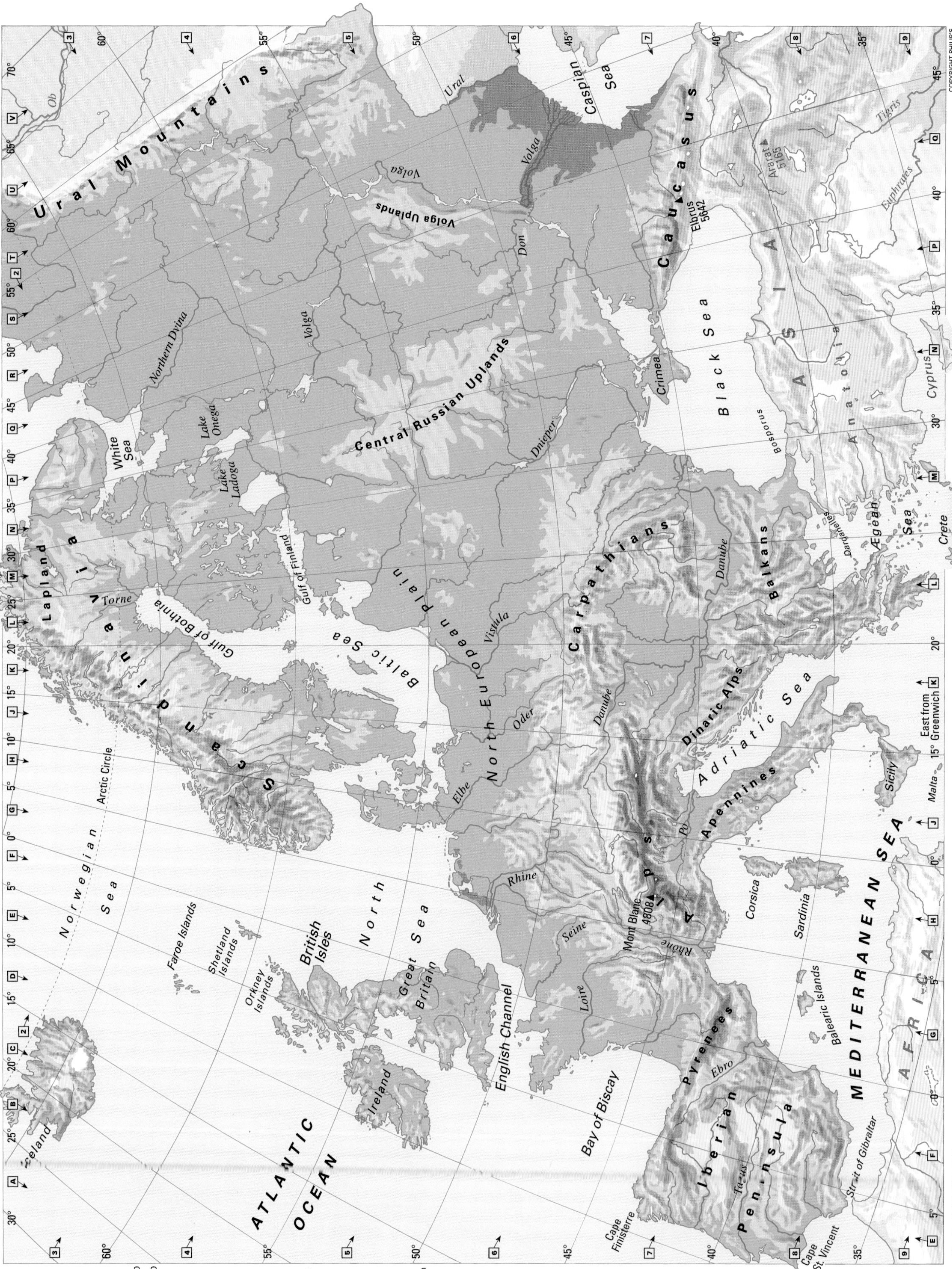

Ural Mountains
Caspian Sea
Caucasus
Elbrus 5642
Ararat 5165
Tigris
Euphrates
Ural
Volga
Volga Uplands
Don
Ob
Northern Dvina
Central Russian Uplands
Dnieper
Crimea
Black Sea
Bosporus
Dardanelles
Aegean Sea
Crete
Cyprus
Anatolia
ASIA
White Sea
Lake Onega
Lake Ladoga
Gulf of Finland
Gulf of Bothnia
Baltic Sea
North European Plain
Vistula
Oder
Elbe
Rhine
Seine
Loire
Rhône
Danube
Carpathians
Balkans
Dinaric Alps
Adriatic Sea
Apennines
Po
Alps
Mont Blanc 4808
Sicily
Malta
Corsica
Sardinia
Balearic Islands
MEDITERRANEAN SEA
AFRICA
Pyrenees
Ebro
Iberian Peninsula
Tagus
Strait of Gibraltar
Cape St. Vincent
Cape Finisterre
Bay of Biscay
English Channel
Great Britain
Ireland
British Isles
North Sea
Orkney Islands
Shetland Islands
Faroe Islands
Norwegian Sea
Iceland
ATLANTIC OCEAN
Scandinavia
Lapland
Torne
North Cape
Arctic Circle
East from Greenwich
COPYRIGHT PHILIP'S

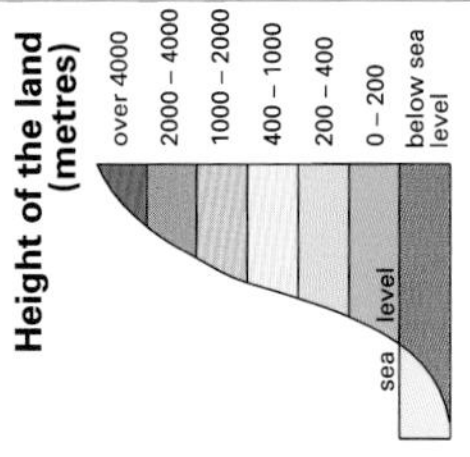

Height of the land (metres)
over 4000
2000 – 4000
1000 – 2000
400 – 1000
200 – 400
0 – 200
below sea level
sea level

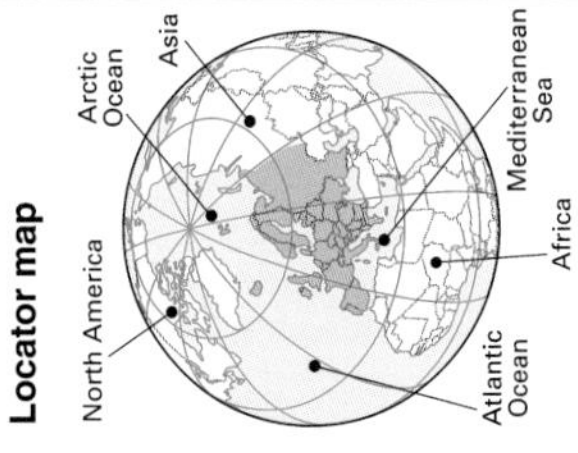

Locator map
Arctic Ocean
Asia
Mediterranean Sea
Africa
Atlantic Ocean
North America

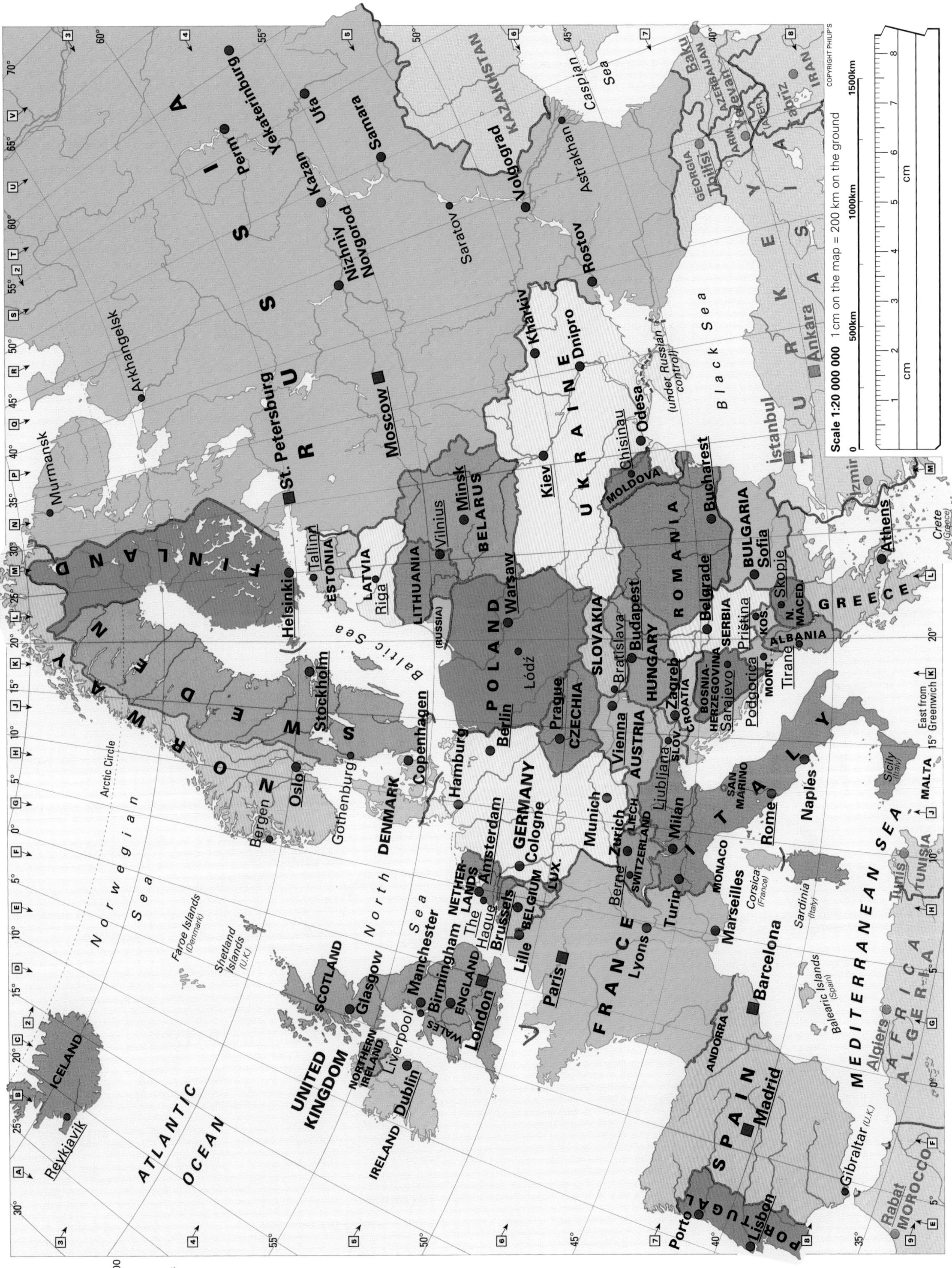

Key to map symbols

- ■ Over 5,000,000 inhabitants
- ● 1,000,000 - 5,000,000 inhabitants
- • Under 1,000,000 inhabitants
- London — Capital cities underlined
- — Country boundaries

Key to abbreviations

ARM. = Armenia
AZER. = Azerbaijan
KOS. = Kosovo
LEB. = Lebanon
LIECH. = Liechtenstein
LUX. = Luxembourg
MACED. = Macedonia
MONT. = Montenegro
SLOV. = Slovenia

EUROPEAN UNION

This map shows the members of the European Union and the year they joined.

- Founder members (Treaty of Rome
- Joined in 19
- Joined in 19
- Joined in 19
- Joined in 19 (German unifi
- Joined in 19
- Joined in 20
- Joined in 20
- Joined in 20
- ○ HQ of European institutions
- € Euro-zone
- Non-memb

Albania, Montenegr North Macedonia, S and Turkey have app for membership of t

The UK was a memb from 1973 to 2020

WEALTH

The value of total production divided by population (US $, 2019)

- Over $50,000 per person
- $40,000 – 50,000 per person
- $30,000 – 40,000 per person
- $20,000 – 30,000 per person
- $10,000 – 20,000 per person
- Under $10,000 per person

Wealthiest countries:

Switzerland US$ 85,500
Norway US$ 82,500
Luxembourg US$ 73,910

Poorest countries:

Ukraine US$ 3,370
Moldova US$ 4,590
Kosovo US$ 4,640

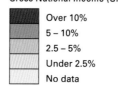

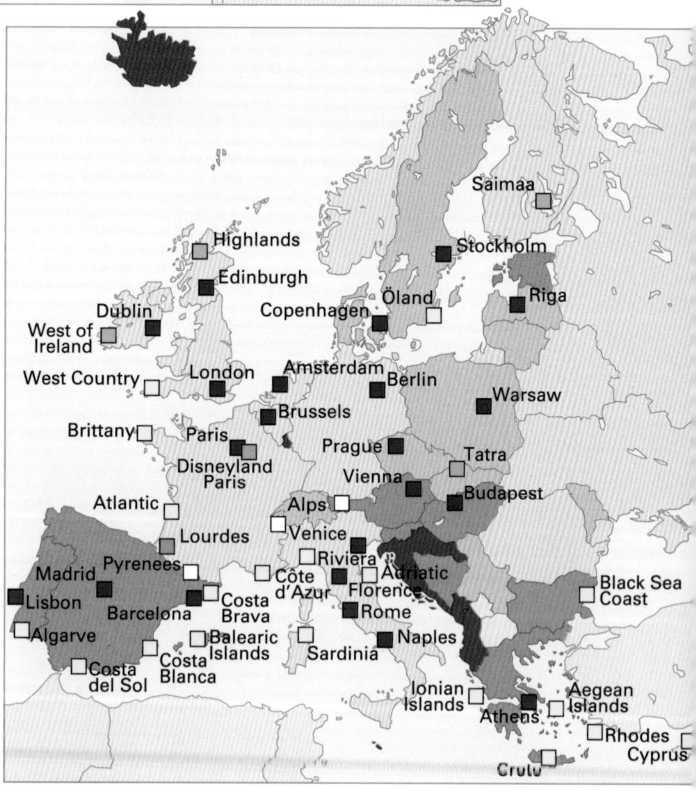

TOURISM

Tourism receipts as a percentage of Gross National Income (GNI) (2019)

- Over 10%
- 5 – 10%
- 2.5 – 5%
- Under 2.5%
- No data

Tourist destinations

- Cultural & historical centr
- Coastal resorts
- Ski resorts
- Centres of entertainment
- Places of pilgrimage
- Places of great natural bea

Northern Europe

ARCTIC OCEAN

North Cape

Hammerfest · Vardø
Vadsø ·
Tromsø · Kirkenes
Lake Inari
Murmansk

Norwegian Sea

Vesterålen

Lofoten Islands

Narvik
Kebnekaise ▲ 2123
Kiruna
Gällivare

ATLANTIC OCEAN

Bodø

Arctic Circle

Kiruna
Gällivare

L Torne

Muonio

Rovaniemi
Kemijärvi

Kemi

Kemi
Luleå
Oulu

Skellefteå

Lapland

Lake Imandra

Kola Peninsula

Kandalaksha

White Sea

Belomorsk

Arkhangelsk

Onega

Kristiansund

Ålesund

Trondheim
Östersund
Storsjön

Galdhøpiggen ▲ 2469
Jotunheimen
Lillehammer

Sogne Fjord

Gläma

Mjøsa Lake

N O R W A Y

S W E D E N

Norrland

Umeå

Vaasa

Lake Oulu
Kajaani

Karelia

Lake Onega

Kuopio
Joensuu

FINLAND
Jyväskylä
Petrozavodsk

Lake Saimaa

Lake Ladoga

Svealand

Sundsvall

Gävle

Pori
Tampere
Lahti

Vyborg

Cherepovets

Helsinki
Kotka
St. Petersburg

gen

Hardanger Fjord
Haugesund
Stavanger
Drammen
Fredrikstad
Kristiansand

Oslo

Västerås
Örebro
Lake Väner

Götä Canal

Stockholm

Uppsala

Turku

Gulf of Finland

Tallinn

Novgorod

Rybinsk Reservoir

Tver

RUSSIA

Volga

Skagerrak
Skagen
Gothenburg
Aalborg
Götaland
Borås
Jönköping

Lake Vätter

Norrköping
Linköping

Hiiumaa
Saaremaa

ESTONIA

Lake Chudskoye

Pskov

Öland

Öland

Gotland

Gulf of Riga

LATVIA

Liepāja

Riga

West Drina

Moscow

DENMARK
Jutland
Aarhus
Copenhagen
Esbjerg
Odense
Sjaelland
Malmö

Kattegat

Helsingborg

Klaipėda

LITHUANIA

Kaunas

Vitsyebsk

Smolensk
Kaluga

Bornholm

Kiel Canal
Kiel
Rostock

Hamburg
Bremen
Hanover

Baltic Sea

Kaliningrad
(RUSSIA)

Gdańsk

Vistula

Vilnius

Niemen

Minsk
Mahilyow

Bryansk

GERMANY
ogne
Berlin
Leipzig
Dresden

nn

Dortmund

Szczecin
Bydgoszcz

Oder

POLAND
Poznań
Warsaw
Łódź
Wrocław

Białystok

Brest

BELARUS

Pripet

Homyel

Dnieper

Frankfurt

CZECHIA
Prague

Kraków

Lublin

Chornobyl

U K R A I N E

Zhytomyr
Kiev

East from Greenwich

COPYRIGHT PHILIP'S

Scale 1:10 000 000   1 cm on the map = 100 km on the ground

0   100km   200km   300km   400km   500km   600km

1   2   3   4   5   6
cm   cm

Height of the land (metres)

over 4000
2000-4000
1000-2000
400-1000
200-400
0-200
sea level
below sea level

Key to map symbols

■   Over 5,000,000 inhabitants

●   1,000,000 - 5,000,000 inhabitants

•   Under 1,000,000 inhabitants

Helsinki   Capital cities underlined

———   Country boundaries

Locator map

Western Europe

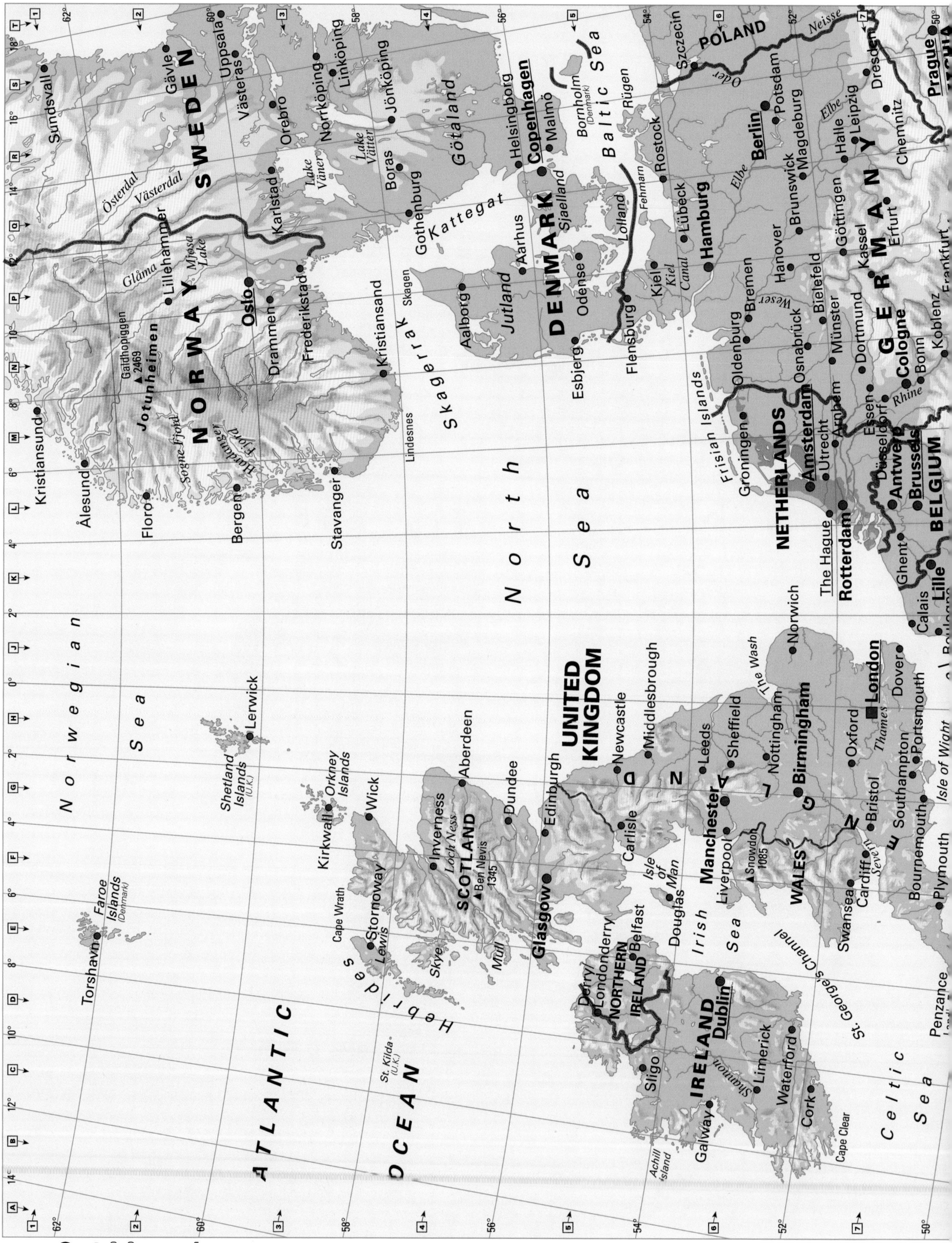

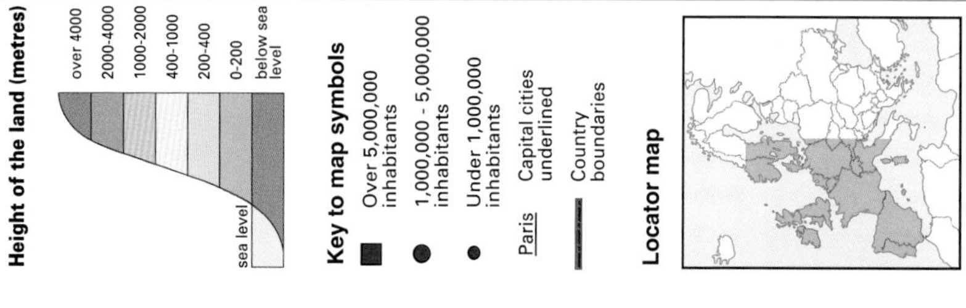

Height of the land (metres)

- over 4000
- 2000-4000
- 1000-2000
- 400-1000
- 200-400
- 0-200
- below sea level

sea level

Key to map symbols

- ■ Over 5,000,000 inhabitants
- ● 1,000,000 - 5,000,000 inhabitants
- • Under 1,000,000 inhabitants
- Paris Capital cities underlined
- ---- Country boundaries

Locator map

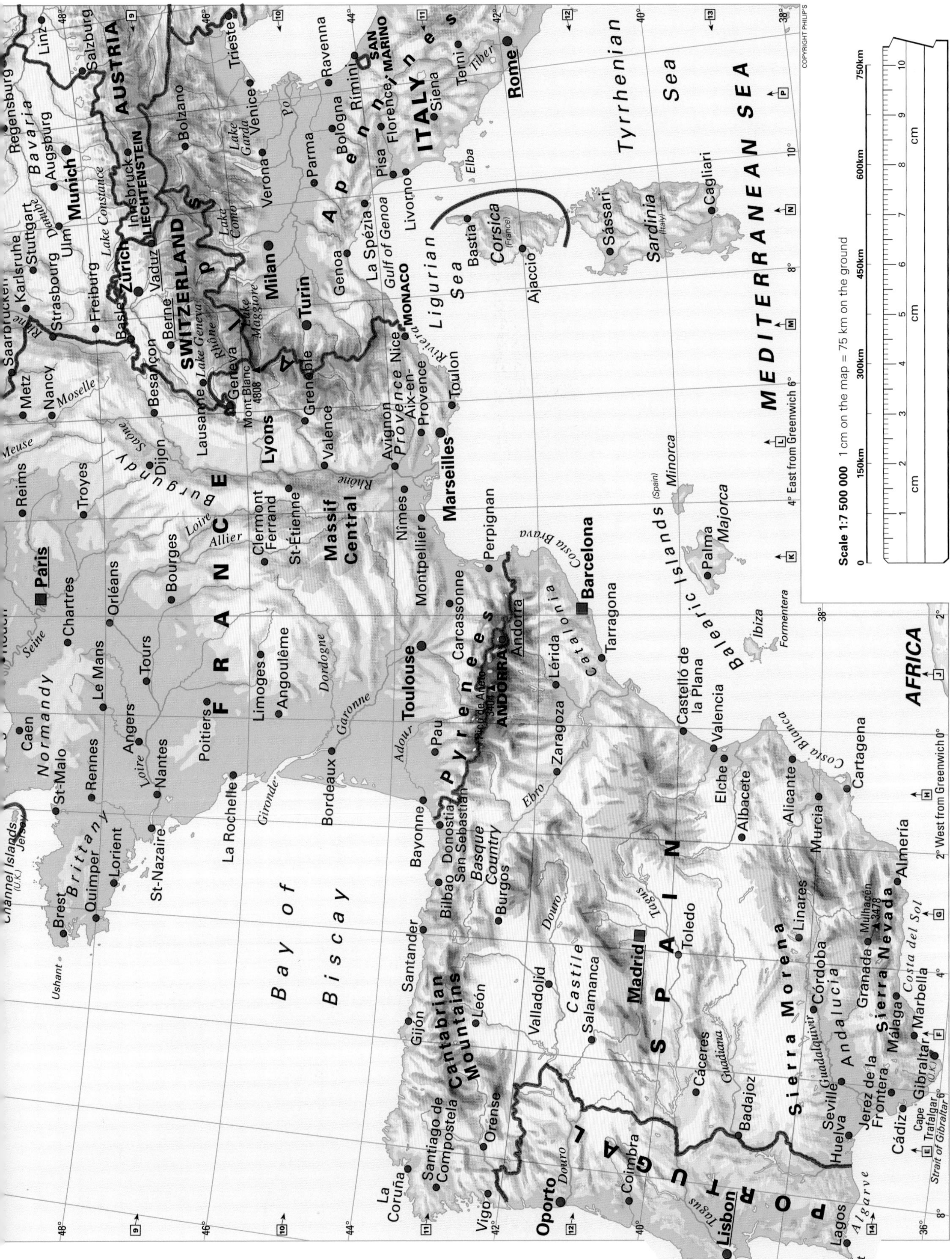
FRANCE
SPAIN
PORTUGAL
ITALY
SWITZERLAND
AUSTRIA
LIECHTENSTEIN
ANDORRA
MONACO
SAN MARINO
AFRICA
MEDITERRANEAN SEA
Bay of Biscay
Tyrrhenian Sea
Ligurian Sea
Gulf of Genoa
Balearic Islands
Alps
Apennines
Pyrenees
Massif Central
Cantabrian Mountains
Sierra Morena
Sierra Nevada
Normandy
Brittany
Burgundy
Provence
Bavaria
Catalonia
Castile
Andalucia
Basque Country
Costa Brava
Costa Blanca
Costa del Sol
Algarve
Riviera
Corsica (France)
Sardinia (Italy)
Elba
Minorca (Spain)
Majorca
Ibiza
Formentera
Channel Islands (U.K.)
Jersey
Ushant
Cape St. Vincent
Cape Trafalgar
Strait of Gibraltar
Gibraltar (U.K.)
Mont Blanc 4808
Pico de Aneto 3404
Mulhacén 3478
Lake Geneva
Lake Constance
Lake Maggiore
Lake Como
Lake Garda
Seine
Loire
Allier
Garonne
Dordogne
Gironde
Adour
Rhône
Saône
Rhine
Moselle
Meuse
Danube
Po
Tiber
Ebro
Douro
Tagus
Guadiana
Guadalquivir
Paris
Madrid
Lisbon
Rome
Berne
Vaduz
Andorra
Barcelona
Marseilles
Lyons
Toulouse
Milan
Turin
Munich
Zürich
Oporto
Reims
Troyes
Dijon
Metz
Nancy
Saarbrücken
Karlsruhe
Stuttgart
Strasbourg
Freiburg
Basle
Ulm
Augsburg
Regensburg
Linz
Salzburg
Innsbruck
Bolzano
Verona
Venice
Trieste
Ravenna
Parma
Bologna
Rímini
Florence
Pisa
Livorno
Siena
Terni
Genoa
La Spézia
Nice
Toulon
Aix-en-Provence
Avignon
Valence
Grenoble
Geneva
Lausanne
Besançon
Bastia
Ajaccio
Sássari
Cagliari
Caen
Rouen
Chartres
Orléans
Le Mans
Rennes
St-Malo
Brest
Quimper
Lorient
St-Nazaire
Nantes
Angers
Tours
Bourges
Poitiers
La Rochelle
Limoges
Angoulême
Clermont Ferrand
St-Étienne
Nîmes
Montpellier
Perpignan
Carcassonne
Bordeaux
Bayonne
Pau
Donostia-San Sebastián
Bilbao
Santander
Gijón
León
Burgos
La Coruña
Santiago de Compostela
Orense
Vigo
Coimbra
Valladolid
Salamanca
Toledo
Cáceres
Badajoz
Zaragoza
Lérida
Tarragona
Castelló de la Plana
Valencia
Elche
Albacete
Alicante
Murcia
Cartagena
Almería
Linares
Córdoba
Granada
Málaga
Marbella
Seville
Huelva
Jerez de la Frontera
Cádiz
Lagos
4° East from Greenwich 6°
2° West from Greenwich 0°
COPYRIGHT PHILIP'S
Scale 1:7 500 000 1 cm on the map = 75 km on the ground
0 150km 300km 450km 600km 750km
cm

ATLANTIC OCEAN

IRELAND

WALES

ENGLAND
Birmingham
Cardiff
Bristol
Plymouth
Thames
London

NETHERLANDS
The Hague
Amsterdam
Rotterdam
Antwerp
Lille
BELGIUM
Brussels
Bonn

LUXEMBOURG
Luxembourg

Hamburg
Bremen
Hanover
Berlin
Szcze

GERMANY
Dortmund
Cologne
Leipzig
Dresden
Frankfurt
Mannheim
Nuremberg
Stuttgart

Prague
CZECH

English Channel

Channel Islands (U.K.)

Brest
Le Havre
Paris
Rennes
Seine
Nancy
Strasbourg
Munich
Linz

Nantes
Loire
Orléans
Tours
Dijon
Basle
Zürich
AUST

FRANCE
Limoges
Clermont Ferrand
Lyons
St. Etienne
Massif Central
Grenoble
Mont Blanc 4808
Geneva
Lake Geneva
Berne
SWITZERLAND
Milan
Turin
LIECHTENSTEIN
Verona
Lake Garda
Venice
SLOV
Trie

Bay of Biscay

Bordeaux
Garonne
Toulouse
Montpellier
MONACO
Nice
Riviera
Genoa
Parma
Po
Bologna
Rímini
Florence
Pisa
SAN MARINO
Siena
Gran Sass 2914

La Coruña
Gijón
Santander
Cantabrian Mountains
León
Bilbao
Burgos
Pyrenees
Pic d'Aneto 3404
ANDORRA
Marseilles
Toulon

Vigo
Oporto
Douro
Salamanca
Valladolid
Douro
Zaragoza
Catalonia
Costa Brava
Corsica (France)
Ajaccio
Rome
ITAL

PORTUGAL
SPAIN
Madrid
Tagus
Toledo
Barcelona
Mount Ve
Naples
Pompeii

Lisbon
Guadiana
Badajoz
Valencia
Balearic Islands (Spain)
Minorca
Sardinia (Italy)

Tagus
Sierra Morena
Guadalquivir
Seville
Cordoba
Granada
Mulhacén 3478
Murcia
Cartagena
Alicante
Palma
Majorca
Ibiza
Cágliari
Tyrrhenian Sea

Algarve
Cádiz
Málaga
Almeria
Costa del Sol
Costa Blanca
MEDITER
Strón
Palermo
Etr
33
Sicily
Ca

Tangier
Gibraltar (U.K.)
Strait of Gibraltar
Ceuta (Spain)
Tétouan
Melilla (Spain)
Oran
Algiers
Blida
Mostaganem
Bejaïa
Annaba
Bizerte
Tunis
Carthage

Ifrane
Fès
Oujda
Constantine
Valletta
MALTA

MOROCCO
Atlas Mountains
ALGERIA
Biskra
Chott Melrhir
Sousse
Sfax

Sahara
Chott Djerid
TUNISIA
Djerba

AFRICA
Tripoli
Al Aziziyah
LIBYA

Mediterranean
Adria
Apennin
Tiber

5° West from Greenwich   0°   East from Greenwich   5°   10

Height of the land (metres)

over 4000
2000-4000
1000-2000
400-1000
200-400
0-200
sea level
below sea level

Key to map symbols

■ Over 5,000,000 inhabitants
● 1,000,000 - 5,000,000 inhabitants
• Under 1,000,000 inhabitants
Sofia Capital cities underlined
── Country boundaries
∴ Historical sites   Seasonal lakes

Scale 1:10 000 000   1 cm on the map = 100 km on the ground

0   250km   500km   750km   1000km

1 2 3 4 5 6 7 8 9 10
cm   cm   cm

Cross-section along latitude 45°N

FRANCE | ITALY | ROMANIA

Bay of Biscay | Mont Dore 1886 ▲ | Massif Central | Rhone | Mont Blanc 4808 ▲ Alps | Po | Adriatic Sea | Dinaric Alps | Sava | Danube | Transylvanian Alps | Danube | Black Sea

45°N

ator map

COPYRIGHT PHILIP'S

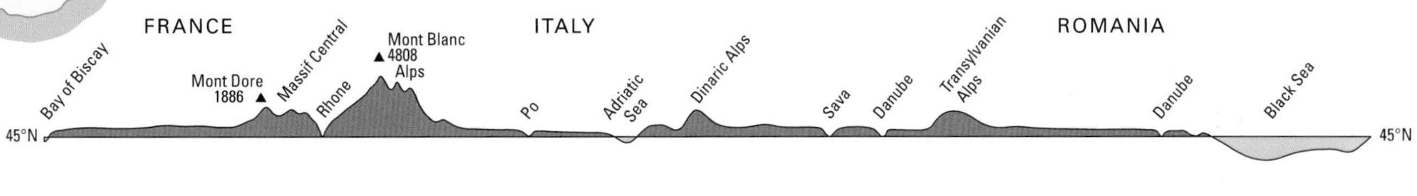

Italy

▲ **Strómboli** Known as the 'Lighthouse of the Mediterranean', it is one of three active volcanoes in Italy. The others are Mount Etna and Mount Vesuvius.

Scale 1:6 250 000 1 cm on the map = 62.5 km on the ground

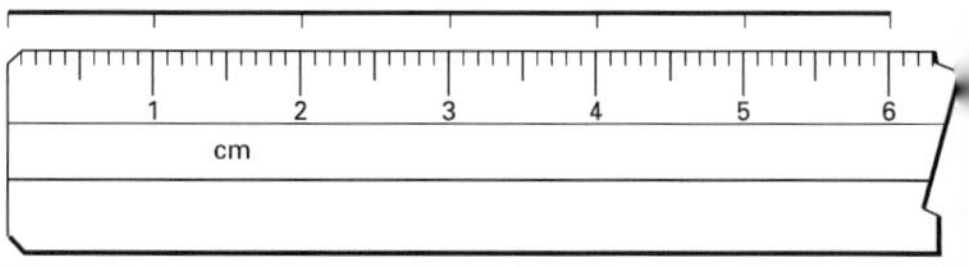

Key to map symbols

- ■ Over 1,000,000 inhabitants
- ● 500,000 – 1,000,000 inhabitants
- • Under 500,000 inhabitants
- Rome — Capital cities
- Country boundaries
- Historical site

Height of the land (metres)

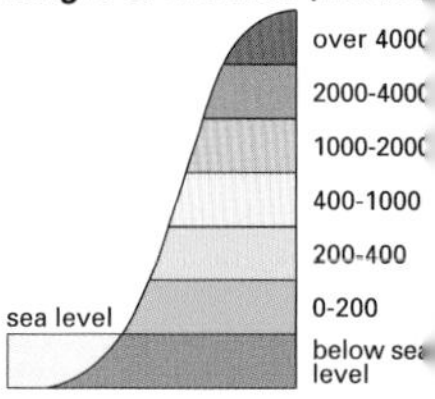

▼ **Venice** This image shows the largest island, on which the main part of the city is built. There are no roads so everything is moved by boat and you can see the wakes made by some of the larger boats.

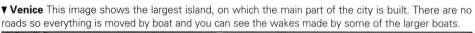

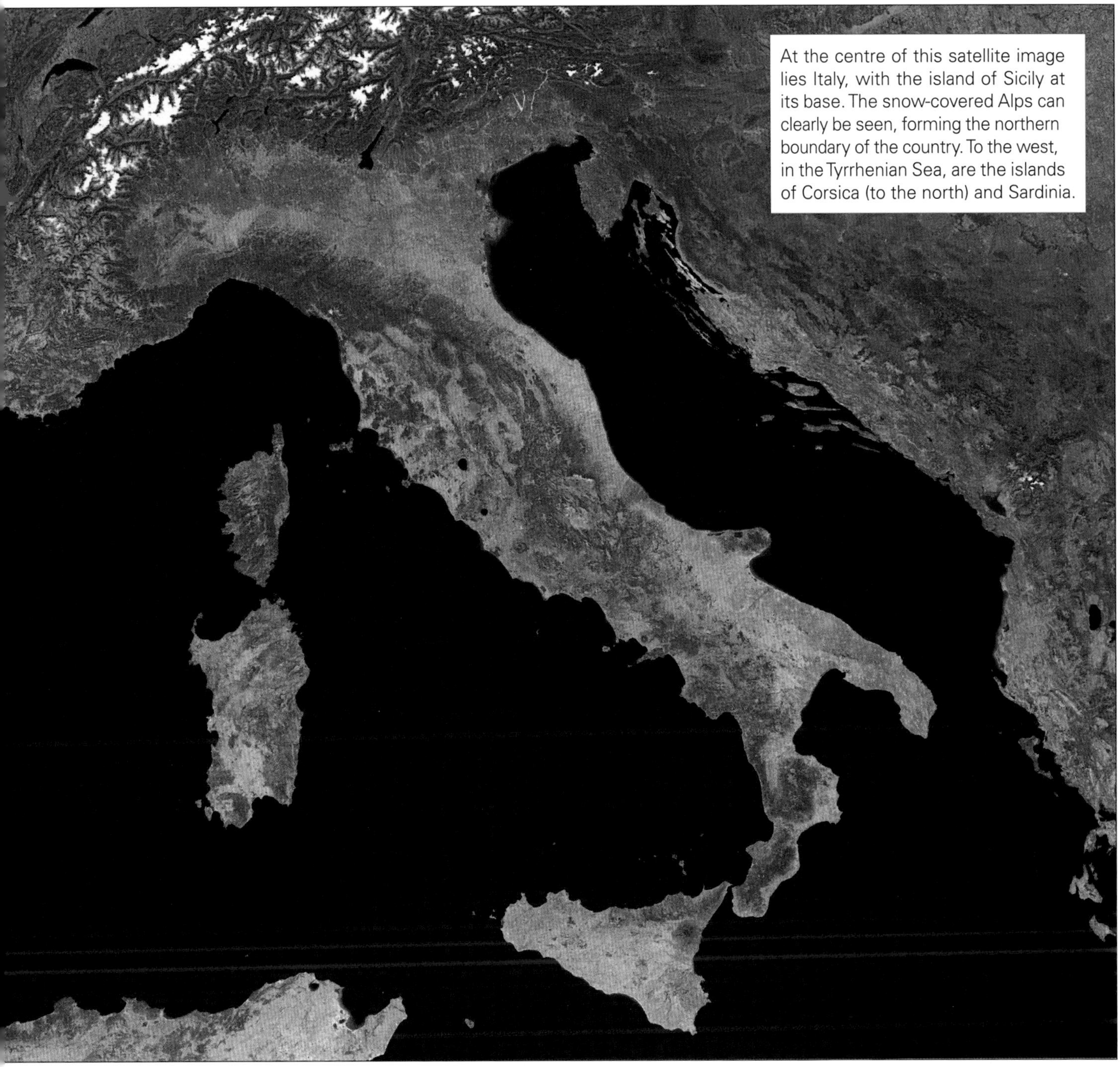

At the centre of this satellite image lies Italy, with the island of Sicily at its base. The snow-covered Alps can clearly be seen, forming the northern boundary of the country. To the west, in the Tyrrhenian Sea, are the islands of Corsica (to the north) and Sardinia.

POPULATION DENSITY
The number of people per square kilometre (2020)

- Over 400
- 300 – 400
- 200 – 300
- 100 – 200
- Under 100

WEALTH
The value of total production divided by the population (€ per person) (2020)

- Over €35,000
- €30,000 – 35,000
- €25,000 – 30,000
- €20,000 – 25,000
- Under €20,000

UNEMPLOYMENT
The percentage of the workforce unemployed (2020)

- Over 12.5%
- 10 – 12.5%
- 7.5 – 10%
- Under 7.5%

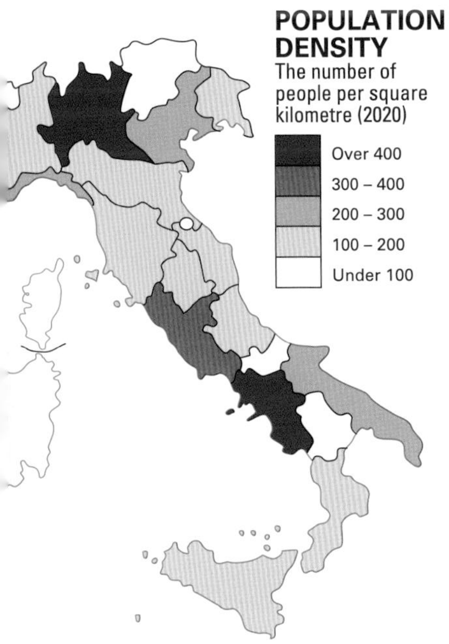

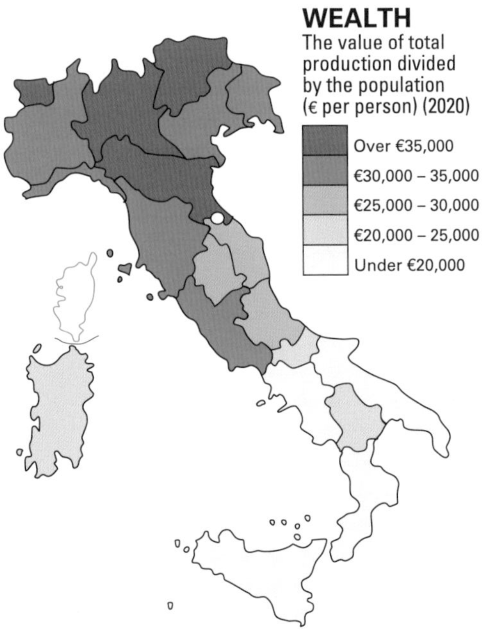

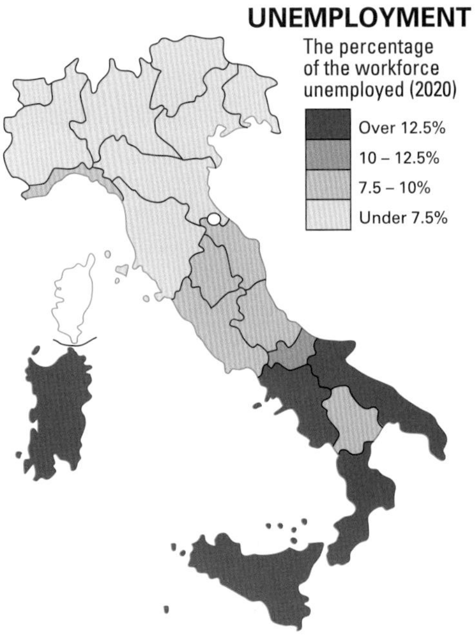

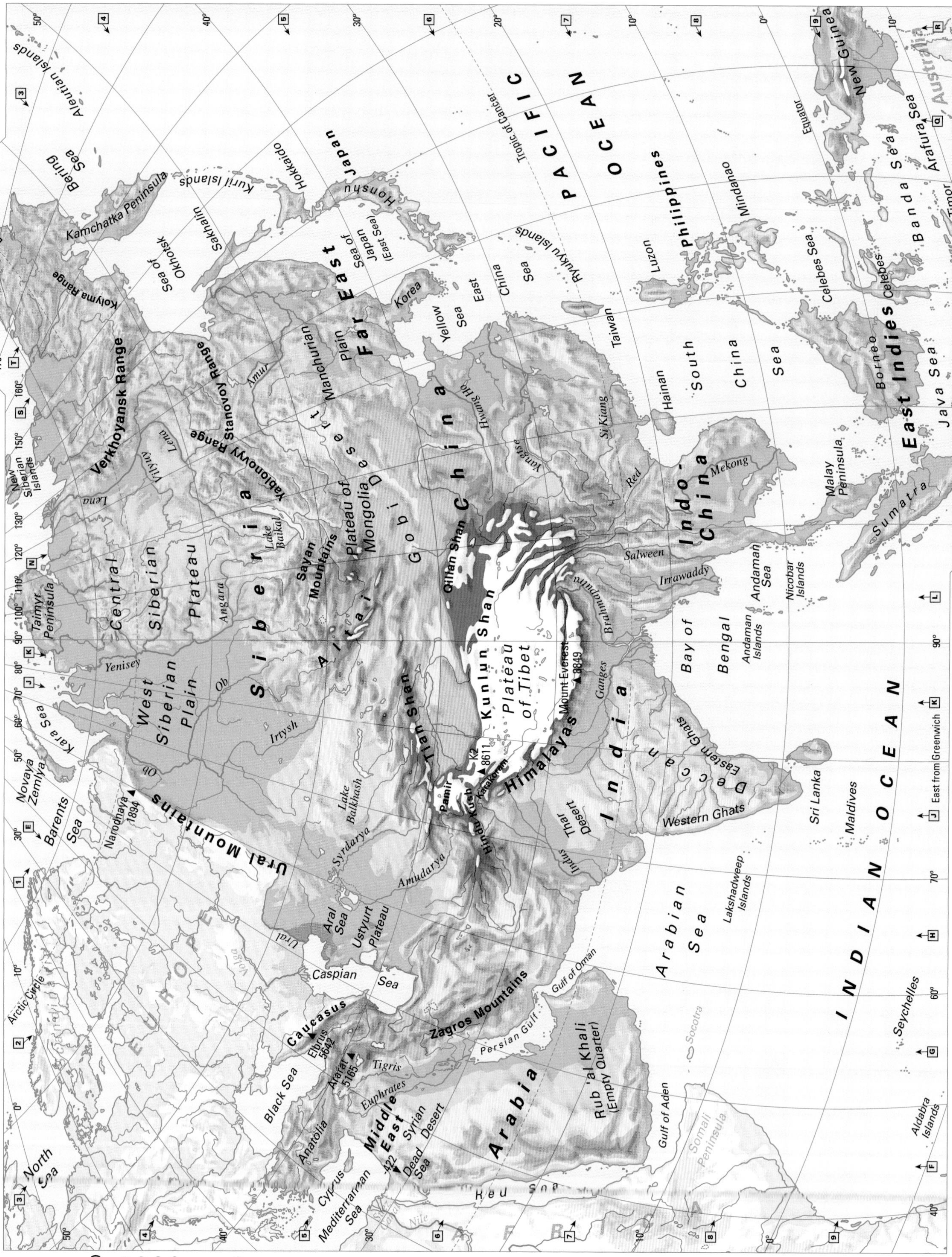
PACIFIC OCEAN
INDIAN OCEAN
Aleutian Islands
Bering Sea
East Cape
Kamchatka Peninsula
Kuril Islands
Sea of Okhotsk
Sakhalin
Hokkaido
Japan
Honshu
Sea of Japan (East Sea)
Kolyma Range
Verkhoyansk Range
Stanovoy Range
Yablonovyy Range
Amur
Manchurian Plain
Far East
Korea
Yellow Sea
East China Sea
Ryukyu Islands
Tropic of Cancer
Taiwan
Philippines
Luzon
Mindanao
Celebes Sea
Celebes
Banda Sea
Timor
Arafura Sea
New Guinea
Australia
Equator
Borneo
East Indies
Java Sea
South China Sea
Hainan
Si Kiang
Hwang Ho
Yangtse
China
Gobi Desert
Plateau of Mongolia
Lake Baikal
Siberia
Sayan Mountains
Altai
New Siberian Islands
Lena
Vilyuy
Central Siberian Plateau
Angara
Taimyr Peninsula
Yenisey
Ob
West Siberian Plain
Irtysh
Kara Sea
Novaya Zemlya
Barents Sea
Narodnaya 1894
Ural Mountains
Lake Balkhash
Tian Shan
Qilian Shan
Kunlun Shan
Plateau of Tibet
Mount Everest 8849
Himalayas
K2 8611
Karakoram
Pamir
Hindu Kush
Brahmaputra
Ganges
India
Thar Desert
Indus
Deccan
Eastern Ghats
Western Ghats
Sri Lanka
Maldives
Lakshadweep Islands
Bay of Bengal
Andaman Islands
Andaman Sea
Nicobar Islands
Irrawaddy
Salween
Red
Mekong
Indo-China
Malay Peninsula
Sumatra
Syrdarya
Amudarya
Aral Sea
Ustyurt Plateau
Ural
Volga
Caspian Sea
EUROPE
Arctic Circle
Caucasus
Elbrus 5642
Ararat 5165
Black Sea
Anatolia
Tigris
Euphrates
Zagros Mountains
Persian Gulf
Gulf of Oman
Middle East
Syrian Desert
Dead Sea -422
Cyprus
Mediterranean Sea
Red Sea
Nile
AFRICA
Arabia
Rub 'al Khali (Empty Quarter)
Gulf of Aden
Socotra
Somali Peninsula
Arabian Sea
Seychelles
Aldabra Islands
North Sea
East from Greenwich
COPYRIGHT PHILIP'S

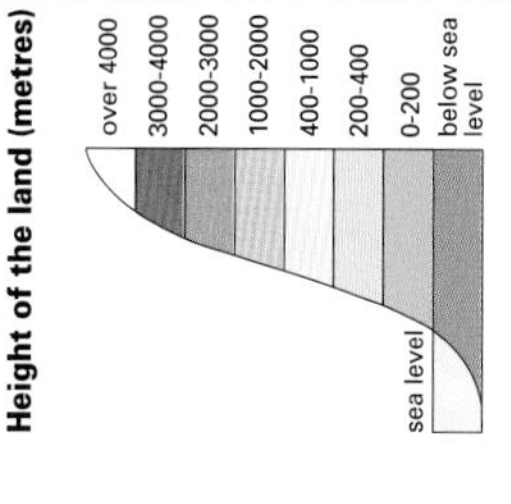
Height of the land (metres)
over 4000
3000-4000
2000-3000
1000-2000
400-1000
200-400
0-200
below sea level
sea level

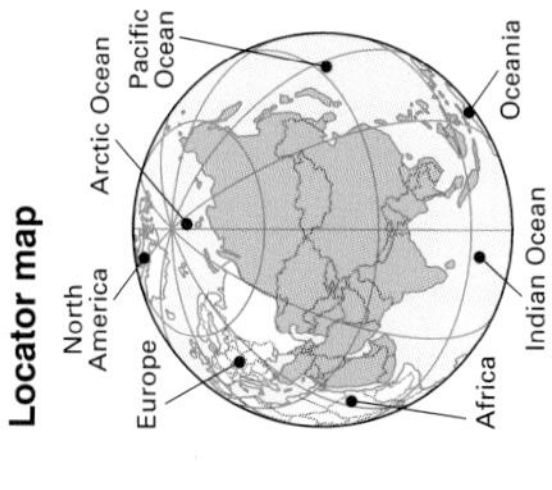
Locator map
Arctic Ocean
Pacific Ocean
Oceania
North America
Europe
Africa
Indian Ocean

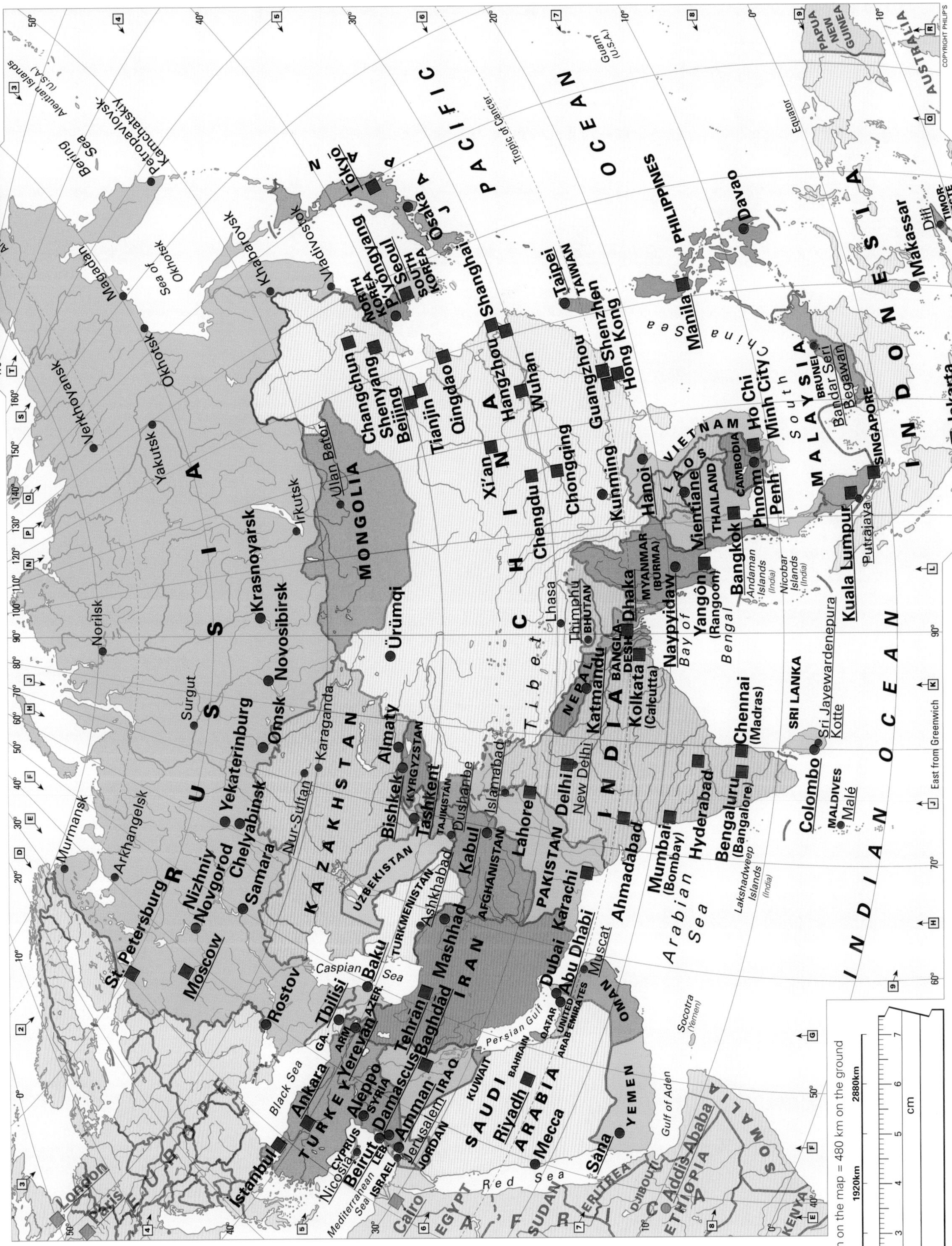

Key to abbreviations
ARM. = Armenia
AZER. = Azerbaijan
GA. = Georgia
LEB. = Lebanon

Key to map symbols
■ Over 5,000,000 inhabitants
● 1,000,000 - 5,000,000 inhabitants
• Under 1,000,000 inhabitants
Kabul — Capital cities underlined
Country boundaries
Disputed country boundaries

Scale 1:48 000 000 1 cm on the map = 480 km on the ground
0 — 960km — 1920km — 2880km

Russia and Northern Asia

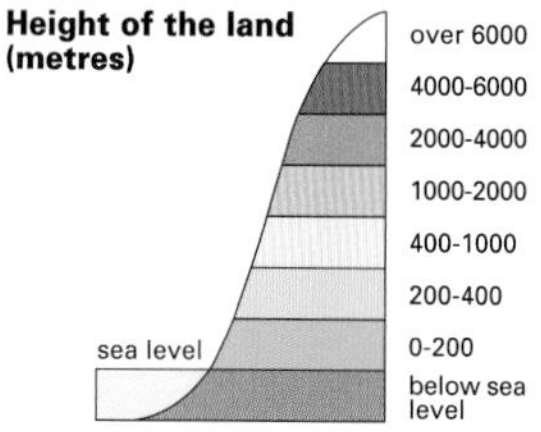

Key to map symbols

- ■ Over 5,000,000 inhabitants
- ● 1,000,000 - 5,000,000 inhabitants
- • Under 1,000,000 inhabitants
- Kiev — Capital cities underlined
- Country boundaries

Scale 1:20 000 000 1 cm on the map = 200 km on the ground

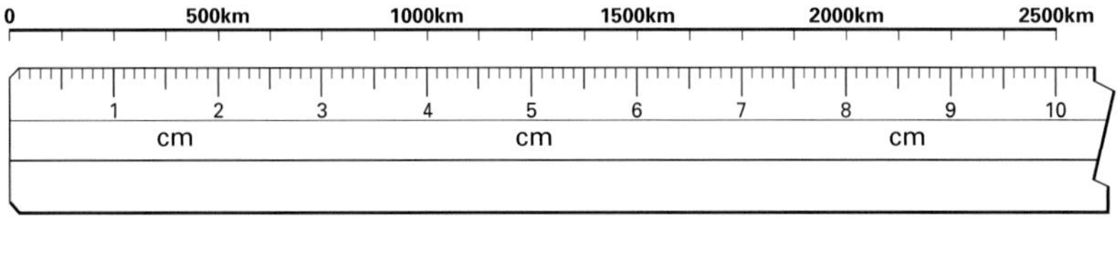

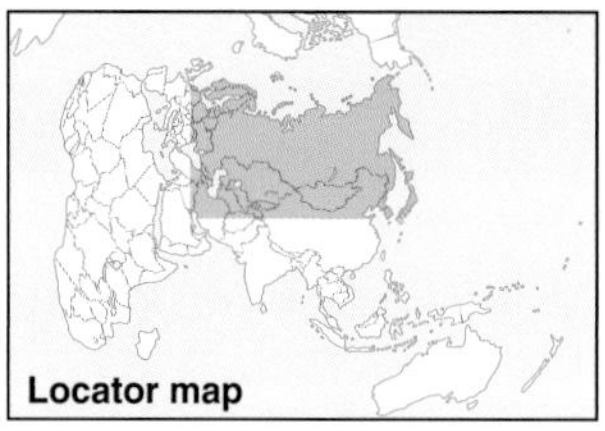

Locator map

Karaganda · **Nur-Sultan** · Semey

RUSSIA · Angarsk · Irkuts

KAZAKHSTAN

Zhezqazghan

Balkhash · Tarbagatai Range · Belukha 4506 · Uvs Nuur · Hövsgöl Nuur · Khangai Mountains

Lake Balkhash · Tacheng · Altay · Har Us Nuur · Hovd · **Ulan Bat** · M O N G

Taraz · **Bishkek** · Bole · Ebinur Hu · Dzungarian Basin · Arvayheer · Plat Mon

KYRGYZSTAN · Issyk Kul · **Almaty** · Shihezi · Tian Shan · **Ürümqi** · Turfan · Sinkiang

Andijon · Pobedy Peak 7439 · Bosten Hu · Turfan Basin · Hami

Kashgar · Aksu · Korla · Tarim · Turfan · Yumen · Wuhai

Kongur Shan 7719 · Taklamakan Desert · Tarim Basin · Lop Nur · Altun Shan · 5547 · Qilian Shan · Zhangye · Yinchuan

Hotan · Muz Tag 7723 · Qaidam Basin · Qinghai Hu · Wuwei

Karakoram · K2 8611 · Kun Lun Shan · Xining · Lanzhou

Kashmir · **Srinagar**

Chandigarh · Yangtse · Tianshui

Meerut · Plateau of Tibet · C

Delhi · Tibet · Sichuan

New Delhi · Dhaulagiri 8172 · Annapurna 8078 · Lhasa · Namcha Barwa 7756 · **Mianyang** · Nanch

Agra · H i m · NEPAL · Mount Everest 8849 · Gongga Shan 7556 · **Chengdu** · **Wanxia**

Kanpur · **Katmandu** · Mekong · Suining

Prayagraj · **Lucknow** · a · Thimphu · **BHUTAN** · Dibrugarh · **Leshan** · **Chongo**

Patna · l a y a s · Brahmaputra · Panzhihua · Luzhou

Varanasi · Ganges · Rajshahi · Zuny

Dhanbad · **Guwahati** · Zhaotong

INDIA · **Jabalpur** · **BANGLADESH** · Assam · **Liupanshui** · **Guiya**

Asansol · **Dhaka** · Imphal · Baoshan · **Kunming**

Jamshedpur · Haora · Khulna · Lashio

Nagpur · **Bhilainagar-Durg** · **Kolkata (Calcutta)** · **Chittagong** · Irrawaddy · **Nanni**

Cuttack · **Mandalay** · Salween · **VIETNAM**

Bay of Bengal · **MYANMAR (BURMA)** · Red · **Hanoi** · **Haiph**

Vishakhapatnam · Brahmapur · **Naypyidaw** · **LAOS** · Gul

East from Greenwich · **THAILAND** · Mekong

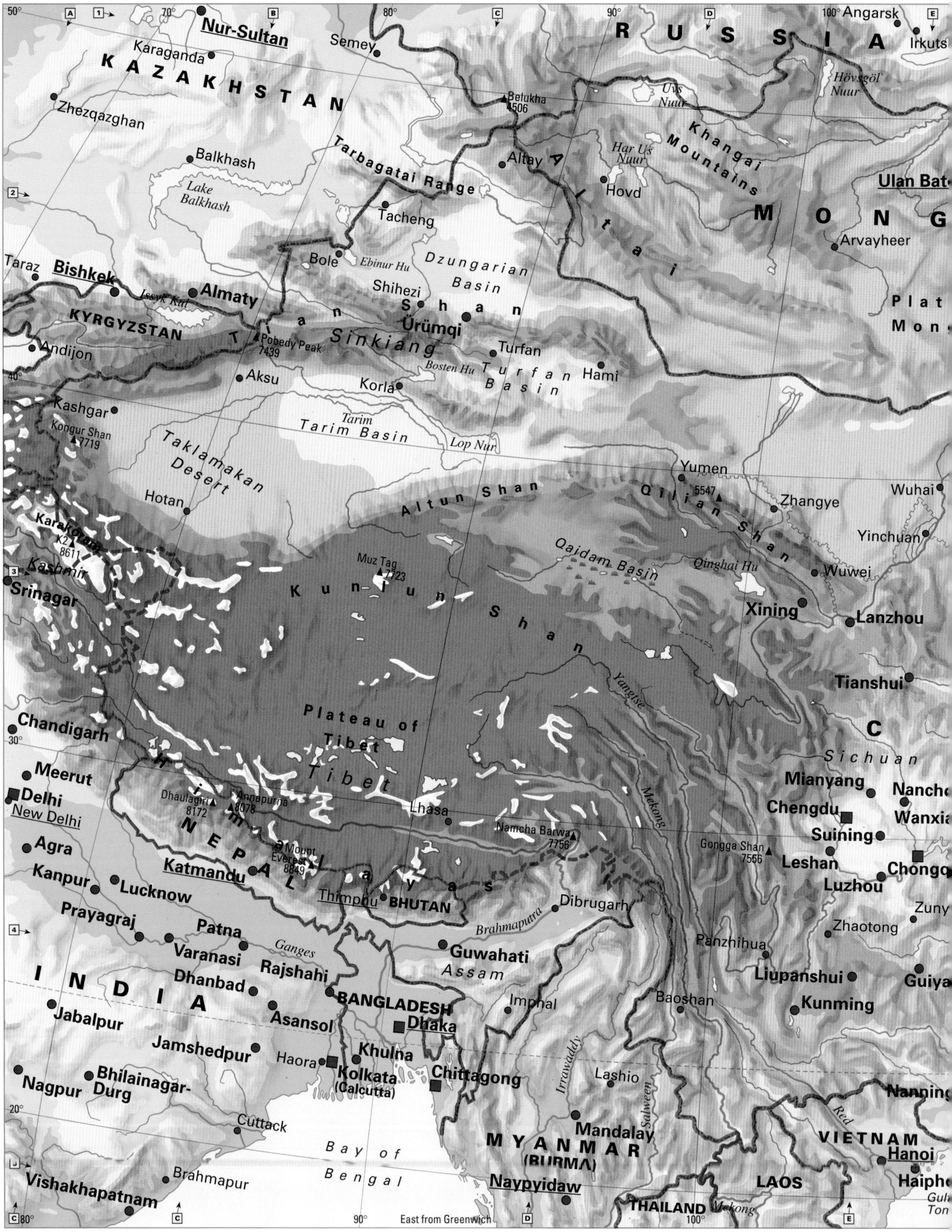

Scale 1:15 000 000   1 cm on the map = 150 km on the ground

0   300km   600km   900km   1200km   1500km

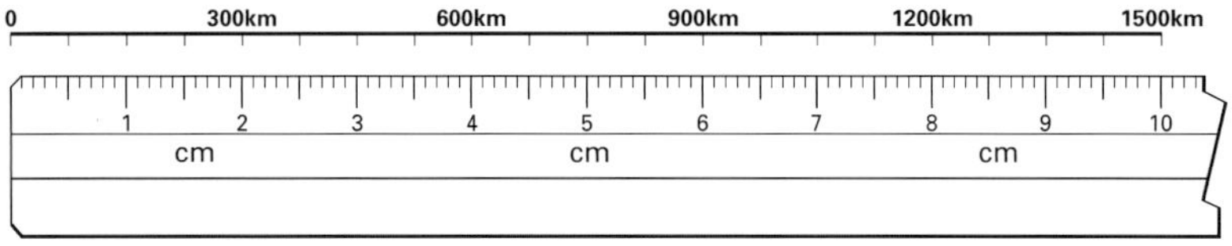

110°
Yablonovvy Range
e Baikal
lan Ude
Chita
120°
G
Manzhouli
Hailar
Choybolsan
Argun
Amur
Blagoveshchensk
Heihe
130°
Komsomsk
Aleksandrovsk-Sakhalinskiy
Khabarovsk
Amur
140°
1
J
RUSSIA
Sakhalin
Yuzhno-Sakhalinsk
Tatar Strait
2
A
of
Gobi
esert
L I A
Inner Mongolia
Great Khingan Mountains
Qiqihar
Daqing
Hegang
Sungari
Jiamusi
Harbin
Jixi
Ussuri
Lake Khanka
Sikhote Alin Range
La Perouse Strait
Asahikawa
Hokkaidō
Sapporo

Fuyu
Manchuria
Mudanjiang
Changchun
Jilin
Sungari Reservoir
Vladivostok
Nakhodka
Tsugaru Strait
40°

Chifeng
Fushun
Shenyang
Chongjin
Kimch'aek
Sea of Japan (East Sea)
Akita
N
Sendai

otou
Hohhot
Zhangjiakou
Jinxi
Anshan
NORTH KOREA
Honshū
H
Datong
Beijing
Tangshan
P'yŏngyang
Namp'o
Tōkyō
Kawasaki
Wall
Yulin
Baoding
Tianjin
Dalian
Seoul
Nagoya
Fuji-San 3776
Yokohama
3
Taiyuan
Shijiazhuang
Bo Hai
Yantai
Incheon
SOUTH KOREA
Kyōto
Ōsaka
P
Handan
Weifang
Zibo
Qingdao
Daejeon
Daegu
Ulsan
Hiroshima
Kōbe
A
Hwang-Ho
Jinan
Tai'an
Yellow Sea
Gwangju
Busan
Kitakyūshū
Shikoku
N
Heze
Jining
Linyi
Korea Strait
Zhengzhou
Grand Canal
Zaozhuang
Jeju-do
Fukuoka
J A P A N
Luoyang
Shangqiu
Xuzhou
Kyūshū
Xi'an
Yuzhou
Yancheng
30°
Nanyang
Xinghua
Kagoshima
I N A
Huainan
Nanjing
Changzhou
Xiangfan
Zaoyang
Suzhou
Jingmen
Hefei
Wuxi
Shanghai
Tai Hu
Wuhan
Huzhou
Three Gorges Dam
Tianmen
Yangtse
Hangzhou
Hangzhou Wan
Ningbo
Dongting Hu
Taizhou
East China Sea
Changde
Nanchang
Yiyang
Changsha
Wenzhou
Pingxiang
Hengyang
Senkaku Islands
Naha Okinawa
Ryukyu Islands
Yongzhou
Fuzhou
Liuzhou
Guangdong
Quanzhou
Xiamen
Taipei
Taichung
Tropic of Cancer
4
Si Kiang
Guangzhou (Canton)
Shantou
Taiwan Strait
Yu Shan 3952
TAIWAN
PACIFIC
Dongguan
Shenzhen
Macau
Hong Kong
Kaohsiung
20°
Pearl River
Zhanjiang
OCEAN
South China Sea
Batan Islands
ainan
Sanya
110°
F
120°
G
130°
H
COPYRIGHT PHILIP'S

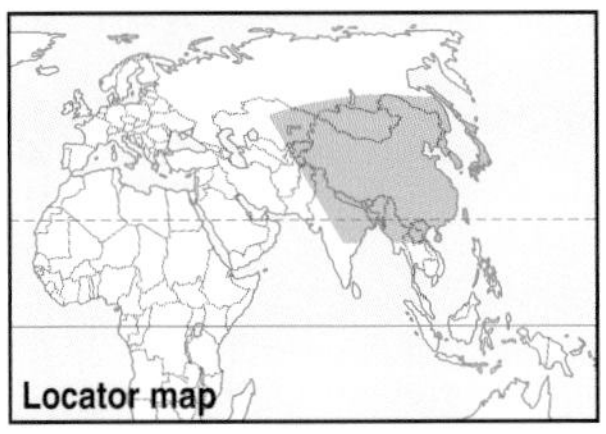

Height of the land (metres)

over 6000	
4000-6000	
2000-4000	
1000-2000	
400-1000	
200-400	
0-200	
below sea level	

sea level

Locator map

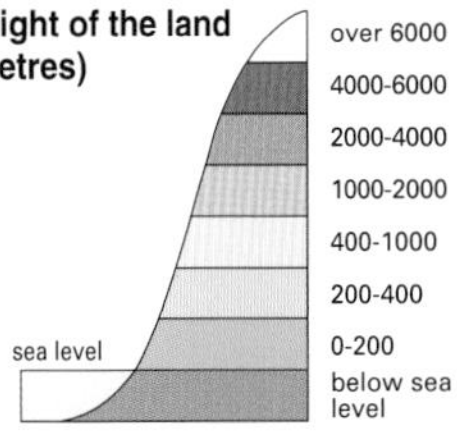

Key to map symbols

■ Over 5,000,000 inhabitants

● 1,000,000 - 5,000,000 inhabitants

• Under 1,000,000 inhabitants

Beijing Capital cities underlined

Country boundaries

Disputed country boundaries

INDUSTRIAL REGIONS

- Core industrial regions
- Major centres for industry
- Centres for iron and steel, and chemicals
- Rapidly developing coastal regions
- Special Economic Zones
- Special Administrative Regions
- Outer industrial regions
- Outer industrial regions with traditional heavy industry
- Remote undeveloped regions
- Direction of future growth
- Important rail links

Ürümqi

Kashi (Kashgar)

Lanzhou

Lhasa

Baotou
Beijing
Tianjin
Taiyuan
Dalian
Qingdao
Zhengzhou
Xi'an
Three Gorges Dam
Chongqing
Chengdu
Nanjing
Suzhou
Pudong
Shanghai
Wuhan
Hangzhou
Ningbo
Changsha
Wenzhou
Fuzhou
Xiamen
Guangzhou (Canton)
Shantou
Zhuhai
Shenzhen
Macau
Hong Kong
Hainan

Harbin
Changchun
Fushun
Shenyang

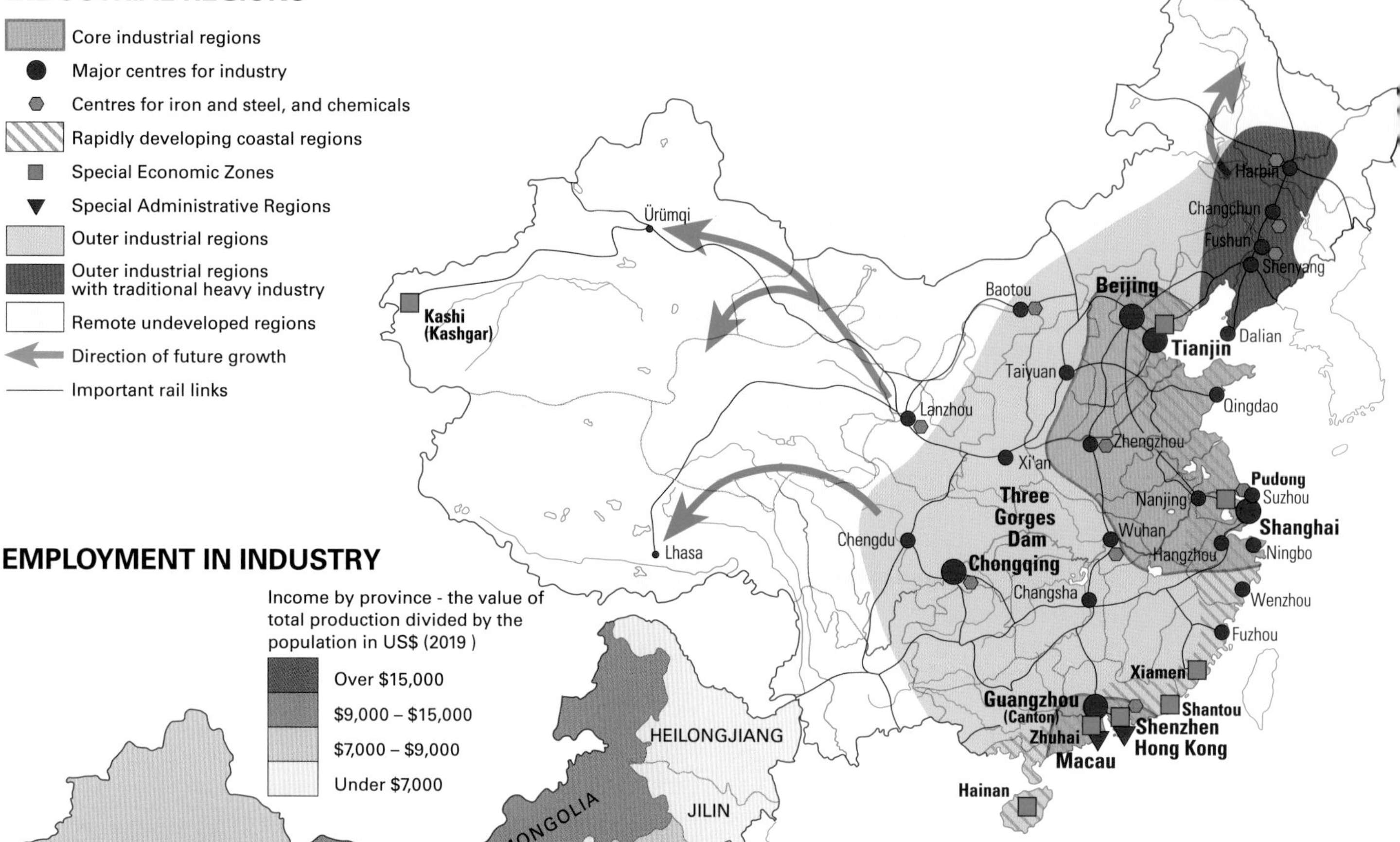

EMPLOYMENT IN INDUSTRY

Income by province - the value of total production divided by the population in US$ (2019)

- Over $15,000
- $9,000 – $15,000
- $7,000 – $9,000
- Under $7,000

XINJIANG

GANSU

QINGHAI

TIBET

HEILONGJIANG

JILIN

INNER MONGOLIA

LIAONING

BEIJING

TIANJIN

HEBEI

NINGXIA HUI

SHANXI

SHANDONG

SHAANXI

HENAN

JIANGSU

SICHUAN

CHONGQING

HUBEI

ANHUI

SHANGHAI

ZHEJIANG

HUNAN

JIANGXI

GUIZHOU

FUJIAN

YUNNAN

GUANGXI ZHUANGZU

GUANGDONG

HONG KONG
MACAU

HAINAN

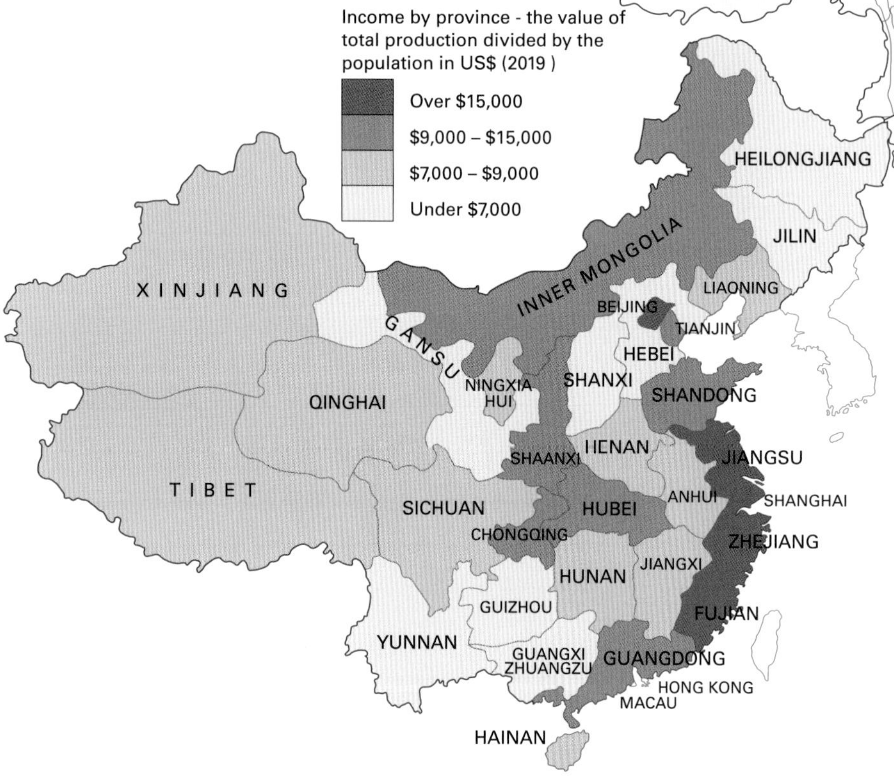

▲ **Three Gorges Dam**
Completed in 2009, it is the world's largest hydroelectric power station.

THREE GORGES DAM

Scale 1:6 000 000

1cm on the map = 60 km on the ground

| 0 | 60km | 120km | 180km | 200km |

cm

The Three Gorges

Height of the land (metres)

- Over 2000
- 1500 – 2000
- 1000 – 1500
- 400 – 1000
- 200 – 400
- 0 – 200
- Sea level
- Below sea level

■ Over 5,000,000 inhabitants

● 1,000,000 – 5,000,000 inhabitants

• Under 1,000,000 inhabitants

SICHUAN

Daba Shan

CHONGQING SHI

Nanchong

Wanxian

Enshi

Sanxia Shuiku
(Three Gorges Reservoir)

Chongqing

Yangtse

WU GORGE

QUTANG GORGE

XILING GORGE

THREE GORGES DAM
(1.1 km wide)

GEZHOU DAM

2550

2393

Xiangfan

Zaoyang

Xinyang

HUBEI

Jingmen

Tianmen

Wuhan

Yichang

Shashi

Xiantao

Yangtse

• Reservoir over 600 km long
• Surface area over 1,000 km²
• Over 630 km² flooded
• 1,200,000 people had to relocate

Changde

Dongting Hu

Yueyang

Yiyang

Changsha

GUIZHOU

HUNAN

Zhuzhou

East from Greenwich

COPYRIGHT PHILIP'S

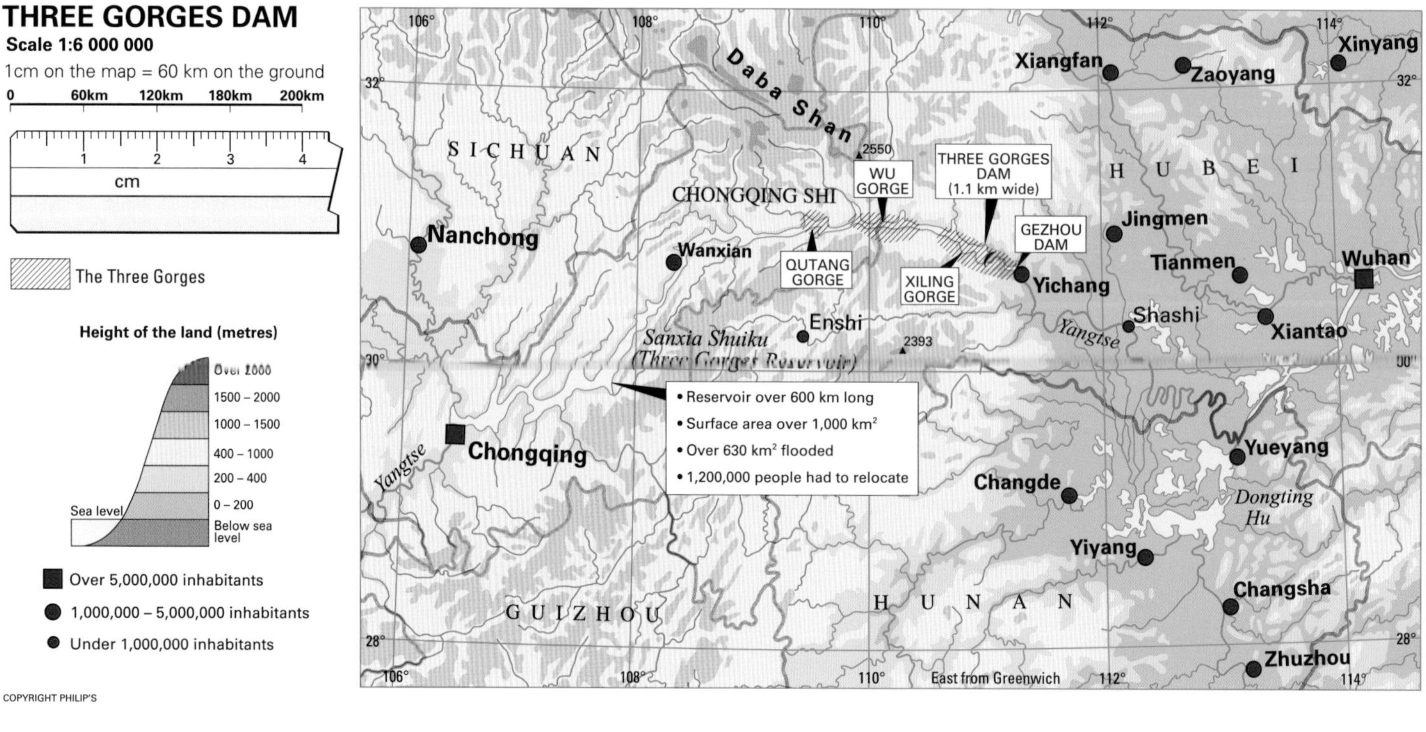

JAPAN EARTHQUAKE AND TSUNAMI 2011

Epicentre of earthquake 11 March 2011 (magnitude 9.0)

Observed tsunami heights
- Over 8 metres
- Over 4 metres
- Over 2 metres
- Over 1 metre

Epicentres of previous earthquakes (magnitude 7.0 or more since AD 1600)

Plate boundary

Destructive plate boundary (plates colliding)

Direction of movement

Active volcanoes

6,742 dead, or missing in Iwate Prefecture

13,818 dead, or missing in Miyagi Prefecture

1,957 dead, or missing in Fukushima Prefecture

Epicentre 11 March 2011

Fukushima Daiichi Nuclear Power Station

NORTH AMERICAN PLATE

EURASIAN PLATE

PACIFIC PLATE

PHILIPPINE PLATE

Tokyo

TOTAL JAPAN
22,589 dead, or missing

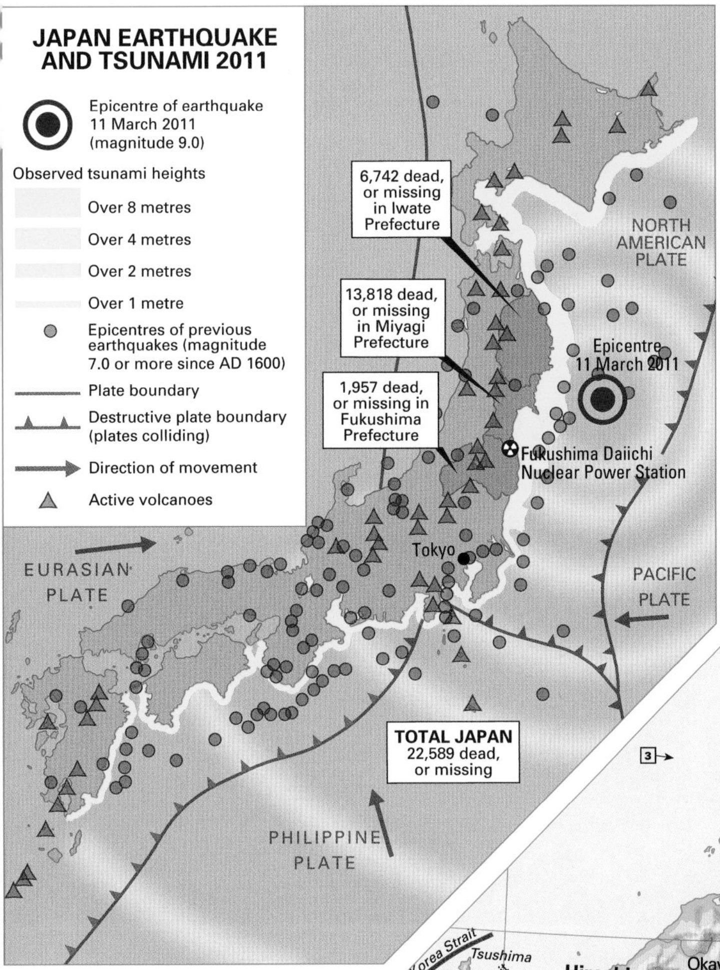

Scale 1:10 000 000
1 cm on the map = 100 km on the ground

0 100km 200km 300km 400km

cm

Height of the land (metres)
- over 4000
- 2000-4000
- 1000-2000
- 400-1000
- 200-400
- 0-200
- below sea level

Key to map symbols
- Over 5,000,000 inhabitants
- 1,000,000 - 5,000,000 inhabitants
- Under 1,000,000 inhabitants
- Tōkyō Capital cities underlined
- Country boundaries

RUSSIA

Sikhote Alin Range

Dalnegorsk

Sakhalin (Russia)

La Perouse Strait

Cape Soya

Rebun
Riishiri
Wakkanai

Sea of Okhotsk

Kunashir (Russia)

Nemuro Strait

Teshio

Asahi Dake 2290
Ishikari Bay
Asahikawa
Kitami

Hokkaidō

Otaru
Sapporo
Obihiro
Kushiro
Yubari

Okushiri

Uchiura Bay

Hakodate
Tsugaru Strait

Cape Erimo

Aomori
Hachinohe

Sea of Japan (East Sea)

Akita
Morioka

Sakata

Yamagata
Sendai

Sado
Niigata
Fukushima

Nagaoka
Kōriyama

Toyama Bay
Iwaki

Kanazawa
Toyama
Nagano
Utsunomiya
Hitachi

Matsumoto
Saitama

Fukui
Tōkyō
Chiba

Gifu
Kawasaki
Yokohama

Fuji-San 3776

Tottori
Nagoya
Shizuoka

Himeji
Kyōto
Yokkaichi

Okayama
Kōbe
Ōsaka
Hamamatsu

Hiroshima
Sakai
Ise Bay

Shimonoseki
Kure
Takamatsu
Wakayama
Cape Daio

Inland Sea
Matsuyama

Kitakyūshū
Shikoku
Nii Islands

Fukuoka
Kōchi
Miyake Islands

Sasebo
Ōita
Tosa Bay
Cape Shiono

Unzen 1360
Kumamoto
Bungo Channel

Nagasaki
Cape Ashizuri

Kyūshū
Miyazaki
Aoga Island

Kagoshima
Miyakonojo

Sakurajima 1118
Osumi Channel

Tanega Island
Sumisu Island

Tokara Strait
Yaku Island

Tokara Island
Nakano Island
Akuseki Island

East from Greenwich 135°

JAPAN

PACIFIC OCEAN

Locator map

COPYRIGHT PHILIP'S

Fukushima Nuclear Power Station
This satellite image shows the damage to the reactor, in the centre of the image, following the March 2011 earthquake and tsunami. The image was used to assess the damage, with minimum risk to human life.

POPULATION DENSITY
The number of people per square kilometre (2019)
- Over 500
- 300 – 500
- 200 – 300
- 100 – 200
- Under 100

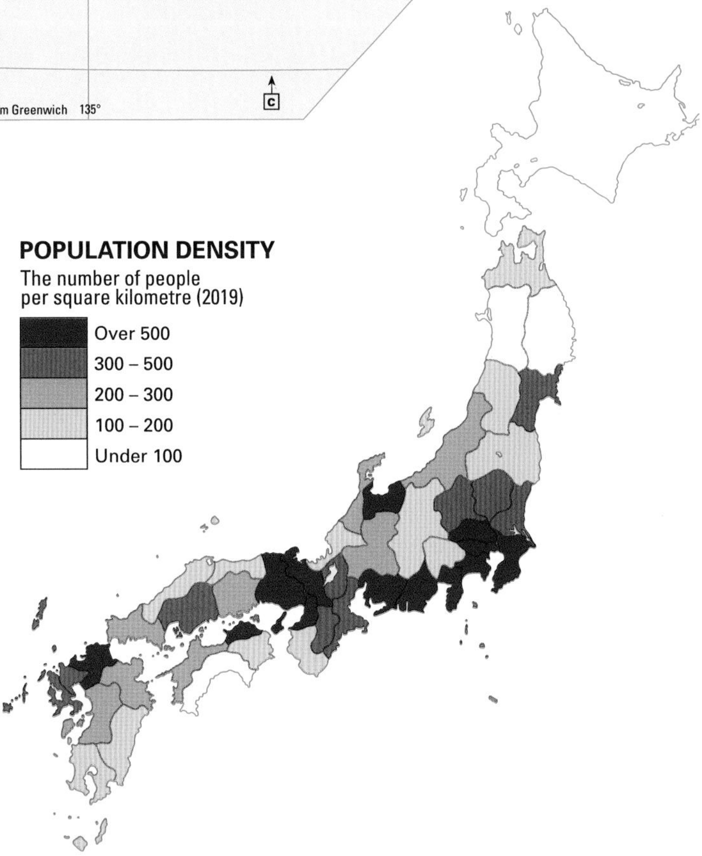

Cross-section along latitude 30°N

IRAN   PAKISTAN   INDIA   TIBET   CHINA

Himalayas
Brahmaputra
▲ Mount Everest
8849

Persian   Tibetan Plateau
Gulf   Salween
Zagros   Mekong
Mountains   Indus   Yangtse   Yangtse
                   Chenab   Ganges   Yangtse   East China S
                   Sutlej   Yangtse
30°N

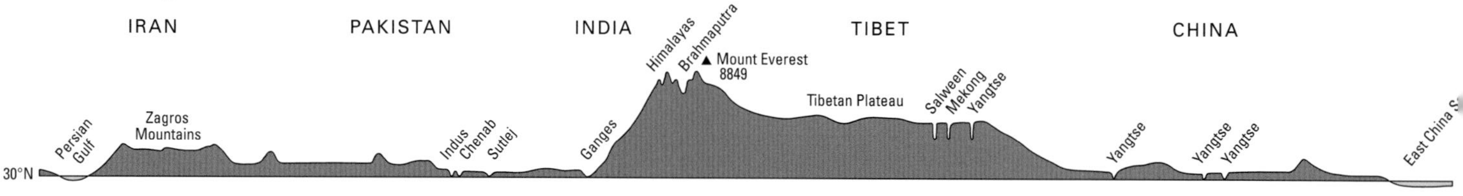

Height of the land (metres)

over 6000
4000-6000
2000-4000
1000-2000
400-1000
200-400
0-200
sea level
below sea level

Locator map

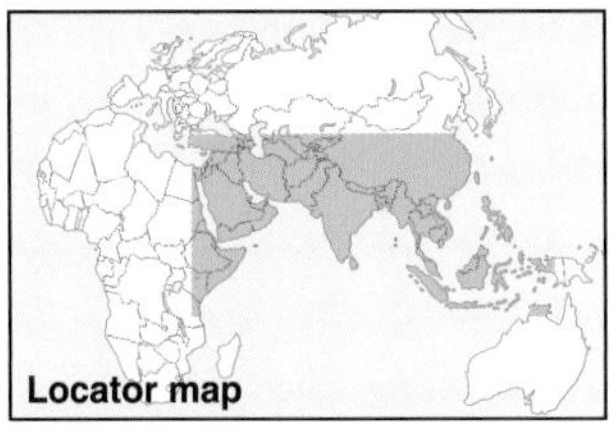

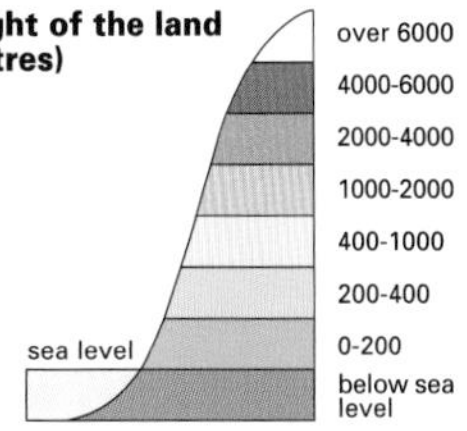

Key to map symbols

■ Over 5,000,000 inhabitants

● 1,000,000 – 5,000,000 inhabitants

• Under 1,000,000 inhabitants

<u>Beijing</u> Capital cities underlined

Country boundaries

Disputed country boundaries

Seasonal lakes

COPYRIGHT PHILIP'S

Middle East

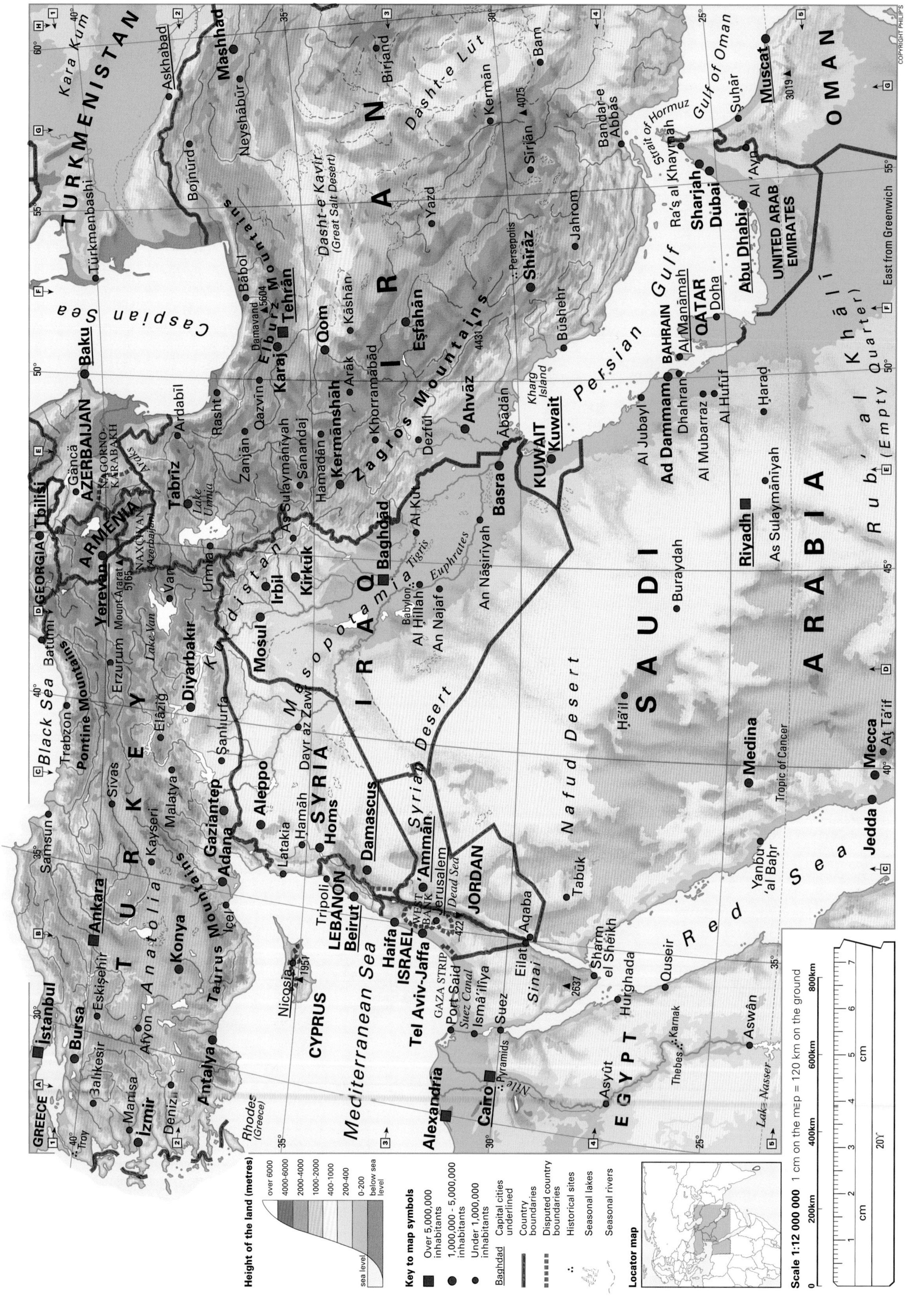
TURKMENISTAN
Kara Kum
Caspian Sea
Black Sea
Mediterranean Sea
Red Sea
Persian Gulf
Gulf of Oman
Strait of Hormuz
TURKEY
Anatolia
Pontine Mountains
Taurus Mountains
GEORGIA
ARMENIA
AZERBAIJAN
NAGORNO-KARABAKH
NAXCHIVAN (Azerbaijan)
IRAN
Elburz Mountains
Zagros Mountains
Dasht-e Kavir (Great Salt Desert)
Dasht-e Lūt
IRAQ
Mesopotamia
Kurdistan
SYRIA
Syrian Desert
LEBANON
ISRAEL
WEST BANK
GAZA STRIP
JORDAN
CYPRUS
EGYPT
Sinai
SAUDI ARABIA
Nafud Desert
Rub' al Khālī (Empty Quarter)
KUWAIT
BAHRAIN
QATAR
UNITED ARAB EMIRATES
OMAN
GREECE
Rhodes (Greece)
İstanbul
Ankara
Bursa
İzmir
Konya
Adana
Antalya
Gaziantep
Diyarbakır
Tbilisi
Yerevan
Baku
Tehrān
Mashhad
Tabrīz
Eşfahān
Shīrāz
Baghdad
Mosul
Basra
Kuwait
Damascus
Aleppo
Homs
Beirut
Nicosia
Haifa
Tel Aviv-Jaffa
Jerusalem
'Ammān
Cairo
Alexandria
Suez Canal
Nile
Lake Nasser
Riyadh
Mecca
Medina
Jedda
Ad Dammam
Al Manāmah
Doha
Abu Dhabi
Dubai
Sharjah
Muscat
Tropic of Cancer
Height of the land (metres)
over 6000
4000-6000
2000-4000
1000-2000
400-1000
200-400
0-200
below sea level
sea level
Key to map symbols
Over 5,000,000 inhabitants
1,000,000 - 5,000,000 inhabitants
Under 1,000,000 inhabitants
Baghdad Capital cities underlined
Country boundaries
Disputed country boundaries
Historical sites
Seasonal lakes
Seasonal rivers
Locator map
Scale 1:12 000 000 1 cm on the map = 120 km on the ground
0 200km 400km 600km 800km
East from Greenwich
COPYRIGHT PHILIP'S

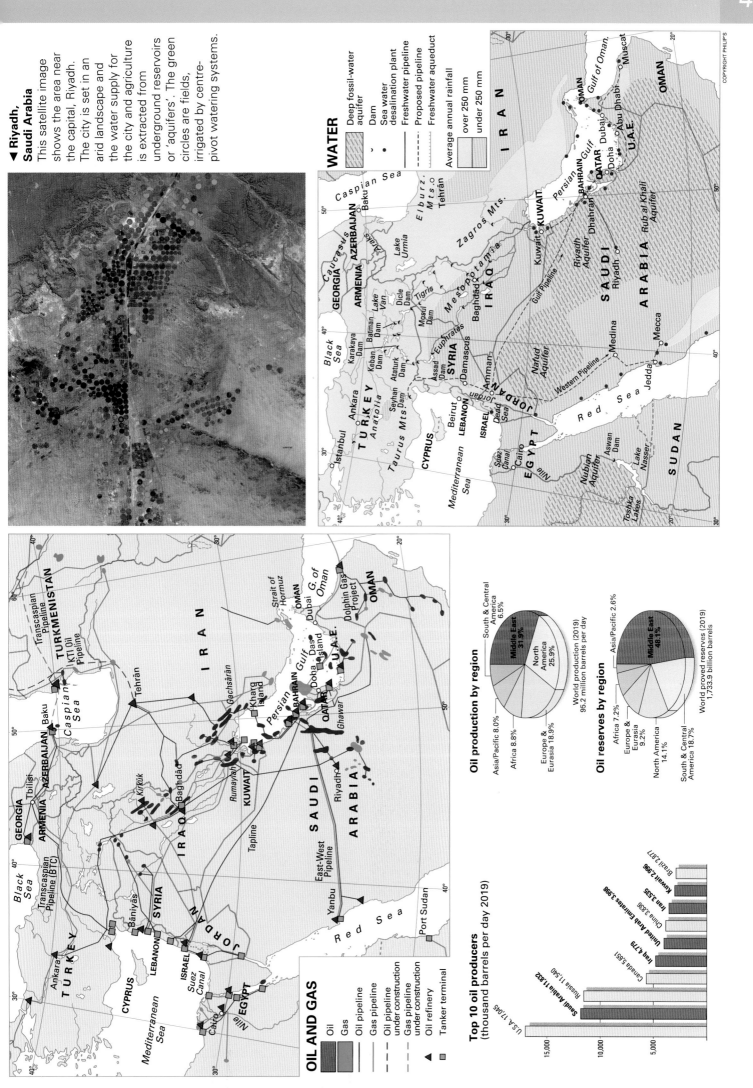

▶ Riyadh, Saudi Arabia
This satellite image shows the area near the capital, Riyadh. The city is set in an arid landscape and the water supply for the city and agriculture is extracted from underground reservoirs or 'aquifers'. The green circles are fields, irrigated by centre-pivot watering systems.

WATER

Deep fossil-water aquifer
Dam
Sea water desalination plant
Freshwater pipeline
Proposed pipeline
Freshwater aqueduct

Average annual rainfall
over 250 mm
under 250 mm

COPYRIGHT PHILIP'S

OIL AND GAS

Oil
Gas
Oil pipeline
Gas pipeline
Oil pipeline under construction
Gas pipeline under construction
Oil refinery
Tanker terminal

Top 10 oil producers
(thousand barrels per day 2019)

U.S.A. 17,045
Saudi Arabia 11,832
Russia 11,540
Iraq 4,779
Canada 5,651
United Arab Emirates 3,998
China 3,836
Iran 3,535
Kuwait 2,996
Brazil 2,877

15,000
10,000
5,000

Oil production by region

South & Central America 6.5%
Middle East 31.9%
North America 25.9%
Europe & Eurasia 18.9%
Africa 8.8%
Asia/Pacific 8.0%

World production (2019)
95.2 million barrels per day

Oil reserves by region

Asia/Pacific 2.6%
Middle East 48.1%
North America 14.1%
South & Central America 18.7%
Europe & Eurasia 9.2%
Africa 7.2%

World proved reserves (2019)
1,733.9 billion barrels

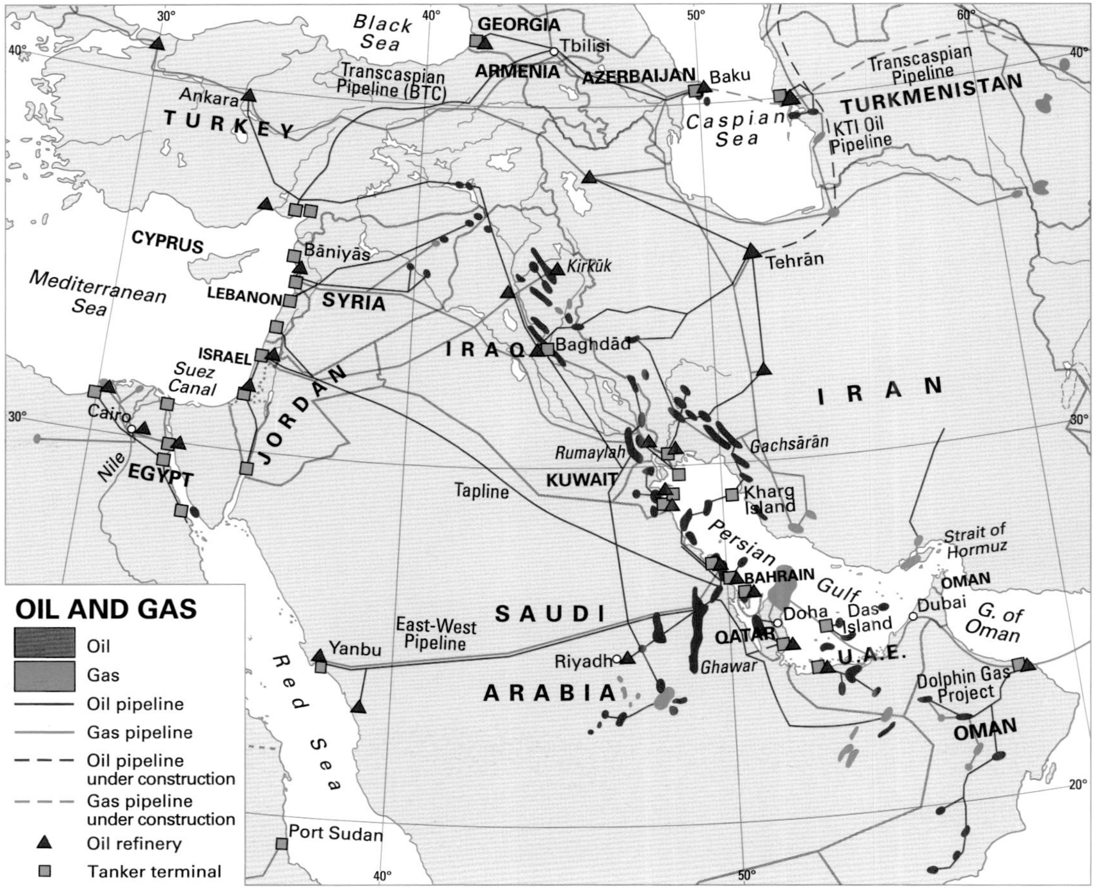

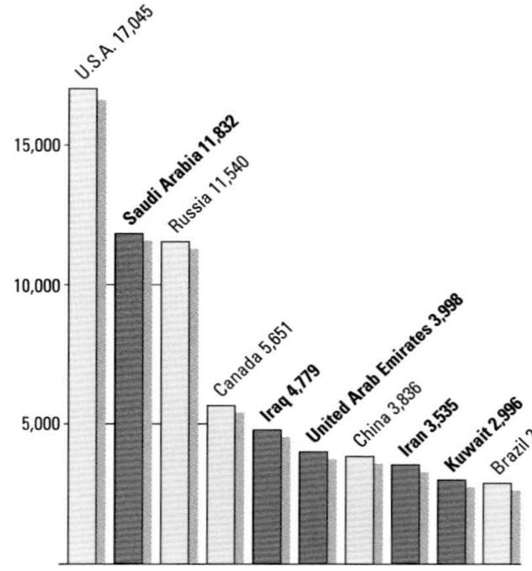

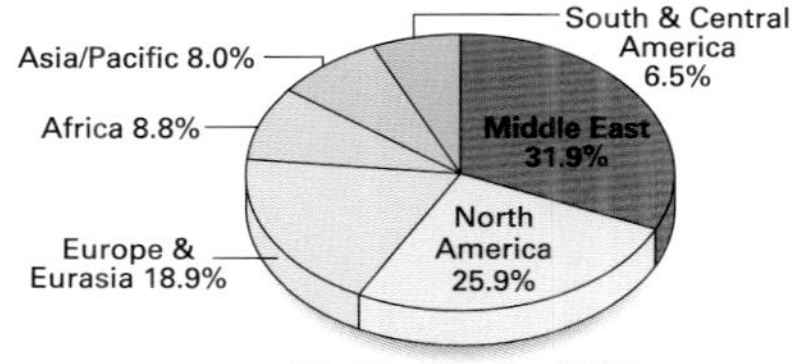

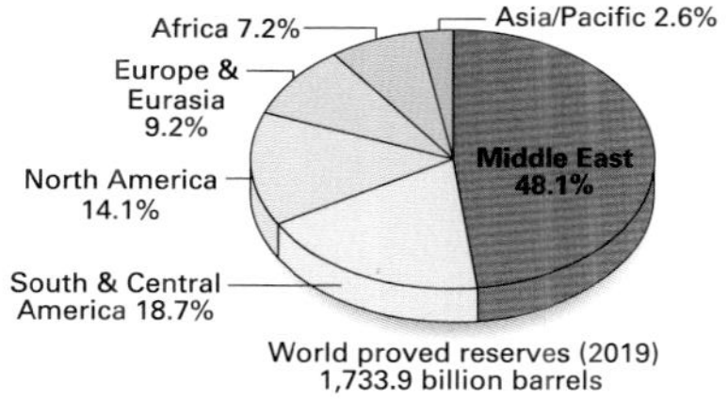

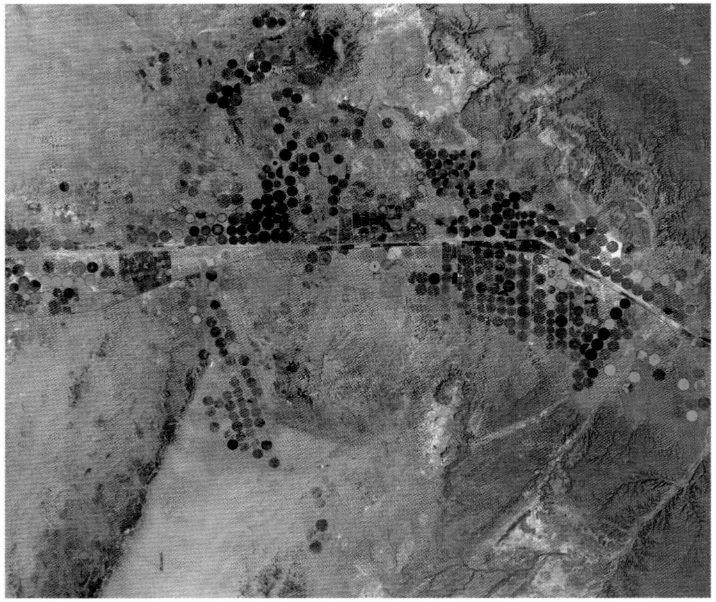

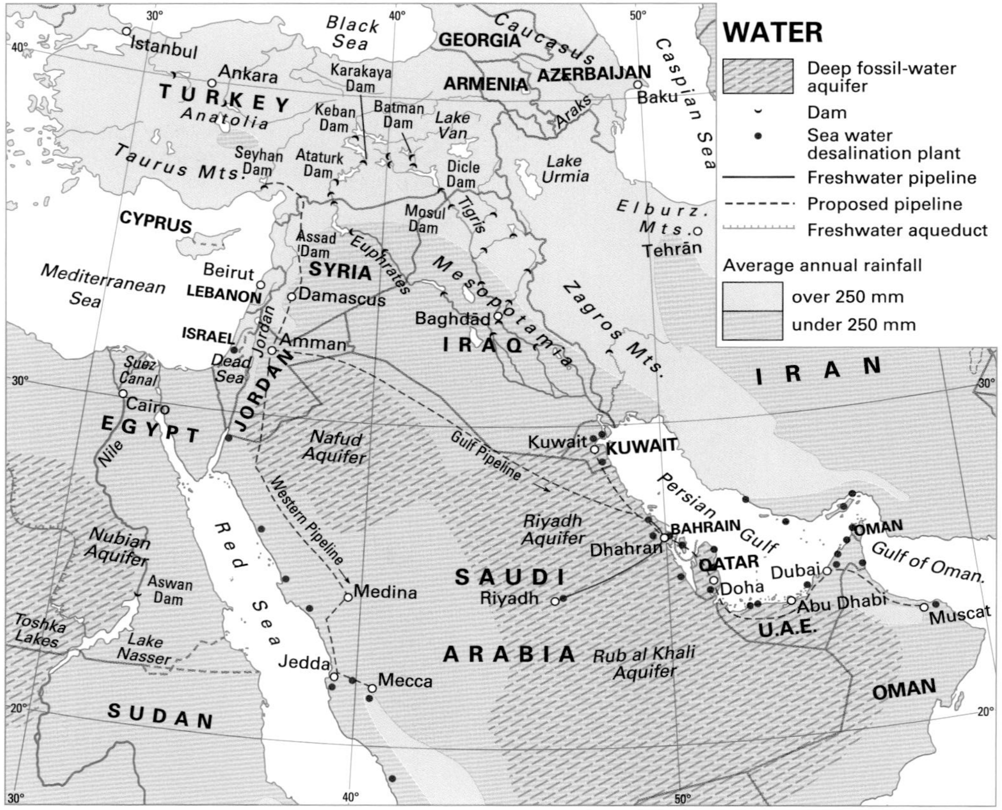

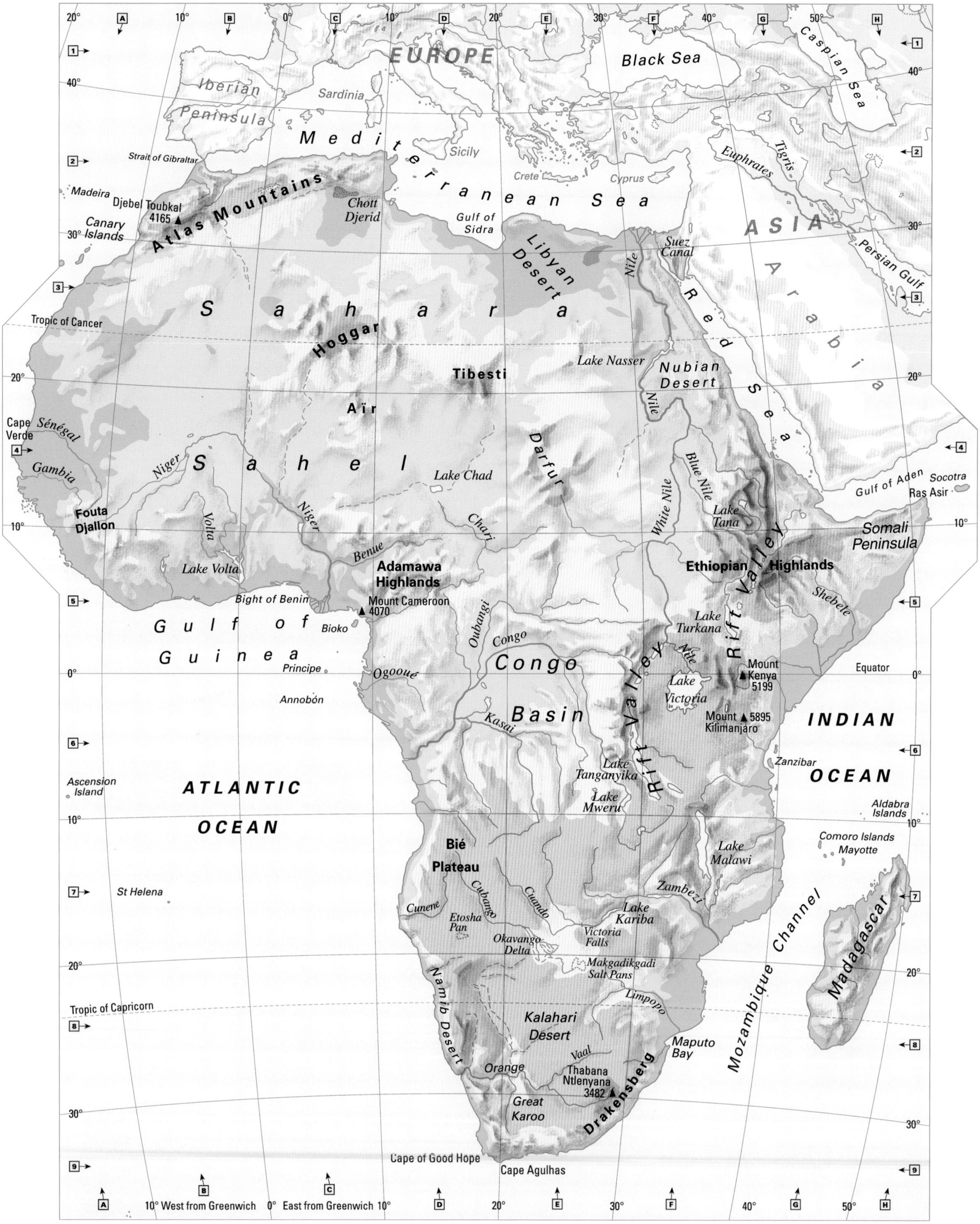

EUROPE

Black Sea

Caspian Sea

Iberian Peninsula

Sardinia

M e d i t e r r a n e a n   S e a

Sicily

Crete

Cyprus

ASIA

Euphrates

Tigris

Strait of Gibraltar

Gulf of Sidra

Arabia

Persian Gulf

Madeira

Djebel Toubkal 4165

Atlas Mountains

Chott Djerid

Gulf of Gabes

Suez Canal

Canary Islands

S a h a r a

Libyan Desert

Nile

Red Sea

Tropic of Cancer

Hoggar

Tibesti

Lake Nasser

Nubian Desert

Cape Verde

Sénégal

Aïr

S a h e l

Darfur

White Nile

Blue Nile

Lake Tana

Gulf of Aden

Socotra

Ras Asir

Niger

Lake Chad

Gambia

Niger

Chari

Ethiopian Highlands

Somali Peninsula

Fouta Djallon

Volta

Benue

Shebele

Lake Volta

Adamawa Highlands

Bight of Benin

Mount Cameroon 4070

Oubangi

Lake Turkana

Rift Valley

G u l f   o f

Bioko

Congo

Mount Kenya 5199

Equator

G u i n e a

Principe

Ogooué

C o n g o

Lake Victoria

INDIAN

Annobón

B a s i n

Kasai

Mount Kilimanjaro 5895

Rift Valley

Ascension Island

Lake Tanganyika

Zanzibar

OCEAN

A T L A N T I C

Lake Mweru

Aldabra Islands

O C E A N

Comoro Islands

Mayotte

Bié Plateau

Lake Malawi

St Helena

Cunene

Cubango

Cuando

Zambezi

Lake Kariba

Namib Desert

Etosha Pan

Okavango Delta

Victoria Falls

Mozambique Channel

Madagascar

Makgadikgadi Salt Pans

Tropic of Capricorn

Kalahari Desert

Limpopo

Maputo Bay

Orange

Vaal

Thabana Ntlenyana 3482

Drakensberg

Great Karoo

Cape of Good Hope

Cape Agulhas

COPYRIGHT PHILIP'S

Scale 1:39 000 000

Height of the land (metres)

over 4000
2000–4000
1000–2000
400–1000
200–400
0–200
sea level
below sea level

Cross-section along latitude 0° (Equator)

GABON   CONGO   DEMOCRATIC REPUBLIC OF THE CONGO   UGANDA   KENYA

Atlantic Ocean   Congo   Congo Basin   Congo   Ruwenzori   Lake Victoria   Indian Ocean

▲ Kilimanjaro 5895
▲ Mount Kenya 5199

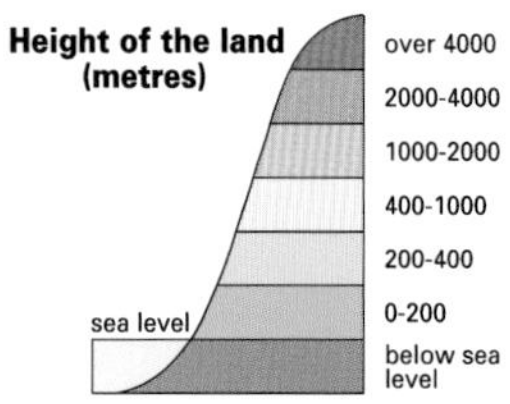

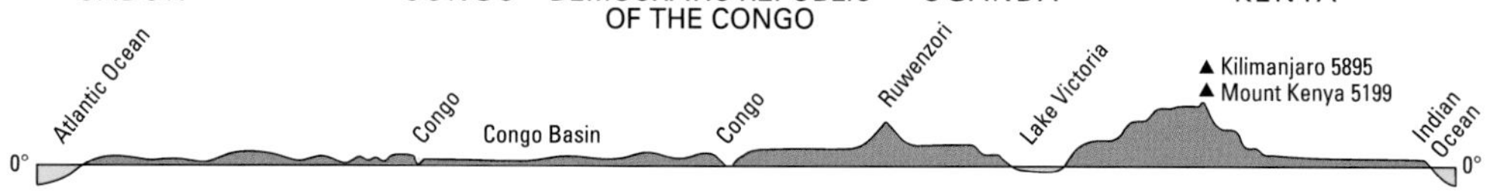

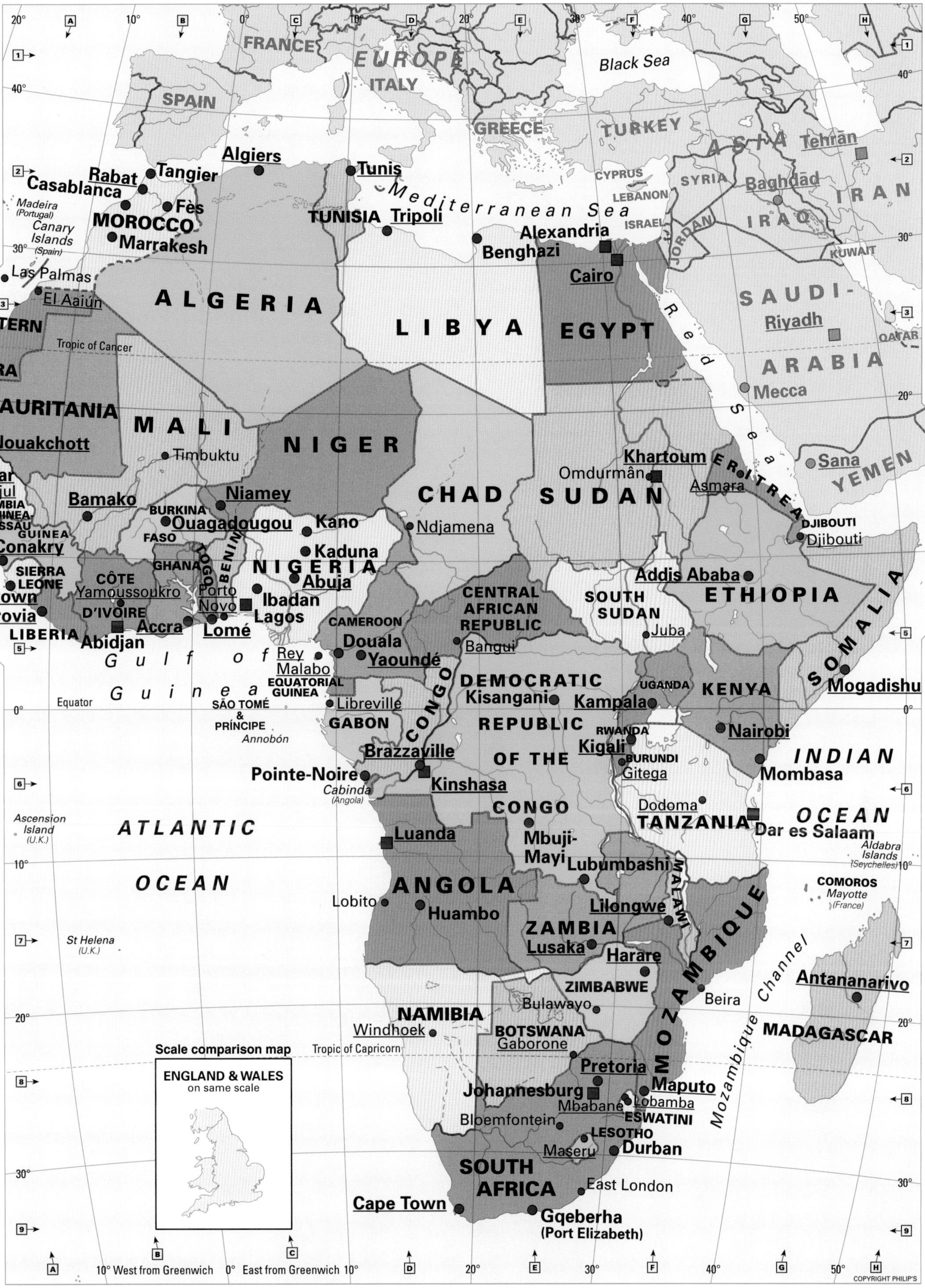

Scale 1:39 000 000 1 cm on the map = 390 km on the ground

0 780km 1560km 2340km 3120km

1 2 3 4 5 6 7 8 cm

Key to map symbols

■	Over 5,000,000 inhabitants	Cairo	Capital cities underlined
●	1,000,000 - 5,000,000 inhabitants	—	Country boundaries
•	Under 1,000,000 inhabitants	- - -	Disputed country boundaries
			Seasonal lakes
			Seasonal rivers

Locator map

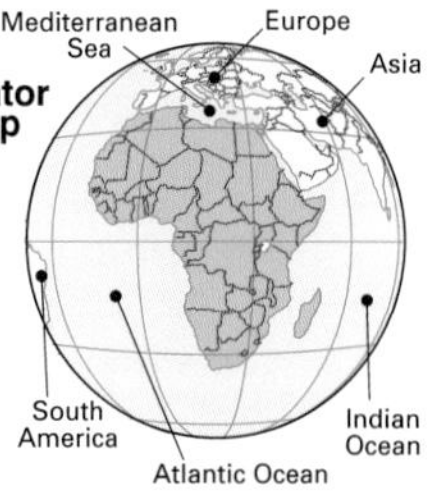

Nigeria and Ghana

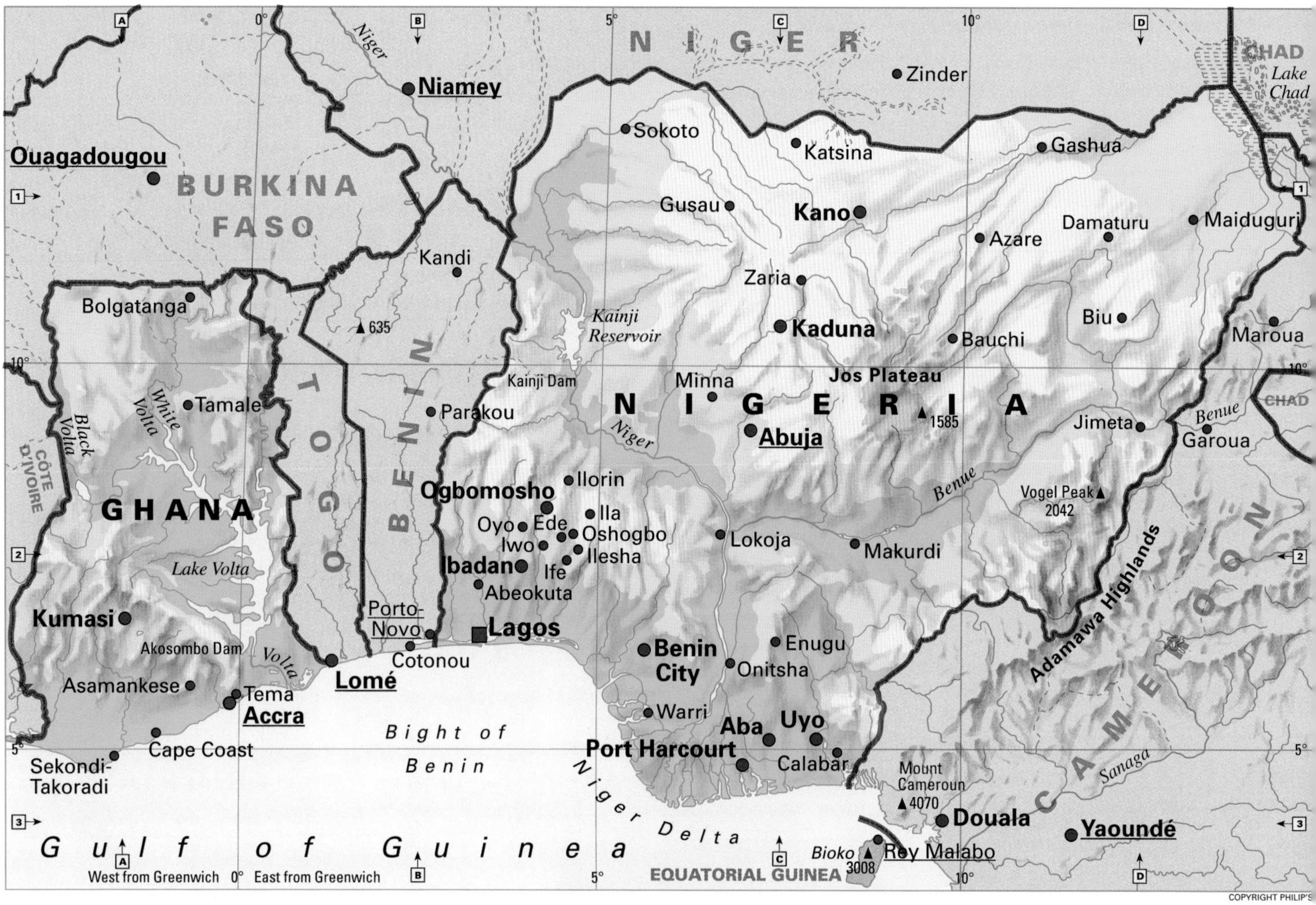

NIGERIA AND GHANA

Scale 1:10 000 000 1 cm on the map = 100 km on the ground

0 100km 200km 300km 400km 500km 600km

1 2 3 4 5 6 cm

See page opposite for key to map symbols, locator map and height of the land reference panel.

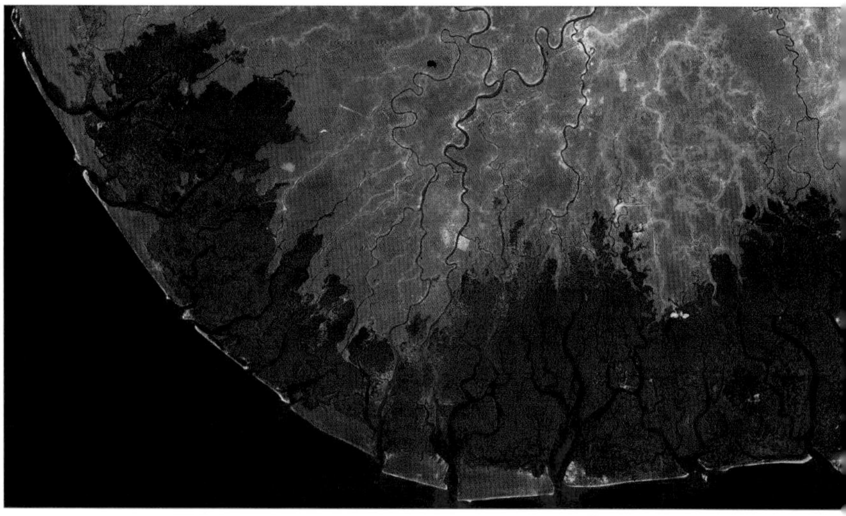

Niger Delta, Nigeria ▲

Satellite imagery helps to plan the drilling for oil and gas in the delta and to monitor the effect of the drilling on this fragile environment. This is a false colour image which shows vegetation such as mangrove swamps in dark red.

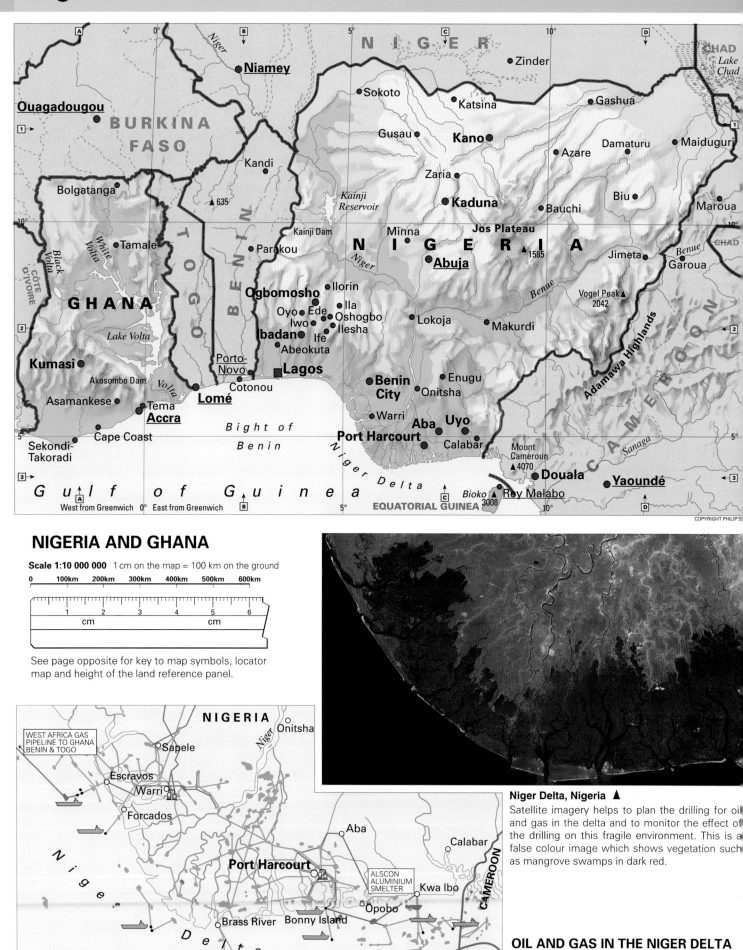

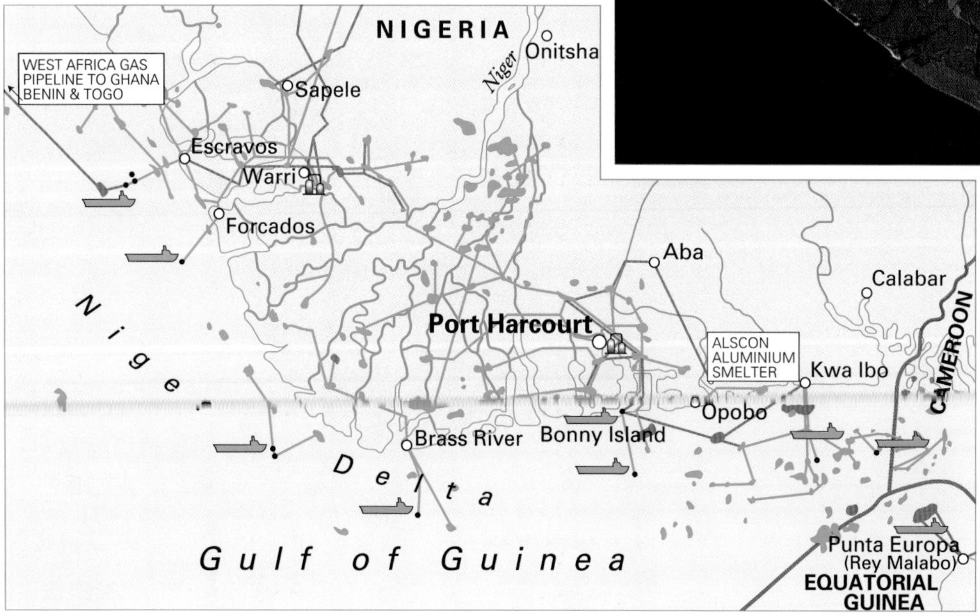

OIL AND GAS IN THE NIGER DELTA

Oilfields
Oil pipelines
Gasfields
Gas pipelines
Tanker terminals
Oil refineries

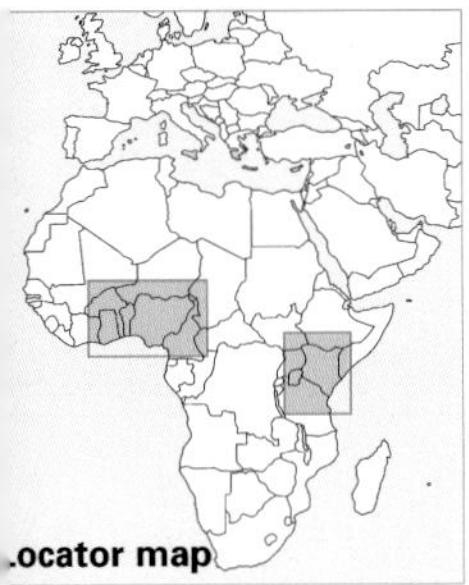

Height of the land (metres)

- over 4000
- 2000 – 4000
- 1000 – 2000
- 400 – 1000
- 200 – 400
- 0 – 200
- sea level
- below sea level

Key to map symbols

- Over 5,000,000 inhabitants
- 1,000,000 - 5,000,000 inhabitants
- Under 1,000,000 inhabitants
- Kampala Capital cities underlined
- Country boundaries
- Administrative boundaries
- Rift Valley
- 5895 ▲ Heights in metres
- 1134 Height of lake surface above sea level

Scale 1:8 000 000 1 cm on the map = 80 km on the ground

80km 160km 240km 320km 400km 480km 560km 640km 720km 800km

1 2 3 4 5 6 7 8 9 10 cm

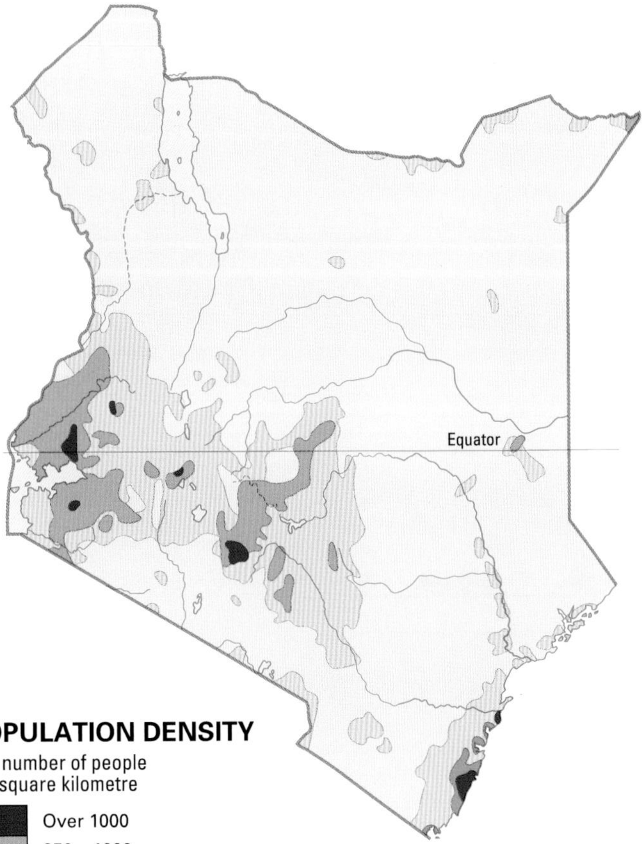

POPULATION DENSITY

The number of people per square kilometre

- Over 1000
- 250 – 1000
- 25 – 250
- Under 25

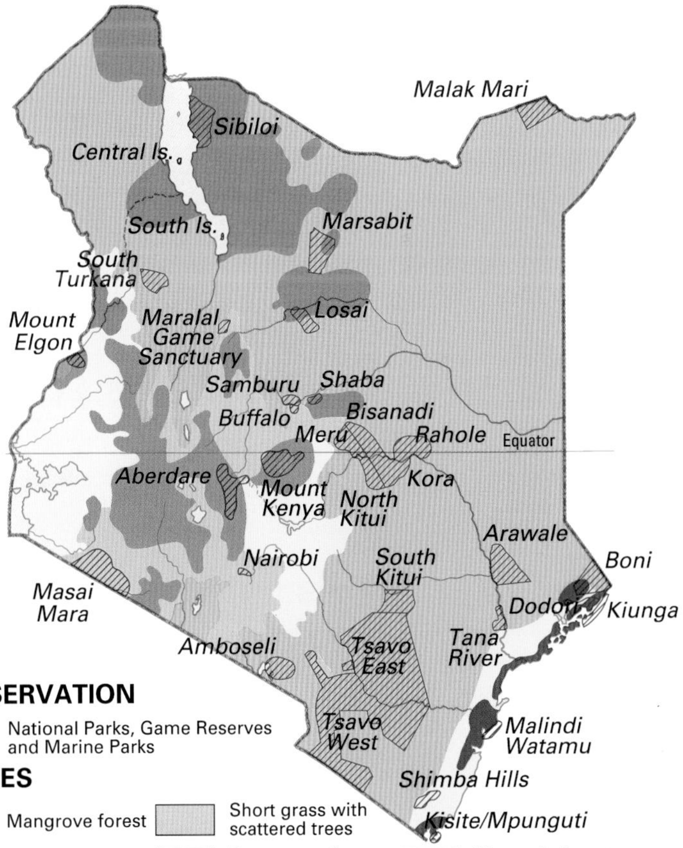

CONSERVATION

- National Parks, Game Reserves and Marine Parks

BIOMES

- Mangrove forest
- Coastal forest
- Tall grass with scattered trees
- Short grass with scattered trees
- Poor grass, thorns, sand and bare rock
- Dry bush with trees
- Mountain forest and grassland
- High mountain vegetation

Australia and Oceania

Height of the land (metres)

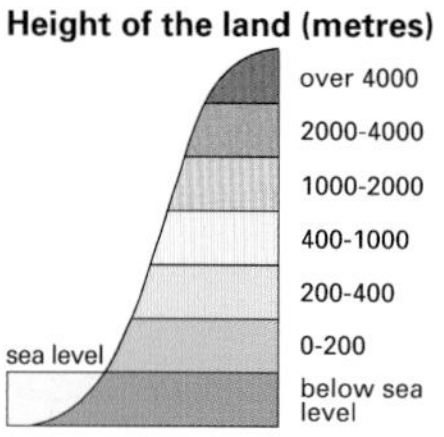

Key to map symbols

- ■ Over 5,000,000 inhabitants
- ● 1,000,000 - 5,000,000 inhabitants
- • Under 1,000,000 inhabitants
- Canberra — Capital cities underlined
- Country boundaries
- State boundaries
- Seasonal lakes
- Seasonal rivers

Locator map

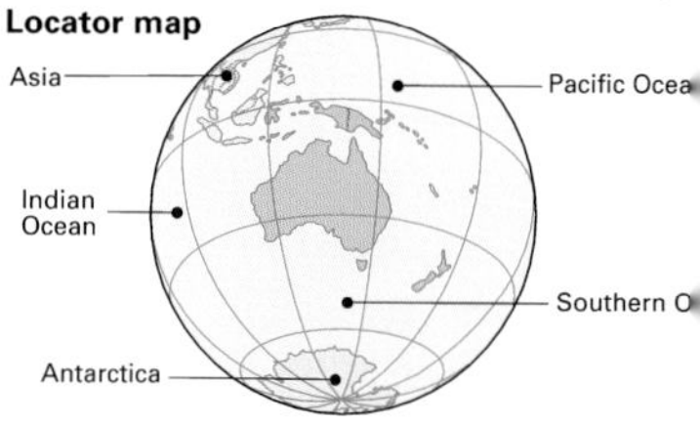

120° □D 125° □E 130° □F 135° □G 140° □H 145° □J 150° □K Ne
Equator 1 Moluccas Irela
0° Seram Papua Jayapura Wewak Bismarck Koko
Seram Sea P a p u a Puncak Jaya Archipelago
Celebes Ambon ▲ 4884 PAPUA NEW GUINEA New
Makassar Buru I N D O N E S I A Madang Britain
5° 2 Aru New Guinea Lae
Flores Sea Islands Solomon Se
Sumbawa Tanimbar D'Entrecaste
3 Flores Dili Islands Arafura Sea Torres Strait Port Islands
Sumba Timor TIMOR- Cape York Moresby Louisiade
Kupang LESTE Melville Archipelago
Timor Sea Island Cape Arnhem Weipa Cape C o r a
10° Darwin Arnhem York
4 Groote Peninsula
I N D I A N Katherine Land Eylandt Gulf of
Wyndham Carpentaria Mitchell Cairns Great
O C E A N Kimberley Lake Barkly Tableland
15° Argyle Tanami N O R T H E R N Townsville Barrier
5 Broome Fitzroy Desert Tennant Mount Isa Cloncurry Reef
Creek Mackay
Great Sandy Desert T E R R I T O R Y Q U E E N S L A N D Rockhampton Great
20° Port Gladsto
Dampier Hedland Gibson Desert MacDonnell Ranges Alice Springs Dividing Bundabe
North Pilbara A U S T R A L I A Simpson Barcoo Charleville Brisba
West 6 Newman Uluru Desert Sturt Quilpie Range Go
Cape W E S T E R N (Ayers Rock) Stony Toowoomba Coa
Carnarvon Musgrave Ranges S O U T H Desert Cooper Creek Warrego
Great Victoria A U S T R A L I A -16 Kati Thanda- Tamwo
25° Meekatharra Desert Lake Eyre N E W S O U T H
Lake Marree Flinders Ranges W A L E S Dubbo
Geraldton Torrens Broken Hill Darling Newcastle
7 Kalgoorlie- Lake Lachlan
Boulder Gairdner Port Augusta Mildura Wagga Sydn
Nullarbor Plain Whyalla Port Pirie Murray Wagga Wollongo
30° Spencer Gulf Murrumbidgee Canberra
Perth Esperance Great Australian Bight Port Lincoln Adelaide Murray Mount Kosciuszko A.C.T.
Rockingham Kangaroo Bendigo 2228 Snowy Mountains
Bunbury 8 Island VICTORIA
Albany Mount Gambier Ballarat Melbourne
Cape Leeuwin S O U T H E R N Geelong Bass Strait Flinders
King Island
35° Island
O C E A N Launceston
9 North Cross-section along longitude 147°E A U S T R A L I A South TASMANIA Hobart
TASMANIA South East Cape

M
<!-- Grid reference L -->
160°   **M**   165°   **N**   170°   **P**   175°   **Q**   180°   **R**   *Baker I.* 175°   **S**   *Equator*

Gilbert Islands **K I R I B A T I**
0°

M
e
Bougainville
Choiseul
SOLOMON
Santa Isabel
New Georgia Islands
ISLANDS
Malaita
Honiara ●
Guadalcanal
Makira
Rennell

l
a
n
e
s
i
a

Phoenix Islands
T U V A L U
Funafuti ● **Fongafale**

Tokelau Islands (N.Z.)

e a

Rotuma
Wallis & Futuna (France)
SAMOA
Apia ●
American Samoa (U.S.A.)
● *Pago Pago*

Espíritu Santo
VANUATU
Malakula
Vanua Levu
Port Vila ●
Viti Levu
FIJI
● **Suva**

TONGA
Niue (N.Z.)

Chesterfield Islands
Loyalty Islands
New Caledonia (France)
● *Nouméa*

Nuku'alofa ●
10 882 ▼
Tonga Trench

P   A   C   I   F   I   C
Tropic of Capricorn

O   C   E   A   N

Norfolk Island (Australia)

Lord Howe Island (Australia)

Kermadec Islands (N.Z.)

Kermadec Trench
10 047 ▼

T a s m a n   S e a
North Cape

Auckland ●
North Island
Hamilton ●
● *Rotorua*

NEW ZEALAND

Palmerston North ●
Nelson ●
Cook Strait
● **Wellington**

South Island
Aoraki
Mount Cook
3724
Southern Alps
● *Christchurch*

Invercargill
● *Dunedin*
Stewart Island

Chatham Islands (N.Z.)

International Date Line

West from Greenwich

Scale comparison map
ENGLAND & WALES
on same scale

160°   **L**   165°   **M**   170°   **N**   175°   **P**   180°   **Q**   175°   **R**   170°   **S**   165°   **T**   160°   **U**   **V**

COPYRIGHT PHILIP'S

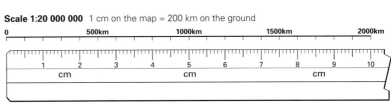

Scale 1:20 000 000   1 cm on the map = 200 km on the ground

0   500km   1000km   1500km   2000km

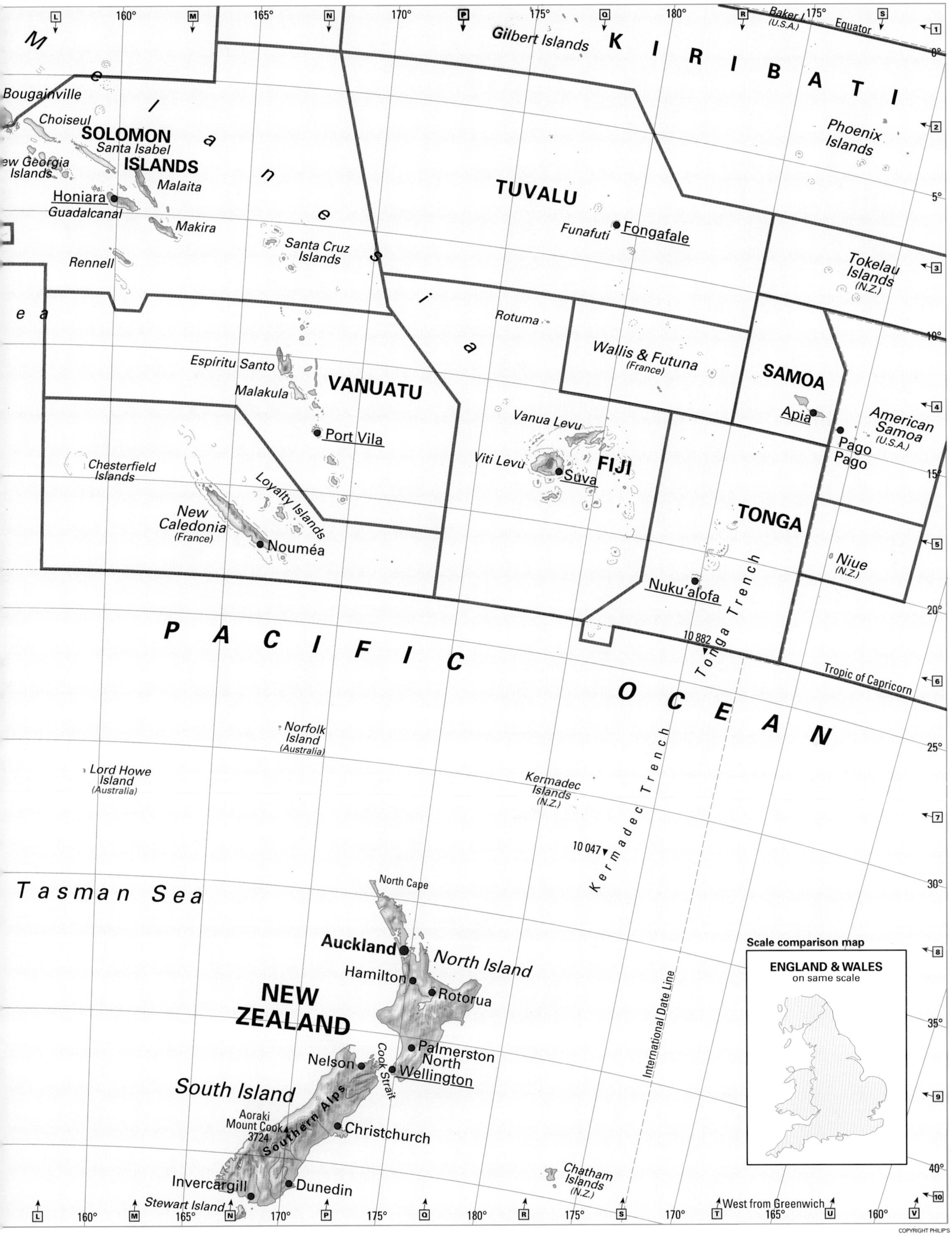

North America : Relief of Land

Scale 1:35 000 000

Height of the land (metres)
over 6000
4000-6000
2000-4000
1000-2000
400-1000
200-400
0-200
sea level
below sea level

Cross-section along latitude 40°N

Pacific Ocean
Mount Shasta 4317
Sierra Nevada
Wasatch Mountains
Colorado
Mount Elbert 4399
Rocky Mountains
Great Plains
Missouri
Mississippi
Ohio
Allegheny Mountains
Appalachian Mountains
Atlantic Ocean
40°N

COPYRIGHT PHILIP'S

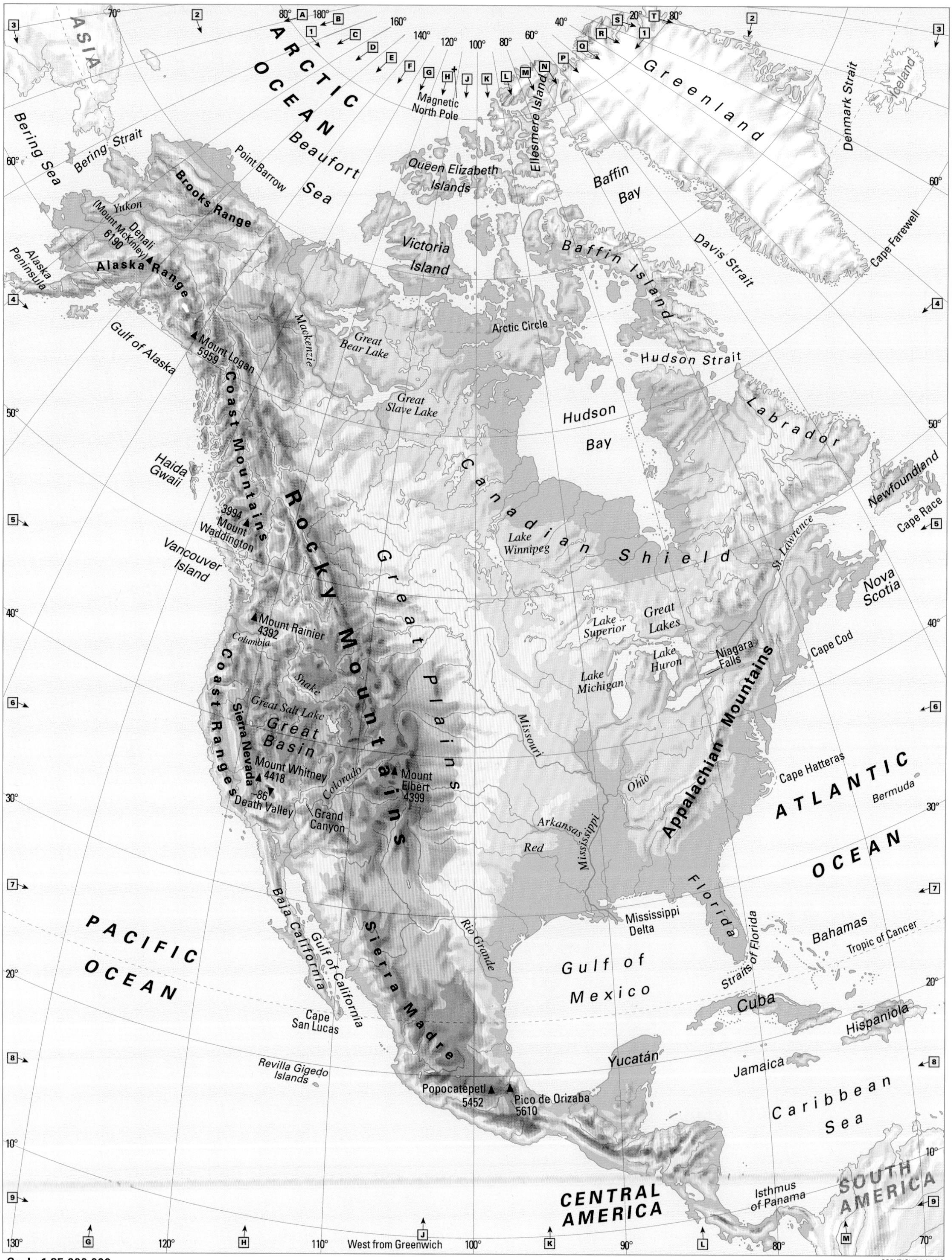

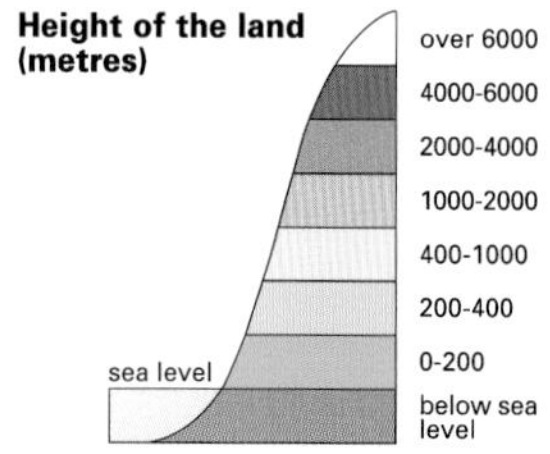

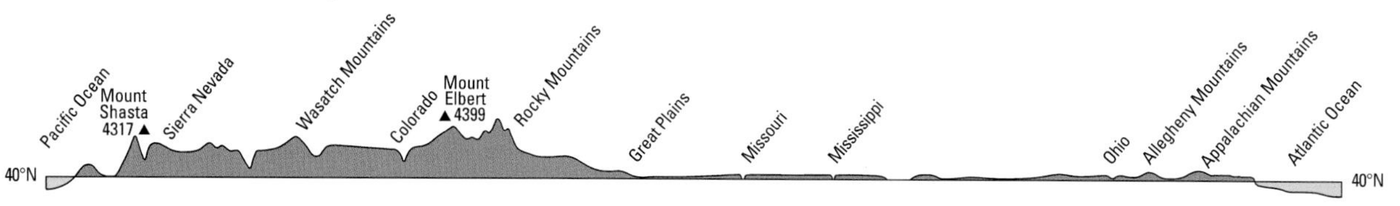

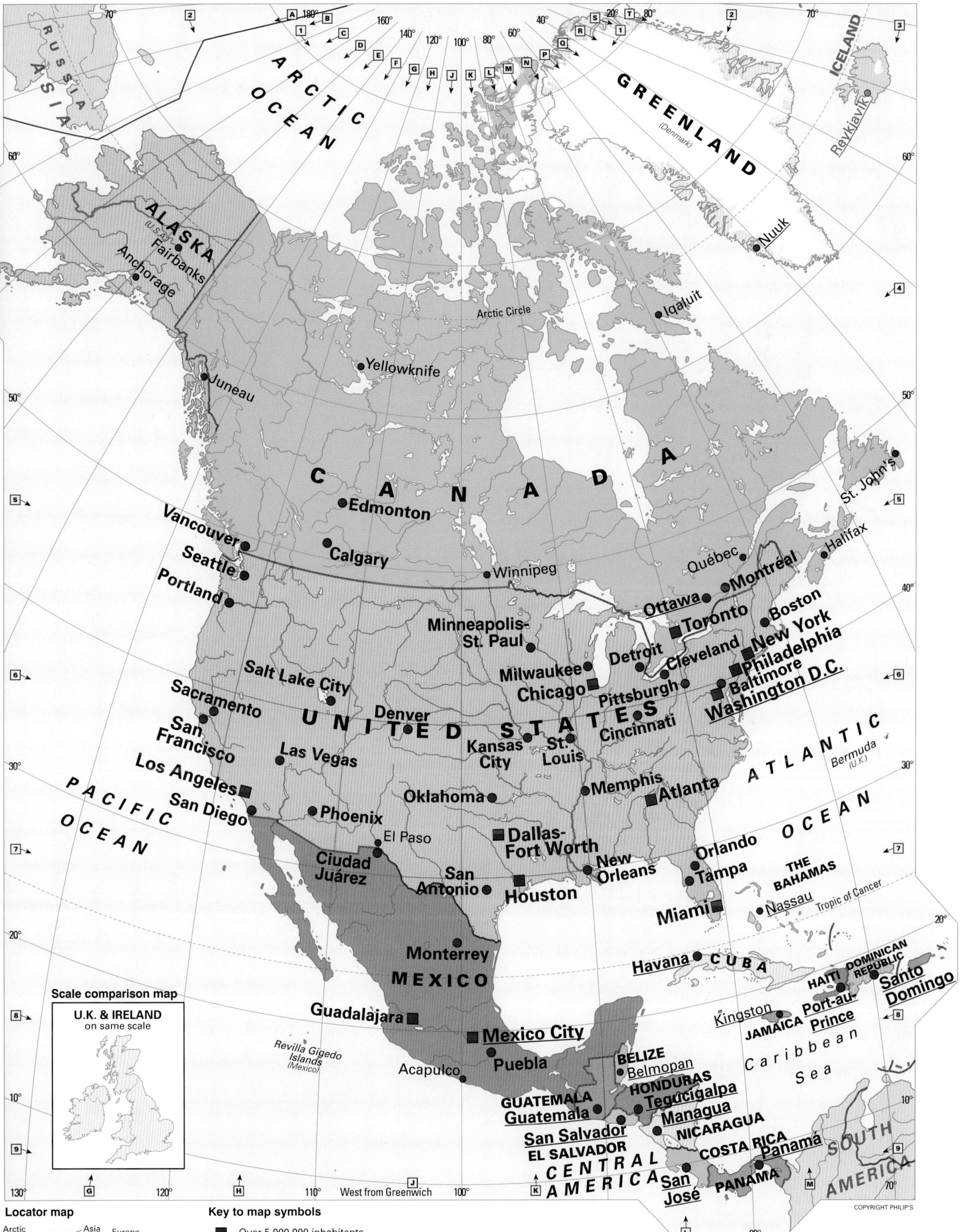

Scale comparison map

U.K. & IRELAND
on same scale

Locator map

Arctic Ocean — Asia — Europe
Africa
Atlantic Ocean
Pacific Ocean — South America

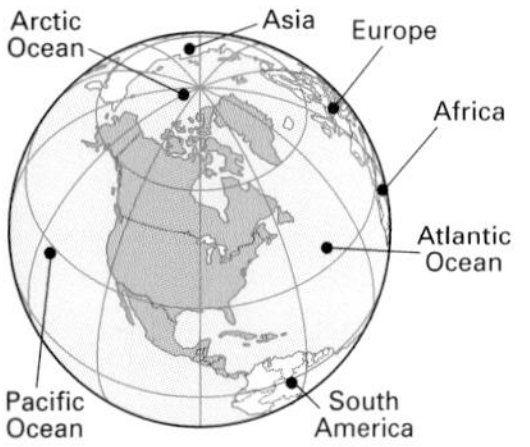

Key to map symbols

■ Over 5,000,000 inhabitants
● 1,000,000 - 5,000,000 inhabitants
• Under 1,000,000 inhabitants
Lima Capital cities underlined
— Country boundaries

Scale 1:35 000 000 1 cm on the map = 350 km on the ground

0   500km   1000km   1500km   2000km   2500km

1   2   3   4   5   6   7   8
cm   cm

COPYRIGHT PHILIP'S

United States of America

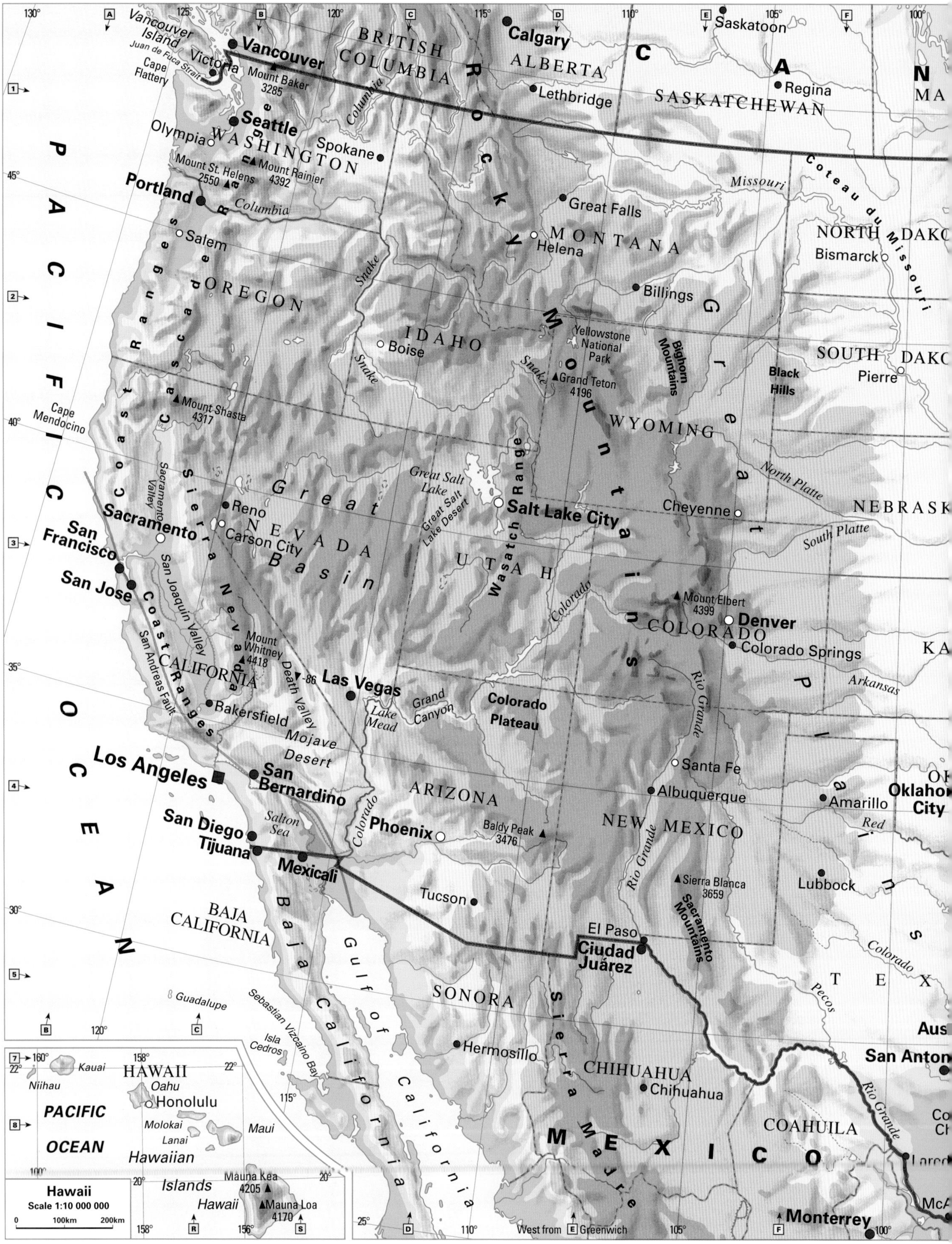

Height of the land (metres)

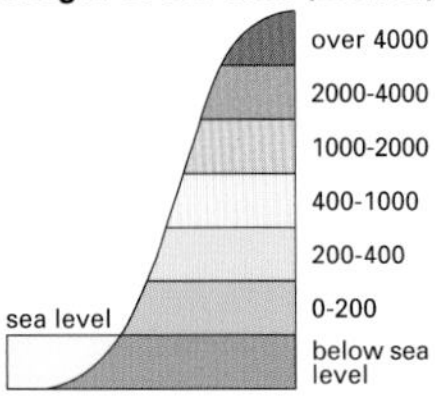

Key to map symbols

- ■ Over 5,000,000 inhabitants
- ● 1,000,000 - 5,000,000 inhabitants
- • Under 1,000,000 inhabitants
- Ottawa — Capital cities underlined
- Country boundaries
- □○○ State capitals in the U.S.A. have white infills. The state capital of Alaska is Juneau - see p56.
- State boundaries

Abbreviations used

CONN. = Connecticut

DEL. = Delaware

MASS. = Massachusetts

R.I. = Rhode Island

Scale 1:12 000 000 1 cm on the map = 120 km on the ground

200km 400km 600km 800km 1000km 1200km

1 2 3 4 5 6 7 8 9 10

cm cm cm

Locator map

United States of America

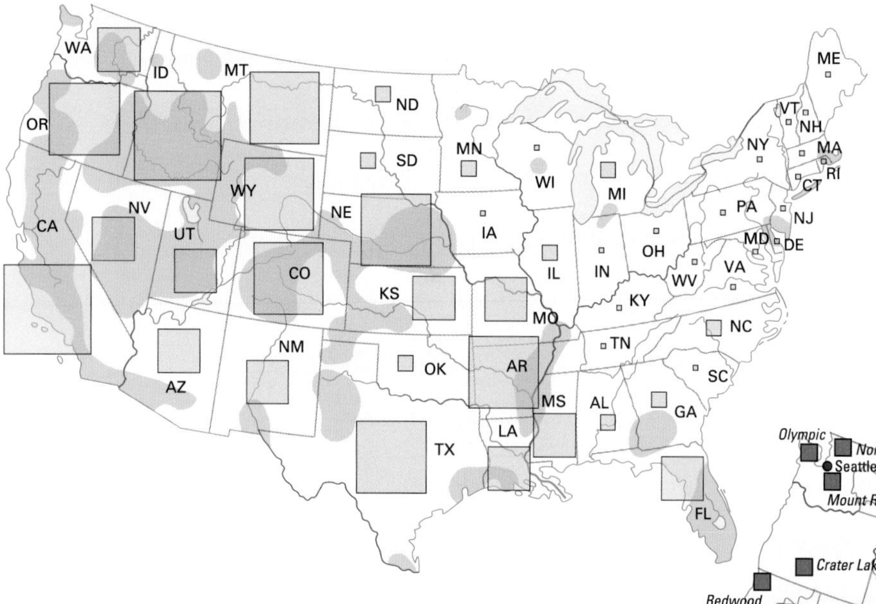

IRRIGATION

Total irrigation per state (million gallons per day)

Over 30,000

10,000

5000

1000

Under 1000

Areas with more than 10% of irrigated land

Irrigation is the watering of the land and crops by means of canals, ditches, pipes and wells. The biggest source of water for irrigation is that which has percolated into natural underground reservoirs or 'aquifers'. It can be extracted using either wells or pumps and, although replenished naturally, is at risk through overuse and depletion

TOURISM

Tourist centres

Concentration of h

National Parks

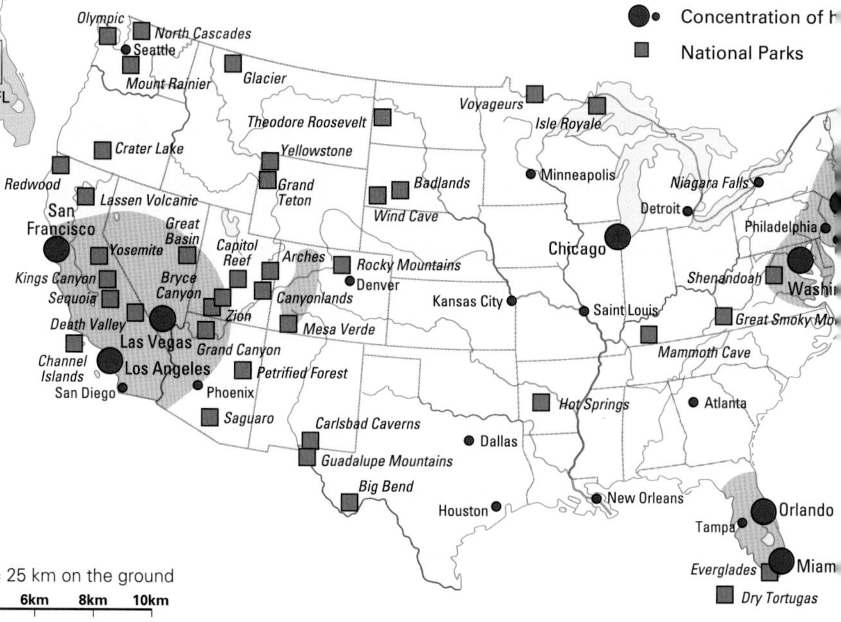

Central business district

Urban area

Park and open space

State boundary

Freeway

Other road

Airport

Place of interest

NEW YORK 1cm on the map = 25 km on the ground

Scale 1:250 000 0 2km 4km 6km 8km 10km

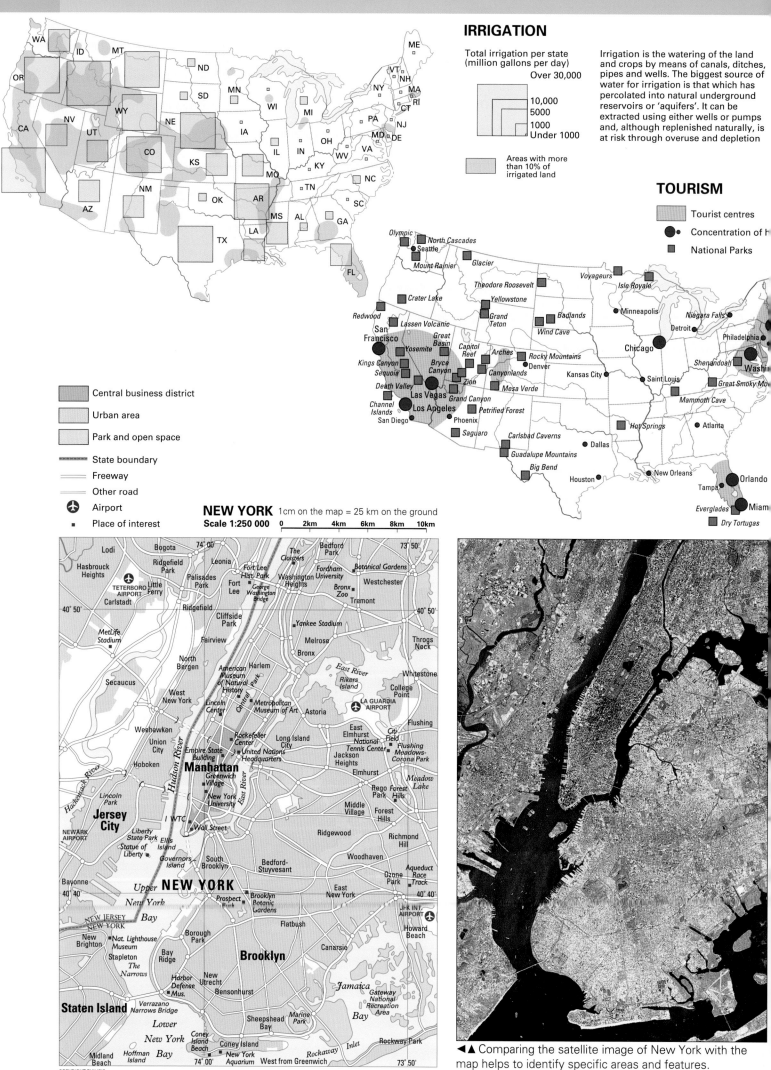

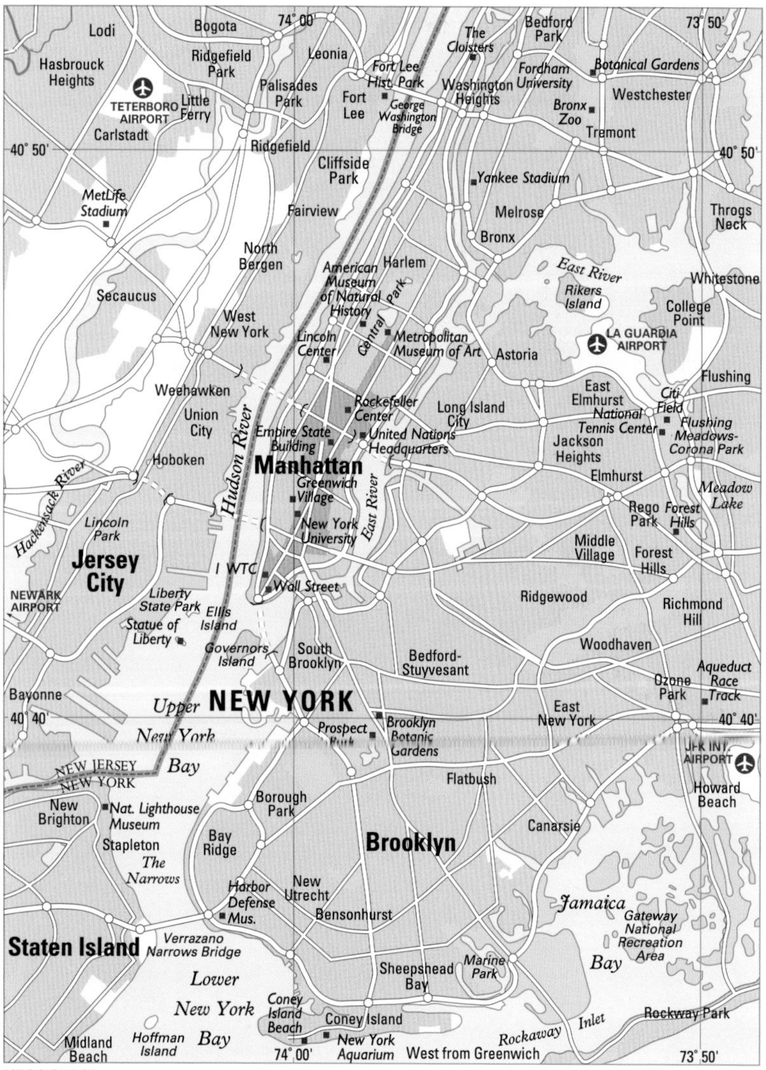

◄▲ Comparing the satellite image of New York with the map helps to identify specific areas and features.

HURRICANE TRACKS
Major hurricanes in the last 30 years

〰〰〰 Hurricanes track

⟵ Direction of storm

IRMA Hurricanes name

2017 Year of hurricane

1:26 000 000

HURRICANE RISK AREAS
Percentage probability of being
in the path of a tropical storm
or hurricane in any year

- Over 60%
- 50 – 60%
- 40 – 50%
- 30 – 40%
- 20 – 30%
- 10 – 20%
- Under 10%

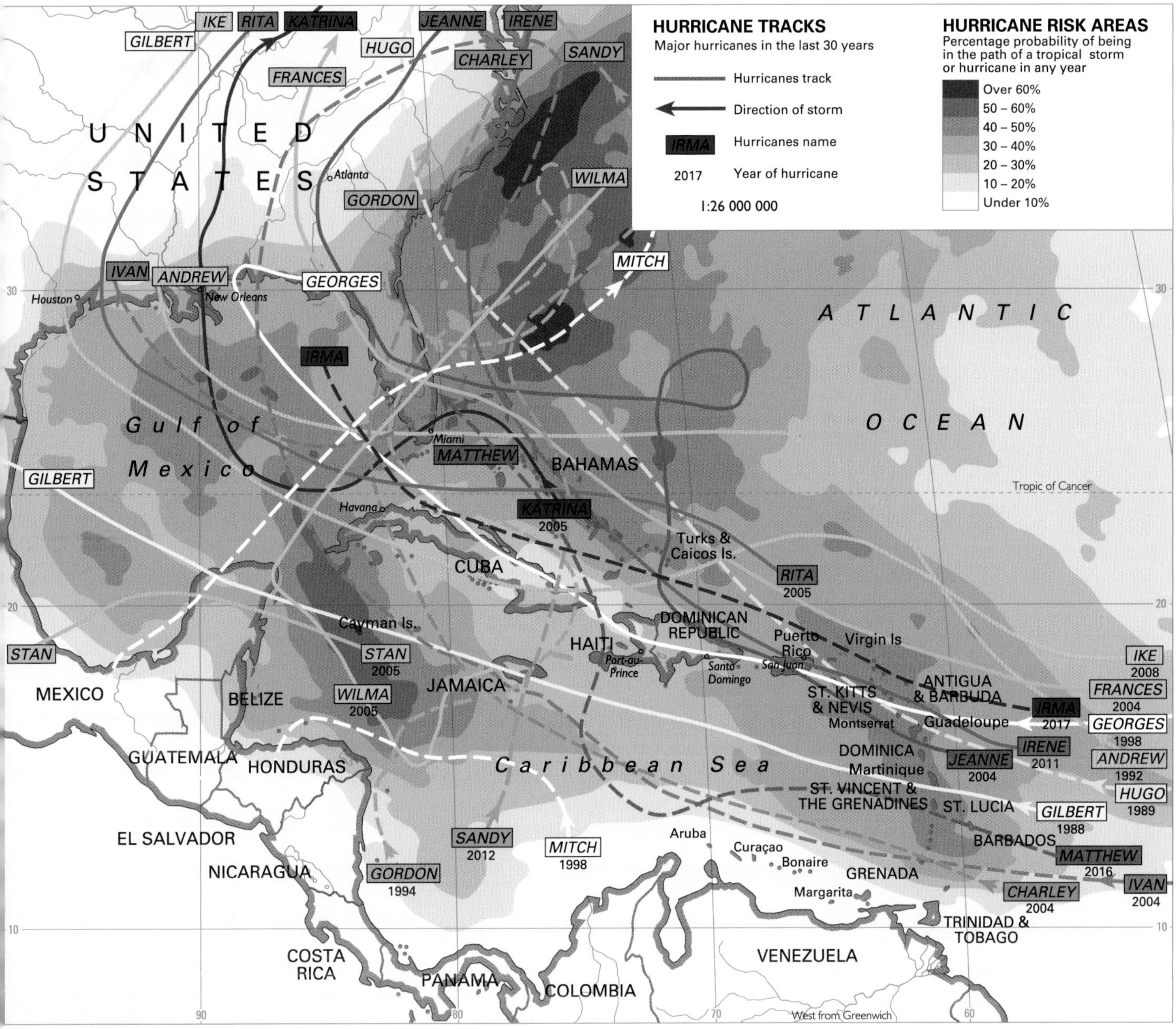

▲ **Hurricane Irma,** with winds of 295km per hour, was the most powerful in over ten years when it made landfall on Barbuda in September 2017. It caused catastrophic damage in St. Barthélemy, St. Martin, Anguilla and the Virgin Islands.

CROSS-SECTION THROUGH A HURRICANE

Total width 200–800 km

Cirrus cloud

Dense cloud

Thunderstorms

Cooled air spirals outwards and descends

Vortex of hurricane

Height 12 km

Warm, moist air spirals towards and around the eye of the hurricane, rising and cooling rapidly

Gusty winds

Violent winds (250 km/h)

Calm eye

Westerly path of system

Energy from warm sea (over 27°C)

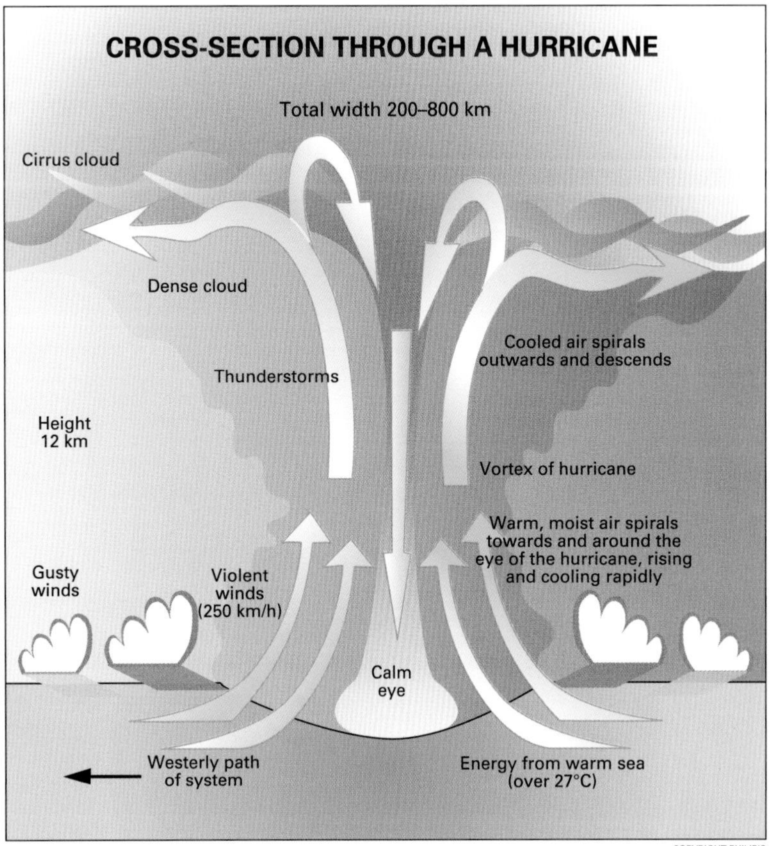

Mexico, Central America and the Caribbean

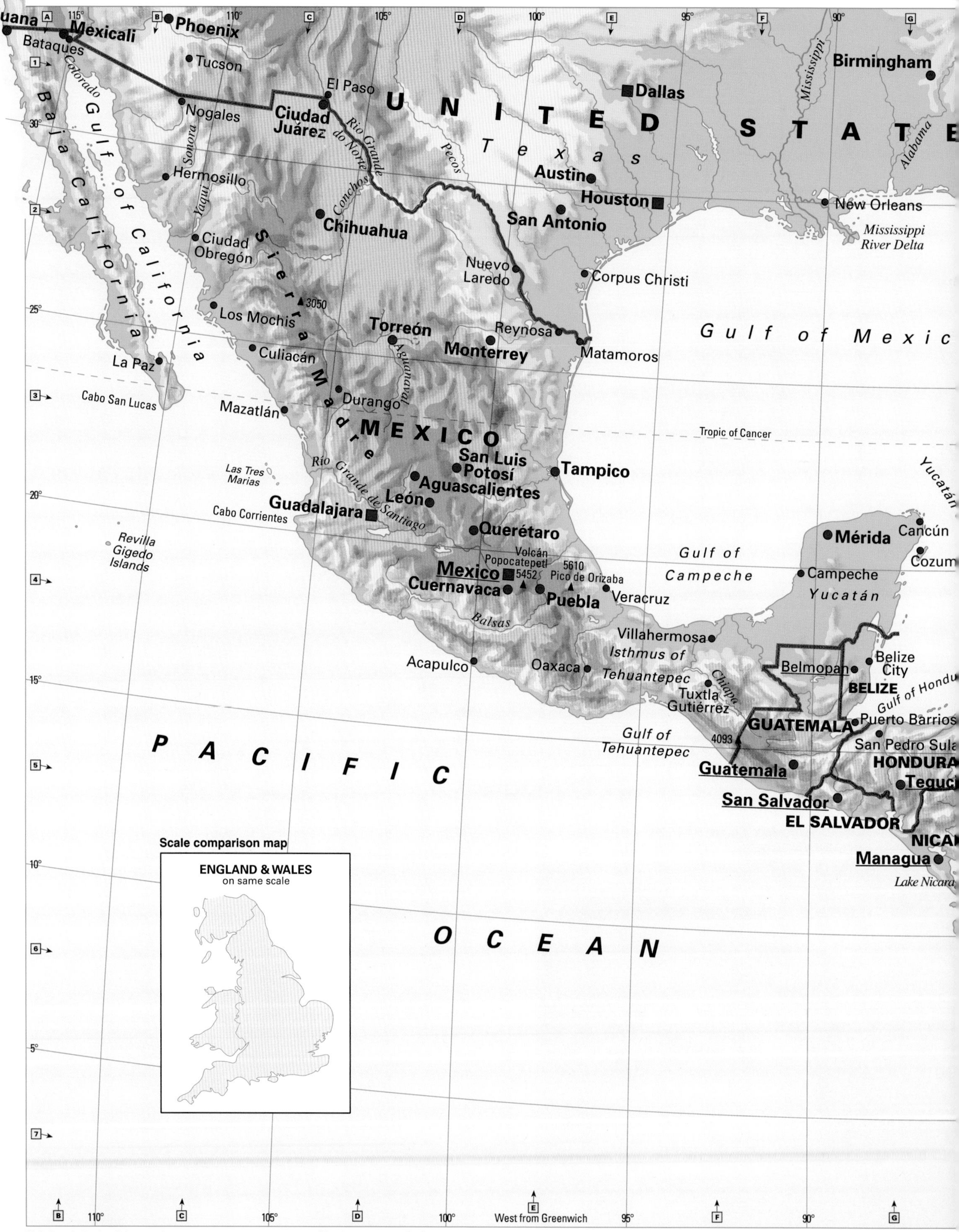

Height of the land (metres)

- over 4000
- 2000-4000
- 1000-2000
- 400-1000
- 200-400
- 0-200
- sea level
- below sea level

Key to map symbols

- ■ Over 5,000,000 inhabitants
- ● 1,000,000 - 5,000,000 inhabitants
- • Under 1,000,000 inhabitants
- Mexico — Capital cities underlined
- Country boundaries

ATLANTIC OCEAN

Sargasso Sea

Bermuda (U.K.) • Hamilton

Manta

• Savannah

• Jacksonville

• Orlando

pa

Fort Lauderdale •
Miami ■

Cape Sable

y West

Straits of Florida

ana Matanzas

Cienfuegos

C U B A

Santa Clara

Camagüey

Holguín

1972 ▲

Santiago
de Cuba

Guantanamo
Bay
(U.S.A.)

Grand
Bahama Island

Freeport

Nassau

THE
BAHAMAS

Turks &
Caicos
Islands
(U.K.)

Cayman
Islands
(U.K.)

Montego
Bay

JAMAICA

Kingston

Windward Passage

HAITI

Port au Prince

Santiago de los
Caballeros

DOMINICAN
REPUBLIC

▲3175

▲2280

Santo
Domingo

8605 ▼ Milwaukee
Deep

Mona Passage

San Juan

PUERTO RICO
(U.S.A.)

▲1338

Virgin Islands
(U.K.–U.S.A.)

Charlotte
Amalie

Basseterre

ST KITTS & NEVIS

GUADELOUPE
(France)

Leeward Islands

Roseau

Fort-de-France

Castries

Windward Islands

Kingstown

ST VINCENT &
THE GRENADINES

St. George's

ANTIGUA &
BARBUDA

• St. John's

Montserrat (U.K.)

Pointe-à-Pitre
Basse-Terre

DOMINICA

MARTINIQUE
(France)

ST LUCIA

Bridgetown

BARBADOS

GRENADA

C a r i b b e a n   S e a

ABC Islands
Aruba (Netherlands)
Curaçao (Netherlands)

Willemstad

Gulf of Venezuela

Margarita

Tobago

Port of Spain

TRINIDAD &
TOBAGO

Barranquilla

Cartagena

Sierra Nevada
de Santa Marta

5775 ▲

Valledupar

Magdalena

Maracaibo

Lake
Maracaibo

Barquisimeto

Maracay

Valencia

Caracas

Barcelona

Maturín

Delta of the
Orinoco

STA RICA

an José

▲3475

Panama
Canal

Panamá

P A N A M A

Isthmus
of
Panama

Gulf of
Darién

Gulf of
Panama

Montería

Cúcuta

4100 ▲

San Cristóbal

Cord. de Mérida

4981 ▲

Orinoco

Ciudad
Bolívar

Ciudad
Guayana

Georgetown

Bucaramanga

Medellín

Quibdó

Manizales

Pereira

Tolima
▲5215

Ibagué

Bogotá ■

C O L O M B I A

A n d e s

V E N E Z U E L A

S O U T H

Angel Falls

Mount
Roraima 2810

Sierra Pacaraima

▲2556

Boa Vista

G U Y A N A

1280 ▲

SURINAME

Essequibo

Buenaventura

Palmira

Cali

Guaviare

A M E R I C A

B R A Z I L

▲4646

West from Greenwich

COPYRIGHT PHILIP'S

ale 1:15 000 000   1 cm on the map = 150 km on the ground

300km   600km   900km   1200km   1500km

1   2   3   4   5   6   7   8   9   10
cm   cm   cm

Locator map

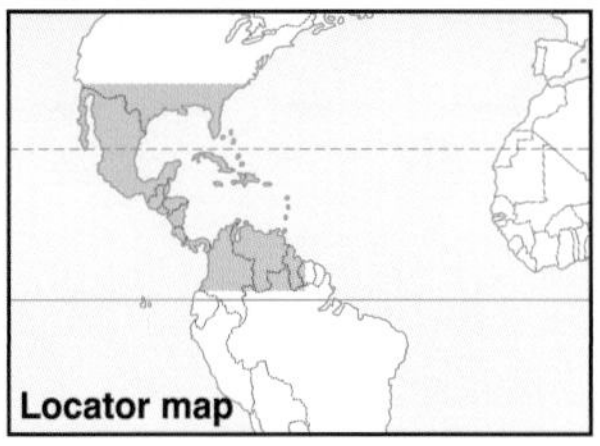

CENTRAL
AMERICA

Greater Antilles

Caribbean Sea

Lesser Antilles

Leeward Islands

Windward Islands

A T L A N T I C

O C E A N

Panama Canal

Gulf of Panama

5775 ▲

Lake Maracaibo

Magdalena

Orinoco

Angel Falls

G u i a n a   H i g h l a n d s

Pico de Neblina
3014 ▲

Negro

Amazon

Equator

Galapagos Islands

Cotopaxi
5897 ▲

Chimborazo
6267 ▲

A m a z o n   B a s i n

Japurá

Amazon

S e l v a s

Purus

Madeira

Tapajós

Xingu

Tocantins

Ucayali

Huascarán
6768 ▲

A   n   d   e   s

Lake Titicaca

Altiplano

Lake Poopó

Plateau of
Mato Grosso

São Francisco

B r a z i l i a n   H i g h l a n d s

2890 ▲

Gran Chaco

Paraguay

Paraná

Iguaçu
Falls

Atacama Desert

Ojos del Salado ▲
6863

Tropic of Capricorn

P A C I F I C

O C E A N

Aconcagua ▲
6962

Colorado

P a m p a s

Paraná

Uruguay

Río de la Plata

A T L A N T I C

O C E A N

Isla de
Chiloé

P a t a g o n i a

A   n   d   e   s

Lago del
Carbón
-105

Strait of Magellan

Falkland Islands

Tierra
del Fuego

Cape Horn

South
Georgia

COPYRIGHT PHILIP'S

110° West from Greenwich 100°

**Height of the land
(metres)**

	over 4000
	3000 – 4000
	2000 – 3000
	1000 – 2000
	500 – 1000
	200 – 500
	0 – 200
sea level	below sea level

Cross-section along latitude 20°S

CHILE   BOLIVIA   PARAGUAY   BRAZIL

▲ Ojos del Salado 6863
▲ Ancohuma & Illampu 6550

Pacific Ocean

Andes

Pilcomayo

Gran Chaco

Paraguay

Verde

Paraná

Brazilian Highlands

São Francisco

Doce

Atlantic Ocean

20°S   20°S

Scale 1:35 000 000

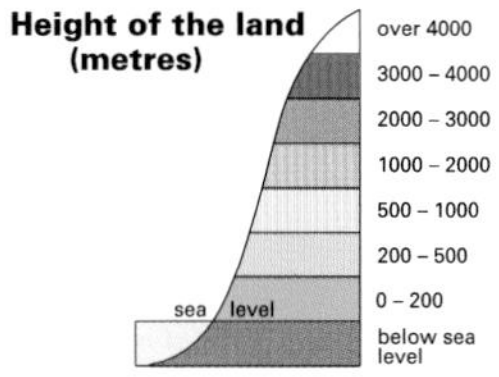

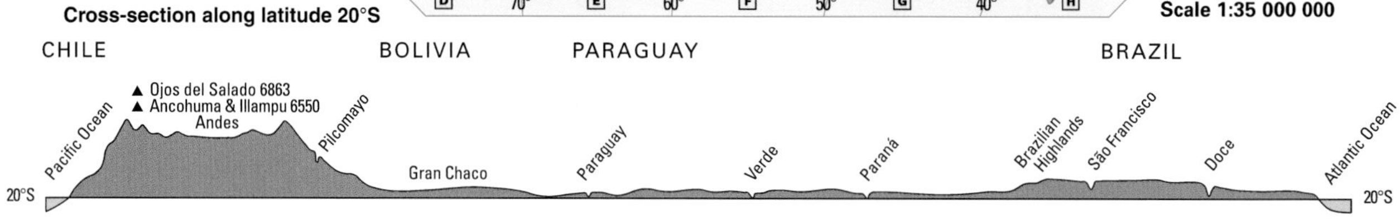

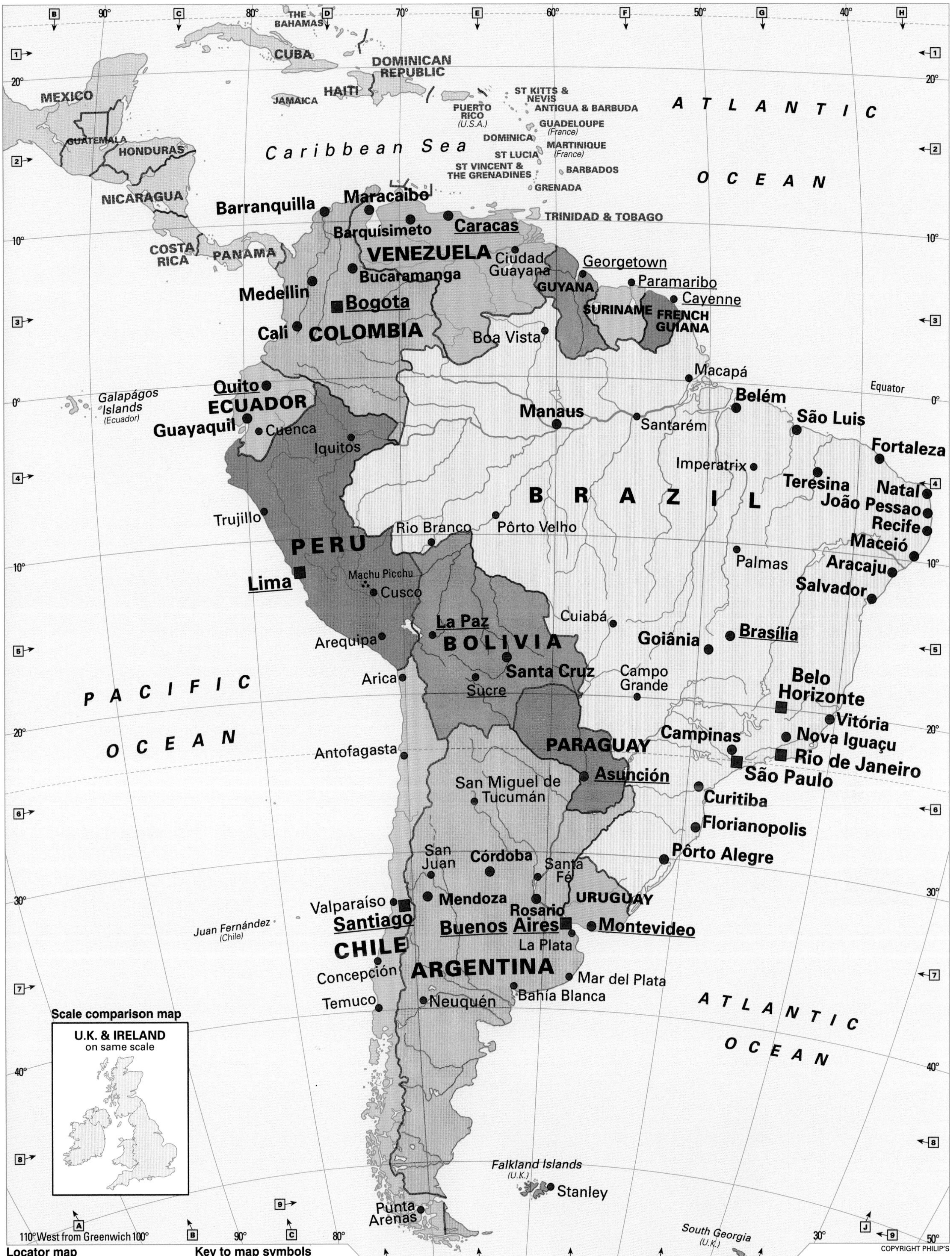

MEXICO

GUATEMALA
HONDURAS
NICARAGUA

COSTA
RICA
PANAMA

THE BAHAMAS
CUBA
JAMAICA
HAITI
DOMINICAN REPUBLIC
PUERTO RICO (U.S.A.)
ST KITTS & NEVIS
ANTIGUA & BARBUDA
GUADELOUPE (France)
DOMINICA
MARTINIQUE (France)
ST LUCIA
ST VINCENT & THE GRENADINES
BARBADOS
GRENADA
TRINIDAD & TOBAGO

Caribbean Sea

A T L A N T I C

O C E A N

Barranquilla
Maracaibo
Barquísimeto
Caracas
VENEZUELA
Ciudad Guayana
Georgetown
Bucaramanga
GUYANA
Paramaribo
Cayenne
Medellín
SURINAME
FRENCH GUIANA
Bogota
COLOMBIA
Boa Vista
Cali

Macapá
Equator
Quito
Belém
São Luis
ECUADOR
Manaus
Guayaquil
Cuenca
Santarém
Fortaleza
Iquitos
B R A Z I L
Teresina
Natal
Imperatrix
João Pessao
Recife
Trujillo
Rio Branco
Pôrto Velho
Maceió
PERU
Palmas
Aracaju
Lima
Salvador
Machu Picchu
Cusco
La Paz
Cuiabá
BOLIVIA
Goiânia
Brasília
Arequipa
Santa Cruz
Campo Grande
Belo Horizonte
Arica
Sucre
Vitória
Antofagasta
PARAGUAY
Campinas
Nova Iguaçu
Rio de Janeiro
São Paulo
San Miguel de Tucumán
Asunción
Curitiba
Florianopolis
San Juan
Córdoba
Pôrto Alegre
Santa Fé
URUGUAY
Valparaíso
Mendoza
Rosario
Santiago
Buenos Aires
Montevideo
CHILE
La Plata
Concepción
ARGENTINA
Mar del Plata
Temuco
Neuquén
Bahía Blanca

P A C I F I C

O C E A N

Galapágos Islands (Ecuador)

Juan Fernández (Chile)

A T L A N T I C

O C E A N

Falkland Islands (U.K.)
Stanley

Punta Arenas

South Georgia (U.K.)

COPYRIGHT PHILIP'S

110° West from Greenwich 100°

Scale comparison map

U.K. & IRELAND
on same scale

Locator map

North America
Atlantic Ocean
Africa
Pacific Ocean
Antarctica

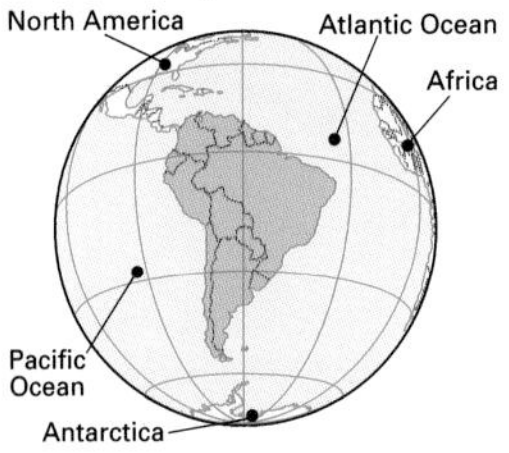

Key to map symbols

■ Over 5,000,000 inhabitants

● 1,000,000 – 5,000,000 inhabitants

• Under 1,000,000 inhabitants

<u>Lima</u> Capital cities underlined

— Country boundaries

Scale 1:35 000 000 1 cm on the map = 350 km on the ground

0   500km   1000km   1500km   2000km   2500km

1   2   3   4   5   6   7
cm   cm

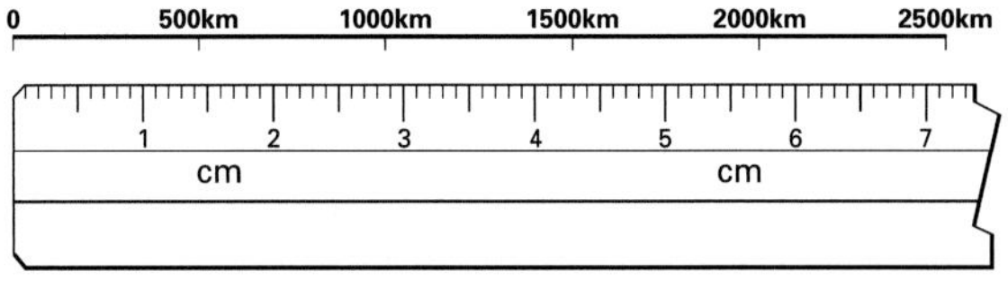

Brazil

ATLANTIC OCEAN
Locator map
VENEZUELA
COLOMBIA
SURINAME
GUYANA
FRENCH GUIANA
PERU
BOLIVIA
PARAGUAY
ARGENTINA
URUGUAY
Guiana Highlands
Pico de Neblina 2994
Boa Vista
RORAIMA
AMAPÁ
Macapá
Equator
Orinoco
Branco
Uaupés
Negro
Japurá
Solimões
Putumayo
Içá
Amazon
Santarém
Manaus
Bragança
Belém
São Luís
Parnaíba
Fortaleza
AMAZONAS
Selvas
Juruá
Purus
Madeira
Tapajós
PARÁ
Marabá
Bacabal
MARANHÃO
Imperatriz
Teresina
Mossoró
CEARÁ
RIO GRANDE DO NORTE
Natal
Juàzeiro do Norte
PARAÍBA
Campina Grande
PERNAMBUCO
PIAUÍ
Sobradinho Reservoir
São Francisco
Juàzeiro
Maceió
ALAGOAS
Aracaju
SERGIPE
ACRE
Rio Branco
Pôrto Velho
Aripuanã
Juruena
Teles Pires
Xingu
Araguaia
Tocantins
BRAZIL
RONDÔNIA
Guaporé
Mamoré
Palmas
TOCANTINS
MATO GROSSO
Feira de Santana
BAHÍA
Salvador
Brazilian Highlands
Vitória da Conquista
Itabuna
Paraguay
Cuiabá
Anápolis
Brasília
Goiânia
GOIÁS
Montes Claros
Teófilo Otoni
MATO GROSSO DO SUL
Uberlândia
MINAS GERAIS
ESPÍRITO SANTO
Belo Horizonte
Pico da Bandeira 2890
Vitória
Campo Grande
Araçatuba
SÃO PAULO
Ribeirão Prêto
Juiz de Fora
Campos
Bauru
Paraná
Londrina
Campinas
Nova Iguaçu
Rio de Janeiro
Tropic of Capricorn
Guarulhos
São Paulo
Santos
PARANÁ
Ponta Grossa
Foz do Iguaçu
Curitiba
Iguaçu
SANTA CATARINA
Joinville
Florianópolis
RIO GRANDE DO SUL
Caxias do Sul
Pôrto Alegre
Uruguaiana
Lagoa dos Patos
Pelotas
West from Greenwich
Scale 1:21 000 000 1 cm on the map = 210 km on the ground
0 210km 420km 630km 840km 1050km 1260km
cm
Height of the land (metres)
over 4000
2000 – 4000
1000 – 2000
400 – 1000
200 – 400
0 – 200
sea level
below sea level
Key to map symbols
Over 5,000,000 inhabitants
1,000,000 – 5,000,000 inhabitants
Under 1,000,000 inhabitants
Brasília Capital cities underlined
Country boundaries
State boundaries

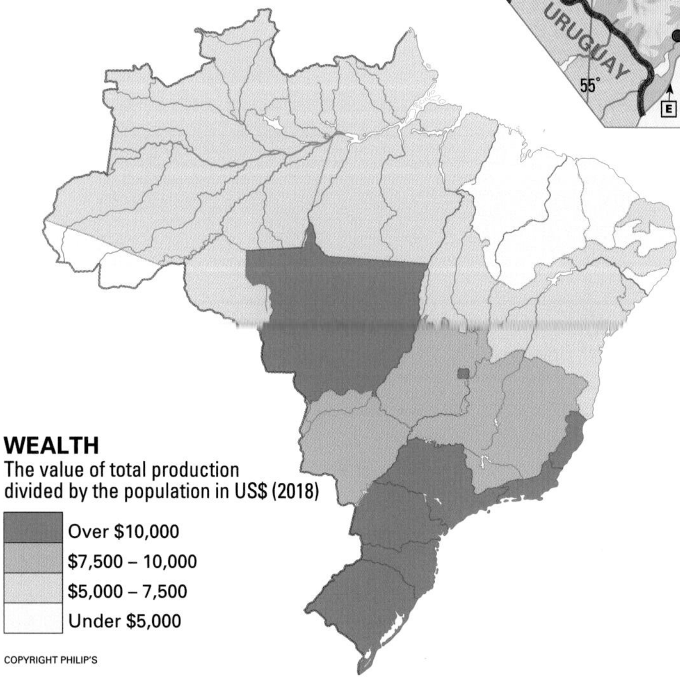
WEALTH
The value of total production divided by the population in US$ (2018)
Over $10,000
$7,500 – 10,000
$5,000 – 7,500
Under $5,000

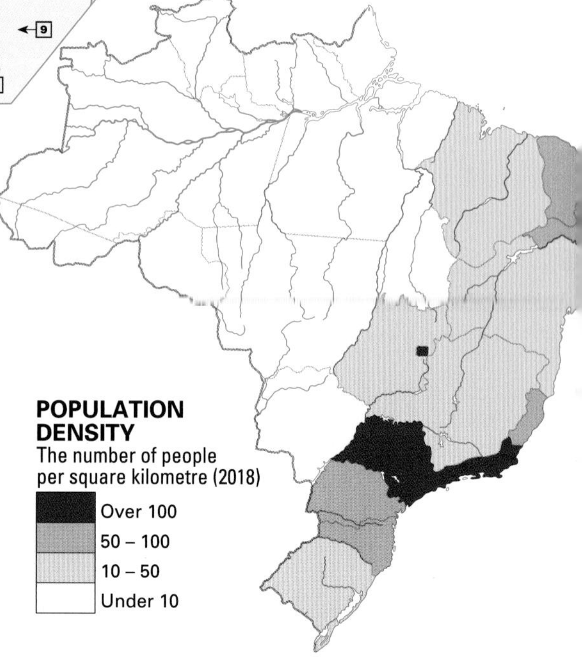
POPULATION DENSITY
The number of people per square kilometre (2018)
Over 100
50 – 100
10 – 50
Under 10

Height of the land (metres)
over 4000
2000-4000
1000-2000
400-1000
200-400
0-200
sea level
below sea level
Yukon
Alaska (U.S.A.)
Cape Barrow
Prudhoe Bay
Beaufort Sea
Wrangel Island (Russia)
East Siberian Sea
New Siberian Islands (Russia)
Nizhne Kolymsk
Tiksi
Lena
Laptev Sea
ARCTIC OCEAN
Mackenzie
Inuvik
Great Bear Lake
NORTH AMERICA
Yellowknife
Great Slave Lake
CANADA
Banks Island (Canada)
Victoria Island (Canada)
Queen Elizabeth Islands (Canada)
Parry Channel
Churchill
Arctic Circle
Hudson Bay
Ellesmere Island (Canada)
Nares Strait
Lincoln Sea
Cape Morris Jessup
North Magnetic Pole 2021
North Pole
Cape Chelyuskin
Taimyr Peninsula
Severnaya Zemlya (Russia)
Siberia
ASIA
RUSSIA
Norilsk
Yenisey
Franz Josef Land (Russia)
Gulf of Ob
Baffin Island (Canada)
Baffin Bay
McKinley Sea
Novaya Zemlya (Russia)
Kara Sea
Surgut
Vorkuta
Ob
Hudson Strait
Iqaluit
80°N
Longyearbyen
Svalbard (Norway)
Barents Sea
Davis Strait
Greenland (Denmark)
Greenland Sea
Bear Island (Norway)
Ural Mountains
Labrador
Nuuk
Mont Forel 3360
3700
Jan Mayen Island (Norway)
70°N
Tromsø
North Cape
Murmansk
NORWAY
FINLAND
White Sea
Arkhangelsk
Northern Dvina
Cape Farewell
Denmark Strait
20° West from Greenwich 0° East from Greenwich 20°
40°
60°
80°
100°
120°
140°
160°
180°

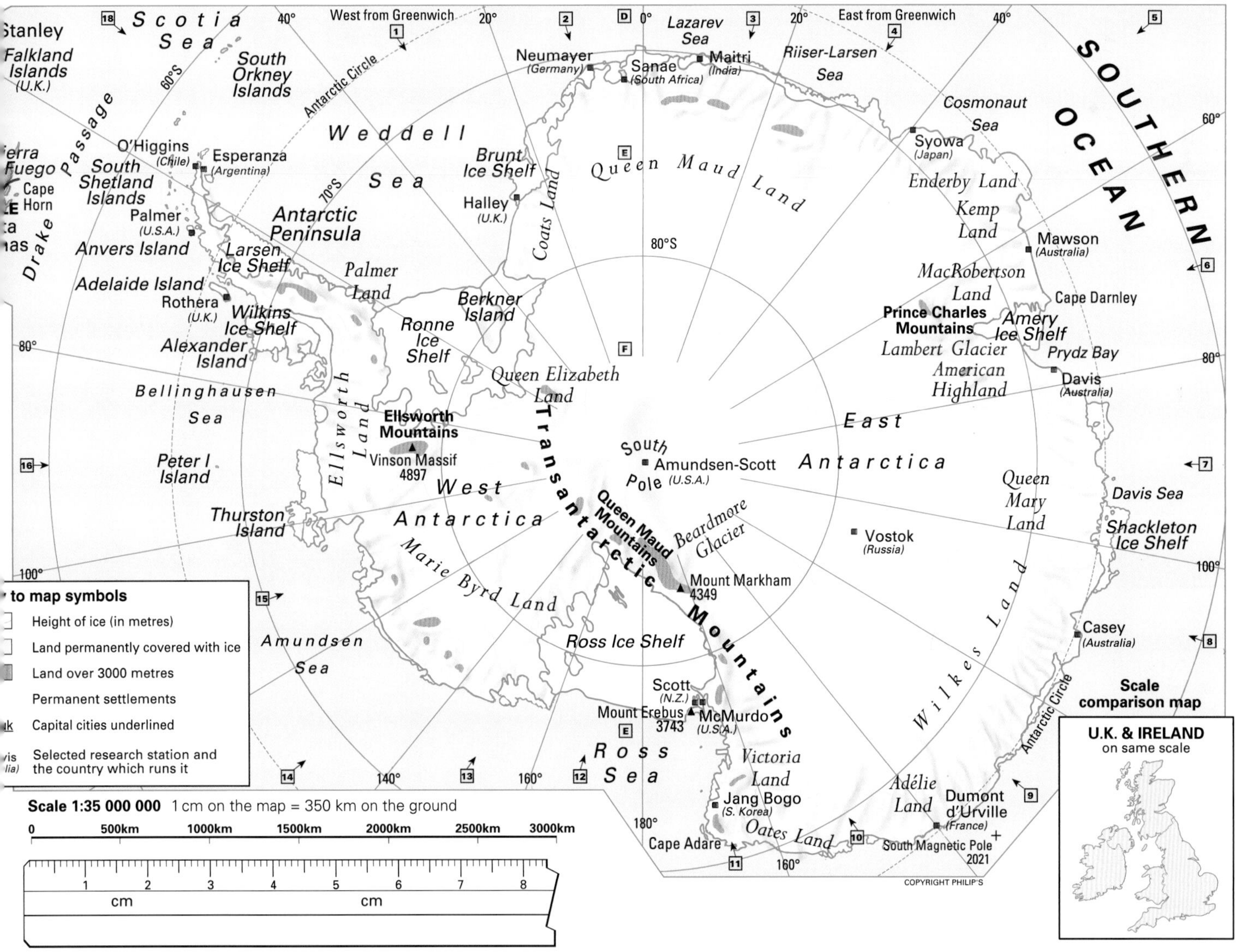
Stanley
Falkland Islands (U.K.)
Scotia Sea
South Orkney Islands
Antarctic Circle
West from Greenwich
Neumayer (Germany)
Sanae (South Africa)
Lazarev Sea
Maitri (India)
Riiser-Larsen Sea
East from Greenwich
SOUTHERN OCEAN
Cosmonaut Sea
Syowa (Japan)
Tierra del Fuego
Cape Horn
Drake Passage
O'Higgins (Chile)
Esperanza (Argentina)
South Shetland Islands
Weddell Sea
Brunt Ice Shelf
Halley (U.K.)
Coats Land
Queen Maud Land
Enderby Land
Kemp Land
Palmer (U.S.A.)
Antarctic Peninsula
Anvers Island
Larsen Ice Shelf
Palmer Land
80°S
Mawson (Australia)
MacRobertson Land
Cape Darnley
Adelaide Island
Rothera (U.K.)
Wilkins Ice Shelf
Berkner Island
Ronne Ice Shelf
Prince Charles Mountains
Amery Ice Shelf
Lambert Glacier
Prydz Bay
Alexander Island
American Highland
Davis (Australia)
Queen Elizabeth Land
Bellinghausen Sea
Ellsworth Land
Ellsworth Mountains
Vinson Massif 4897
Transantarctic Mountains
East Antarctica
South Pole
Amundsen-Scott (U.S.A.)
Peter I Island
West Antarctica
Queen Mary Land
Davis Sea
Shackleton Ice Shelf
Queen Maud Mountains
Beardmore Glacier
Vostok (Russia)
Thurston Island
Marie Byrd Land
Mount Markham 4349
Wilkes Land
Casey (Australia)
Ross Ice Shelf
Amundsen Sea
Scott (N.Z.)
Mount Erebus 3743
McMurdo (U.S.A.)
Ross Sea
Victoria Land
Adélie Land
Dumont d'Urville (France)
Jang Bogo (S. Korea)
Oates Land
South Magnetic Pole 2021
Cape Adare
Key to map symbols
Height of ice (in metres)
Land permanently covered with ice
Land over 3000 metres
Permanent settlements
Capital cities underlined
Selected research station and the country which runs it
Scale 1:35 000 000 1 cm on the map = 350 km on the ground
0 500km 1000km 1500km 2000km 2500km 3000km
cm
COPYRIGHT PHILIP'S
Scale comparison map
U.K. & IRELAND on same scale

CONTINENT	AREA '000 kilometres	COLDEST PLACE degrees Celsius		HOTTEST PLACE degrees Celsius		WETTEST PLACE average annual rainfall, mm		DRIEST PLACE average annual rainfall,
Asia	44,500	Oymyakon, Russia –70°C	1	Tirat Zevi, Israel 54°C	8	Mawsynram, India 11,870	15	Aden, Yemen 46
Africa	30,302	Ifrane, Morocco –24°C	2	Kebili, Tunisia 55°C	9	Debundscha, Cameroon 10,290	16	Wadi Haifa, Sudan 2
North America	24,241	Snag, Yukon –63°C	3	Death Valley, California 57°C	10	Henderson Lake, Canada 6,500	17	Bataques, Mexico 30
South America	17,793	Sarmiento, Argentina –33°C	4	Rivadavia, Argentina 49°C	11	Quibdó, Colombia 8,990	18	Quillagua, Chile 0.6
Antarctica	14,000	Vostok –89°C	5	Vanda Station 15°C	12			
Europe	9,957	Ust Shchugor, Russia –55°C	6	Seville, Spain 50°C	13	Crkvice, Montenegro 4,650	19	Astrakhan, Russia 160
Oceania	8,557	Charlotte Pass, Australia –22°C	7	Oodnadatta, Australia 51°C	14	Tully, Australia 4,550	20	Mulka, Australia 100

ARGEST SEAS 0 square kilometres	LARGEST LAKES '000 square kilometres	LONGEST RIVERS kilometres	LARGEST ISLANDS '000 square kilometres	HIGHEST PEAKS metres	DEEPEST TRENCHES metres
c Ocean 155,557 (27)	Caspian Sea 371 (37)	Nile 6,695 (47)	Greenland 2,176 (57)	Himalayas: Mount Everest 8,849 (67)	Mariana Trench 11,022 (77)
tic Ocean 76,762 (28)	Lake Superior 82 (38)	Amazon 6,450 (48)	New Guinea 821 (58)	Karakoram: K2 8,611 (68)	Tonga Trench 10,822 (78)
n Ocean 68,556 (29)	Lake Victoria 68 (39)	Yangtse 6,380 (49)	Borneo 744 (59)	Pamirs: Ismail Samani Peak 7,495 (69)	Japan Trench 10,554 (79)
ern Ocean 20,237 (30)	Lake Huron 60 (40)	Mississippi-Missouri 5,971 (50)	Madagascar 587 (60)	Tian Shan: Pobedy Peak 7,439 (70)	Kuril Trench 10,542 (80)
Ocean 14,351 (31)	Lake Michigan 58 (41)	Yenisey-Angara 5,550 (51)	Baffin Island 508 (61)	Andes: Aconcagua 6,962 (71)	Mindanao Trench 10,497 (81)
rranean Sea 2,966 (32)	Lake Tanganyika 33 (42)	Hwang-Ho 5,464 (52)	Sumatra 474 (62)	Rocky Mountains: Denali 6,190 (72)	Kermadec Trench 10,047 (82)
China Sea 2,318 (33)	Great Bear Lake 32 (43)	Ob-Irtysh 5,410 (53)	Honshu 231 (63)	East Africa: Kilimanjaro 5,895 (73)	Bougainville Trench 9,140 (83)
g Sea 2,274 (34)	Lake Baikal 31 (44)	Congo 4,670 (54)	Great Britain 230 (64)	Caucasus: Elbrus 5,642 (74)	Milwaukee Deep 8,605 (84)
bean Sea 1,942 (35)	Lake Malawi 30 (45)	Mekong 4,500 (55)	Victoria Island 212 (65)	Antarctica: Vinson Massif 4,897 (75)	South Sandwich Trench 7,235 (85)
of Mexico 1,813 (36)	Great Slave Lake 29 (46)	Amur 4,442 (56)	Ellesmere Island 197 (66)	Alps: Mont Blanc 4,808 (76)	Aleutian Trench 7,822 (86)

ALB. = ALBANIA
B.-H. = BOSNIA-HERZEGOVINA
BELG. = BELGIUM
CR. = CROATIA
CZECH. = CZECHIA
EST. = ESTONIA
HUNG. = HUNGARY
K. = KOSOVO
LAT. = LATVIA
LEB. = LEBANON
LITH. = LITHUANIA
LUX. = LUXEMBOURG

COUNTRY	'000 people	COUNTRY	'000 people	COUNTRY	'000 people	COUNTRY	'000 people	COUNTRY	'000 pe
China	1,397,898	Japan	124,687	France	68,084	Sudan	46,751	Saudi Arabia	31,
India	1,339,331	Ethiopia	110,871	United Kingdom	66,052	Argentina	45,865	Angola	33,
USA	334,998	Philippines	110,818	Italy	62,390	Uganda	44,712	Malaysia	33,
Indonesia	275,122	Egypt	106,437	Tanzania	62,093	Ukraine	43,746	Ghana	32,
Pakistan	238,181	Congo (Dem. Rep.)	105,045	Myanmar	57,069	Algeria	43,577	Peru	32,
Nigeria	219,464	Vietnam	102,790	South Africa	56,979	Iraq	39,650	Mozambique	30,
Brazil	213,445	Iran	85,889	Kenya	54,685	Poland	38,186	Uzbekistan	30,
Bangladesh	164,099	Turkey	82,482	South Korea	51,715	Canada	37,943	Nepal	30,
Russia	142,321	Germany	79,903	Colombia	50,356	Afghanistan	37,466	Yemen	30,
Mexico	130,207	Thailand	69,481	Spain	47,261	Morocco	36,562	Venezuela	29,

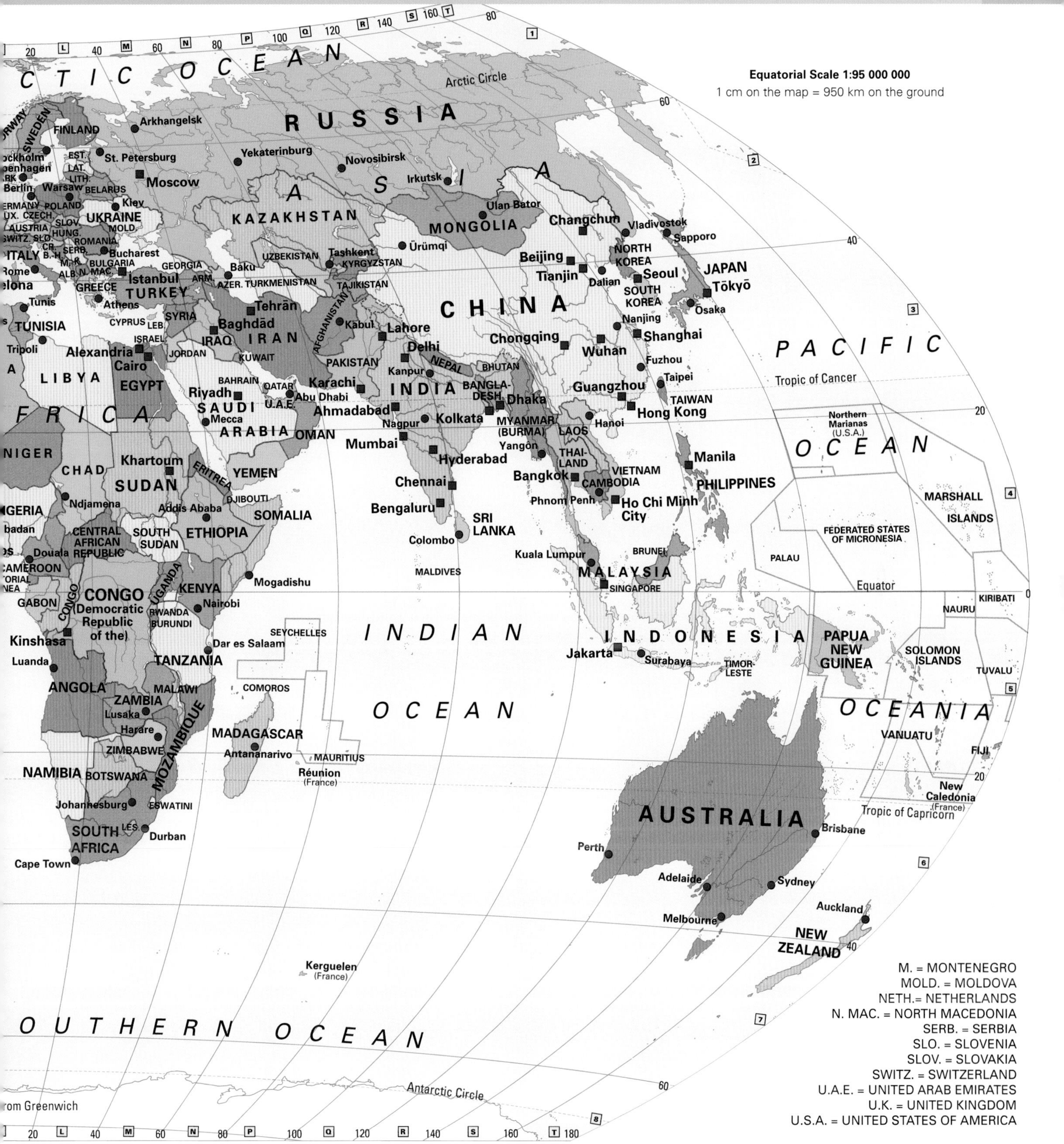

Equatorial Scale 1:95 000 000
1 cm on the map = 950 km on the ground

M. = MONTENEGRO
MOLD. = MOLDOVA
NETH. = NETHERLANDS
N. MAC. = NORTH MACEDONIA
SERB. = SERBIA
SLO. = SLOVENIA
SLOV. = SLOVAKIA
SWITZ. = SWITZERLAND
U.A.E. = UNITED ARAB EMIRATES
U.K. = UNITED KINGDOM
U.S.A. = UNITED STATES OF AMERICA

COUNTRY	'000 people	COUNTRY	'000 people	COUNTRY	'000 people	COUNTRY	'000 people	COUNTRY	'000 people
meroon	28,524	Syria	20,384	Ecuador	17,093	Bolivia	11,759	Sweden	10,262
e d'Ivoire	28,088	Malawi	20,309	Senegal	16,082	Haiti	11,198	United Arab Emirates	9,857
dagascar	27,534	Mali	20,138	Zimbabwe	14,830	Cuba	11,032	Hungary	9,728
rth Korea	25,831	Kazakhstan	19,246	Benin	13,302	South Sudan	10,984	Belarus	9,442
stralia	25,810	Zambia	19,078	Rwanda	12,943	Jordan	10,910	Honduras	9,346
er	23,606	Chile	18,308	Guinea	12,878	Czechia	10,703	Tajikistan	8,991
wan	23,572	Guatemala	17,423	Burundi	12,241	Dominican Republic	10,597	Austria	8,885
Lanka	23,044	Chad	17,414	Somalia	12,095	Greece	10,570	Israel	8,787
kina Faso	21,383	Netherlands	17,337	Tunisia	11,811	Azerbaijan	10,282	Switzerland	8,454
mania	21,230	Cambodia	17,304	Belgium	11,779	Portugal	10,264	Togo	8,283

CLIMATE REGIONS

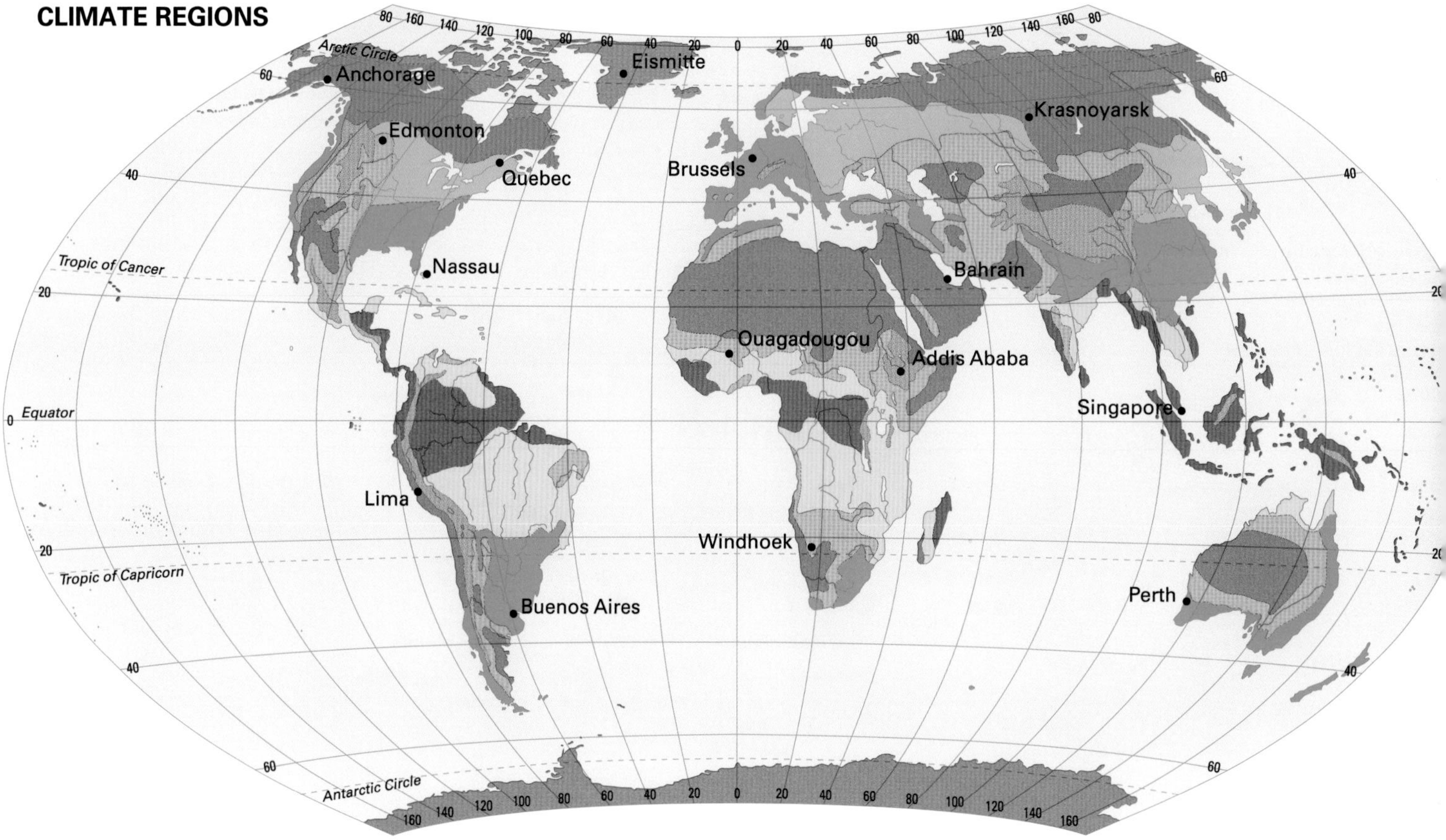

The map shows how the world can be divided into 9 broad climate types

Humid tropical climate (hot with rain all year)	Savanna climate (hot with dry season)	Mild climate (warm and wet)
Hot desert climate (hot and very dry)	Steppe climate (warm and dry)	Continental climate (wet with cold winter)
Subarctic climate (very cold winter)	Mountainous climate (altitude affects climate)	
Polar climate (very cold and dry)		

These colours are also used to show the climate type of each city shown in the graphs below

CLIMATE GRAPHS

The graphs below give examples of places within each climate region, showing how temperature and rainfall vary from month to month.

Colour of climate type on map
Name of place
Average monthly temperature
Average annual rainfall
Average monthly rainfall
Months of the year

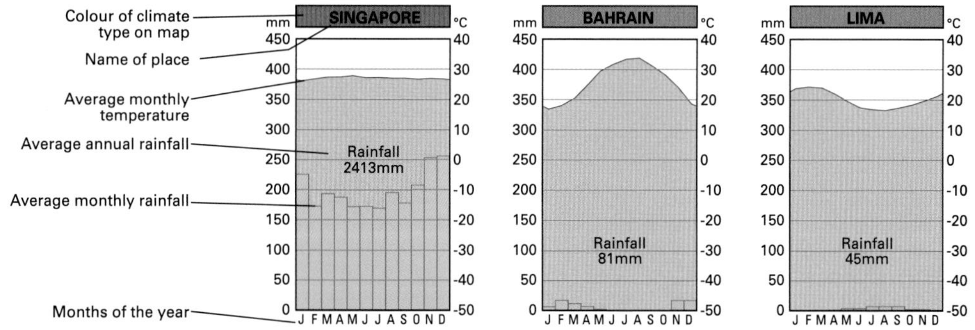

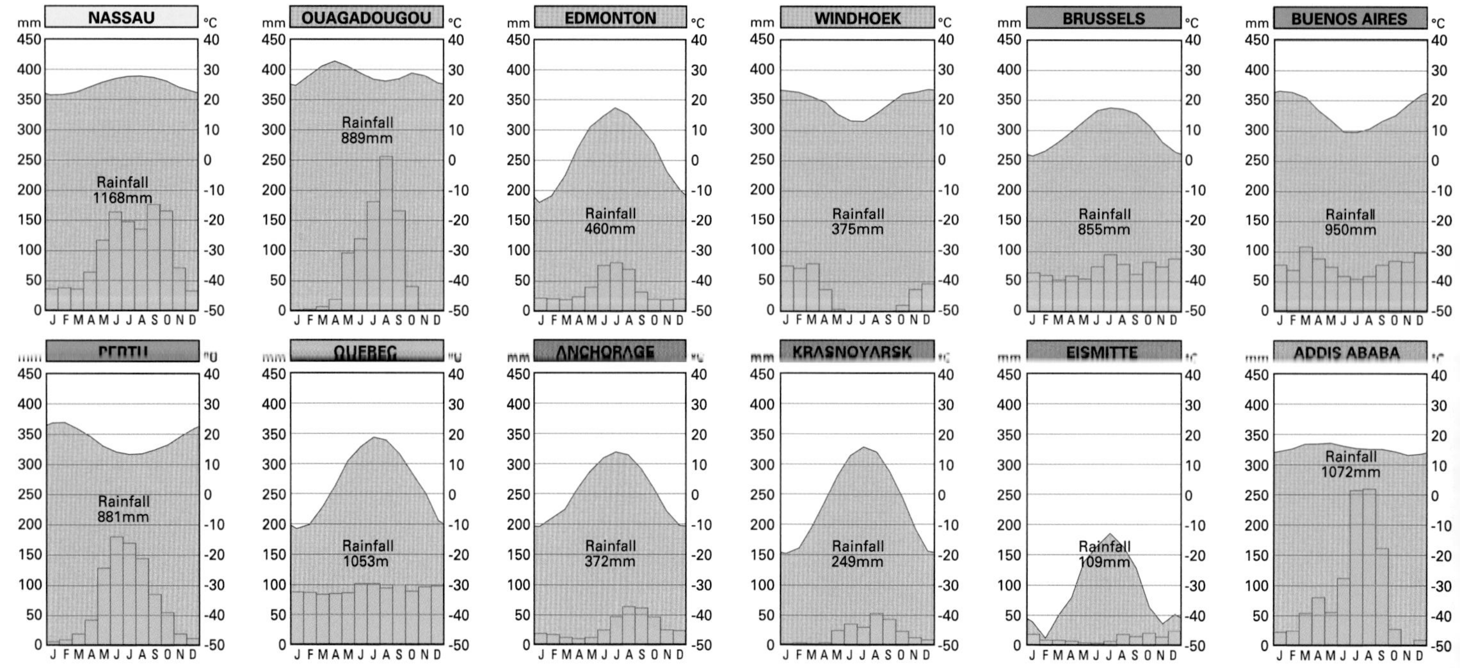

HUMID TROPICAL CLIMATE

HOT DESERT CLIMATE

SAVANNA CLIMATE

MILD CLIMATE

POLAR CLIMATE

MOUNTAINOUS CLIMATE

ANNUAL RAINFALL

Average annual rainfall

- 3000 mm
- 2000 mm
- 1000 mm
- 500 mm
- 250 mm

Mawsynram, India
Over 11,800 mm
has fallen in a year
Wettest place
on Earth

Atacama Desert
Driest place on Earth
No rain has ever
been recorded

Tropic of Cancer

Equator

Tropic of Capricorn

JANUARY TEMPERATURE

BLIZZARDS November-March

Northern
Hemisphere –
WINTER

Average
temperature
in January

- 30°C
- 20°C
- 10°C
- 0°C
- -10°C
- -20°C
- -30°C
- -40°C

Paths of
winter
blizzards

Southern
Hemisphere –
SUMMER

Tropic of Cancer

Equator

Tropic of Capricorn

JULY TEMPERATURE

Hottest place
on Earth:
Death Valley
57°C

Northern
Hemisphere –
SUMMER

*HURRICANES
August-October*

*TYPHOONS
July-October*

*CYCLONES
June-November*

*WILLY
WILLIES
January-March*

Average
temperature
in July

- 30°C
- 20°C
- 10°C
- 0°C
- -10°C

Paths of
tropical
storms

Vostok in
Antarctica
Coldest place
on Earth -89°C

Southern
Hemisphere –
WINTER

Tropic of Cancer

Equator

Tropic of Capricorn

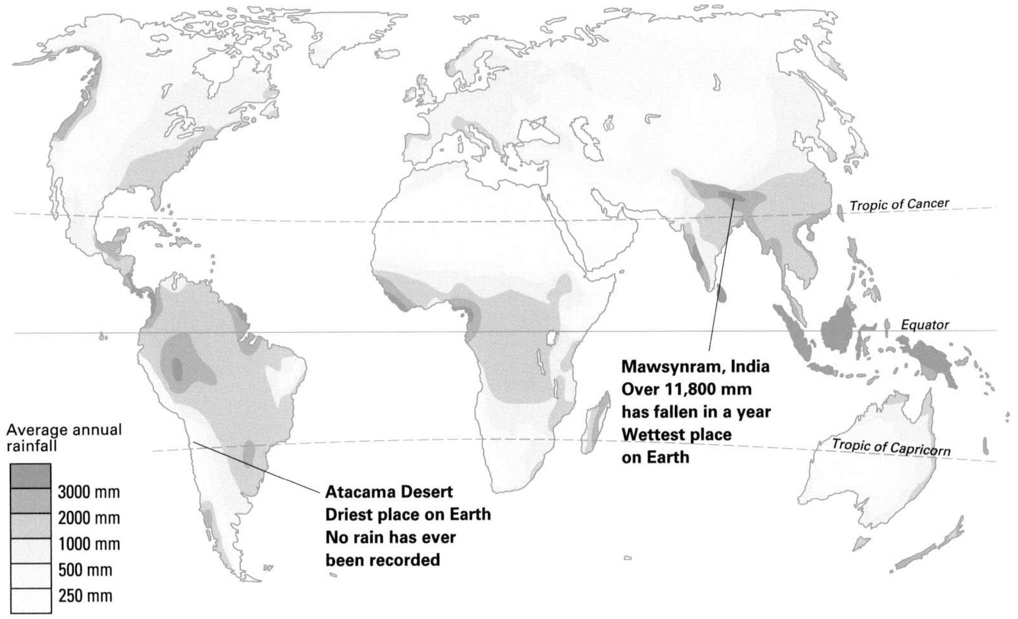

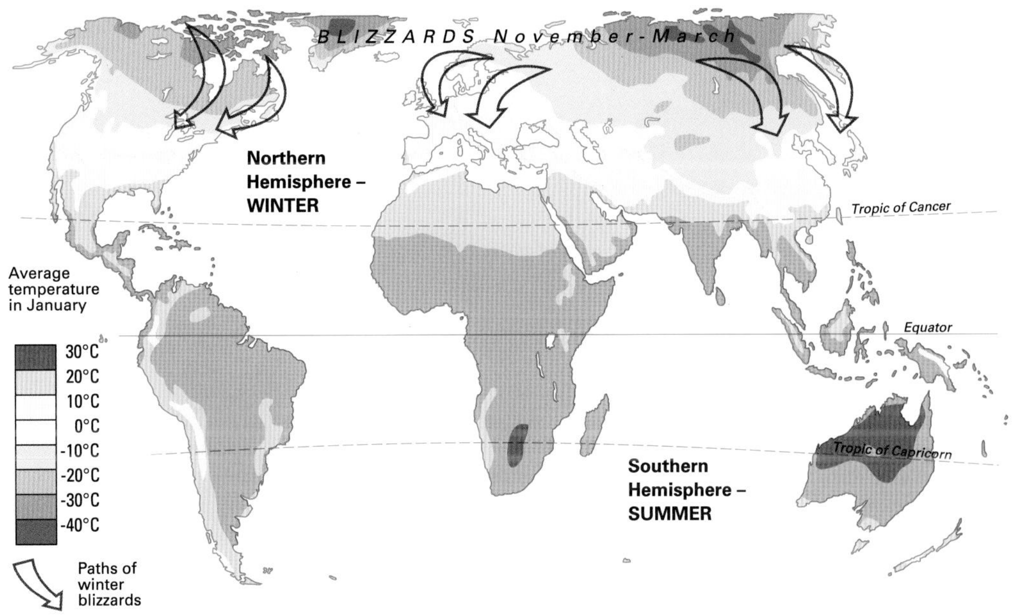

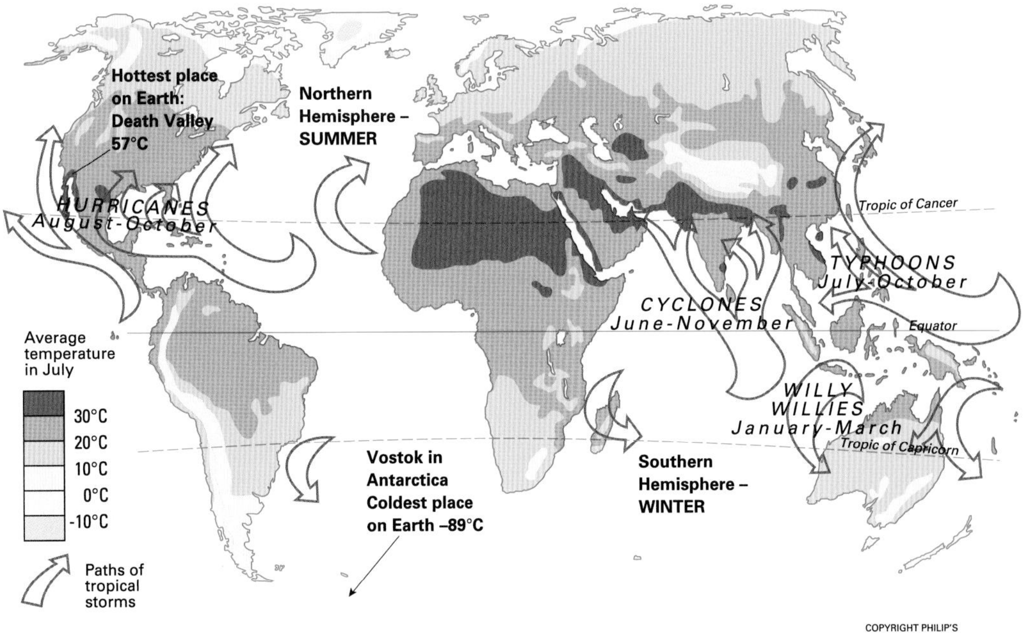

This graph shows the estimated percentage share of total world CO_2 emissions (2018).

World total CO_2 emissions in 2018 were 36,302 million tonnes.

CARBON DIOXIDE EMISSIONS

Carbon dioxide emissions in tonnes per person (2018)

■ Over 15 tonnes	1 – 5 tonnes
10 – 15 tonnes	Under 1 tonne
5 – 10 tonnes	No data

THE GREENHOUSE EFFECT

Carbon dioxide is increased by burning fossil fuels and cutting forests

Carbon Dioxide

The carbon dioxide traps the heat being reflected from the Earth, although some heat is lost.

The warming increases water vapour in the air, leading to even greater absorption of heat.

Rising temperatures would melt snow and ice.

Melting glacial ice could cause oceans to rise.

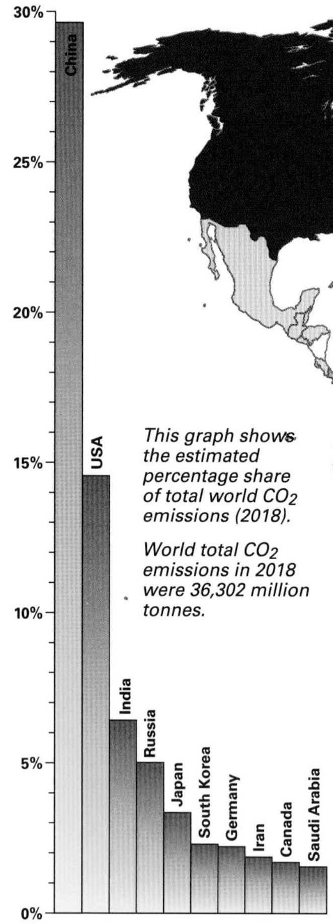

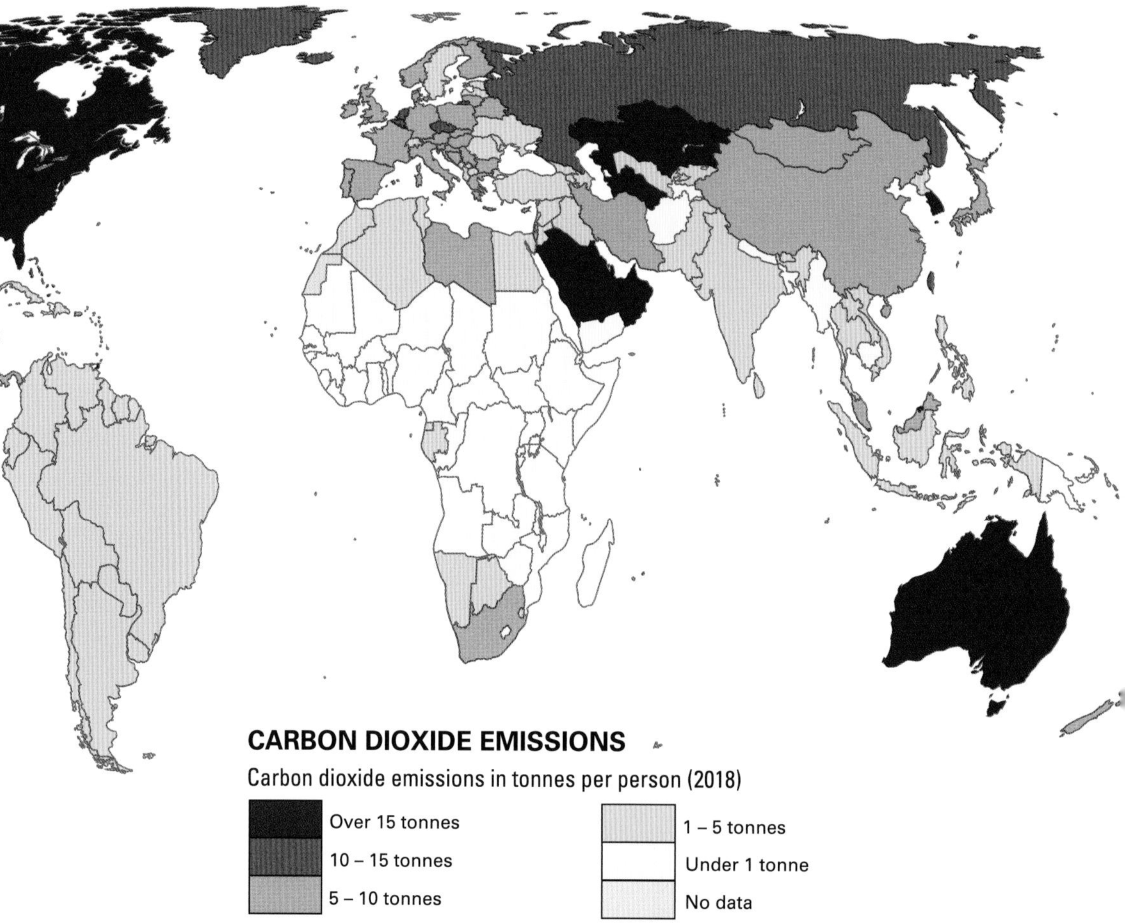

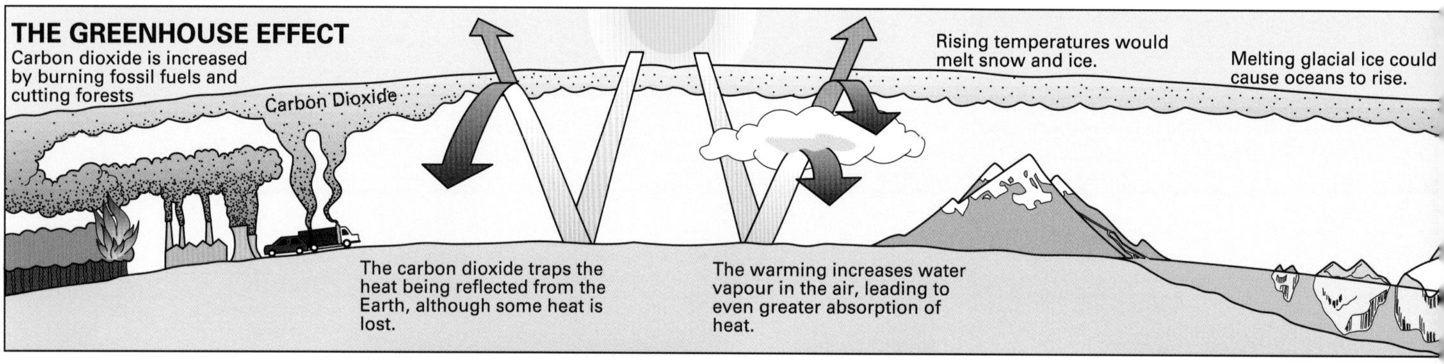

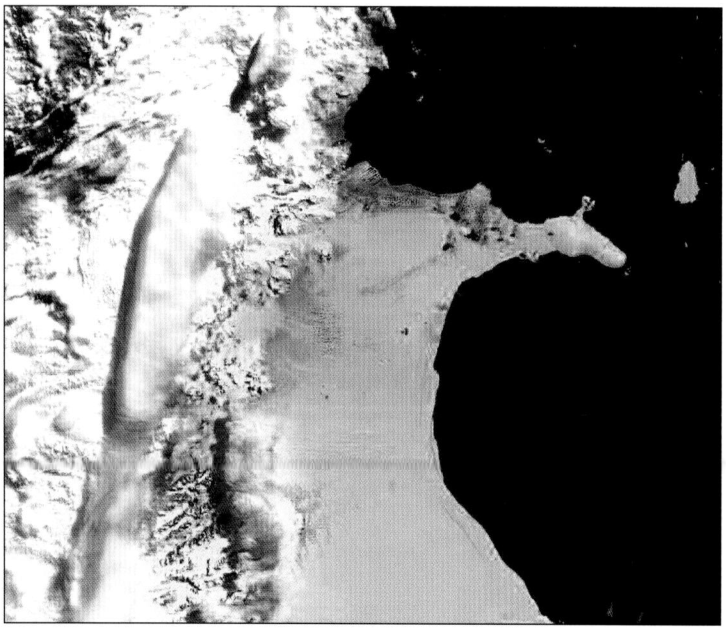

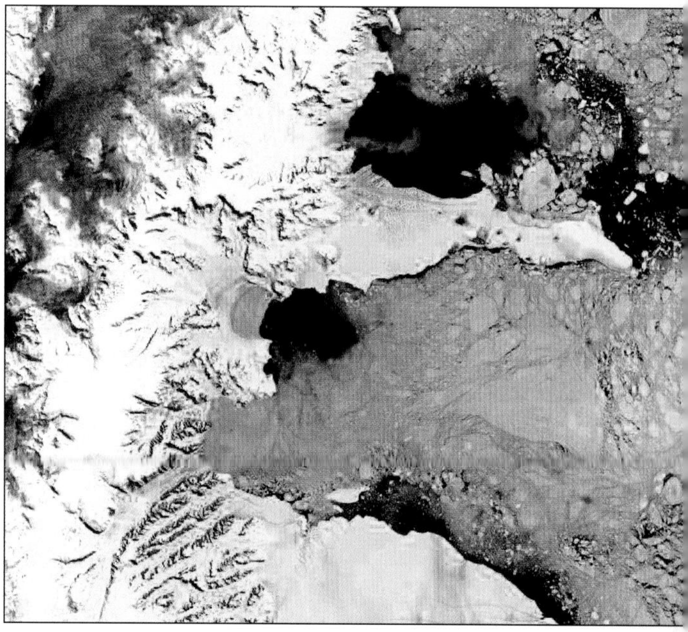

▲ **Larsen B ice shelf, Antarctica.** Between January and March 2002, Larsen B ice shelf on the Antarctic Peninsula collapsed. The image on the left shows its area before the collapse, while the image on the right shows the area after the collapse. The 200 m thick ice sheet had been retreating before this date, but over 500 billion tonnes of ice collapsed in under a month. This was due to rising temperatures of 0.5°C per year in this part of Antarctica. Satellite images like these the only way for scientists to monitor inaccessible areas of the wo

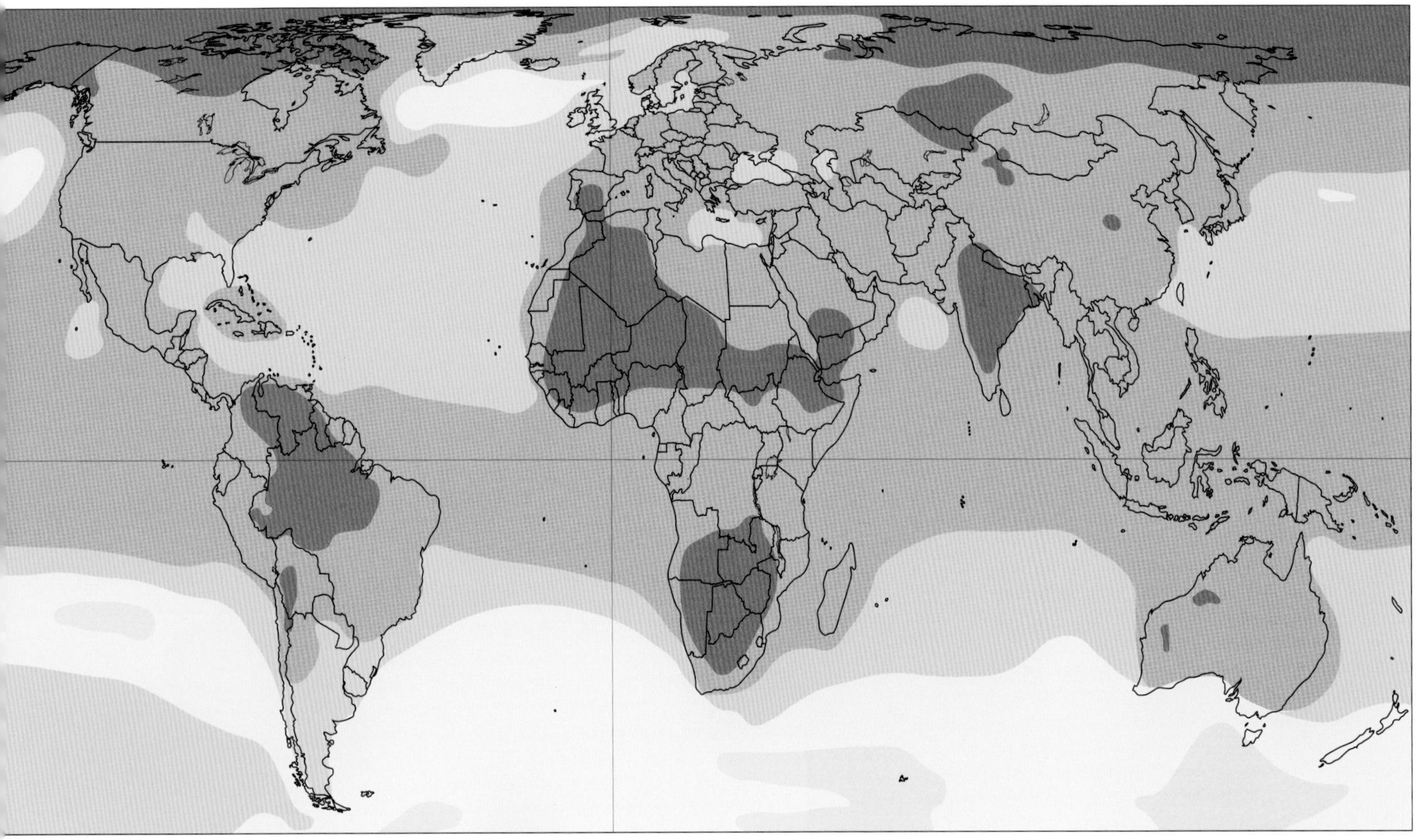

DICTED CHANGE IN TEMPERATURE

difference between actual annual
age surface air temperature, 1969–1990,
redicted annual average surface
mperature, 2070–2100

5 – 10°C warmer	
3 – 5°C warmer	
2 – 3°C warmer	

1 – 2°C warmer	
0 – 1°C warmer	

These maps shows the predicted
increase assuming a 'medium growth'
of the global economy and assuming
that no measures to combat the
emission of greenhouse gases
are taken.

It should be noted that these predicted
annual average changes mask quite
significant seasonal detail.

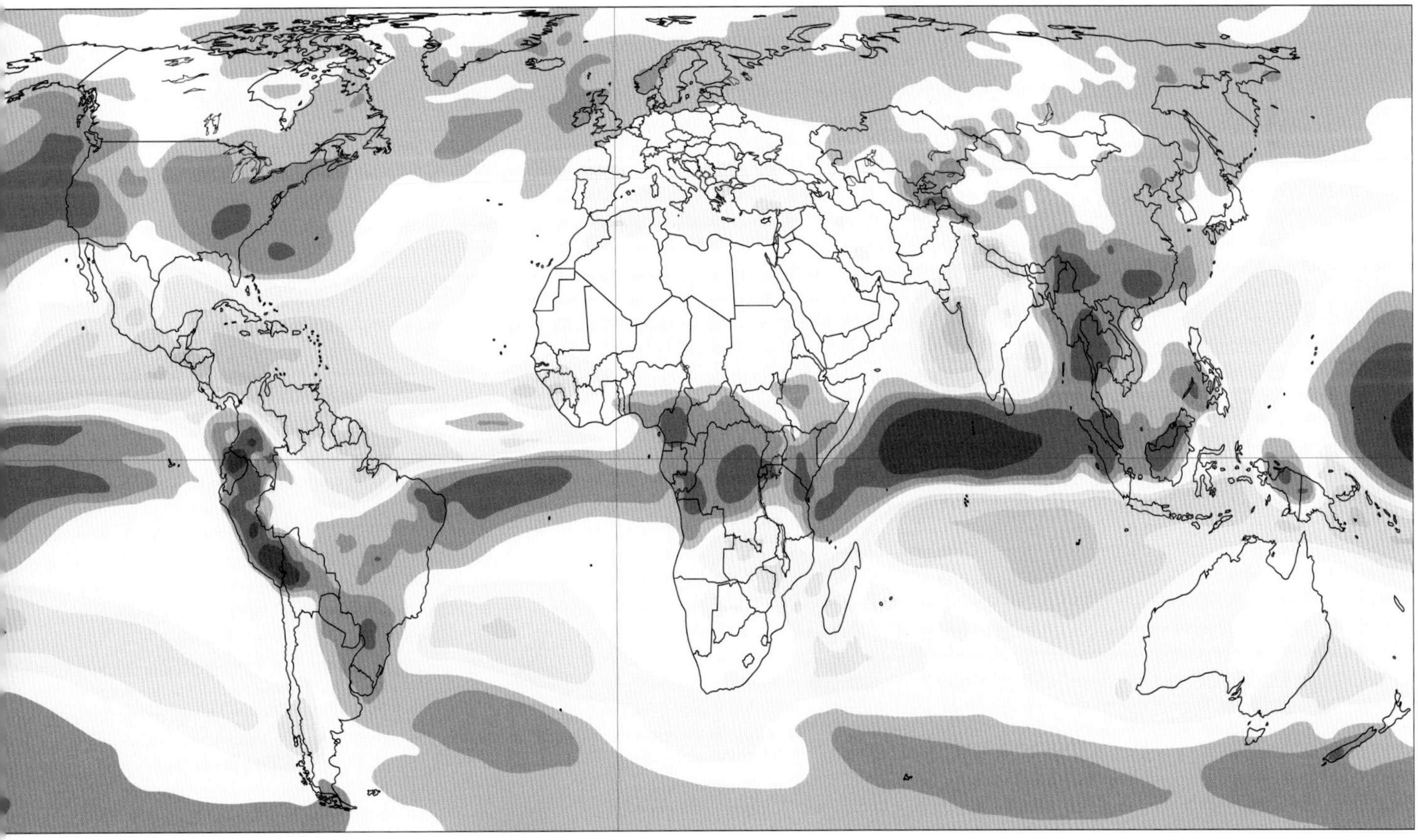

EDICTED CHANGE IN RAINFALL

difference between actual annual average
fall, 1969–1990, and predicted annual
age rainfall, 2070–2100

ce: The Hadley Centre of Climate Prediction
esearch, Met Office

Over 2 mm more rain per day	
1 – 2 mm more rain per day	
Over 2 mm more rain per day	

0.2 – 0.5 mm more rain per day	
No change	
0.2 – 0.5 mm less rain per day	

0.5 – 1 mm less rain per day	
1 – 2 mm less rain per day	
Over 2 mm less rain per day	

TUNDRA AND MOUNTAIN VEGETATION

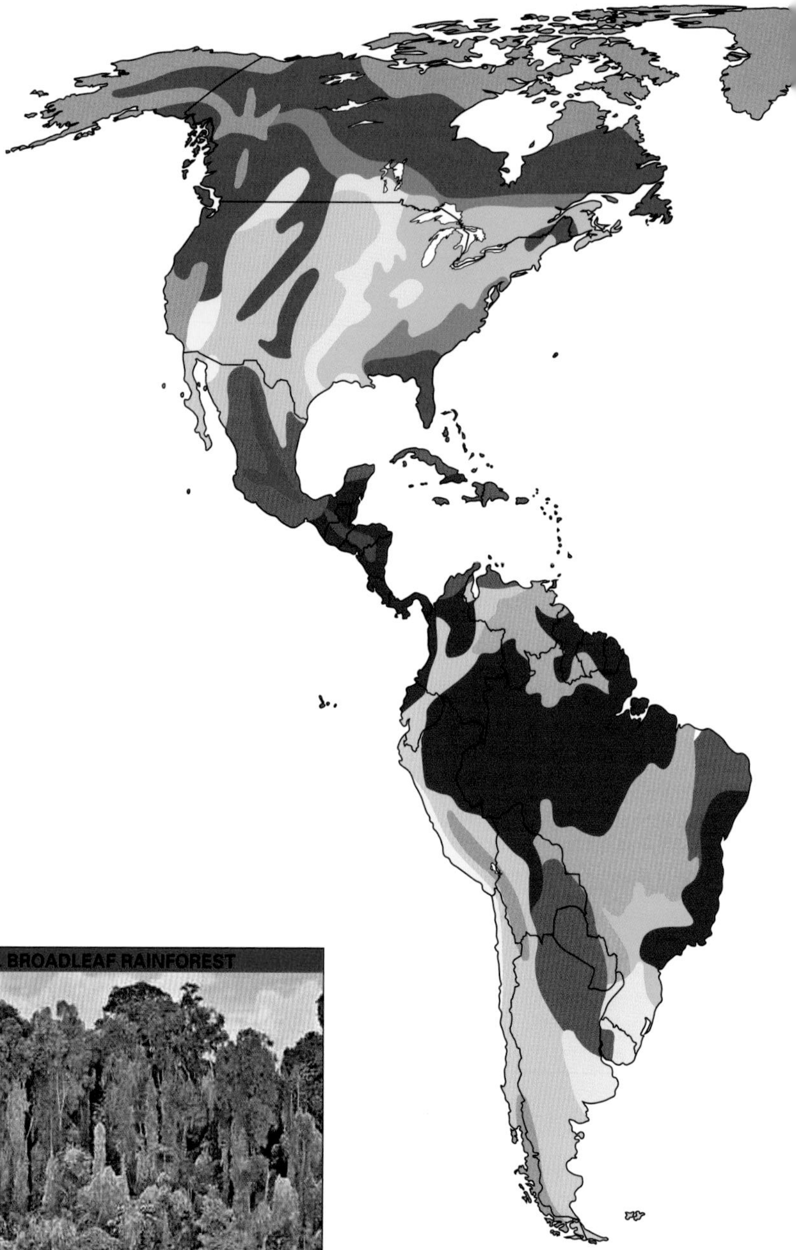

NEEDLELEAF EVERGREEN FOREST

MID-LATITUDE GRASSLAND

TROPICAL BROADLEAF RAINFOREST

DESERT

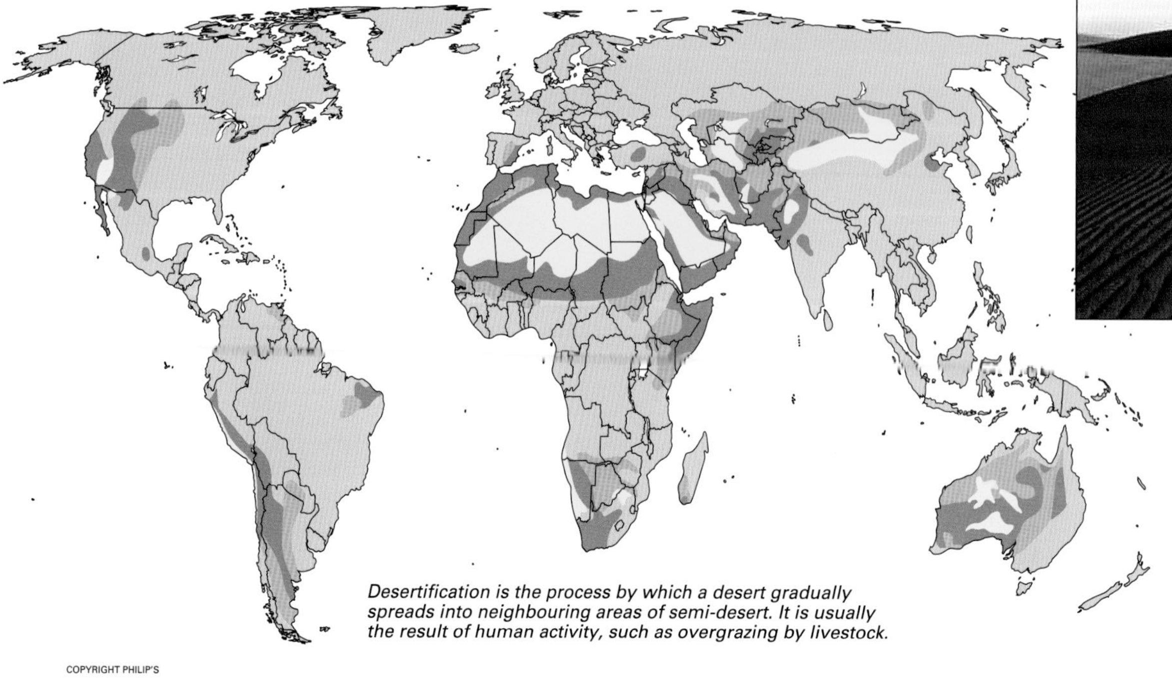

Desertification is the process by which a desert gradually spreads into neighbouring areas of semi-desert. It is usually the result of human activity, such as overgrazing by livestock.

DESERTIFICATION

- Existing desert
- Areas with a high risk of desertification
- Areas with a moderate risk of desertification

NATURAL VEGETATION

The map shows the type of vegetation that would grow if people were not there. People have cleared forests and natural grasslands for thousands of years. Most of the broadleaf deciduous woodland that would naturally cover Britain and Ireland has been cleared for farming and for building. In more recent years, much of the tropical broadleaf rainforest and monsoon forests have been felled.

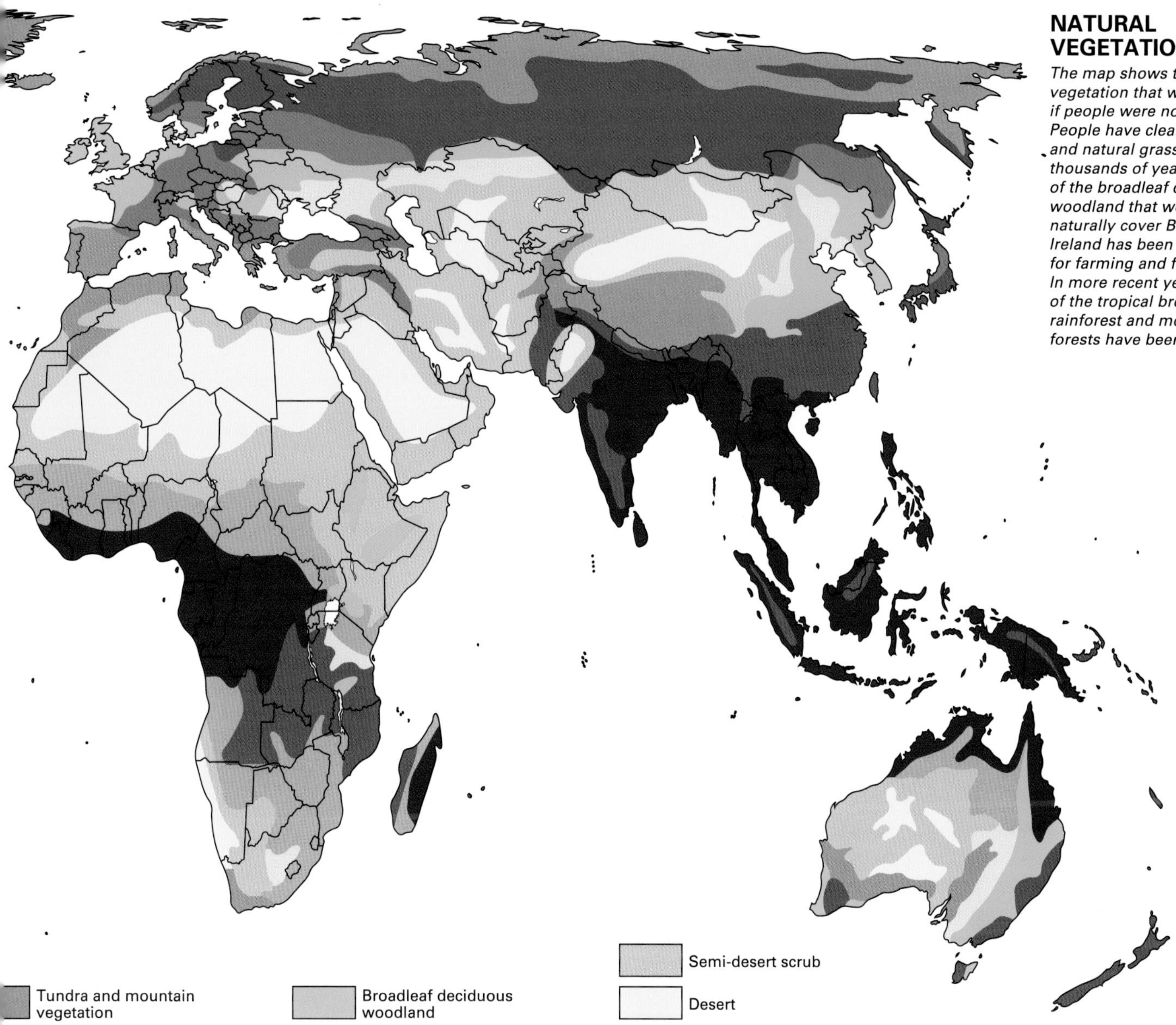

- Tundra and mountain vegetation
- Needleleaf evergreen forest
- Mixed forest of needleleaf evergreen and broadleaf deciduous trees
- Broadleaf deciduous woodland
- Mid-latitude grassland
- Evergreen broadleaf and deciduous trees, shrubs and herbs
- Semi-desert scrub
- Desert
- Tropical grassland (savanna)
- Tropical broadleaf rainforest and needleleaf forest
- Sub-tropical broadleaf and needleleaf forest

ORESTATION

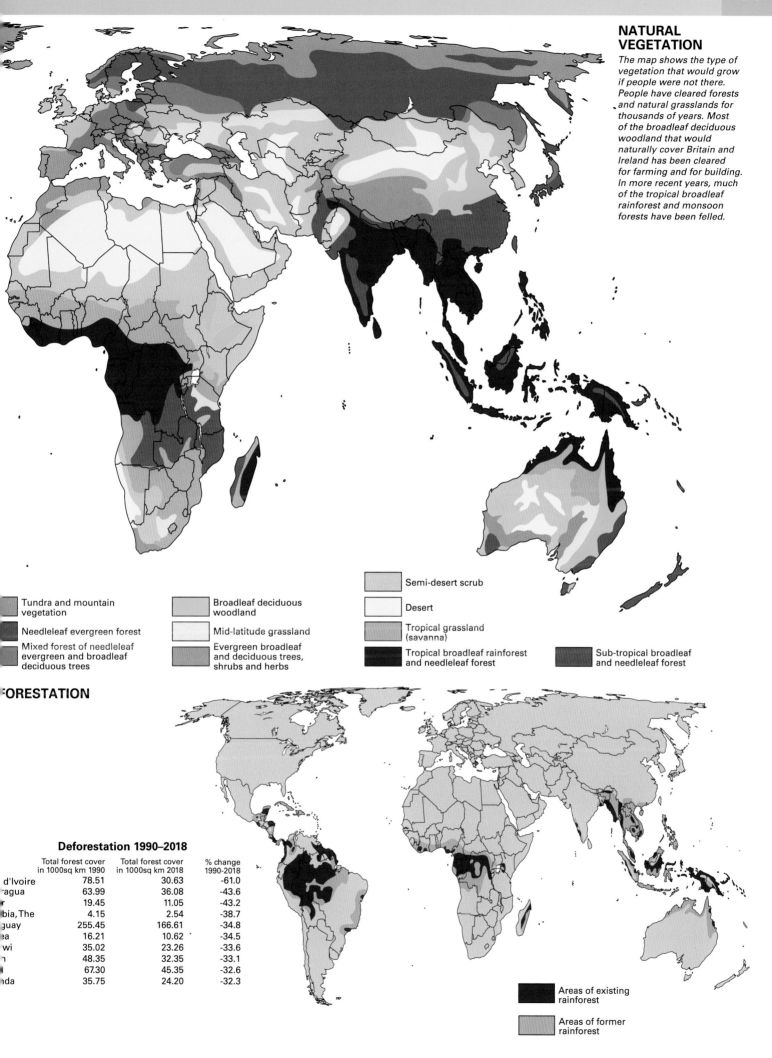

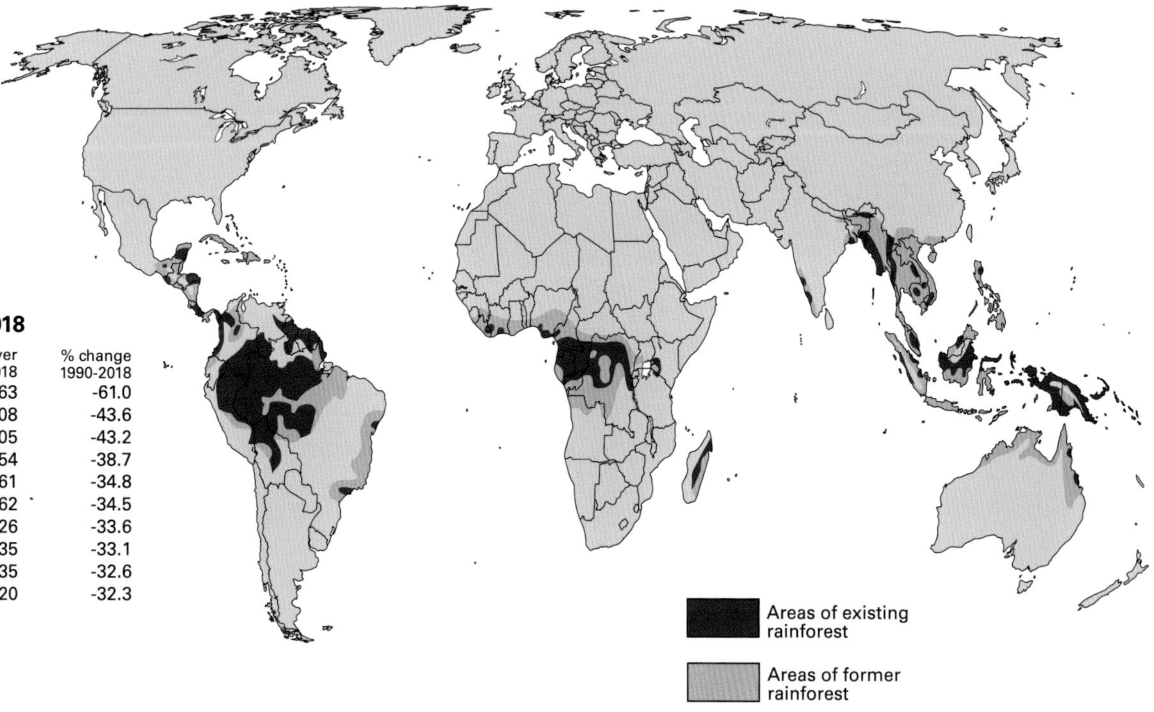

- Areas of existing rainforest
- Areas of former rainforest

Deforestation 1990–2018

	Total forest cover in 1000sq km 1990	Total forest cover in 1000sq km 2018	% change 1990-2018
d'Ivoire	78.51	30.63	-61.0
agua	63.99	36.08	-43.6
r	19.45	11.05	-43.2
bia, The	4.15	2.54	-38.7
guay	255.45	166.61	-34.8
ea	16.21	10.62	-34.5
wi	35.02	23.26	-33.6
n	48.35	32.35	-33.1
	67.30	45.35	-32.6
nda	35.75	24.20	-32.3

CONTINENTAL DRIFT

180 MILLION YEARS AGO JURASSIC

Laurasia

Gondwanaland

65 MILLION YEARS AGO CRETACEOUS

PRESENT DAY

Ocean trench	New ocean floor
Rift	Zones of slippage

(after Dietz and Holden, Scientific American 1970)

m In 1995, after almost 400 years lying dormant, the Soufrière Hills volcano on the Caribbean island of Montserrat began a series of eruptions. Further eruptio in 1996 and 1997 left the south of the island uninhabita and 5,000 people had to be evacuated to the northern zone. Steam can be seen rising from the volcano in the false colour satellite image, above.

SOUFRIÈRE HILLS VOLCANO, MONTSERRAT

403

NORTHERN ZONE (low risk of ash flow)

Brades (current capital)

St. John's

St. Peter's

CENTRAL ZONE (controlled access)

739

Salem

Bethel

Soufrière Hills 914

Plymouth (former capital)

754

EXCLUSION ZONE (enforced evacuation)

→ Pyroclastic (ash) flow

Areas at mo risk from effects of eruption

····· Risk zone boundaries in Septembe 1997

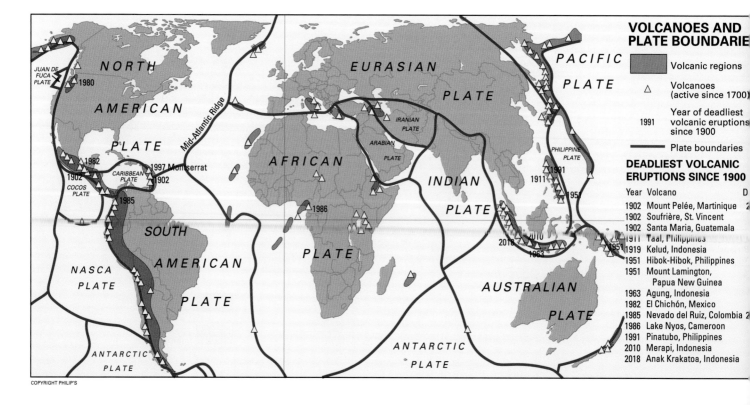

JUAN DE FUCA PLATE

NORTH AMERICAN PLATE

1980

Mid-Atlantic Ridge

EURASIAN PLATE

PACIFIC PLATE

IRANIAN PLATE

ARABIAN PLATE

PHILIPPINE PLATE

1991

1911

1951

1982

1997 Montserrat

1902

CARIBBEAN PLATE

1902

COCOS PLATE

AFRICAN PLATE

INDIAN PLATE

1985

1986

2018

2010

1963

1951

SOUTH AMERICAN PLATE

NASCA PLATE

AUSTRALIAN PLATE

ANTARCTIC PLATE

ANTARCTIC PLATE

VOLCANOES AND PLATE BOUNDARIE

Volcanic regions

△ Volcanoes (active since 1700)

1991 Year of deadliest volcanic eruptions since 1900

— Plate boundaries

DEADLIEST VOLCANIC ERUPTIONS SINCE 1900

Year	Volcano	D
1902	Mount Pelée, Martinique	2
1902	Soufrière, St. Vincent	
1902	Santa Maria, Guatemala	
1911	Taal, Philippines	
1919	Kelud, Indonesia	
1951	Hibok-Hibok, Philippines	
1951	Mount Lamington, Papua New Guinea	
1963	Agung, Indonesia	
1982	El Chichón, Mexico	
1985	Nevado del Ruiz, Colombia	2
1986	Lake Nyos, Cameroon	2
1991	Pinatubo, Philippines	
2010	Merapi, Indonesia	
2018	Anak Krakatoa, Indonesia	

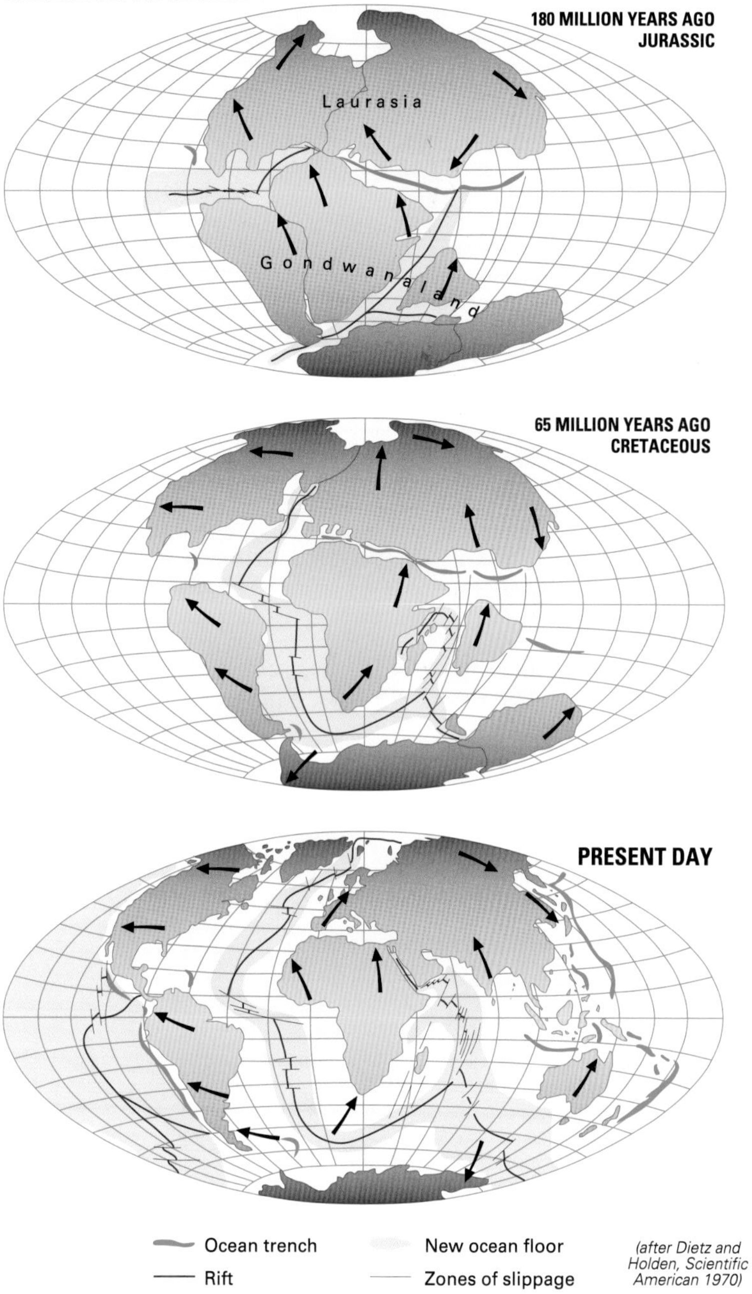

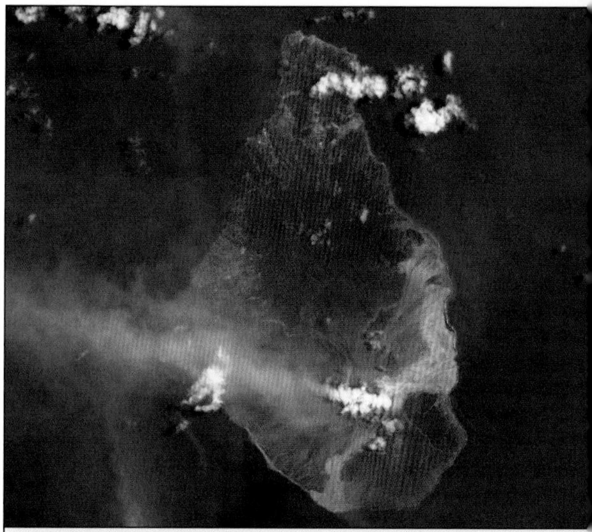

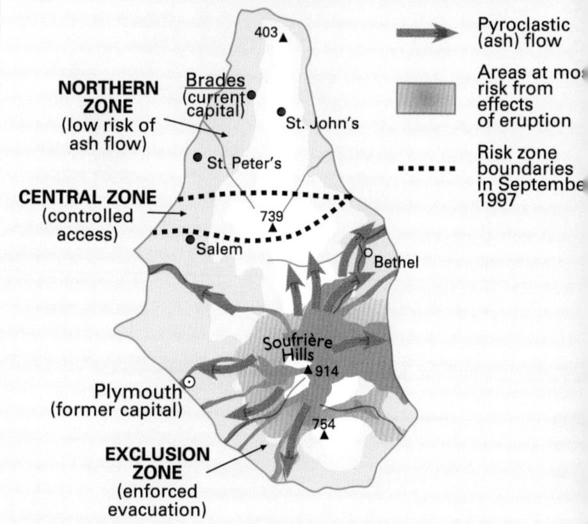

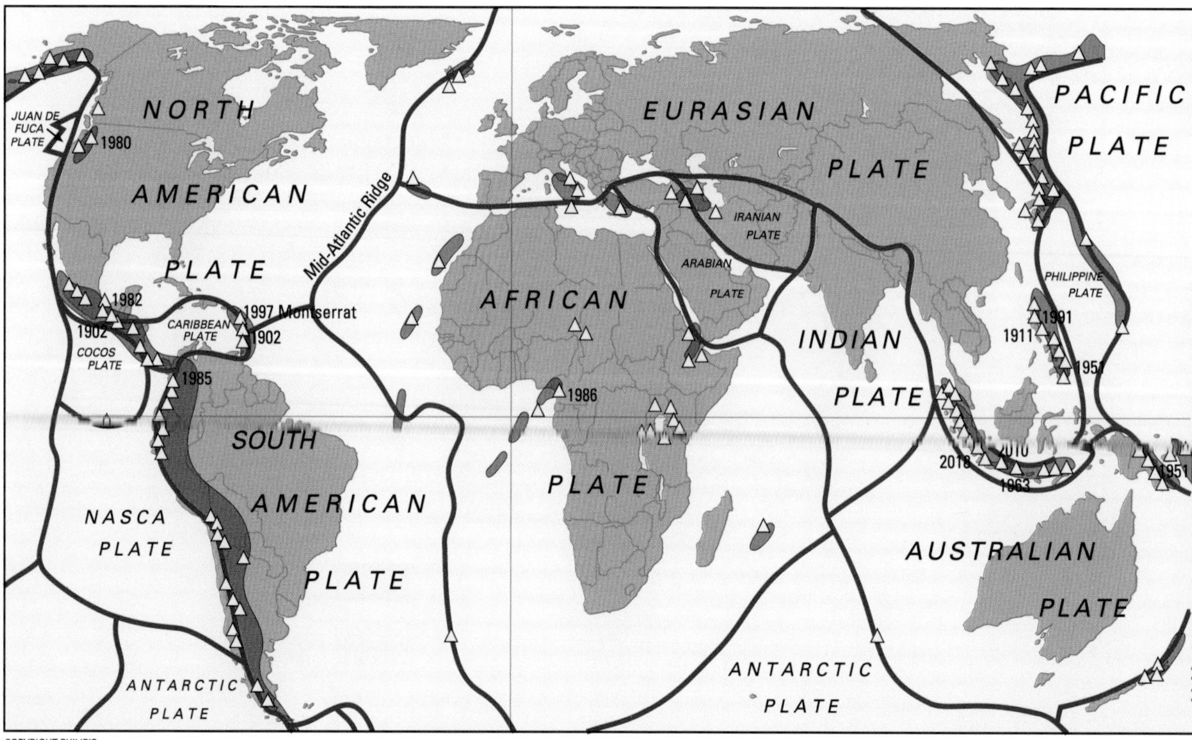

TE TECTONICS IN THE CARIBBEAN

Labels: Shockwaves reach surface, PACIFIC OCEAN, Central America, COCOS PLATE, Subduction zone, Origin or focus of an earthquake, Shockwaves travel away from focus, CARIBBEAN SEA, CARIBBEAN PLATE, Montserrat, Puerto Rico Trench, Destructive boundary (rocks melt here), ATLANTIC OCEAN, Mid-Atlantic Ridge, NORTH AMERICAN PLATE, Earth's mantle

North American Plate is moving away from the Mid-Atlantic Ridge owards the Caribbean Plate at a rate of 30–40mm a year. The of the North American Plate is forced downwards under the ean Plate. As the North American Plate descends, the rocks melt re destroyed. This is called a *destructive boundary*. The destructive ary to the east of the Caribbean has caused the Puerto Rico Trench and the chain of volcanoes in the Leeward Islands such as Montserrat. The molten rocks along the destructive boundary are forced upwards through cracks at the edge of the Caribbean Plate to pour out as lava from volcanoes. Earthquakes are also common along destructive plate boundaries, as is the case in Central America, along the boundary between the Caribbean and Cocos Plates.

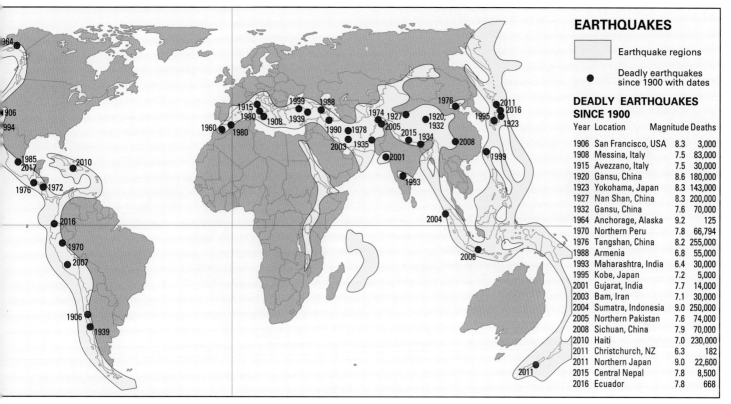

EARTHQUAKES

- Earthquake regions
- • Deadly earthquakes since 1900 with dates

DEADLY EARTHQUAKES SINCE 1900

Year	Location	Magnitude	Deaths
1906	San Francisco, USA	8.3	3,000
1908	Messina, Italy	7.5	83,000
1915	Avezzano, Italy	7.5	30,000
1920	Gansu, China	8.6	180,000
1923	Yokohama, Japan	8.3	143,000
1927	Nan Shan, China	8.3	200,000
1932	Gansu, China	7.6	70,000
1964	Anchorage, Alaska	9.2	125
1970	Northern Peru	7.8	66,794
1976	Tangshan, China	8.2	255,000
1988	Armenia	6.8	55,000
1993	Maharashtra, India	6.4	30,000
1995	Kobe, Japan	7.2	5,000
2001	Gujarat, India	7.7	14,000
2003	Bam, Iran	7.1	30,000
2004	Sumatra, Indonesia	9.0	250,000
2005	Northern Pakistan	7.6	74,000
2008	Sichuan, China	7.9	70,000
2010	Haiti	7.0	230,000
2011	Christchurch, NZ	6.3	182
2011	Northern Japan	9.0	22,600
2015	Central Nepal	7.8	8,500
2016	Ecuador	7.8	668

Other affected countries	Number killed
Somalia	289
Tanzania	13
Seychelles	3
South Africa	2
Yemen	2
Kenya	1

BANGLADESH 2 dead; INDIA 18,045 dead or missing; BURMA (MYANMAR) 61 dead; Bay of Bengal; Andaman Is. (India); Pondicherry; Nagappattinam; Trincomalee; EURASIAN PLATE; Destructive plate boundary; THAILAND 8,212 dead or missing; Phuket; Nicobar Is. (India); Krabi; Banda Aceh; LDIVES dead missing; Galle; SRI LANKA 35,222 dead or missing, 516,000 displaced; Earthquake epicentre; MALAYSIA 68 dead; INDIAN PLATE; Sumatra; INDONESIA 167,736 dead or missing, 500,000 displaced

COPYRIGHT PHILIP'S

INDIAN OCEAN TSUNAMI

On 26 December 2004, an earthquake off the coast of Sumatra triggered a deadly tsunami that swept across the Indian Ocean, causing devastation in many countries (see map left).
The image below shows the turbulent receding waters of the tsunami, on the west coast of Sri Lanka. Such imagery enabled rescuers to assess the worst affected areas.

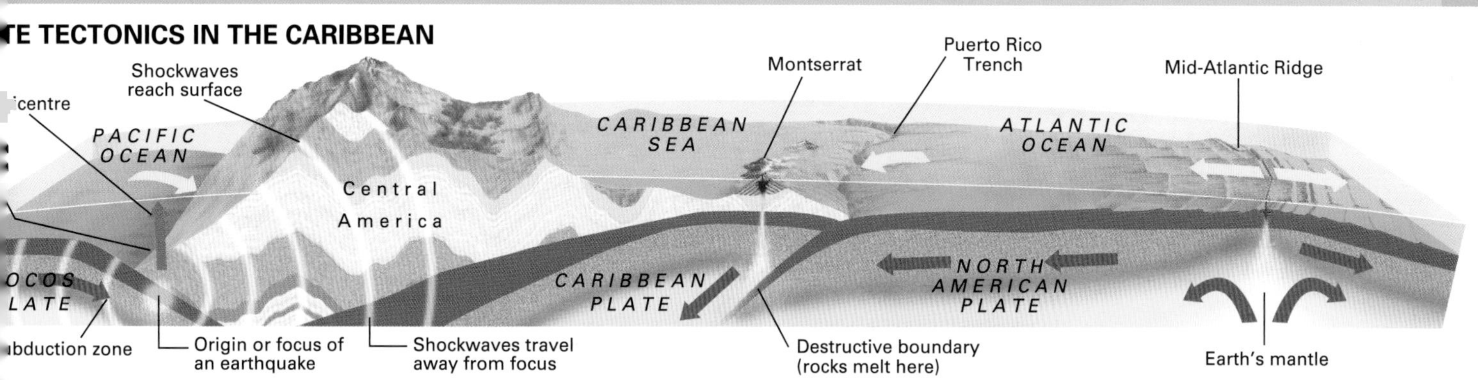

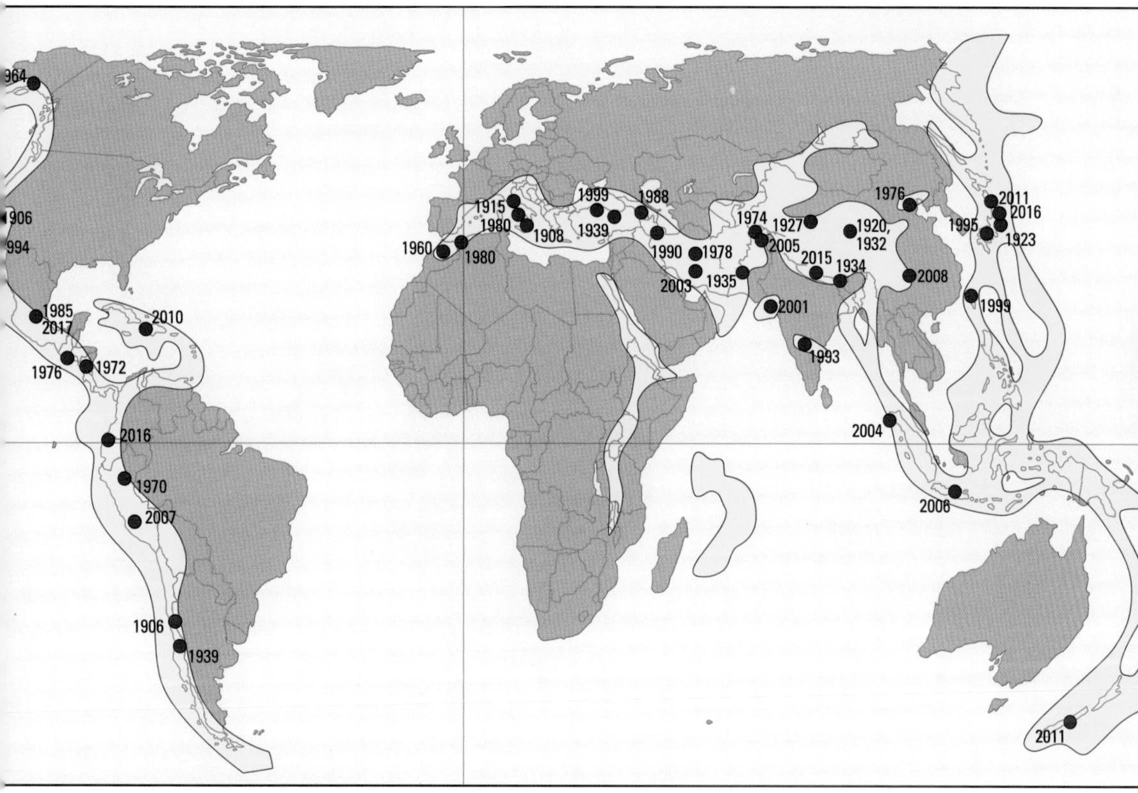

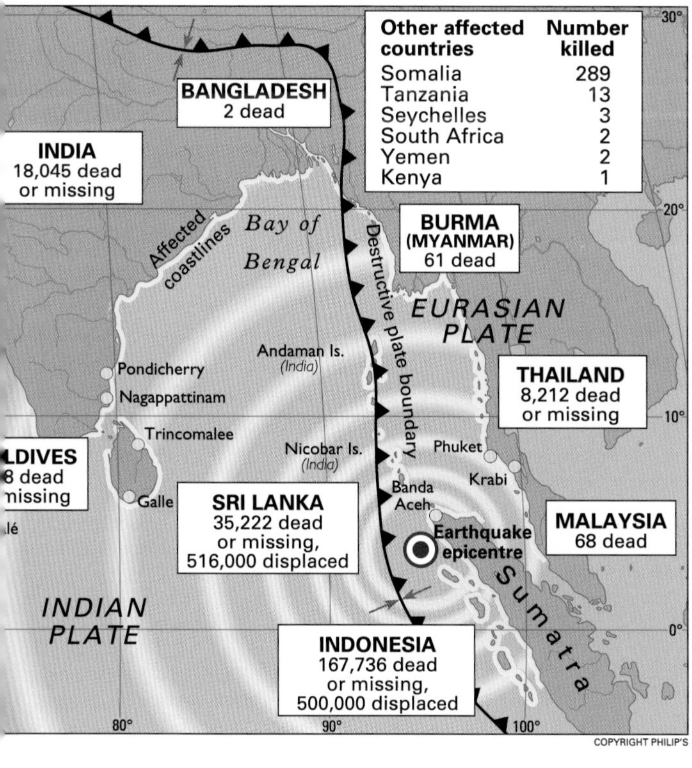

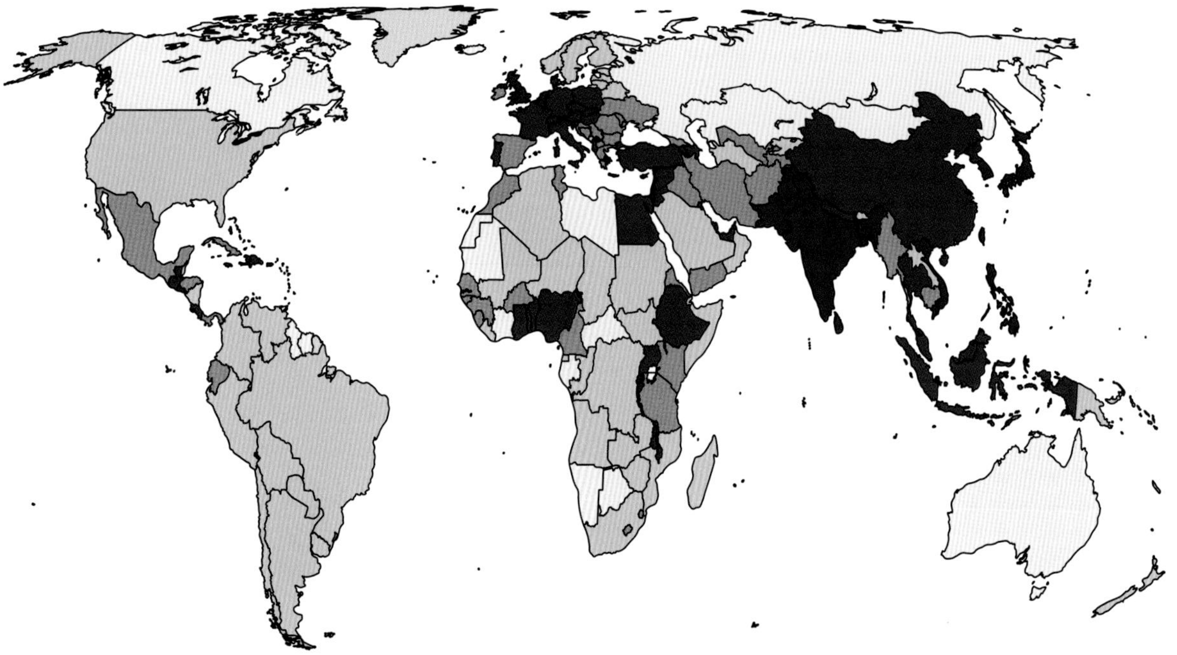

POPULATION DENSITY BY COUNTRY

Density of people per square kilometre (2020)

- 250 per km² and over
- 100 – 250 per km²
- 50 – 100 per km²
- 10 – 50 per km²
- Under 10 per km²
- No data

Most and least densely populated countries

Most per km²		Least per km²	
Monaco	15,457	Mongolia	2
Singapore	8,627	Australia	3
Bahrain	2,213	Namibia	3
Malta	1,440	Iceland	3
Maldives	1,302	Guyana	4

UK 273 per km²

POPULATION CHANGE

Expected change in total population (2004–2050)

- Over 125% gain
- 100 – 125% gain
- 50 – 100% gain
- 25 – 50% gain
- 0 – 25% gain
- No change or loss

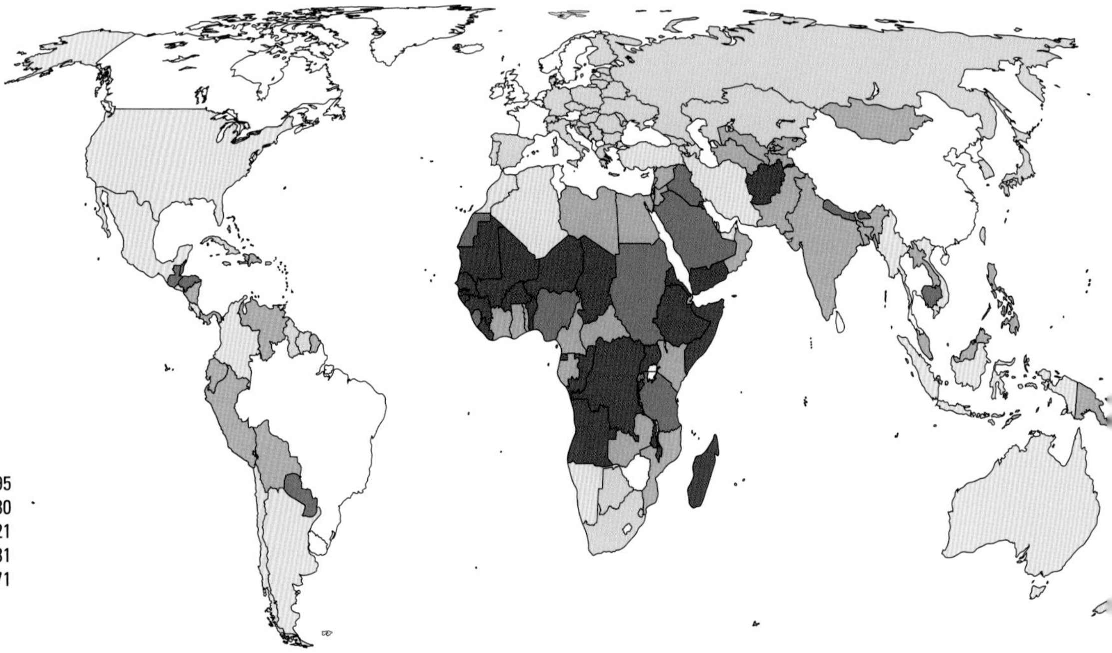

Based on estimates for the year 2050, the ten most populous nations in the world will be, in millions:

India	1,628	Pakistan	295
China	1,437	Bangladesh	280
USA	420	Brazil	221
Indonesia	308	Congo Dem. Rep.	181
Nigeria	307	Ethiopia	171

UK (2050) 77 million

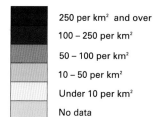

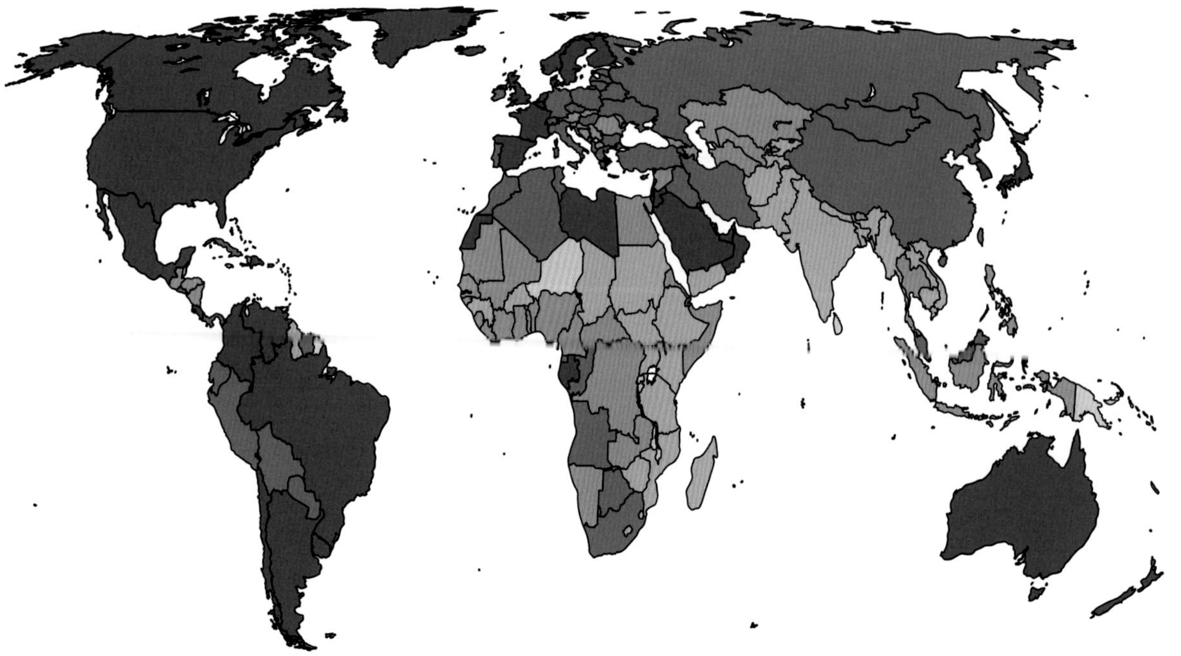

URBAN POPULATION

Percentage of total population living in towns and cities (2020)

- 80% urban and over
- 60 – 80% urban
- 40 – 60% urban
- 20 – 40% urban
- Under 20% urban
- No data

Countries that are the most and least urbanized (%)

Most urbanized		Least urbanized	
Kuwait	100	Papua N. Guinea	13
Monaco	100	Burundi	14
Singapore	100	Liechtenstein	14

UK 84% urban

In 2008, for the first time in history, more than half the world's population lived in urban areas.

POPULATION BY CONTINENT

In this diagram the size of each continent is in proportion to its population (2020).

Each square represents 10 million people.

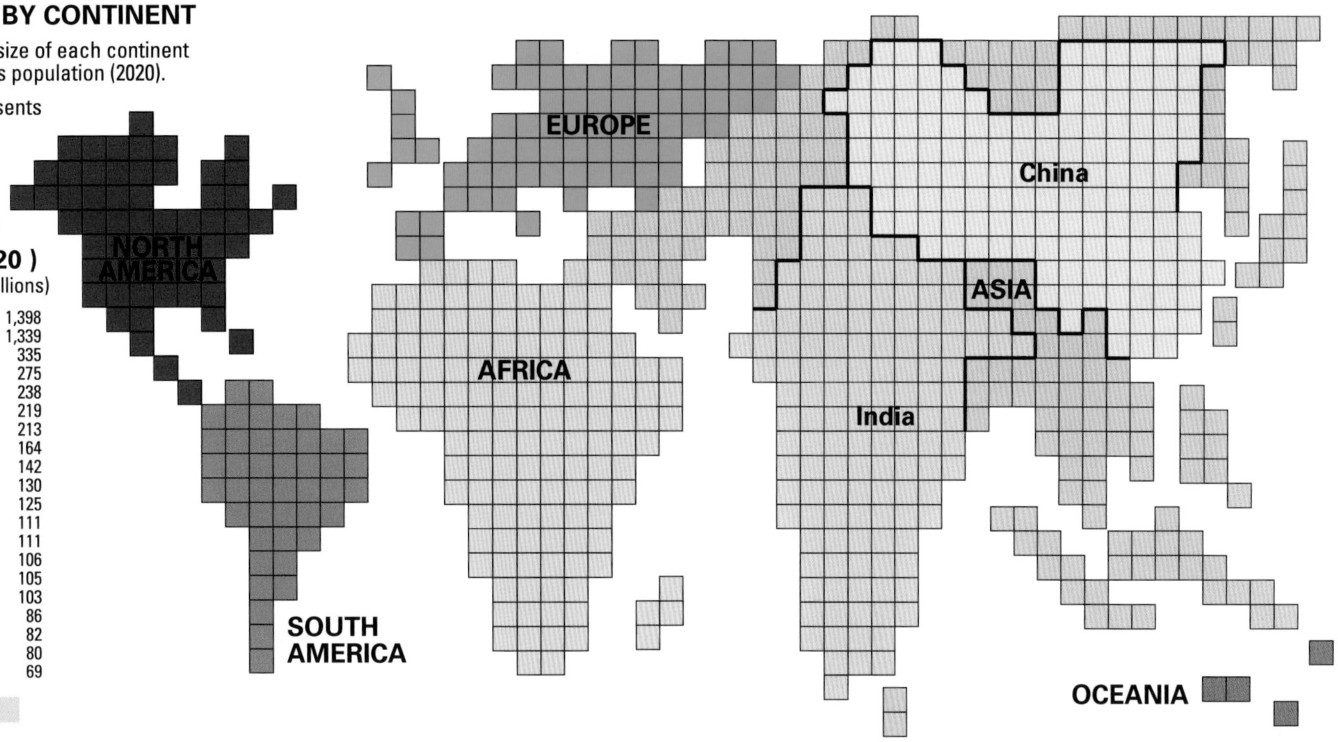

Population of countries (2020)

Top 20 countries (millions)

China	1,398
India	1,339
USA	335
Indonesia	275
Pakistan	238
Nigeria	219
Brazil	213
Bangladesh	164
Russia	142
Mexico	130
Japan	125
Ethiopia	111
Philippines	111
Egypt	106
Congo, Dem. Rep.	105
Vietnam	103
Iran	86
Turkey	82
Germany	80
Thailand	69

UK 66 million

LIFE EXPECTANCY

The average expected lifespan of babies born in 2021

- Over 80 years
- 75 – 80 years
- 70 – 75 years
- 65 – 70 years
- Under 65 years
- No data

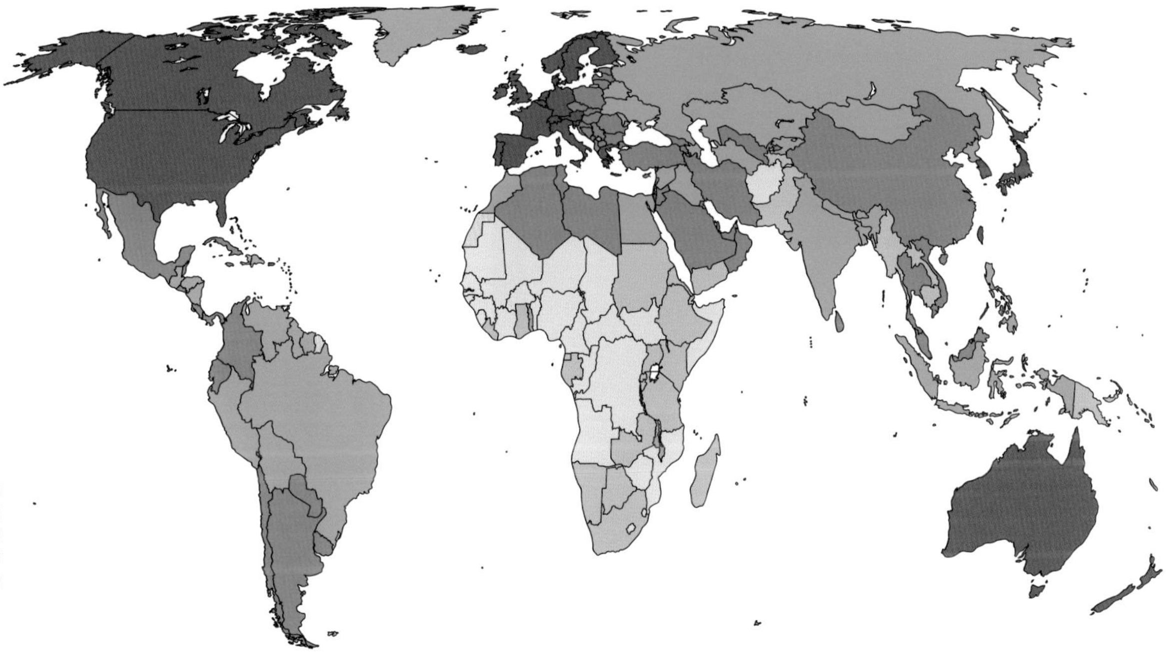

Countries with the highest and lowest life expectancy at birth in years

Highest		Lowest	
Monaco	89	Afghanistan	53
Singapore	86	Central African Rep.	55
Japan	85	Somalia	55
San Marino	84	Mozambique	56
Canada	84	South Sudan	59

UK 81 years

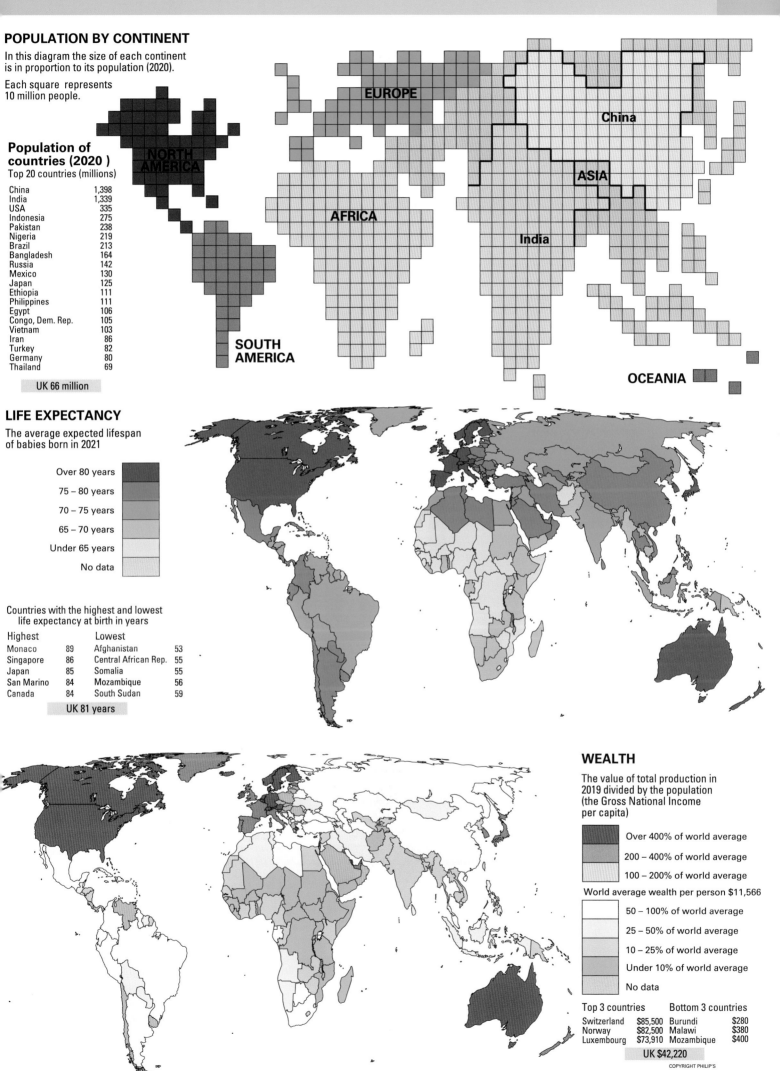

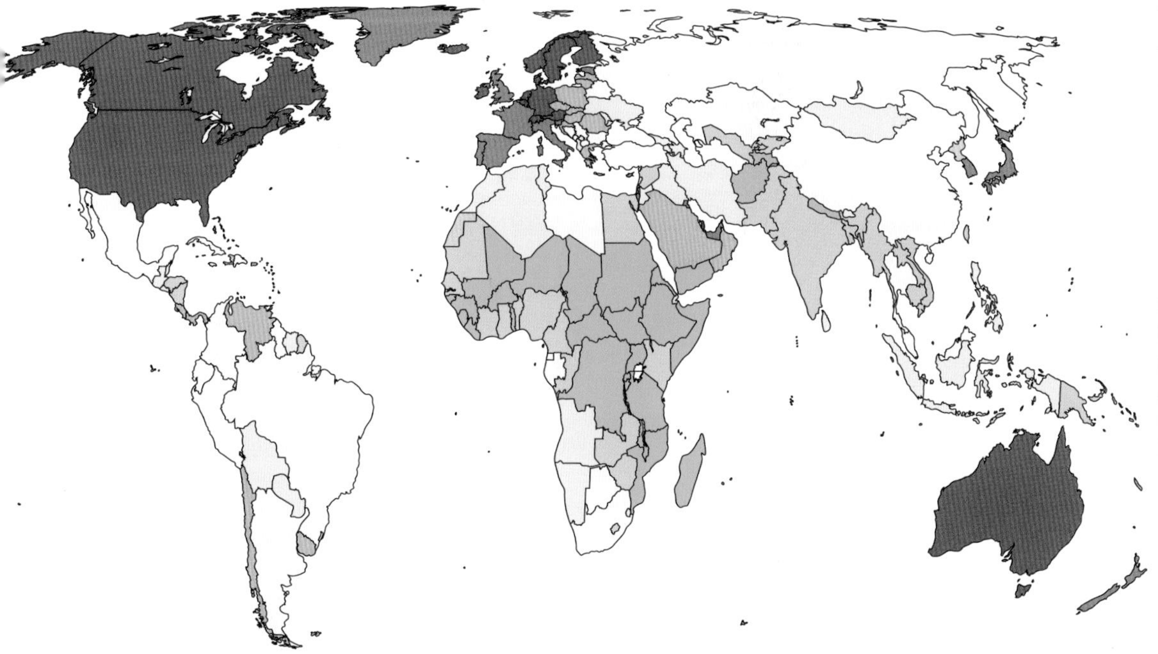

WEALTH

The value of total production in 2019 divided by the population (the Gross National Income per capita)

- Over 400% of world average
- 200 – 400% of world average
- 100 – 200% of world average

World average wealth per person $11,566

- 50 – 100% of world average
- 25 – 50% of world average
- 10 – 25% of world average
- Under 10% of world average
- No data

Top 3 countries		Bottom 3 countries	
Switzerland	$85,500	Burundi	$280
Norway	$82,500	Malawi	$380
Luxembourg	$73,910	Mozambique	$400

UK $42,220

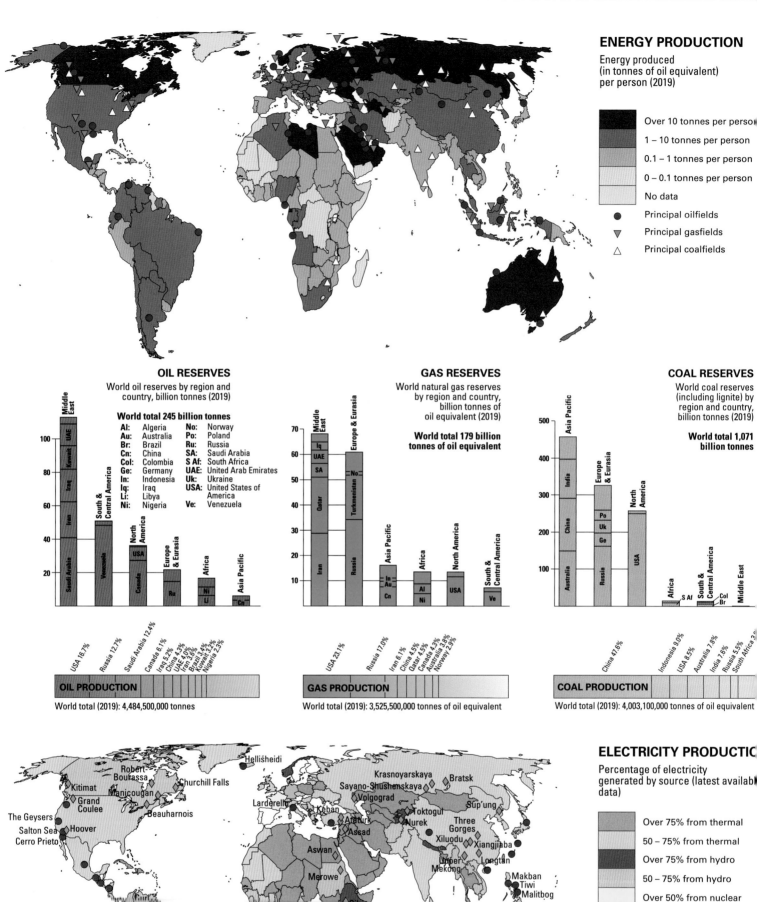

ENERGY PRODUCTION

Energy produced
(in tonnes of oil equivalent)
per person (2019)

- Over 10 tonnes per person
- 1 – 10 tonnes per person
- 0.1 – 1 tonnes per person
- 0 – 0.1 tonnes per person
- No data
- ● Principal oilfields
- ▽ Principal gasfields
- △ Principal coalfields

OIL RESERVES

World oil reserves by region and
country, billion tonnes (2019)

World total 245 billion tonnes

Al:	Algeria
Au:	Australia
Br:	Brazil
Cn:	China
Col:	Colombia
Ge:	Germany
In:	Indonesia
Iq:	Iraq
Li:	Libya
Ni:	Nigeria
No:	Norway
Po:	Poland
Ru:	Russia
SA:	Saudi Arabia
S Af:	South Africa
UAE:	United Arab Emirates
Uk:	Ukraine
USA:	United States of America
Ve:	Venezuela

OIL PRODUCTION

USA 16.7% Russia 12.7% Saudi Arabia 12.4% Canada 6.1% China 5.2% Iraq 4.3% UAE 4.0% Iran 3.6% Brazil 3.2% Kuwait 3.2% Nigeria 2.3%

World total (2019): 4,484,500,000 tonnes

GAS RESERVES

World natural gas reserves
by region and country,
billion tonnes of
oil equivalent (2019)

World total 179 billion
tonnes of oil equivalent

GAS PRODUCTION

USA 23.1% Russia 17.0% Iran 6.1% China 4.5% Qatar 4.5% Canada 4.3% Australia 3.9% Norway 2.9%

World total (2019): 3,525,500,000 tonnes of oil equivalent

COAL RESERVES

World coal reserves
(including lignite) by
region and country,
billion tonnes (2019)

World total 1,071
billion tonnes

COAL PRODUCTION

China 47.6% Indonesia 9.0% USA 8.5% Australia 7.8% India 7.6% Russia 5.5% South Africa 3.%

World total (2019): 4,003,100,000 tonnes of oil equivalent

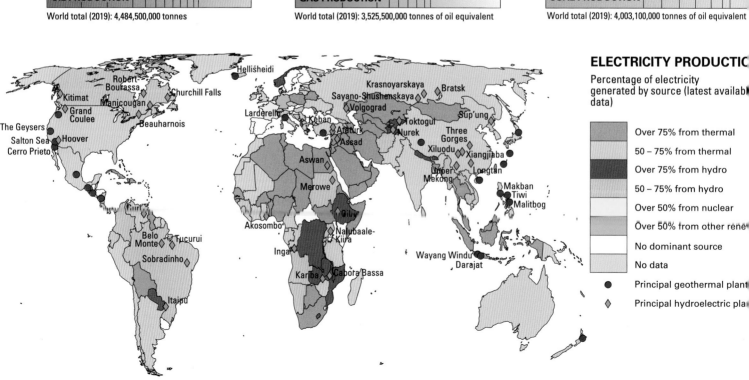

ELECTRICITY PRODUCTION

Percentage of electricity
generated by source (latest available
data)

- Over 75% from thermal
- 50 – 75% from thermal
- Over 75% from hydro
- 50 – 75% from hydro
- Over 50% from nuclear
- Over 50% from other renew
- No dominant source
- No data
- ● Principal geothermal plant
- ◆ Principal hydroelectric plant

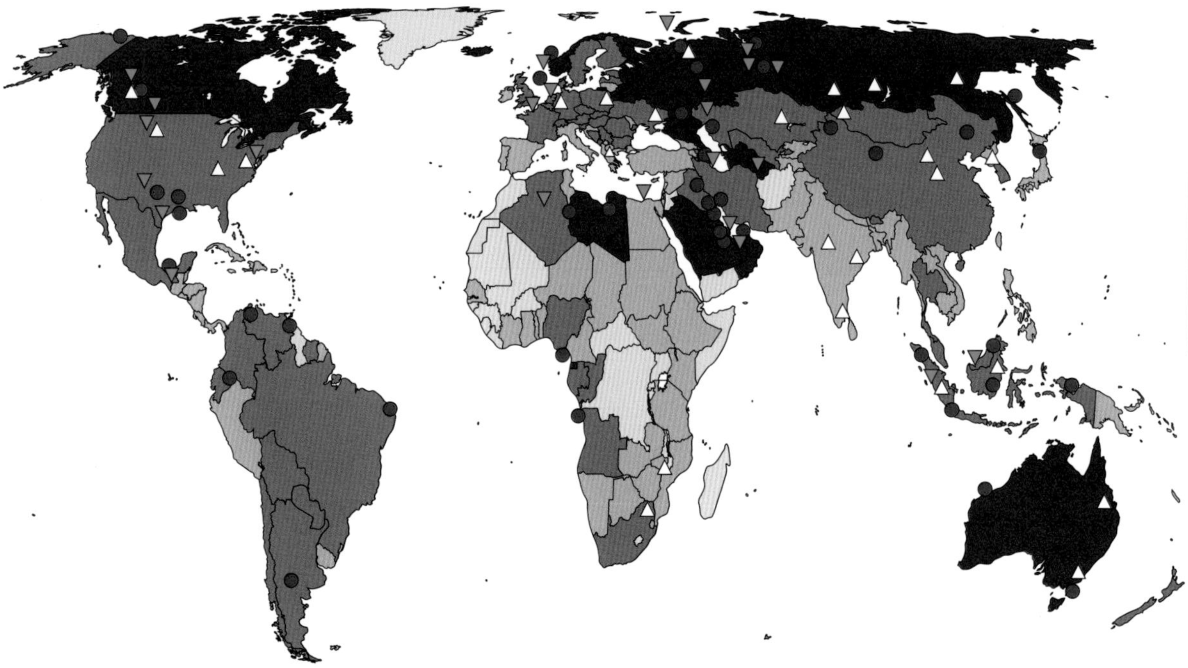

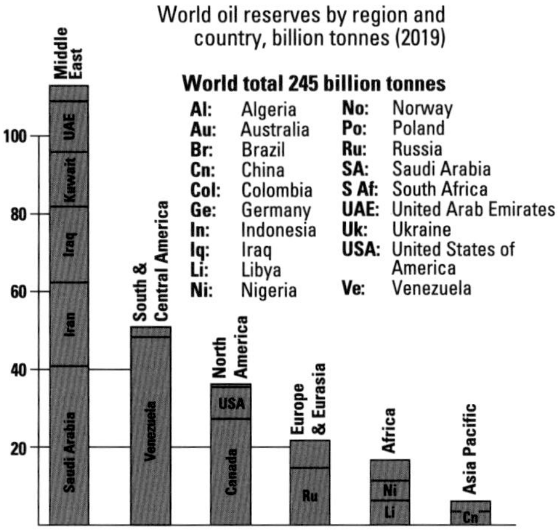

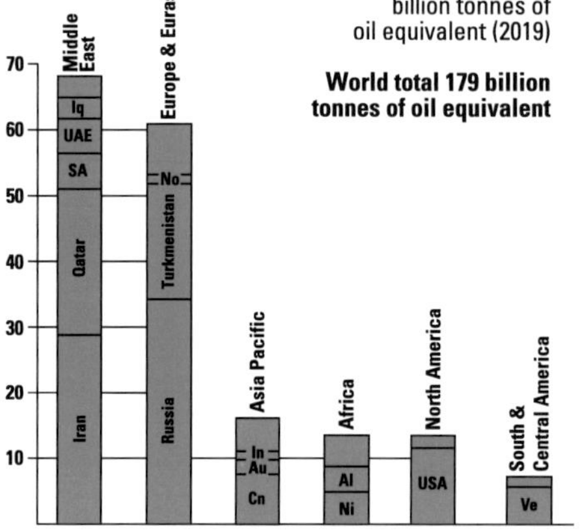

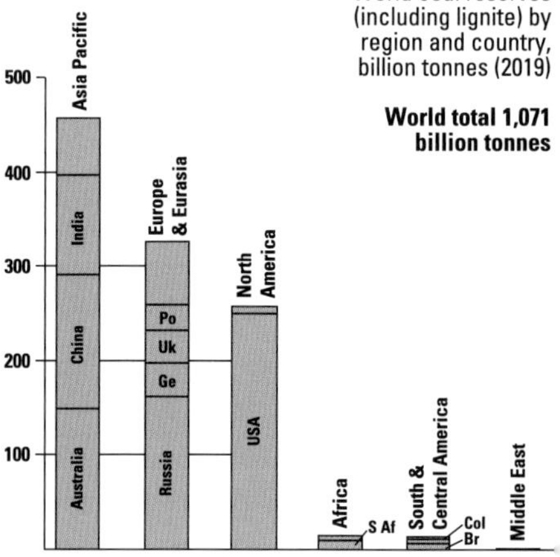

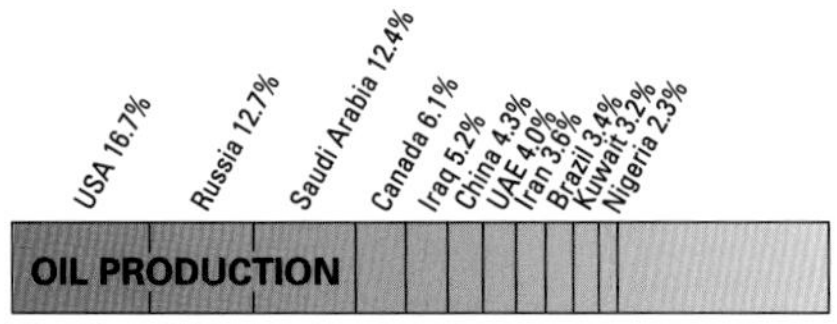

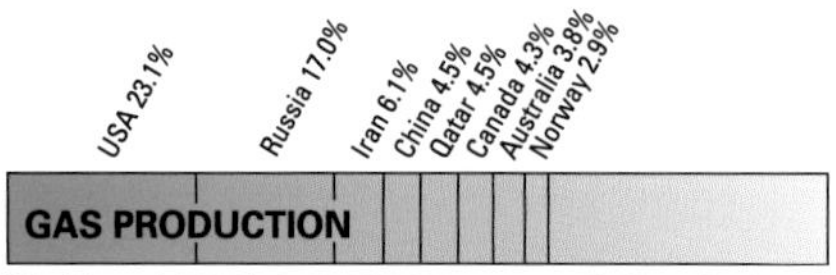

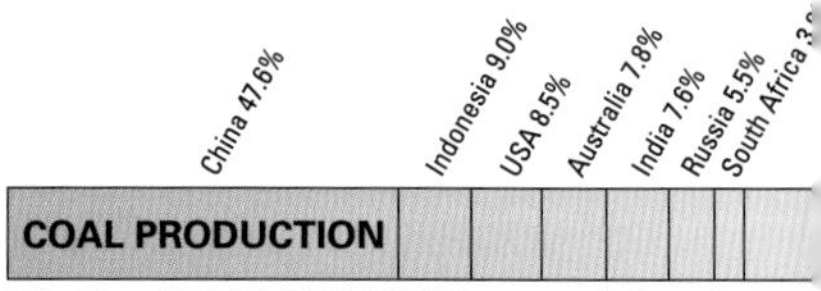

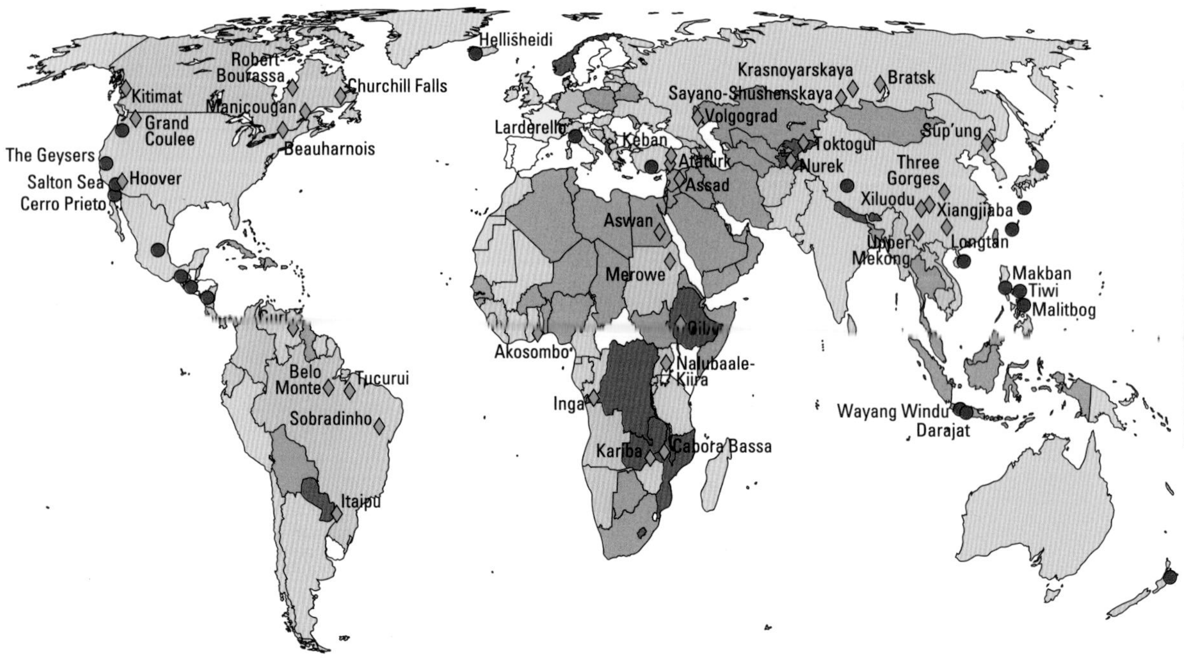

FOOD PRODUCTION

- Principal fishing areas
- Nomadic herding
- Forestry
- Hunting, fishing and gathering
- Subsistence agriculture (growing food to feed the family)
- Livestock ranching (large-scale breeding and rearing of animals for sale)
- Commercial farming (arable land, dairying, and small-scale grazing to produce food for sale)
- Urban areas (commercial, industrial and residential land use)
- Unproductive land

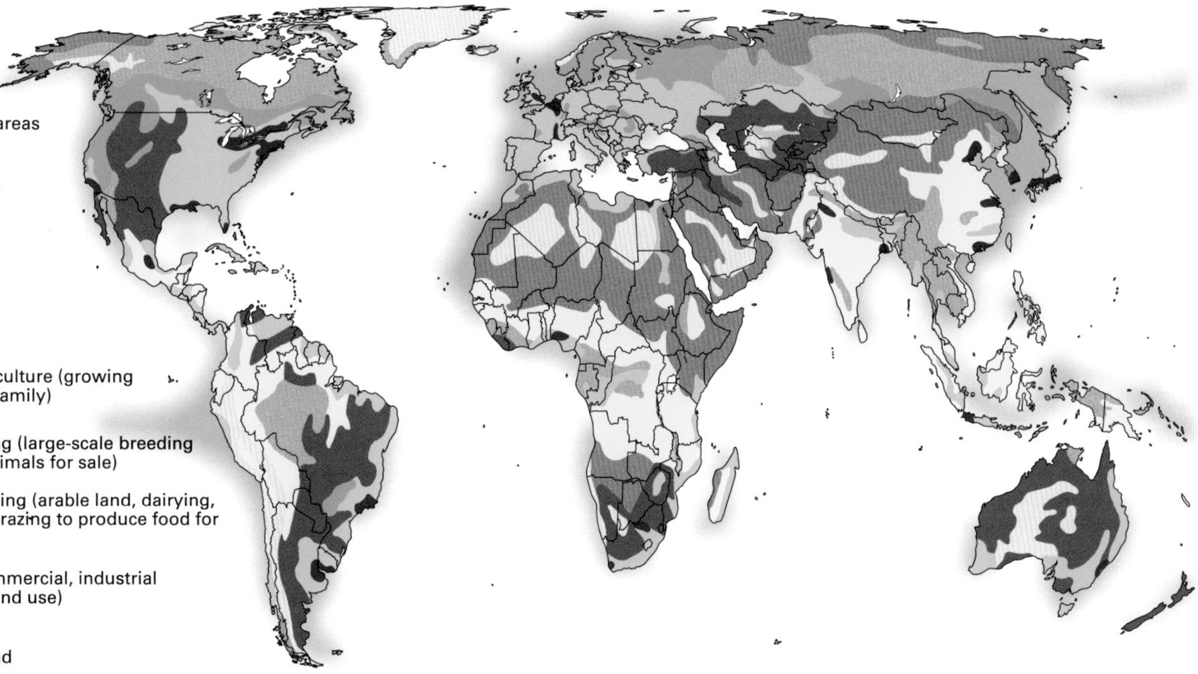

MALNUTRITION

Level of malnutrition as a percentage of the population (2018)

- Over 30%
- 20 – 30%
- 15 – 20%
- 10 – 15%
- Under 10%
- No data

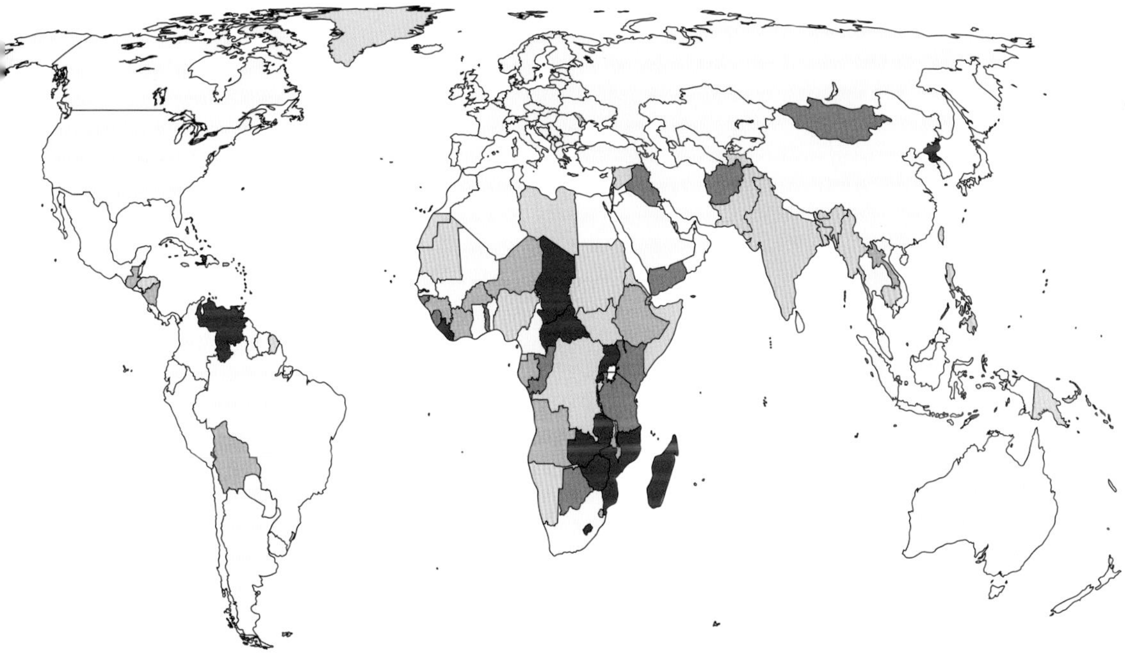

Countries with highest rates

CAR	60%	Madagascar	42%
Zimbabwe	51%	Uganda	41%
Haiti	48%	Chad	40%
North Korea	48%	Liberia	38%
Zambia	47%	Rwanda	36%

UK 3%

WATER SUPPLY

Mortality rate due to unsafe drinking water, deaths per 100,000 people (2019)

- Over 50
- 25 – 50
- 10 – 25
- 2.5 – 10
- 1 – 2.5
- Under 1
- No data

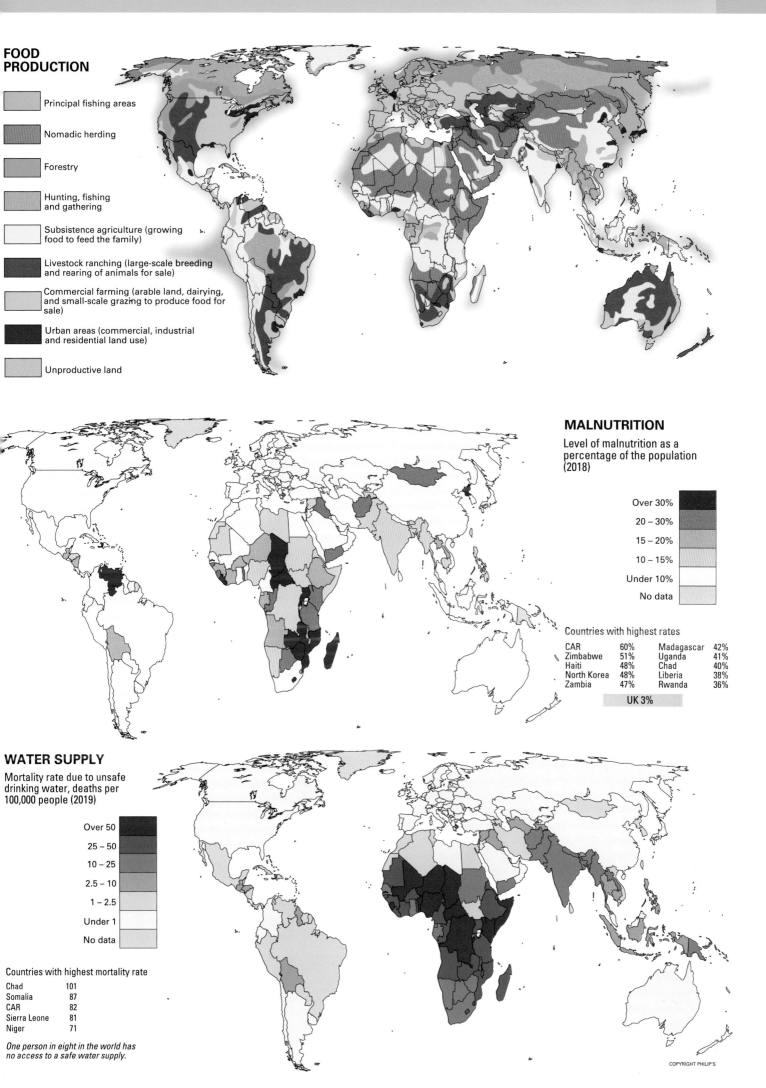

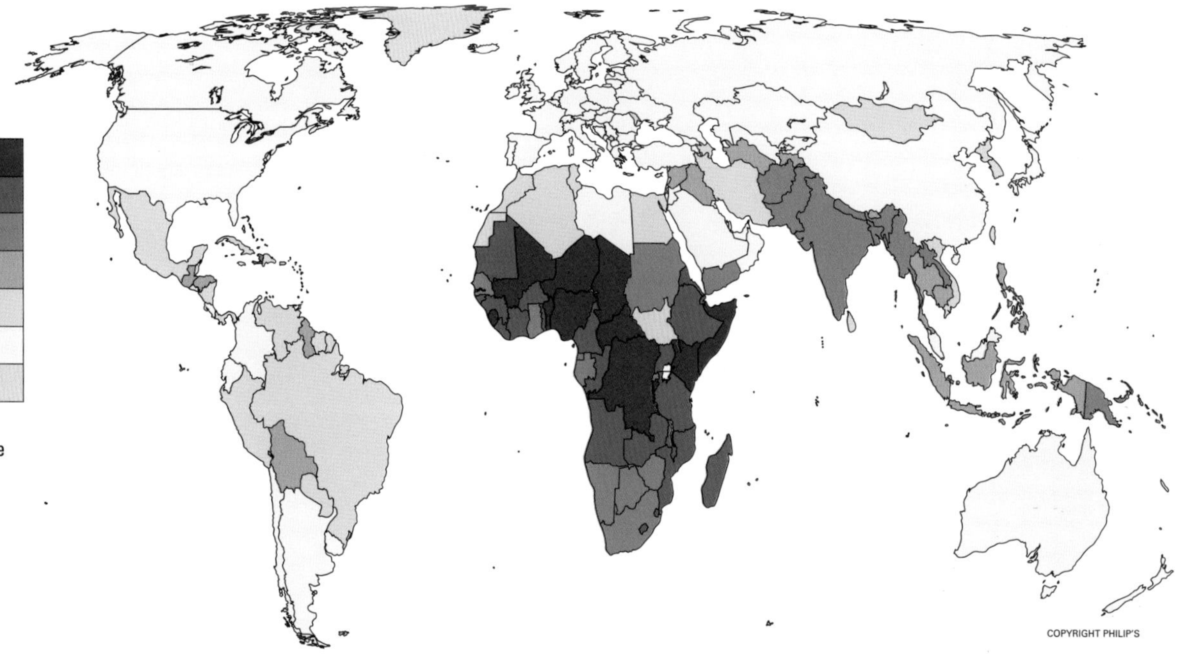

Countries with highest mortality rate

Chad	101
Somalia	87
CAR	82
Sierra Leone	81
Niger	71

One person in eight in the world has no access to a safe water supply.

INDUSTRY AND TRADE

Manufactured exports as a percentage of total exports (2019)

- Over 75%
- 50 – 75%
- 25 – 50%
- 10 – 25%
- 0 – 10%
- No data

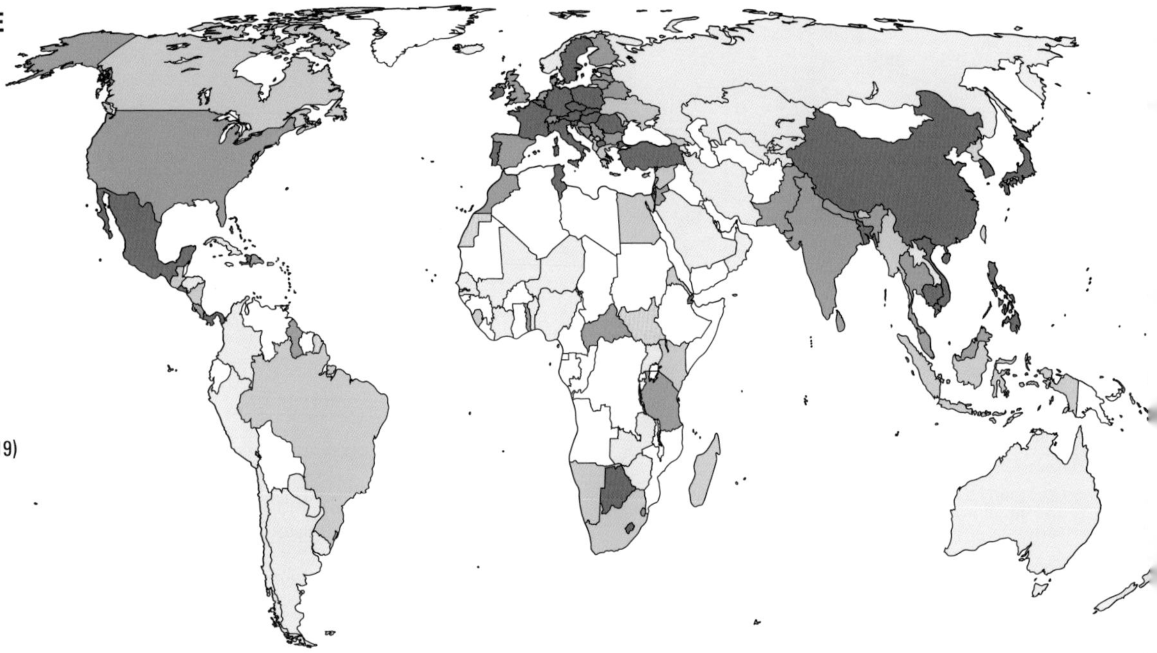

Countries most dependent on the export of manufactured goods (2019)

Bangladesh	96%
Botswana	96%
Panama	94%
China	93%
Israel	93%
Andorra	92%

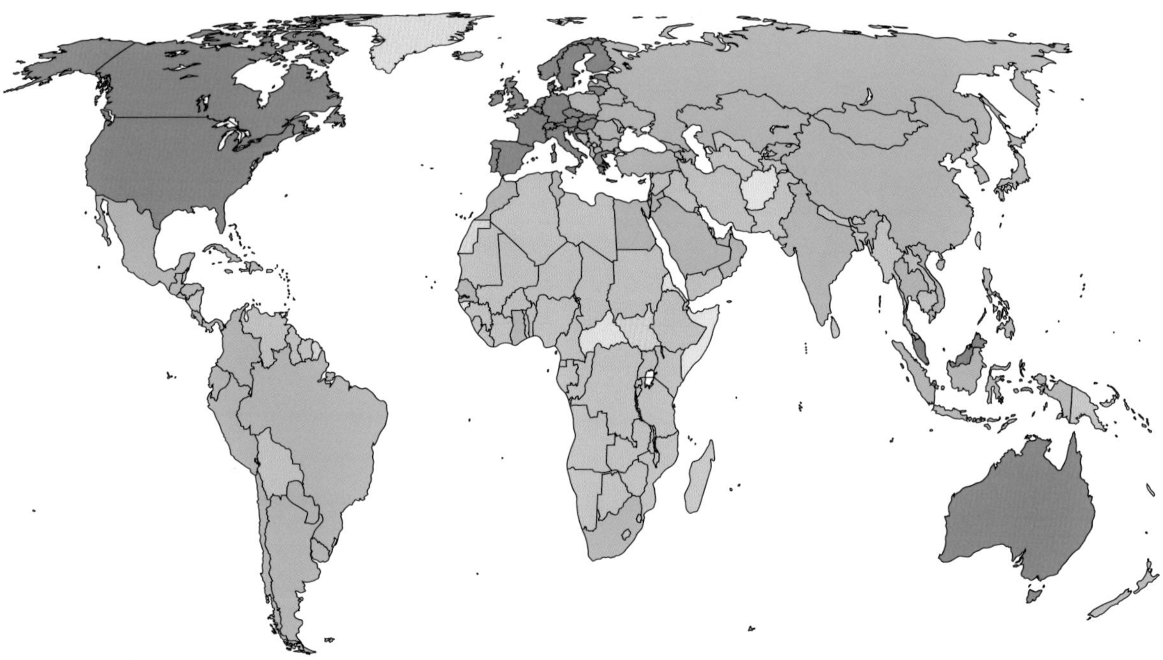

GLOBALIZATION INDEX

Index of globalization

- Over 80
- 60 – 80
- 40 – 60
- 20 – 40
- No data

The index is a measure of econom political and social globalization. T higher values show a greater level globalization.

INTERNATIONAL AID

Official Development Assistance (ODA) provided and received, US$ per person (2020)

PROVIDERS

- Over $250
- $100 – $250
- Under $100

RECEIVERS

- Under $10
- $10 – $50
- $50 – $100
- Over $100
- No data

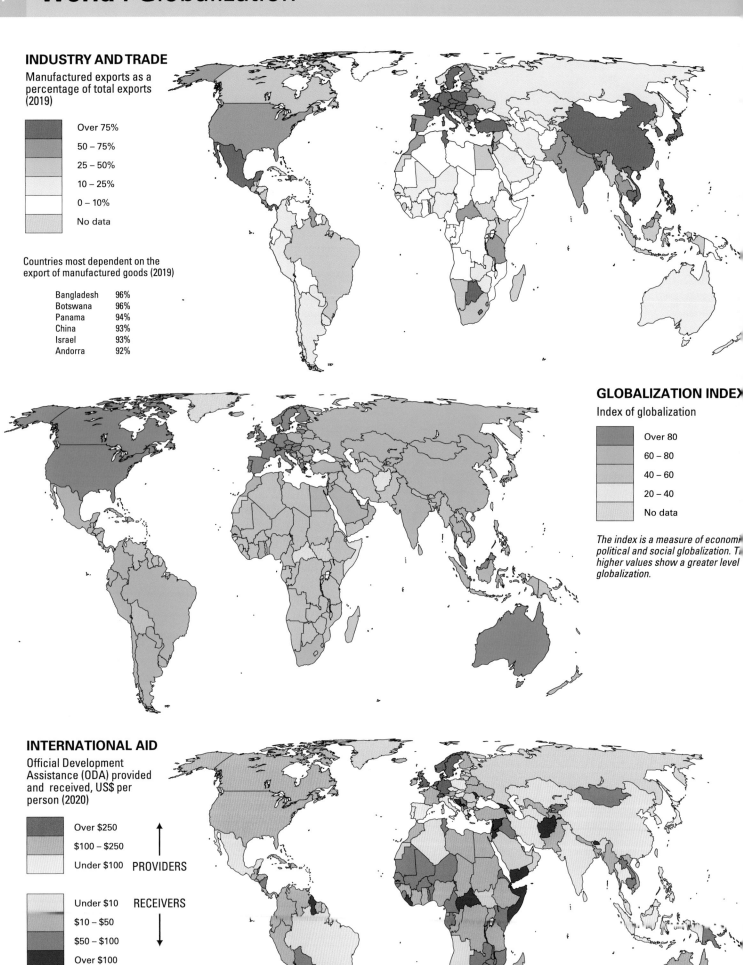

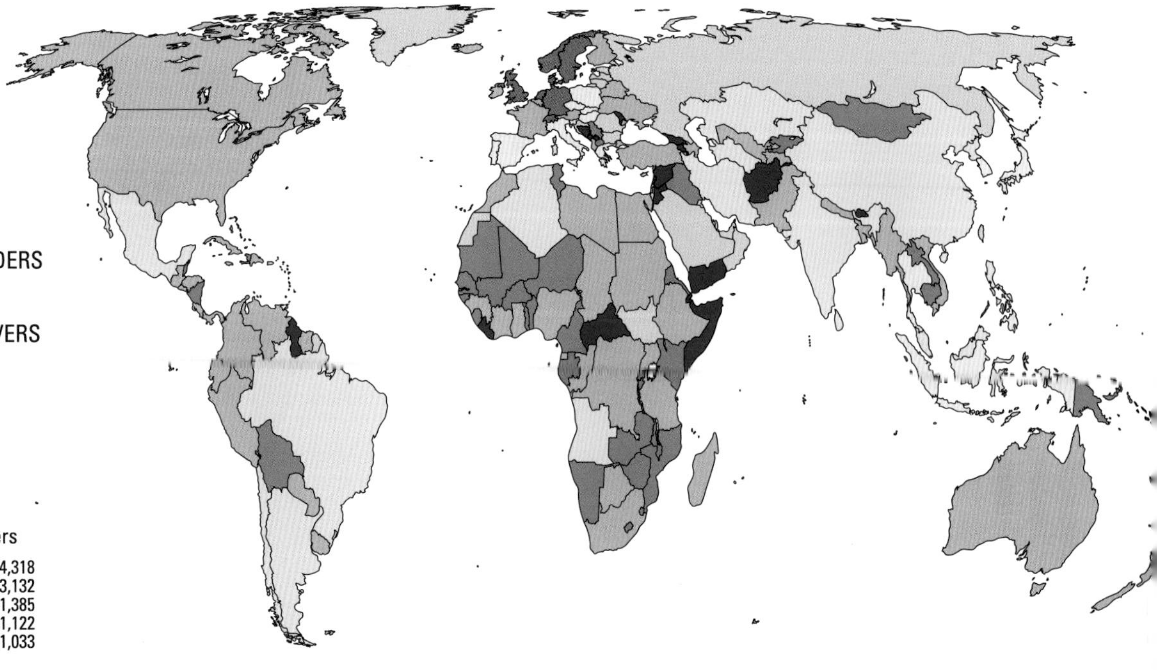

Top 5 providers		Top 5 receivers	
Norway	$785	Nauru	$4,318
Luxembourg	$754	Tuvalu	$3,132
Sweden	$529	Palau	$1,385
Switzerland	$368	Marshall Is.	$1,122
Netherlands	$306	Tonga	$1,033

UK provides $294

TOURIST SPENDING
Countries spending the most on overseas tourism, US$ million (2019)

China, USA, Germany, UK, France, Australia, Russia, Italy, Korea, Rep., Canada, UAE, Japan

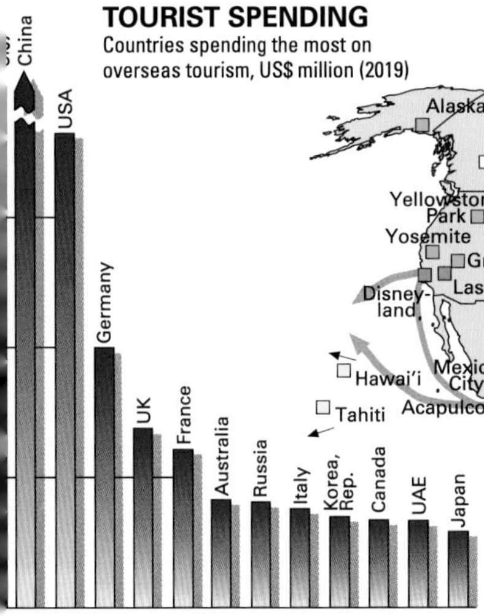

TOURIST EARNINGS
Countries receiving the most from overseas tourism, US$ million (2019)

USA, France, Thailand, Germany, Italy, Japan, Australia, Turkey, UAE, India, UK, Spain

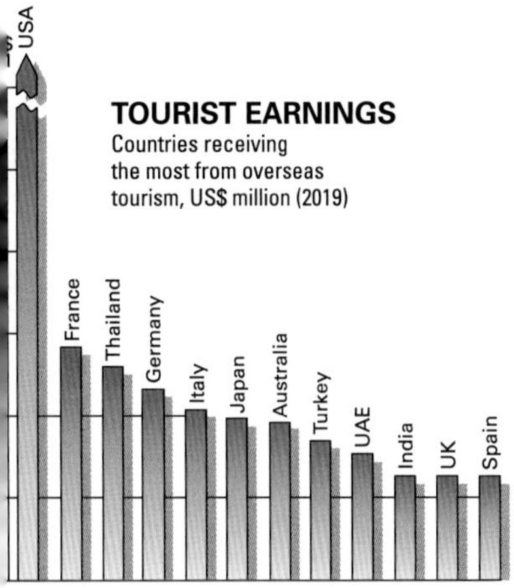

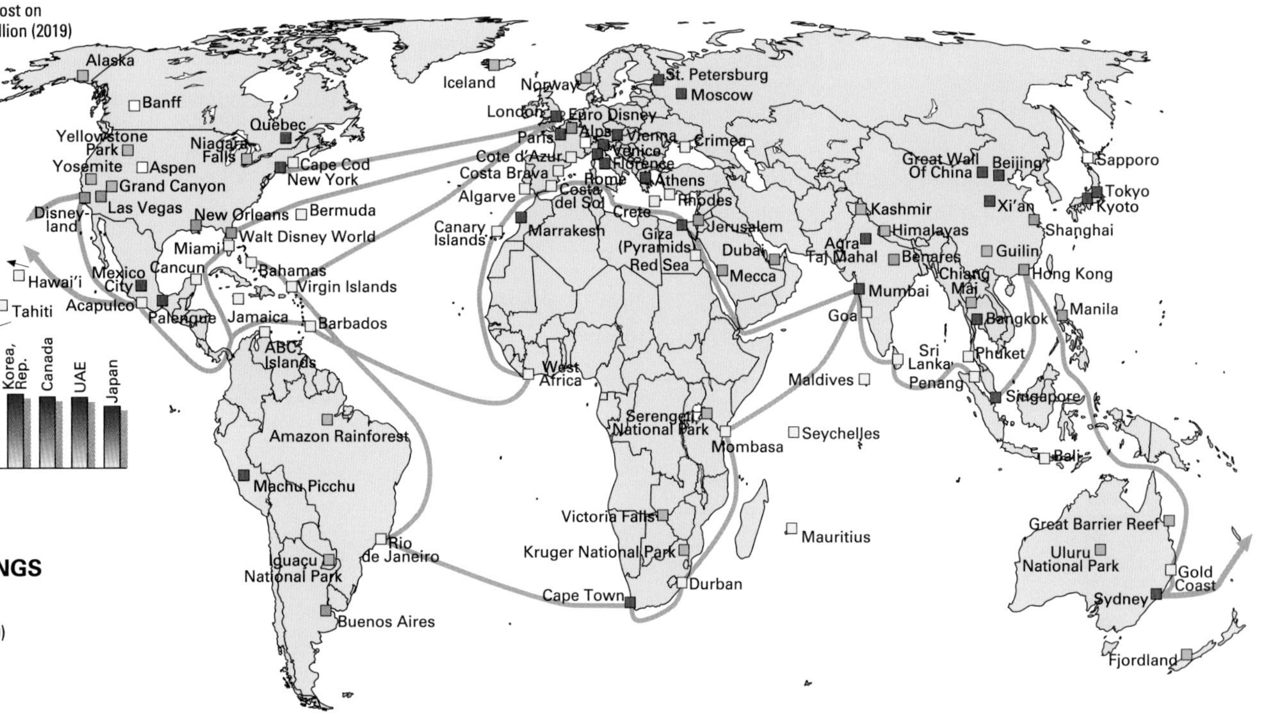

TOURIST DESTINATIONS

—— Popular holiday cruise routes

■ Cultural and historical centres
□ Coastal resorts
□ Ski resorts
■ Centres of entertainment
■ Places of pilgrimage
■ Places of great natural beauty

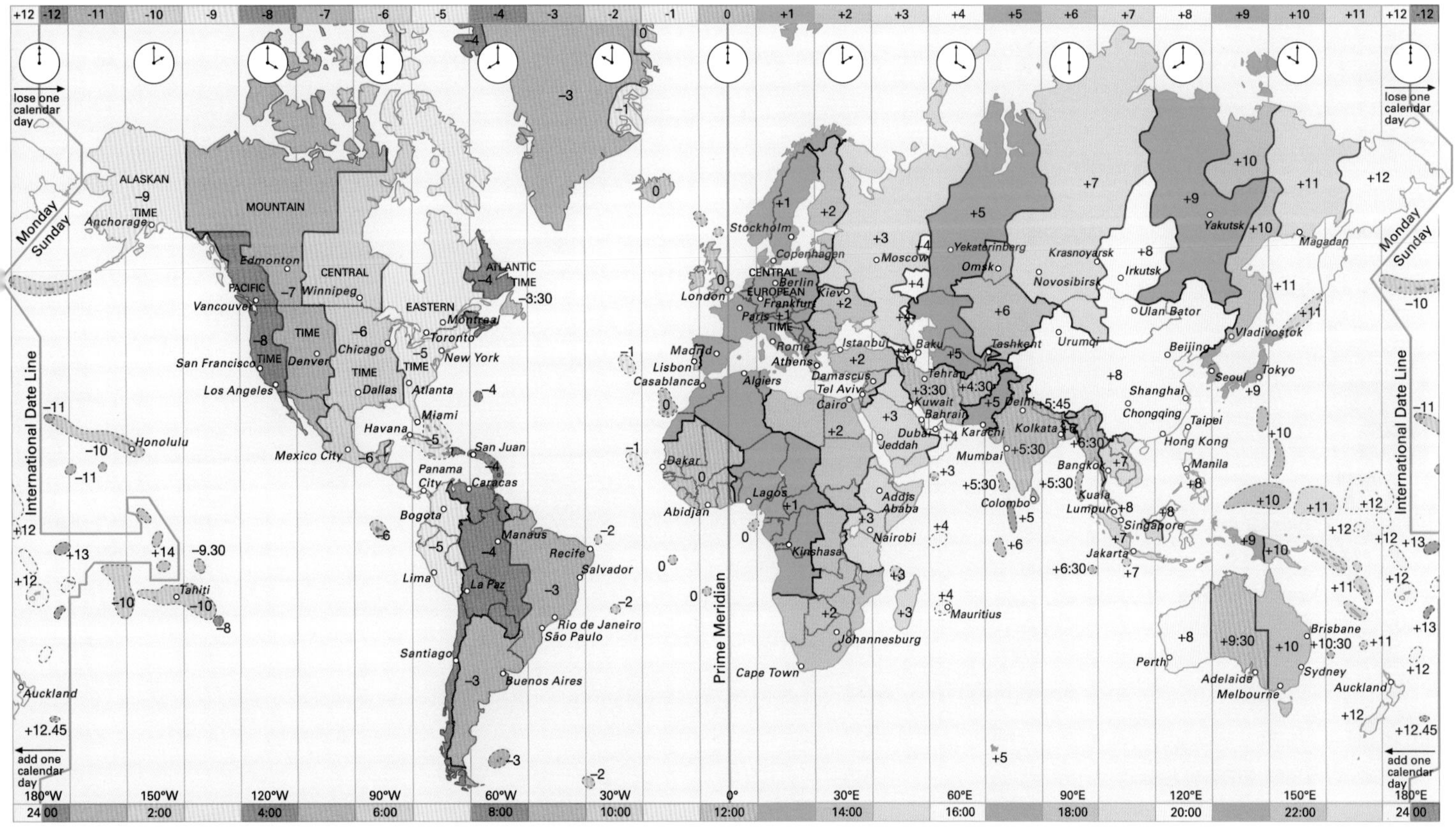

STANDARD TIME ZONES

10 Hours slow or fast of UT or Co-ordinated Universal Time

Zones using UT (Universal Time)
Half-hour zones
Zones behind UT (Universal Time)
Zones ahead of UT (Universal Time)
—— International boundaries
—— Time zone boundaries
—— International Date Line

The Earth rotates through 360° in 24 hours, and so moves 15° every hour. The World is divided into 24 standard time zones, each centred on lines of longitude at 15° intervals. The Greenwich Meridian (or Prime Meridian) lies on the centre of the first zone. All places to the west of Greenwich are one hour behind for every 15° of longitude; places to the east are ahead by one hour for every 15°.

World : Statistics

FLAG	COUNTRY	CAPITAL CITY	AREA thousand square kilometres 2021	POPULATION in millions 2021	POPULATION CHANGE percent per year 2021	BIRTHS per thousand people 2021	DEATHS per thousand people 2021	LIFE EXPECTANCY years 2021	INCOME US $ per person 2019
	Afghanistan	Kabul	652	37.5	2.3	36	13	53	2,190
	Albania	Tirane	28.7	3.1	0.2	13	7	79	14,450
	Algeria	Algiers	2,382	43.6	1.4	19	4	78	11,720
	Angola	Luanda	1,247	33.6	3.4	42	8	62	6,380
	Argentina	Buenos Aires	2,780	45.9	0.8	16	7	78	21,780
	Armenia	Yerevan	29.8	3.0	-0.4	11	9	76	14,500
	Australia	Canberra	7,741	25.8	1.3	12	7	83	51,680
	Austria	Vienna	83.9	8.9	0.3	9	10	82	60,720
	Azerbaijan	Baku	86.6	10.3	0.7	14	7	74	14,400
	Bahamas	Nassau	13.9	0.4	0.8	15	6	76	37,420
	Bahrain	Manama	0.7	1.5	0.9	13	3	80	44,250
	Bangladesh	Dhaka	144	164.1	1.0	18	5	74	5,200
	Barbados	Bridgetown	0.4	0.3	0.3	11	8	78	15,770
	Belarus	Minsk	208	9.4	-0.3	9	13	74	19,400
	Belgium	Brussels	30.5	11.8	0.6	11	10	82	57,050
	Belize	Belmopan	23.0	0.4	1.7	22	4	76	6,700
	Benin	Porto-Novo	113	13.3	3.4	42	8	62	3,400
	Bhutan	Thimphu	47.0	0.9	1.0	16	6	72	11,230
	Bolivia	La Paz/Sucre	1,099	11.8	1.4	20	6	71	8,930
	Bosnia-Herzegovina	Sarajevo	51.2	3.8	-0.2	9	10	78	16,280
	Botswana	Gaborone	582	2.4	1.4	21	9	65	17,140
	Brazil	Brasília	8,514	213.4	0.7	13	7	75	14,890
	Brunei	Bandar Seri Begawan	5.8	0.5	1.5	16	4	78	66,590
	Bulgaria	Sofia	111	6.9	-0.7	8	15	75	24,900
	Burkina Faso	Ouagadougou	274	21.4	2.6	34	8	63	2,180
	Burundi	Gitega	27.8	12.2	3.7	35	6	67	790
	Cabo Verde	Praia	4.0	0.6	1.2	19	6	73	7,330
	Cambodia	Phnom Penh	181	17.3	1.3	21	7	66	4,320
	Cameroon	Yaoundé	475	28.5	2.8	36	8	63	3,730
	Canada	Ottawa	9,971	37.9	0.8	10	8	84	51,140
	Central African Republic	Bangui	623	5.4	1.8	33	12	55	1,060
	Chad	N'djamena	1,284	17.4	3.1	41	10	59	1,620
	Chile	Santiago	757	18.3	0.7	13	6	80	25,920
	China	Beijing	9,597	1397.9	0.3	11	8	76	16,790
	Colombia	Bogotá	1,139	50.4	1.0	17	6	77	15,510
	Congo	Brazzaville	342	5.4	3.2	41	8	62	2,980
	Congo (Dem. Rep.)	Kinshasa	2,345	105.0	2.4	32	9	61	1,110
	Costa Rica	San José	51.1	5.2	1.0	15	6	79	20,470
	Côte d'Ivoire	Yamoussoukro	322	28.1	2.2	29	8	62	5,300
	Croatia	Zagreb	56.5	4.2	-0.5	9	13	77	30,660
	Cuba	Havana	111	11.0	-0.2	10	9	79	12,300
	Cyprus	Nicosia	9.3	1.3	1.1	11	7	80	39,830
	Czechia	Prague	78.9	10.7	0.0	9	11	80	41,570

FLAG	COUNTRY	CAPITAL CITY	AREA thousand square kilometres 2021	POPULATION in millions 2021	POPULATION CHANGE percent per year 2021	BIRTHS per thousand people 2021	DEATHS per thousand people 2021	LIFE EXPECTANCY years 2021	INCOME US $ per person 2019
	Denmark	Copenhagen	43.1	5.9	0.4	11	10	81	63,920
	Djibouti	Djibouti	23.2	0.9	2.0	22	7	65	5,620
	Dominican Republic	Santo Domingo	48.5	10.6	0.9	18	6	72	18,300
	Ecuador	Quito	284	17.1	1.2	17	5	78	11,540
	Egypt	Cairo	1,001	106.4	2.2	26	4	74	11,840
	El Salvador	San Salvador	21.0	6.5	0.7	18	6	75	8,720
	Equatorial Guinea	Malabo	28.1	0.9	2.3	30	7	66	14,640
	Eritrea	Asmara	118	6.1	1.0	27	7	67	1,610
	Estonia	Tallinn	45.1	1.2	-0.7	9	13	78	39,080
	Eswatini	Mbabane/ Lobamba	17.4	1.1	0.8	24	10	59	8,090
	Ethiopia	Addis Ababa	1,104	110.9	2.5	31	6	68	2,310
	Fiji	Suva	18.3	0.9	0.5	17	6	74	13,120
	Finland	Helsinki	338	5.6	0.3	10	10	82	53,430
	France	Paris	552	68.1	0.3	12	10	82	52,050
	Gabon	Libreville	268	2.3	2.4	26	6	69	14,350
	Gambia	Banjul	11.3	2.2	1.8	26	7	66	2,280
	Georgia	Tbilisi	69.7	4.9	0.1	11	11	77	15,260
	Germany	Berlin	357	79.9	-0.2	9	12	81	59,090
	Ghana	Accra	239	32.4	2.3	29	6	69	5,530
	Greece	Athens	132	10.6	-0.3	8	12	81	31,540
	Guatemala	Guatemala	109	17.4	1.6	23	5	73	8,870
	Guinea	Conakry	246	12.9	2.8	36	8	64	2,650
	Guinea-Bissau	Bissau	36.1	2.0	2.5	37	8	63	2,230
	Guyana	Georgetown	215	0.8	0.2	17	7	72	13,540
	Haiti	Port-au-Prince	27.8	11.2	1.2	21	7	66	3,040
	Honduras	Tegucigalpa	112	9.3	1.2	18	5	75	5,530
	Hungary	Budapest	93	9.7	-0.3	9	13	77	34,020
	Iceland	Reykjavik	103	0.4	1.0	13	7	83	61,240
	India	New Delhi	3,287	1339.3	1.0	18	7	70	6,920
	Indonesia	Jakarta	1,905	275.1	0.8	16	7	73	11,970
	Iran	Tehrān	1,648	85.9	1.0	16	5	75	12,950
	Iraq	Baghdād	438	39.7	2.1	25	4	73	11,310
	Ireland	Dublin	70.3	5.2	1.0	13	7	81	71,150
	Israel	Jerusalem	20.6	8.8	1.5	18	5	83	42,700
	Italy	Rome	301	62.4	0.1	8	11	83	46,110
	Jamaica	Kingston	11.0	2.8	0.1	16	7	75	9,940
	Japan	Tokyo	378	124.7	-0.4	7	11	85	45,180
	Jordan	Amman	89.3	10.9	0.8	23	3	76	10,520
	Kazakhstan	Nur-Sultan	2,725	19.2	0.8	16	8	72	24,080
	Kenya	Nairobi	580	54.7	2.2	27	5	69	4,430
	Korea, North	P'yŏngyang	121	25.8	0.5	14	9	72	1,700
	Korea, South	Seoul	99.3	51.7	0.3	7	7	83	44,390
	Kosovo	Priština	10.9	1.9	0.7	15	7	73	12,140

FLAG	COUNTRY	CAPITAL CITY	AREA thousand square kilometres 2021	POPULATION in millions 2021	POPULATION CHANGE percent per year 2021	BIRTHS per thousand people 2021	DEATHS per thousand people 2021	LIFE EXPECTANCY years 2021	INCOME US $ per person 2019
	Kuwait	Kuwait	17.8	3.0	1.2	18	2	79	58,550
	Kyrgyzstan	Bishkek	200	6.0	0.9	20	6	72	5,080
	Laos	Vientiane	237	7.6	1.5	23	7	66	7,980
	Latvia	Riga	64.6	1.9	-1.1	9	15	76	32,550
	Lebanon	Beirut	10.4	5.3	0.7	13	6	79	14,920
	Lesotho	Maseru	30.4	2.2	0.7	23	11	59	3,330
	Liberia	Monrovia	111	5.2	2.7	37	7	65	1,320
	Libya	Tripoli	1,760	7.0	1.8	22	3	77	16,130
	Lithuania	Vilnius	65.2	2.7	-1.0	9	15	76	38,630
	Luxembourg	Luxembourg	2.6	0.6	1.7	12	7	83	79,670
	Macedonia, North	Skopje	25.7	2.1	0.1	11	10	77	17,270
	Madagascar	Antananarivo	587	27.5	2.3	29	6	68	1,660
	Malawi	Lilongwe	118	20.3	2.4	29	5	72	1,080
	Malaysia	Kuala Lumpur/ Putrajaya	330	33.5	1.1	15	6	76	28,830
	Mali	Bamako	1,240	20.1	3.0	42	9	62	2,350
	Malta	Valletta	0.3	0.5	0.8	10	8	83	43,970
	Mauritania	Nouakchott	1,026	4.1	2.0	28	8	65	5,360
	Mauritius	Port Louis	2.0	1.4	0.5	12	7	77	26,840
	Mexico	Mexico City	1,958	130.2	1.0	17	5	77	20,340
	Moldova	Chisinau	33.9	3.3	-1.1	10	12	72	14,330
	Mongolia	Ulan Bator	1,567	3.2	0.9	16	6	71	11,420
	Montenegro	Podgorica	14.0	0.6	-0.4	11	10	78	24,120
	Morocco	Rabat	447	36.6	0.9	18	7	74	7,680
	Mozambique	Maputo	802	30.9	2.6	38	11	56	1,310
	Myanmar	Naypyidaw	677	57.1	0.8	17	7	70	5,170
	Namibia	Windhoek	824	2.7	1.8	25	7	66	9,780
	Nepal	Katmandu	147	30.4	0.8	18	6	72	3,610
	Netherlands	Amsterdam/ The Hague	41.5	17.3	0.4	11	9	82	61,520
	New Zealand	Wellington	271	5.0	1.3	13	7	82	44,090
	Nicaragua	Managua	130	6.2	0.9	17	5	75	5,440
	Niger	Niamey	1,267	23.6	3.7	47	10	60	1,330
	Nigeria	Abuja	924	219.5	2.5	34	9	61	5,190
	Norway	Oslo	324	5.5	0.8	12	8	82	72,920
	Oman	Muscat	310	3.7	1.9	23	3	77	26,210
	Pakistan	Islamabad	796	238.2	2.0	27	6	69	4,800
	Panama	Panamá	75.5	3.9	1.2	17	5	79	30,690
	Papua New Guinea	Port Moresby	463	7.4	1.6	22	6	70	4,360
	Paraguay	Asunción	407	7.3	1.2	10	5	78	12,790
	Peru	Lima	1,285	32.2	0.9	17	6	75	12,790
	Philippines	Manila	300	110.8	1.5	23	6	70	10,230
	Poland	Warsaw	323	38.2	-0.2	9	11	79	33,770
	Portugal	Lisbon	88.8	10.3	-0.2	8	11	81	37,040
	Qatar	Doha	11.0	2.5	1.2	9	1	80	91,670

FLAG	COUNTRY	CAPITAL CITY	AREA thousand square kilometres 2021	POPULATION in millions 2021	POPULATION CHANGE percent per year 2021	BIRTHS per thousand people 2021	DEATHS per thousand people 2021	LIFE EXPECTANCY years 2021	INCOME US $ per person 2019
	Romania	Bucharest	238	21.2	-0.4	8	12	76	32,860
	Russia	Moscow	17,075	142.3	-0.2	10	13	72	28,270
	Rwanda	Kigali	26.3	12.9	1.8	27	6	65	2,250
	Saudi Arabia	Riyadh	2,150	34.8	1.6	15	3	76	49,520
	Senegal	Dakar	197	16.1	2.3	31	8	64	3,470
	Serbia	Belgrade	77.5	7.0	-0.5	9	13	77	18,440
	Sierra Leone	Freetown	71.7	6.8	2.4	35	10	60	1,770
	Singapore	Singapore	0.68	5.9	1.0	9	4	86	92,270
	Slovakia	Bratislava	49.0	5.4	-0.1	9	10	78	32,920
	Slovenia	Ljubljana	20.3	2.1	-0.0	9	10	82	41,750
	Solomon Islands	Honiara	28.9	0.7	1.8	23	4	76	2,750
	Somalia	Mogadishu	638	12.1	2.4	38	12	55	-
	South Africa	Cape Town/ Pretoria	1,221	57.0	1.0	19	9	65	12,670
	South Sudan	Juba	620	11.0	5.1	38	10	59	1,080
	Spain	Madrid	498	47.3	-0.0	8	10	82	43,560
	Sri Lanka	Colombo/ Sri Jayewardenepura Kotte	65.6	23.0	0.6	14	6	78	13,260
	Sudan	Khartoum	1,886	46.8	2.6	34	6	67	3,990
	Suriname	Paramaribo	163	0.6	0.9	15	6	74	15,310
	Sweden	Stockholm	450	10.3	0.7	12	9	83	58,060
	Switzerland	Berne	41.3	8.5	0.7	10	8	83	73,800
	Syria	Damascus	185	20.4	5.3	23	4	74	2,900
	Taiwan	Taipei	36.0	23.6	0.0	7	8	81	50,500
	Tajikistan	Dushanbe	143	9.0	1.4	21	6	69	4,110
	Tanzania	Dodoma	945	62.1	2.8	34	5	70	2,700
	Thailand	Bangkok	513	69.5	0.3	10	8	77	18,570
	Timor-Leste	Dili	14.9	1.4	2.2	31	6	70	4,970
	Togo	Lomé	56.8	8.3	2.5	32	5	71	1,670
	Trinidad and Tobago	Port of Spain	5.1	1.2	-0.3	11	9	75	27,140
	Tunisia	Tunis	164	11.8	0.8	15	6	77	10,850
	Turkey	Ankara	775	82.5	0.7	15	6	76	27,660
	Turkmenistan	Ashkhabad	488	5.6	1.0	18	6	72	14,570
	Uganda	Kampala	241	44.7	3.3	42	5	69	2,220
	Ukraine	Kiev	604	43.7	-0.5	9	14	73	13,750
	United Arab Emirates	Abu Dhabi	83.6	9.9	0.6	11	2	79	70,430
	United Kingdom	London	242	66.1	0.5	12	9	81	49,040
	USA	Washington D.C.	9,629	335.0	0.7	12	8	80	66,080
	Uruguay	Montevideo	175	3.4	0.3	13	9	78	21,180
	Uzbekistan	Tashkent	447	30.8	0.9	16	5	75	7,420
	Venezuela	Caracas	912	29.1	2.5	18	7	72	17,080
	Vietnam	Hanoi	332	102.8	1.0	16	6	75	7,910
	Yemen	Sana	528	30.4	1.9	25	6	67	3,520
	Zambia	Lusaka	753	19.1	2.9	35	6	66	3,560
	Zimbabwe	Harare	391	14.8	1.9	33	9	63	2,740

A
B
C
7°
6°
5°
1
2
58°
57°
Cape Wrath
Butt of Lewis
Flannan Islands
Stornoway
Lewis
Outer Hebrides
North Minch
799
Harris
Little Minch
Ullapool
Ben Dearg
1081
Loch Maree
Loch Fannich
North Uist
Benbecula
Loch Torridon
North West Highlands
Portree
Skye
Stromeferry
Loch Carron
South Uist
Carn Eige
1182
Kyle of Lochalsh
992
Glen Affric
Glen Garry
Inner Hebrides
Barra
Rùm
Mallaig
Eigg
Loch Morar
Loch Arkaig
Loch Lochy
Ben Nevis
1345
Fort William
Barra Head
Point of
Sut
Beau

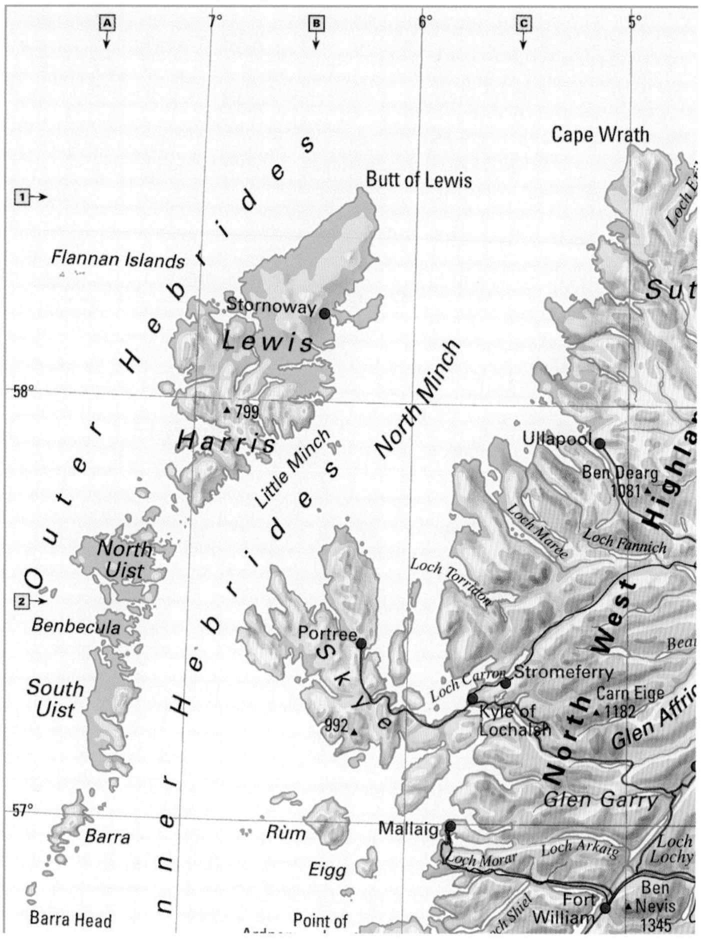

This index contains the names of all the principal places and features shown on the maps in the atlas. They are listed in alphabetical order. If a name has a description as part of it, for example, Bay of Biscay, the name is in alphabetical order, followed by the description:

Biscay, Bay of ......

Sometimes, the same name occurs in more than one country. In these cases, the country names are added after each place name. For example:

Córdoba, *Argentina* ..
Córdoba, *Spain* .....

All rivers are indexed to their mouths or confluences and are followed by the symbol →. All country names are followed by the symbol ■.

Each place name is followed by its latitude and longitude, and then its map page number and figure-letter grid reference. Both latitude and longitude are measured in degrees and minutes. There are 60 minutes in a degree. The latitude is followed by N(orth) or S(outh) and the longitude by E(ast) or W(est). The map extract on the left shows how to find a place by estimating the required distance from the nearest line of latitude or longitude on the map page. Portree is used as an example:

Portree .... 57°25′N 6°12′W **18 2B**

There are 60 minutes between the lines and so to find the position of Portree an estimate has to be made. 25 parts of the 60 minutes north of the 57°N latitude line, and 12 parts of the 60 minutes west of the 6°W longitude line.

The latitude and longitude are followed by a number in bold type which refers to the number of the map page on which the place or feature appears. Portree is on page **18**.

The figure and letter which follow the page number give the grid rectangle on the map within which the place or feature appears. The grid is formed by the lines of latitude and longitude. The columns are labelled at the top and bottom of the map with a letter and the rows at the sides of the map with a number. Portree is in the grid square where row **2** crosses column **B**.

A

Aalborg 57° 2′N 9°54′ E **32 4N**
Aarhus 56° 8′N 10°11′ E **32 4P**
Aba 5°10′N 7°19′ E **52 2C**
Ābādān 30°22′N 48°20′ E **48 3E**
Abakan 53°40′N 91°10′ E **41 4K**
ABC Islands 12°15′N 69° 0′W **63 5L**
Abeokuta 7° 3′N 3°19′ E **52 2B**
Aberdare 51°43′N 3°27′W **17 5C**
Aberdare Range 0°15′S 36°50′ E **53 3B**
Aberdeen 57° 9′N 2° 5′W **18 2F**
Abergavenny 51°49′N 3° 1′W **17 5C**
Aberystwyth 52°25′N 4° 5′W **17 4B**
Abidjan 5°26′N 3°58′W **51 5B**
Abu Dhabi 24°28′N 54°22′ E **48 5F**
Abuja 9° 5′N 7°32′ E **52 2C**
Acapulco 16°51′N 99°55′W **62 4D**
Accra 5°35′N 0° 6′W **52 2A**
Accrington 53°45′N 2°22′W **16 3D**
Achill Island 53°58′N 10° 1′W **19 3A**
Aconcagua 32°39′S 70° 0′W **64 7D**
Acre 9° 1′S 71° 0′W **66 4A**
Ad Dammām 26°20′N 50° 5′ E **48 4F**
Adamawa Highlands 7°20′N 12°20′ E **52 2D**
Adana 37° 0′N 35°16′ E **35 4L**
Adare, Cape 71° 0′S 171° 0′ E **67 11E**
Addis Ababa 9° 2′N 38°42′ E **51 5F**
Adelaide 34°52′S 138°30′ E **54 8G**
Adelaide Island 67°15′S 68°30′W **67 17D**
Adélie Land 68° 0′S 140° 0′ E **67 10D**
Aden 12°45′N 45° 0′ E **46 5C**
Aden, Gulf of 12°30′N 47°30′ E **46 5C**
Adriatic Sea 43° 0′N 16° 0′ E **36 3F**
Ægean Sea 38°30′N 25° 0′ E **35 4J**
Aeolian Islands 38°30′N 14°57′ E **36 5E**
Afghanistan ■ 33° 0′N 65° 0′ E **46 3E**
Africa 10° 0′N 20° 0′ E **50 5E**
Agra 27°17′N 77°58′ E **46 4F**
Aguascalientes 21°53′N 102°18′W **62 3D**
Ahmadabad 23° 0′N 72°40′ E **46 4F**
Ahvāz 31°20′N 48°40′ E **48 3E**
Ailsa Craig 55°15′N 5° 6′W **18 4C**
Aïr 18°30′N 8° 0′ E **50 4C**
Airdrie 55°52′N 3°57′W **18 4E**
Aire → 53°43′N 0°55′W **13 5F**
Aix-en-Provence 43°32′N 5°27′ E **33 11L**
Ajaccio 41°55′N 8°40′ E **33 12N**
Akita 39°45′N 140° 7′ E **45 3D**
Akosombo Dam 6°20′N 0° 5′ E **52 2B**
Akron 41° 5′N 81°31′W **59 2K**
Aksu 41° 5′N 80°10′ E **42 2C**
Al ′Ayn 24°15′N 55°45′ E **48 5G**
Al Aziziyah 32°30′N 13° 1′ E **34 5F**
Al Ḥillah 32°30′N 44°25′ E **48 3D**
Al Hufūf 25°25′N 49°45′ E **48 4E**
Al Jubayl 27° 0′N 49°50′ E **48 4E**
Al Kūt 32°30′N 46° 0′ E **48 3E**
Al Mubarraz 25°30′N 49°40′ E **48 4E**
Alabama 33° 0′N 87° 0′W **59 4J**
Alabama → 31° 8′N 87°57′W **59 4J**
Alagoas 9° 0′S 36° 0′W **66 4H**
Åland Islands 60°15′N 20° 0′ E **31 3D**
Alaska 64° 0′N 154° 0′W **57 3D**
Alaska, Gulf of 58° 0′N 145° 0′W **56 4E**
Alaska Peninsula 56° 0′N 159° 0′W **56 4D**
Alaska Range 62°50′N 151° 0′W **56 3D**
Albacete 39° 0′N 1°50′W **33 13H**
Albania ■ 41° 0′N 20° 0′ E **35 3G**
Albany, *Australia* 35° 1′S 117°58′ E **54 9C**
Albany, *U.S.A.* 42°39′N 73°45′W **59 2M**
Albuquerque 35° 5′N 106°39′W **58 3E**
Aldabra Islands 9°22′S 46°28′ E **51 6G**
Aldeburgh 52°10′N 1°37′ E **17 4H**
Alderney 49°42′N 2°11′W **17 7D**
Aleppo 36°10′N 37°15′ E **48 2C**
Ålesund 62°28′N 6°12′ E **31 3B**
Aleutian Islands 52° 0′N 175° 0′W **68 2A**
Alexander Island 69° 0′S 70° 0′W **67 17D**
Alexandria 31°13′N 29°58′ E **48 3A**
Algarve 36°58′N 8°20′W **33 14D**
Algeria ■ 28°30′N 2° 0′ E **51 3C**
Algiers 36°42′N 3° 8′ E **51 2C**
Alicante 38°23′N 0°30′W **33 13H**
Alice Springs 23°40′S 133°50′ E **54 6F**
Allegheny Mountains 38°15′N 80°10′W **59 3L**
Allen, Bog of 53°15′N 7° 0′W **19 3D**
Allen, Lough 54° 8′N 8° 4′W **19 2C**
Alloa 56° 7′N 3°47′W **18 3E**
Almaty 43°15′N 76°57′ E **40 5H**
Almería 36°52′N 2°27′W **33 14G**
Alness 57°41′N 4°16′W **18 2D**
Alnwick 55°24′N 1°42′W **16 1E**
Alps 46°30′N 9°30′ E **33 9N**
Altai 46°40′N 92°45′ E **40 4J**
Altay 47°48′N 88°10′ E **42 2C**
Altun Shan 38°30′N 88° 0′ E **42 3C**
Amapá 1°40′N 52° 0′W **66 2E**
Amarillo 35°13′N 101°50′W **58 3F**
Amazon → 0° 5′S 50° 0′W **66 3E**
Amazonas 5° 0′S 65° 0′W **66 4B**
Ambon 3°43′S 128°12′ E **47 7L**
American Highland 73° 0′S 75° 0′ E **67 6E**
American Samoa 14°20′S 170° 0′W **55 4S**
Amery Ice Shelf 69°30′S 72° 0′ E **67 6D**
Amiens 49°54′N 2°16′ E **33 8J**
Amlwch 53°24′N 4°20′W **16 3B**
′Ammān 31°57′N 35°52′ E **48 3C**
Amritsar 31°35′N 74°57′ E **46 3F**
Amsterdam 52°23′N 4°54′ E **32 6L**
Amudarya → 43°58′N 59°34′ E **40 5F**
Amundsen Sea 72° 0′S 115° 0′W **67 15E**
Amur → 52°56′N 141°10′ E **41 4Q**
An Najaf 32° 3′N 44°15′ E **48 3D**
An Nāşirīyah 31° 0′N 46°15′ E **48 3E**
Anápolis 16°15′S 48°50′W **66 6F**
Anatolia 39° 0′N 30° 0′ E **48 2B**
Anchorage 61°13′N 149°54′W **57 3E**
Ancona 43°38′N 13°30′ E **36 3D**
Andalucía 37°35′N 5° 0′W **33 14F**
Andaman Islands 12°30′N 92°45′ E **46 5H**
Andaman Sea 13° 0′N 96° 0′ E **38 7L**
Andes 10° 0′S 75°53′W **64 5D**
Andizhan 41°10′N 72°15′ E **42 2B**
Andorra ■ 42°30′N 1°30′ E **33 11J**
Andover 51°12′N 1°29′W **17 5E**
Aneto, Pico de 42°37′N 0°40′ E **33 11J**
Angara → 58° 5′N 94°20′ E **41 4K**
Angel Falls 5°57′N 62°30′W **63 6M**
Angers 47°30′N 0°35′W **33 9H**
Anglesey 53°17′N 4°20′W **16 3B**
Angola ■ 12° 0′S 18° 0′ E **51 7D**
Angoulême 45°39′N 0°10′ E **33 10J**
Angus 56°46′N 2°56′W **15 3E**
Ankara 39°57′N 32°54′ E **35 4K**
Annaba 36°50′N 7°46′ E **34 4E**
Annan 54°59′N 3°16′W **18 5E**
Annan → 54°58′N 3°16′W **18 4E**
Annapolis 38°59′N 76°30′W **59 3L**
Annobón 1°25′S 5°36′ E **50 6C**
Anshan 41° 5′N 122°58′ E **43 2G**
Antalya 36°52′N 30°45′ E **35 4K**
Antananarivo 18°55′S 47°31′ E **51 7G**
Antarctic Peninsula 67° 0′S 60° 0′W **67 18D**
Antarctica 90° 0′S 0° 0′W **67 3F**
Antigua & Barbuda ■ 17°20′N 61°48′W **63 4M**
Antofagasta 23°50′S 70°30′W **65 6D**
Antrim 54°43′N 6°14′W **19 2E**
Antrim, Mountains of 55° 3′N 6°14′W **19 2E**
Antrim & Newtownabbey 54°40′N 6°11′W **15 4C**
Antwerp 51°13′N 4°25′ E **32 7L**
Anvers Island 64°30′S 63°40′W **67 17D**
Aomori 40°45′N 140°45′ E **45 2D**
Aoraki Mount Cook 43°36′S 170° 9′ E **55 10P**
Apennines 44°30′N 10° 0′ E **36 3D**
Apia 13°50′S 171°50′W **55 4S**
Appalachian Mountains 38° 0′N 80° 0′W **59 3K**
Appleby-in-Westmorland 54°35′N 2°29′W **16 2D**
Aqaba 29°31′N 35° 0′ E **48 4C**
Arabia 25° 0′N 45° 0′ E **38 6F**
Arabian Sea 16° 0′N 65° 0′ E **46 5E**
Aracaju 10°55′S 37° 4′W **66 5H**
Araçatuba 21°10′S 50°30′W **66 7E**
Araguaia → 5°21′S 48°41′W **66 4F**
Arāk 34° 0′N 49°40′ E **48 3E**
Araks → 40° 5′N 48°29′ E **48 1E**
Aral Sea 45° 0′N 58°20′ E **40 5F**
Aran Islands 53° 6′N 9°38′W **19 3B**
Ararat, Mount 39°50′N 44°15′ E **48 2D**
Arbroath 56°34′N 2°35′W **18 3F**
Arctic Ocean 78° 0′N 160° 0′W **67 18B**
Ardabīl 38°15′N 48°18′ E **48 2E**
Ardnamurchan, Point of 56°43′N 6°14′W **18 3B**
Ardrossan 55°39′N 4°49′W **18 4D**
Ards & North Down 54°32′N 5°39′W **15 4D**
Ards Peninsula 54°33′N 5°34′W **19 2F**
Arequipa 16°20′S 71°30′W **65 5D**
Argentina ■ 35° 0′S 66° 0′W **65 7E**
Argun → 53°20′N 121°28′ E **43 1F**
Argyle, Lake 16°20′S 128°40′ E **54 5E**
Argyll 56°10′N 5°20′W **18 3C**
Argyll & Bute 56°13′N 5°28′W **15 3D**
Arica 18°32′S 70°20′W **65 5D**
Aripuanã → 5° 7′S 60°25′W **66 4C**
Arizona 34° 0′N 112° 0′W **58 4D**
Arkaig, Loch 56°59′N 5°10′W **18 3C**
Arkansas 35° 0′N 92°30′W **59 4H**
Arkansas → 33°47′N 91° 4′W **59 4H**
Arkhangelsk 64°38′N 40°36′ E **31 3J**
Arklow 52°48′N 6°10′W **19 4E**
Armagh 54°21′N 6°39′W **19 2E**
Armagh, Bansbridge & Craigavon 54°20′N 6°28′W **15 4C**
Armenia ■ 40°20′N 45° 0′ E **48 1D**
Arnhem 51°58′N 5°55′ E **32 7L**
Arnhem Land 13°10′S 134°30′ E **54 4F**
Arran 55°34′N 5°12′W **18 4C**
Arranmore 55° 0′N 8°30′W **19 1C**
Aru Islands 6° 0′S 134°30′ E **47 7M**
Aruba 12°30′N 70° 0′W **63 5L**
Arusha 3°20′S 36°40′ E **53 3B**
Arvayheer 46°15′N 102°48′ E **42 2E**
As Sulaymānīyah, *Iraq* 35°35′N 45°29′ E **48 2E**
As Sulaymānīyah, *Saudi Arabia* 24° 9′N 47°18′ E **48 5E**
Asahikawa 43°46′N 142°22′ E **45 2D**
Asamankese 5°50′N 0°40′W **52 2A**
Ascension Island 7°57′S 14°23′W **51 6A**
Ashford 51° 8′N 0°53′ E **17 5G**
Ashington 55°11′N 1°33′W **16 1E**
Ashkhabad 37°58′N 58°24′ E **48 2G**
Ashton under Lyne 53°29′N 2° 6′W **16 3D**
Asmara 15°19′N 38°55′ E **51 4F**
Assam 26° 0′N 93° 0′ E **46 4H**
Astrakhan 46°25′N 48° 5′ E **38 5E**
Asunción 25°10′S 57°30′W **65 6F**
Aswân 24° 4′N 32°57′ E **48 5B**
Asyût 27°11′N 31° 4′ E **48 4B**
Aţ Tā′if 21° 5′N 40°27′ E **48 5D**
Atacama Desert 24° 0′S 69°20′W **64 6E**
Athens 37°58′N 23°43′ E **35 4H**
Athlone 53°25′N 7°56′W **19 3D**
Athy 53° 0′N 7° 0′W **19 4E**
Atlanta 33°45′N 84°23′W **59 4K**
Atlantic Ocean 0° 0′ 20° 0′W **68 3G**
Atlas Mountains 32°30′N 5° 0′W **50 2B**
Auckland 36°52′S 174°46′ E **55 [illegible]**
Augsburg 48°25′N 10°52′ E **33 8P**
Augusta 44°19′N 69°47′W **59 2N**
Austin 30°17′N 97°45′W **58 4G**
Australia ■ 23° 0′S 135° 0′ E **54 6D**
Australian Capital Territory (A.C.T.) 35°30′S 149° 0′ E **54 9J**
Austria ■ 47° 0′N 14° 0′ E **34 2F**
Aviemore 57°12′N 3°50′W **18 2E**
Avignon 43°57′N 4°50′ E **33 11L**
Avon →, *Bristol* 51°29′N 2°41′W **17 5D**
Avon →, *Dorset* 50°44′N 1°46′W **17 6E**
Avon →, *Warwickshire* 52° 0′N 2° 8′W **17 4D**
Awe, Loch 56°17′N 5°16′W **18 3C**
Ayers Rock = Uluru 25°23′S 131° 5′ E **54 7F**

Aylesbury 51°49′N 0°49′W 17 5F
Ayr 55°28′N 4°38′W 18 4D
Azerbaijan ■ 40°20′N 48° 0′ E 48 1E
Azores 38° 0′N 27° 0′W 68 3H
Azov, Sea of 46° 0′N 36°30′ E 35 2L

B

Bābol 36°40′N 52°50′ E 48 2F
Babylon 32°34′N 44°22′ E 48 3D
Bacabal 4°15′S 44°45′W 66 3G
Bacău 46°35′N 26°55′ E 35 2J
Badajoz 38°50′N 6°59′W 33 13E
Baffin Bay 72° 0′N 64° 0′W 56 2N
Baffin Island 68° 0′N 75° 0′W 56 2M
Baghdād 33°20′N 44°23′ E 48 3D
Bahamas, The ■ 24° 0′N 75° 0′W 63 3J
Bahía 12° 0′S 42° 0′W 66 5G
Bahía Blanca 38°35′S 62°13′W 65 7E
Bahrain ■ 26° 0′N 50°35′ E 48 4F
Baikal, Lake 53° 0′N 108° 0′ E 41 4L
Baja California 31°10′N 115°12′W 58 4C
Bakersfield 35°23′N 119° 1′W 58 3C
Baku 40°29′N 49°56′ E 48 1E
Bala, L. 52°53′N 3°37′W 13 5E
Balbriggan 53°37′N 6°11′W 19 3E
Balearic Islands 39°30′N 3° 0′ E 33 13J
Bali 8°20′S 115° 0′ E 47 7K
Balıkeşir 39°39′N 27°53′ E 35 4J
Balkan Mountains 43°15′N 23° 0′ E 35 3H
Balkhash, Lake 46° 0′N 74°50′ E 40 5H
Ballachulish 56°41′N 5° 8′W 18 3C
Ballarat 37°33′S 143°50′ E 54 9H
Ballater 57° 3′N 3° 3′W 18 2E
Ballina 54° 7′N 9° 9′W 19 2B
Ballinasloe 53°20′N 8°13′W 19 3C
Ballycastle 55°12′N 6°15′W 19 1E
Ballymena 54°53′N 6°18′W 19 2E
Ballymoney 55° 5′N 6°23′W 19 1E
Balmoral 57° 3′N 3°13′W 18 2E
Balsas → 17°55′N 102°10′W 62 4D
Baltic Sea 57° 0′N 19° 0′ E 31 4D
Baltimore 39°17′N 76°36′W 59 3L
Bam 29° 7′N 58°14′ E 48 4G
Bamako 12°34′N 7°55′W 51 4B
Banbridge 54°21′N 6°16′W 19 2E
Banbury 52° 4′N 1°20′W 17 4E
Banda Aceh 5°35′N 95°20′ E 47 6H
Banda Sea 6° 0′S 130° 0′ E 47 7L
Bandar-e Abbās 27°15′N 56°15′ E 48 4G
Bandar Seri Begawan 4°52′N 115° 0′ E 47 6K
Bandeira, Pico da 20°26′S 41°47′W 66 7G
Bandon 51°44′N 8°44′W 19 5C
Bandung 6°54′S 107°36′ E 47 7J
Banff 57°40′N 2°33′W 18 2F
Bangalore = Bengaluru 12°59′N 77°40′ E 46 5F
Bangka 2° 0′S 105°50′ E 47 7J
Bangkok 13°45′N 100°35′ E 47 5J
Bangladesh ■ 24° 0′N 90° 0′ E 46 4G
Bangor, *Northern Ireland* 54°40′N 5°40′W 19 2F
Bangor, *Wales* 53°14′N 4° 8′W 16 3B
Bangui 4°23′N 18°35′ E 51 5D
Banjarmasin 3°20′S 114°35′ E 47 7K
Banjul 13°28′N 16°40′W 51 4A
Bann → 54°30′N 6°31′W 19 2E
Bantry 51°41′N 9°27′W 19 5B
Bantry Bay 51°37′N 9°44′W 19 5B
Baoding 38°50′N 115°28′ E 43 3F
Baotou 40°32′N 110° 2′ E 43 2F
Barbados ■ 13°10′N 59°30′W 63 5N
Barcelona, *Spain* 41°22′N 2°10′ E 33 12K
Barcelona, *Venezuela* 10°10′N 64°40′W 63 5M
Bardsey Island 52°45′N 4°47′W 16 4B
Barents Sea 73° 0′N 39° 0′ E 31 2H
Bari 41° 8′N 16°51′ E 36 4F
Barkly Tableland 17°50′S 136°40′ E 54 5G
Barnsley 53°34′N 1°27′W 16 3E
Barnstaple 51° 5′N 4° 4′W 17 5B
Barquísimeto 10° 4′N 69°19′W 63 5L
Barra 57° 0′N 7°29′W 18 3A
Barra Head 56°47′N 7°40′W 18 3A
Barranquilla 11° 0′N 74°50′W 63 5K
Barrow → 52°25′N 6°58′W 19 4E
Barrow-in-Furness 54° 7′N 3°14′W 16 2C
Barry 51°24′N 3°16′W 17 5C
Basel 47°35′N 7°35′ E 33 9M
Basildon 51°34′N 0°28′ E 17 5G
Basingstoke 51°15′N 1° 5′W 17 5E
Basque Country 43°15′N 1°20′W 33 11G
Basra 30°30′N 47°50′ E 48 3E
Bass Strait 39°15′S 146°30′ E 54 9J
Basseterre 17°17′N 62°43′W 63 4M
Bataques 32°33′N 115° 4′W 62 1A
Bath 51°23′N 2°22′W 17 5D
Baton Rouge 30°27′N 91°11′W 59 4H
Batumi 41°39′N 41°44′ E 35 3M
Bauchi 10°22′N 9°48′ E 52 1C
Bauru 22°10′S 49° 0′W 66 7F
Bavaria 48°50′N 12° 0′ E 33 8P
Bayonne 43°30′N 1°28′W 33 11H
Beachy Head 50°44′N 0°15′ E 17 6G
Bear Island, *Arctic* 74°30′N 19° 0′ E 67 8B
Bear Island, *Ireland* 51°38′N 9°50′W 19 5B
Beardmore Glacier 84°30′S 170° 0′ E 67 11F
Beaufort Sea 72° 0′N 140° 0′W 56 2E
Beauly → 57°29′N 4°27′W 18 2D
Bebington 53°22′N 3° 0′W 16 3D
Bedford 52° 8′N 0°28′W 17 4F
Beijing 39°53′N 116°21′ E 43 3F
Beira 19°50′S 34°52′ E 51 7F
Beirut 33°53′N 35°31′ E 48 3C
Bejaïa 36°42′N 5° 2′ E 34 4D
Belarus ■ 53°30′N 27° 0′ E 31 5F
Belém 1°20′S 48°30′W 66 3F
Belfast 54°37′N 5°56′W 19 2F
Belfast Lough 54°40′N 5°50′W 19 2F
Belgium ■ 50°30′N 5° 0′ E 32 7K
Belgrade 44°50′N 20°37′ E 35 3H
Belize ■ 17° 0′N 88°30′W 62 4G
Belize City 17°25′N 88°10′W 62 4G
Bellingshausen Sea 66° 0′S 80° 0′W 67 17D
Belmopan 17°18′N 88°30′W 62 4G
Belo Horizonte 19°55′S 43°56′W 66 6G
Belomorsk 64°35′N 34°54′ E 31 3G
Ben Cruachan 56°26′N 5° 8′W 18 3C
Ben Lawers 56°32′N 4°14′W 18 3D
Ben Macdhui 57° 4′N 3°40′W 18 2E
Ben Nevis 56°48′N 5° 1′W 18 3D
Benbecula 57°26′N 7°21′W 18 2A
Bendigo 36°40′S 144°15′ E 54 9H
Bengal, Bay of 15° 0′N 90° 0′ E 46 4G
Bengaluru 12°59′N 77°40′ E 46 5F
Benghazi 32°11′N 20° 3′ E 51 2E
Benin ■ 10° 0′N 2° 0′ E 52 2B
Benin, Bight of 5° 0′N 3° 0′ E 52 2B
Benin City 6°20′N 5°31′ E 52 2C
Benue → 7°48′N 6°46′ E 52 2C
Berezniki 59°24′N 56°46′ E 40 4F
Bergen 60°20′N 5°20′ E 31 3B
Bering Sea 58° 0′N 171° 0′W 56 3B
Bering Strait 65°30′N 169° 0′W 56 3C
Berkner Island 79°30′S 50° 0′W 67 18E
Berlin 52°31′N 13°23′ E 32 6Q
Bermuda 32°18′N 64°45′W 63 1M
Berne 46°57′N 7°28′ E 33 9M
Berwick-upon-Tweed 55°46′N 2° 0′W 16 1D
Besançon 47°15′N 6° 2′ E 33 9M
Beverley 53°51′N 0°26′W 16 3F
Bexhill 50°51′N 0°29′ E 17 6G
Bhutan ■ 27°25′N 90°30′ E 46 4G
Białystok 53°10′N 23°10′ E 31 5E
Bideford 51° 1′N 4°13′W 17 5B
Bié Plateau 12° 0′S 16° 0′ E 50 7D
Bielefeld 52° 1′N 8°33′ E 32 6N
Bighorn Mountains 44°25′N 107° 0′W 58 2E
Bilbao 43°16′N 2°56′W 33 11G
Billingham 54°36′N 1°17′W 16 2E
Bioko 3°30′N 8°40′ E 52 3C
Birkenhead 53°23′N 3° 2′W 16 3C
Birmingham, *U.K.* 52°29′N 1°52′W 17 4E
Birmingham, *U.S.A.* 33°31′N 86°48′W 59 4J
Biscay, Bay of 45° 0′N 2° 0′W 33 10F
Bishkek 42°54′N 74°46′ E 42 2B
Bishop Auckland 54°39′N 1°40′W 16 2E
Bishop's Stortford 51°52′N 0°10′ E 17 5G
Bismarck 46°48′N 100°47′W 58 1F
Bismarck Archipelago 2°30′S 150° 0′ E 54 2K
Bissau 11°45′N 15°45′W 51 4A
Bizerte 37°15′N 9°50′ E 34 4E
Black Hills 44° 0′N 103°45′W 58 2F
Black Sea 43°30′N 35° 0′ E 35 3K
Black Volta → 8°41′N 1°33′W 52 2A
Blackburn 53°45′N 2°29′W 16 3D
Blackpool 53°49′N 3° 3′W 16 3C
Blackwater → 52° 4′N 7°52′W 19 4C
Blaenau Ffestiniog 53° 0′N 3°56′W 16 4C
Blaenau Gwent 51°48′N 3°12′W 15 6E
Blair Atholl 56°46′N 3°50′W 18 3E
Blairgowrie 56°35′N 3°21′W 18 3E
Blanc, Mont 45°48′N 6°50′ E 33 10M
Blarney 51°56′N 8°33′W 19 5C
Blida 36°30′N 2°49′ E 34 4D
Bloemfontein 29° 6′S 26° 7′ E 51 8E
Bloody Foreland 55°10′N 8°17′W 19 1C
Blue Nile → 15°38′N 32°31′ E 50 4F
Blue Ridge 36°40′N 80°50′W 59 3K
Blyth 55° 8′N 1°31′W 16 1E
Bo Hai 39° 0′N 119° 0′ E 43 3F
Boa Vista 2°48′N 60°30′W 66 2E
Bodmin 50°28′N 4°43′W 17 6B
Bodmin Moor 50°33′N 4°36′W 17 6B
Bodø 67°17′N 14°24′ E 31 2C
Boggeragh Mountains 52° 2′N 8°55′W 19 4C
Bognor Regis 50°47′N 0°40′W 17 6F
Bogotá 4°34′N 74° 0′W 63 7K
Bole 44°55′N 81°37′ E 42 2C
Bolgatanga 10°44′N 0°53′W 52 1A
Bolivia ■ 17° 6′S 64° 0′W 65 5E
Bologna 44°29′N 11°20′ E 36 2C
Bolton 53°35′N 2°26′W 16 3D
Bolzano 46°31′N 11°22′ E 36 1C
Bombay = Mumbai 18°56′N 72°50′ E 46 5F
Bonifacio, Strait of 41°12′N 9°15′ E 36 4B
Bonn 50°46′N 7° 6′ E 32 7M
Bordeaux 44°50′N 0°36′W 33 10H
Borneo 1° 0′N 115° 0′ E 47 6K
Bornholm 55°10′N 15° 0′ E 31 4C
Bosnia-Herzegovina ■ 44° 0′N 18° 0′ E 35 3G
Bosporus 41° 5′N 29° 3′ E 35 3J
Bosten Hu 41°55′N 87°40′ E 42 2C
Boston, *U.K.* 52°59′N 0° 2′W 16 4F
Boston, *U.S.A.* 42°22′N 71° 3′W 59 2M
Bothnia, Gulf of 62° 0′N 20° 0′ E 31 3E
Botswana ■ 22° 0′S 24° 0′ E 51 8E
Bougainville Island 6° 0′S 155° 0′ E 55 3L
Boulogne 50°42′N 1°36′ E 32 7J
Bourges 47° 9′N 2°25′ E 33 9K
Bournemouth 50°43′N 1°52′W 17 6E
Bowmore 55°45′N 6°17′W 18 4B
Boyne → 53°43′N 6°15′W 19 3E
Bracknell Forest 51°25′N 0°44′W 15 6F
Bradford 53°47′N 1°45′W 16 3E
Bragança 1° 0′S 47° 2′W 66 3F
Brahmaputra → 23°40′N 90°35′ E 46 4H
Braintree 51°53′N 0°34′ E 17 5G
Branco → 1°20′S 61°50′W 66 3C
Brandon Mountain 52°15′N 10°15′W 19 4A
Brasília 15°47′S 47°55′W 66 6F
Braşov 45°38′N 25°35′ E 35 2J
Bratislava 48°10′N 17° 7′ E 35 2G
Bratsk Reservoir 56°15′N 101°45′ E 41 4L
Bray 53°13′N 6° 7′W 19 3E
Brazil ■ 12° 0′S 50° 0′W 66 5E
Brazos → 28°53′N 95°23′W 59 5G
Brazzaville 4° 9′S 15°12′ E 51 6D
Brechin 56°44′N 2°39′W 18 3F
Brecon 51°57′N 3°23′W 17 5C
Brecon Beacons 51°53′N 3°26′W 17 5C
Bremen 53° 4′N 8°47′ E 32 6N
Brentwood 51°37′N 0°19′ E 17 5G
Bressay 60° 9′N 1° 6′W 18 8J
Brest, *Belarus* 52°10′N 23°40′ E 31 5E
Brest, *France* 48°24′N 4°31′W 33 8F
Bridgend 51°36′N 3°36′W 17 5C
Bridgetown 13° 6′N 59°37′W 63 5N
Bridgwater 51° 8′N 2°59′W 17 6D
Bridgwater Bay 51°15′N 3°15′W 17 5C
Bridlington 54° 5′N 0°12′W 16 2F
Brigg 53°34′N 0°28′W 16 3F
Brighton 50°49′N 0° 7′W 17 6F
Bríndisi 40°39′N 17°55′ E 36 4G
Brisbane 27°25′S 153° 2′ E 54 7K
Bristol 51°26′N 2°35′W 17 5D
Bristol Channel 51°18′N 4°30′W 17 5B
British Isles 54° 0′N 4° 0′W 28 4F
Brittany 48°10′N 3° 0′W 33 8G
Brno 49°10′N 16°35′ E 35 2G
Broad Law 55°30′N 3°21′W 18 4E
Broken Hill 31°58′S 141°29′ E 54 8H
Brooks Range 68° 0′N 152° 0′W 56 3D
Broome 18° 0′S 122°15′ E 54 5D
Brown Willy 50°35′N 4°37′W 17 6B
Brunei ■ 4°50′N 115° 0′ E 47 6K
Brunswick 52°15′N 10°31′ E 32 6P
Brunt Ice Shelf 75°30′S 25° 0′W 67 1E
Brussels 50°51′N 4°21′ E 32 7L
Bryansk 53°13′N 34°25′ E 31 5G
Bucaramanga 7° 0′N 73° 0′W 63 6K
Buchan Ness 57°29′N 1°46′W 18 2G
Buckie 57°41′N 2°58′W 18 2F
Buckinghamshire 51°53′N 0°55′W 15 6F
Bucureşti 44°27′N 26°10′ E 35 3J
Budapest 47°29′N 19° 3′ E 35 2G
Bude 50°49′N 4°34′W 17 6B
Buenaventura 3°53′N 77° 4′W 63 7J
Buenos Aires 34°36′S 58°22′W 65 7F
Buffalo 42°53′N 78°53′W 59 2L
Bug → 46°59′N 31°58′ E 35 2K
Builth Wells 52° 9′N 3°25′W 17 4C
Bulawayo 20° 7′S 28°32′ E 51 8E
Bulgaria ■ 42°35′N 25°30′ E 35 3H
Bunbury 33°20′S 115°35′ E 54 8C
Buncrana 55° 8′N 7°27′W 19 1D
Bundaberg 24°54′S 152°22′ E 54 6K
Bundoran 54°28′N 8°18′W 19 2C
Buraydah 26°20′N 43°59′ E 48 4D
Bure → 52°38′N 1°43′ E 16 4H
Burgas 42°33′N 27°29′ E 35 2J
Burgos 42°21′N 3°41′W 33 11G
Burgundy 47° 0′N 4°50′ E 33 9L
Burkina Faso ■ 12° 0′N 1° 0′W 51 4B
Burma = Myanmar ■ 21° 0′N 96°30′ E 47 4H
Burnley 53°47′N 2°14′W 16 3D
Bursa 40°15′N 29° 5′ E 35 3J
Burton upon Trent 52°48′N 1°38′W 16 4E
Buru 3°30′S 126°30′ E 47 7L
Burundi ■ 3°15′S 30° 0′ E 51 6F
Bury 53°35′N 2°17′W 16 3D
Bury St. Edmunds 52°15′N 0°43′ E 17 4G
Busan 35° 5′N 129° 0′ E 43 3G
Būshehr 28°55′N 50°55′ E 48 4F
Bute 55°48′N 5° 2′W 18 4C
Buxton 53°16′N 1°54′W 16 3E
Bydgoszcz 53°10′N 18° 0′ E 31 5D

C

Cabinda 5° 0′S 12°30′ E 51 6D
Cabo Verde ■ 16° 0′N 24° 0′W 70 4H
Cáceres 39°26′N 6°23′W 33 13E
Cader Idris 52°42′N 3°53′W 16 4C
Cádiz 36°30′N 6°20′W 33 14E
Caen 49°10′N 0°22′W 33 8H
Caernarfon 53° 8′N 4°16′W 16 3B
Caerphilly 51°35′N 3°13′W 17 5C
Cágliari 39°13′N 9° 7′ E 36 5B
Caha Mountains 51°45′N 9°40′W 19 5B
Cahir 52°22′N 7°56′W 19 4D
Cahirciveen 51°56′N 10°14′W 19 5A
Cairn Gorm 57° 7′N 3°39′W 18 2E
Cairns 16°57′S 145°45′ E 54 5J
Cairo 30° 2′N 31°13′ E 48 3B
Caithness 58°25′N 3°35′W 18 1E
Calabar 4°57′N 8°20′ E 52 3C
Calábria 39° 0′N 16°30′ E 36 5F
Calais 50°57′N 1°56′ E 32 7J
Calcutta = Kolkata 22°34′N 88°21′ E 46 4G
Calder → 53°44′N 1°22′W 16 3E
Caledonian Canal 57°29′N 4°15′W 18 2D
Calgary 51° 0′N 114°10′W 57 4H
Cali 3°25′N 76°35′W 63 7J
California 37°30′N 119°30′W 58 3B
California, Gulf of 27° 0′N 111° 0′W 62 2B
Callander 56°15′N 4°13′W 18 3D
Cam → 52°21′N 0°16′ E 17 4G
Camagüey 21°20′N 77°55′W 63 3J
Cambodia ■ 12°15′N 105° 0′ E 47 5J
Camborne 50°12′N 5°19′W 17 6A
Cambrian Mountains 52° 3′N 3°57′W 17 4C
Cambridge 52°12′N 0° 8′ E 17 4G
Cambridgeshire 52°25′N 0° 7′W 15 5F
Cameroon ■ 6° 0′N 12°30′ E 51 5D
Cameroun, Mount 4°13′N 9°10′ E 52 3C
Campbeltown 55°26′N 5°36′W 18 4C
Campeche 19°51′N 90°32′W 62 4F
Campeche, Gulf of 19°30′N 93° 0′W 62 3F
Campina Grande 7°20′S 35°47′W 66 4H
Campinas 22°50′S 47° 0′W 66 7F
Campo Grande 20°25′S 54°40′W 66 7E
Campos 21°50′S 41°20′W 66 7G
Canada ■ 60° 0′N 100° 0′W 57 4K
Canadian Shield 53° 0′N 75° 0′W 56 4M
Canary Islands 28°30′N 16° 0′W 51 3A
Canaveral, Cape 28°27′N 80°32′W 59 5K
Canberra 35°15′S 149° 8′ E 54 9J
Cancún 21° 8′N 86°44′W 62 3G
Cannock 52°41′N 2° 1′W 16 4D
Cantabrian Mountains 43° 0′N 5°10′W 33 11F
Canterbury 51°16′N 1° 6′ E 17 5H
Canton = Guangzhou 23° 6′N 113°13′ E 43 4F
Cape Coast 5° 5′N 1°15′W 52 2A
Cape Town 33°55′S 18°22′ E 51 9D
Cape Verde Is. 16° 0′N 24° 0′W 68 4H
Cape York Peninsula 12° 0′S 142°30′ E 54 4H
Capri 40°33′N 14°14′ E 36 4E
Caracas 10°30′N 66°55′W 63 5L
Carbón, Lago del 49°35′S 68°21′W 64 8E
Carcassonne 43°13′N 2°20′ E 33 11K
Cardiff 51°29′N 3°10′W 17 5C
Cardigan 52° 5′N 4°40′W 17 4B
Cardigan Bay 52°30′N 4°30′W 17 4B
Caribbean Sea 15° 0′N 75° 0′W 63 5J
Carlisle 54°54′N 2°56′W 16 2D
Carlow 52°50′N 6°56′W 19 4E
Carmarthen 51°52′N 4°19′W 17 5B
Carmarthen Bay 51°40′N 4°30′W 17 5B
Carn Eige 57°17′N 5° 8′W 18 2C
Carnarvon 24°51′S 113°42′ E 54 6B
Carpathians 49°30′N 21° 0′ E 35 2H
Carpentaria, Gulf of 14° 0′S 139° 0′ E 54 4G
Carrauntoohill 52° 0′N 9°45′W 19 4B
Carrick-on-Shannon 53°57′N 8° 7′W 19 3C
Carrick-on-Suir 52°21′N 7°24′W 19 4D
Carrickfergus 54°43′N 5°49′W 19 2F
Carrickmacross 53°59′N 6°43′W 19 3E
Carrigaline 51°48′N 8°23′W 19 5C
Carron, Loch 57°22′N 5°35′W 18 2C
Carson City 39°10′N 119°46′W 58 3C
Cartagena, *Colombia* 10°25′N 75°33′W 63 5J
Cartagena, *Spain* 37°38′N 0°59′W 33 14H
Casablanca 33°36′N 7°36′W 51 2B
Cascade Range 47° 0′N 121°30′W 58 1B
Cashel 52°30′N 7°53′W 19 4D
Caspian Sea 43° 0′N 50° 0′ E 40 6F
Castelló de la Plana 39°58′N 0° 3′W 33 13H
Castile 42° 0′N 5° 0′W 33 12F
Castle Douglas 54°56′N 3°56′W 18 5E
Castlebar 53°52′N 9°18′W 19 3B
Castleford 53°43′N 1°21′W 16 3E
Castletown Bearhaven 51°39′N 9°55′W 19 5B
Castries 14° 2′N 60°58′W 63 5M
Catalonia 41°40′N 1°15′ E 33 12J
Catánia 37°30′N 15° 6′ E 36 6E
Caucasus Mountains 42°50′N 44° 0′ E 28 7Q
Causeway Coast & Glens 55° 5′N 6°33′W 15 4C
Cavan 54° 0′N 7°22′W 19 3D
Caxias do Sul 29°10′S 51°10′W 66 8E
Cayenne 5° 5′N 52°18′W 65 3F
Cayman Islands 19°40′N 80°30′W 63 4H
Ceará 5° 0′S 40° 0′W 66 4G
Cebu 10°18′N 123°54′ E 47 5L
Celano 42° 5′N 13°33′ E 36 3D
Celebes 2° 0′N 120° 0′ E 47 7L
Celebes Sea 3° 0′N 123° 0′ E 47 6L
Celtic Sea 50° 9′N 9°34′W 13 6B
Central African Republic ■ 7° 0′N 20° 0′ E 51 5E
Central America 12° 0′N 85° 0′W 56 8L
Central Bedfordshire 52° 5′N 0°20′W 15 5F
Ceredigion 52°16′N 4°15′W 15 5D
Ceuta 35°52′N 5°18′W 34 4B
Chad ■ 15° 0′N 17°15′ E 51 4D
Chad, Lake 13°30′N 14°30′ E 50 4D
Chagos Archipelago 6° 0′S 72° 0′ E 46 7F
Changchun 43°57′N 125°17′ E 43 2G
Changde 29° 4′N 111°35′ E 43 4F
Changsha 28°12′N 113° 0′ E 43 4F
Changzhou 31°47′N 119°58′ E 43 3F
Channel Islands 49°19′N 2°24′W 17 7D
Chard 50°52′N 2°58′W 17 6D
Chari → 12°58′N 14°31′ E 50 4D
Charleston 38°21′N 81°38′W 59 3K
Charleville 26°24′S 146°15′ E 54 7J
Charlotte 35°13′N 80°50′W 59 3K
Chartres 48°29′N 1°30′ E 33 8J
Chatham 51°22′N 0°32′ E 17 5G
Chatham Islands 44° 0′S 176°40′W 55 10R
Chattahoochee → 30°54′N 84°57′W 59 4K
Chelmsford 51°44′N 0°29′ E 17 5G
Cheltenham 51°54′N 2° 4′W 17 5D
Chelyabinsk 55°10′N 61°24′ E 40 4G
Chelyuskin, Cape 77°30′N 103° 0′ E 41 2L
Chemnitz 50°51′N 12°54′ E 32 7Q
Chengdu 30°38′N 104° 2′ E 42 3E
Chennai 13° 8′N 80°19′ E 46 5G
Cherbourg 49°39′N 1°40′W 33 8H
Cherepovets 59° 5′N 37°55′ E 31 4H
Chernihiv 51°28′N 31°20′ E 35 1K
Chernivtsi 48°15′N 25°52′ E 35 2J
Cherwell → 51°44′N 1°14′W 17 5E
Chesapeake Bay 38° 0′N 76°10′W 59 3L
Cheshire East 53°15′N 2°15′W 15 5E
Cheshire West and Chester 53°15′N 2°40′W 15 5E
Chester 53°12′N 2°53′W 16 3D
Chesterfield 53°15′N 1°25′W 16 3E
Chesterfield Islands 19°52′S 158°15′ E 55 5L
Cheviot, The 55°29′N 2° 9′W 16 1D
Cheviot Hills 55°20′N 2°30′W 16 1D
Cheyenne 41° 8′N 104°49′W 58 2F
Chiapa → 16°42′N 93° 0′W 62 4F
Chicago 41°52′N 87°38′W 59 2J
Chichester 50°50′N 0°47′W 17 6F
Chiengmai 18°47′N 98°59′ E 47 5H
Chifeng 42°18′N 118°58′ E 43 2F
Chihuahua 28°38′N 106° 5′W 62 2C
Chile ■ 35° 0′S 72° 0′W 65 7D
Chiloé, Isla de 42°30′S 73°50′W 64 8D
Chiltern Hills 51°40′N 0°53′W 17 5F
Chimborazo 1°29′S 78°55′W 64 4D
China ■ 30° 0′N 110° 0′ E 47 3J
China, Great Wall of 38°30′N 109°30′ E 43 3E
Chios 38°27′N 26° 9′ E 35 4J
Chippenham 51°27′N 2° 6′W 17 5D
Chisinau 47° 2′N 28°50′ E 35 2J
Chita 52° 0′N 113°35′ E 41 4M
Chittagong 22°19′N 91°48′ E 46 4H
Choiseul 7° 0′S 156°40′ E 55 3L
Chongqing 29°35′N 106°25′ E 42 4E
Chorley 53°39′N 2°38′W 16 3D
Chornobyl 51°20′N 30°15′ E 31 5G
Christchurch 43°33′S 172°47′ E 55 10P
Chudskoye, Lake 58°13′N 27°30′ E 31 4F
Cienfuegos 22°10′N 80°30′W 63 3H
Cincinnati 39° 9′N 84°27′W 59 3K
Cirencester 51°43′N 1°57′W 17 5E
Ciudad Bolívar 8° 5′N 63°36′W 63 6M
Ciudad Guayana 8° 0′N 62°30′W 65 3E

Ciudad Juárez 31°44'N 106°29'W 62 1C
Ciudad Obregón 27°29'N 109°56'W 62 2C
Clackmannanshire 56°10'N 3°43'W 15 3E
Clacton-on-Sea 51°47'N 1°11' E 17 5H
Clare 52°45'N 9° 0'W 15 5B
Clare → 53°20'N 9° 2'W 19 3C
Claremorris 53°45'N 9° 0'W 19 3B
Clear, Cape 51°25'N 9°32'W 19 5B
Clear Island 51°26'N 9°30'W 19 5B
Cleethorpes 53°33'N 0° 3'W 16 3F
Clermont-Ferrand 45°46'N 3° 4' E 33 10K
Cleveland 41°29'N 81°41'W 59 2K
Clew Bay 53°50'N 9°49'W 19 3B
Clifden 53°29'N 10° 1'W 19 3A
Clonakilty 51°37'N 8°53'W 19 5C
Cloncurry 20°40'S 140°28' E 54 6H
Clonmel 52°21'N 7°42'W 19 4D
Cluj-Napoca 46°47'N 23°38' E 35 2H
Clwyd → 53°19'N 3°31'W 16 3C
Clyde → 55°55'N 4°30'W 18 4E
Clyde, Firth of 55°22'N 5° 1'W 18 4C
Clydebank 55°54'N 4°23'W 18 4D
Coalville 52°44'N 1°23'W 16 4E
Coast Ranges 39° 0'N 123° 0'W 58 3B
Coatbridge 55°52'N 4° 6'W 18 4D
Coats Land 77° 0'S 25° 0'W 67 1E
Cobh 51°51'N 8°17'W 19 5C
Cod, Cape 42° 5'N 70°10'W 56 5M
Coimbatore 11° 2'N 76°59' E 46 5F
Colchester 51°54'N 0°55' E 17 5G
Coldstream 55°39'N 2°15'W 18 4F
Coleraine 55° 8'N 6°40'W 19 1E
Coll 56°39'N 6°34'W 18 3B
Cologne 50°56'N 6°57' E 32 7M
Colombia ■ 3°45'N 73° 0'W 65 3D
Colombo 6°56'N 79°58' E 46 6F
Colonsay 56° 5'N 6°12'W 18 3B
Colorado 39°30'N 105°30'W 58 3E
Colorado →, *Argentina* 39°50'S 62° 8'W 64 7E
Colorado →, *N. Amer.* 31°45'N 114°40'W 58 4D
Colorado Plateau 37° 0'N 111° 0'W 58 3D
Colorado Springs 38°50'N 104°49'W 58 3F
Columbia 34° 0'N 81° 2'W 59 4G
Columbia → 46°15'N 124° 5'W 58 1B
Columbus 39°58'N 83° 0'W 59 3K
Colwyn Bay 53°18'N 3°44'W 16 3C
Como, Lake 46° 0'N 9°11' E 36 1B
Comorin, Cape 8° 3'N 77°40' E 46 6F
Comoros ■ 12°10'S 44°15' E 51 7G
Conakry 9°29'N 13°49'W 51 5A
Concepción 36°50'S 73° 0'W 65 7D
Conchos → 29°35'N 104°25'W 62 2C
Concord 43°12'N 71°32'W 59 2M
Congleton 53°10'N 2°13'W 16 3D
Congo ■ 1° 0'S 16° 0' E 51 6D
Congo → 6° 4'S 12°24' E 50 6D
Congo, Democratic Republic of the ■ 3° 0'S 23° 0' E 51 6E
Congo Basin 0°10'S 24°30' E 50 6E
Conn, Lough 54° 3'N 9°15'W 19 2B
Connaught 53°43'N 9°12'W 19 3B
Connecticut 41°30'N 72°45'W 59 2M
Connemara 53°29'N 9°45'W 19 3B
Consett 54°51'N 1°50'W 16 2E
Constance, Lake 47°35'N 9°25' E 33 9N
Constanța 44°14'N 28°38' E 35 3J
Constantine 36°25'N 6°42' E 34 4E
Conwy → 53°17'N 3°50'W 16 3C
Cook Islands 17° 0'S 160° 0'W 70 5A
Cook Strait 41°15'S 174°29' E 55 10P
Cookstown 54°40'N 6°43'W 19 2E
Copenhagen 55°40'N 12°26' E 32 5Q
Coquet → 55°20'N 1°32'W 16 1E
Coral Sea 15° 0'S 150° 0' E 54 4K
Corby 52°30'N 0°41'W 17 4F
Córdoba, *Argentina* 31°20'S 64°10'W 65 7E
Córdoba, *Spain* 37°50'N 4°50'W 33 14F
Corfu 39°38'N 19°50' E 35 4G
Corinth, Gulf of 38°16'N 22°30' E 35 4H
Cork 51°54'N 8°29'W 19 5C
Cornwall 50°26'N 4°40'W 15 6D
Corpus Christi 27°47'N 97°24'W 58 5G
Corrib, Lough 53°27'N 9°16'W 19 3B
Corrientes, Cape 20°25'N 105°42'W 62 3C
Corsica 42° 0'N 9° 0' E 33 11N
Cosenza 39°18'N 16°15' E 36 5F
Cosmonaut Sea 66°30'S 40° 0' E 67 5D
Costa Blanca 38°25'N 0°10'W 33 14H
Costa Brava 41°30'N 3° 0' E 33 12K
Costa del Sol 36°30'N 4°30'W 33 14G
Costa Rica ■ 10° 0'N 84° 0'W 63 5H
Côte d'Ivoire ■ 7°30'N 5° 0'W 51 5B
Cotonou 6°20'N 2°25' E 52 2B
Cotopaxi 0°40'S 78°30'W 64 4D
Cotswold Hills 51°42'N 2°10'W 17 5D
Coventry 52°25'N 1°28'W 17 4E
Crawley 51° 7'N 0°11'W 17 5F
Crete 35°15'N 25° 0' E 35 4H
Crewe 53° 6'N 2°26'W 16 3D
Crianlarich 56°24'N 4°37'W 18 3D
Crieff 56°22'N 3°50'W 18 3E
Crimea 45° 0'N 34° 0' E 35 2K
Croatia ■ 45°20'N 16° 0' E 35 2G
Cromarty 57°40'N 4° 2'W 18 2D
Cromer 52°56'N 1°17' E 16 4H
Crosby 53°30'N 3° 3'W 16 3C
Cross Fell 54°43'N 2°28'W 16 2D
Crow Head 51°35'N 10° 9'W 19 5A
Cuba ■ 22° 0'N 79° 0'W 63 3J
Cúcuta 7°54'N 72°31'W 63 6K
Cuenca 2°50'S 79° 9'W 65 4D
Cuernavaca 18°55'N 99°15'W 62 4E
Cuiabá 15°30'S 56° 0'W 66 6D
Culiacán 24°50'N 107°23'W 62 3C
Cumberland → 37° 9'N 88°25'W 59 2J
Cumberland Plateau 36° 0'N 85° 0'W 59 3J
Cumbernauld 55°57'N 3°58'W 18 4E
Cumbria 54°42'N 2°52'W 15 4E
Cumbrian Mountains 54°30'N 3° 0'W 16 2C
Cumnock 55°28'N 4°17'W 18 4D
Cupar 56°19'N 3° 1'W 18 3E
Curaçao 12°10'N 69° 0'W 63 5M
Curitiba 25°20'S 49°10'W 66 8F
Cusco 13°32'S 72° 0'W 65 5D
Cwmbran 51°39'N 3° 2'W 17 5C
Cyclades 37° 0'N 24°30' E 35 4J
Cyprus ■ 35° 0'N 33° 0' E 35 4K
Czechia ■ 50° 0'N 15° 0' E 34 2F

D

Da Nang 16° 4'N 108°13' E 47 5J
Dacca = Dhaka 23°43'N 90°26' E 46 4H
Daegu 35°50'N 128°37' E 43 3G
Daejeon 36°20'N 127°28' E 43 3G
Dakar 14°34'N 17°29'W 51 4A
Dakhla 23°50'N 15°53'W 51 3A
Dalian 38°50'N 121°40' E 43 3G
Dallas 32°47'N 96°48'W 59 4G
Damascus 33°30'N 36°18' E 48 3C
Damaturu 11°45'N 11°55' E 52 1D
Damavand 35°56'N 52°10' E 48 2F
Dampier 20°41'S 116°42' E 54 6C
Danube → 45°20'N 29°40' E 35 3J
Dar es Salaam 6°50'S 39°12' E 51 6F
Dardanelles 40°17'N 26°32' E 35 3J
Darién, Gulf of 9° 0'N 77° 0'W 63 6J
Darling → 34° 4'S 141°54' E 54 8H
Darling Range 32°30'S 116°20' E 54 8C
Darlington 54°32'N 1°33'W 16 2E
Darnley, Cape 68° 0'S 69° 0' E 67 6D
Dart → 50°24'N 3°39'W 17 6C
Dartmoor 50°38'N 3°57'W 17 6C
Dartmouth 50°21'N 3°36'W 17 6C
Darwin 12°25'S 130°51' E 54 4F
Dasht-e Kavīr 34°30'N 55° 0' E 48 3F
Dasht-e Lūt 31°30'N 58° 0' E 48 3G
Datong 40° 6'N 113°18' E 43 2F
Davao 7° 0'N 125°40' E 47 6L
Davis Sea 66° 0'S 92° 0' E 67 7D
Davis Strait 65° 0'N 58° 0'W 56 3P
Dayr az Zawr 35°20'N 40° 5' E 48 2D
Dayton 39°45'N 84°12'W 59 3K
Dead Sea 31°30'N 35°30' E 48 3C
Deal 51°13'N 1°25' E 17 5H
Death Valley 36°15'N 116°50'W 58 3C
Debrecen 47°33'N 21°42' E 35 2H
Deccan 18° 0'N 79° 0' E 46 5F
Dee →, *Scotland* 54°51'N 4° 3'W 18 5D
Dee →, *Scotland* 57° 9'N 2° 5'W 18 2F
Dee →, *Wales* 53°22'N 3°17'W 16 3D
Delaware 39° 0'N 75°20'W 59 3L
Delhi 28°39'N 77°13' E 46 4F
Denali 63° 4'N 151° 0'W 56 3D
Denizli 37°42'N 29° 2' E 35 4J
Denmark ■ 55°45'N 10° 0' E 32 5N
Denmark Strait 66° 0'N 30° 0'W 67 6C
Denpasar 8°39'S 115°13' E 47 7K
D'Entrecasteaux Islands 9° 0'S 151° 0' E 54 3K
Denver 39°42'N 104°59'W 58 3F
Derby 52°56'N 1°28'W 16 4E
Derbyshire 53°11'N 1°38'W 15 5F
Dereham 52°41'N 0°57' E 16 4G
Derg, Lough 53° 0'N 8°20'W 19 4C
Derry = Londonderry 55° 0'N 7°20'W 19 2D
Derry & Strabane 54°47'N 7°22'W 15 4C
Derwent →, *Cumbria* 54°39'N 3°33'W 16 2C
Derwent →, *Derbyshire* 52°57'N 1°28'W 16 3E
Derwent →, *North Yorkshire* 53°45'N 0°58'W 16 3F
Des Moines 41°35'N 93°37'W 59 2H
Detroit 42°19'N 83°12'W 59 2K
Deveron → 57°41'N 2°32'W 18 2F
Devon 50°50'N 3°40'W 15 6E
Dezfūl 32°20'N 48°30' E 48 3E
Dhahran 26°10'N 50° 7' E 48 4F
Dhaka 23°43'N 90°26' E 46 4H
Dieppe 49°54'N 1° 4' E 33 8J
Dijon 47°20'N 5° 3' E 33 9L
Dili 8°39'S 125°34' E 47 7L
Dinaric Alps 44° 0'N 16°30' E 35 3G
Dingle 52° 9'N 10°17'W 19 4A
Dingle Peninsula 52°12'N 10° 5'W 19 4A
Dingwall 57°36'N 4°26'W 18 2D
Diyarbakır 37°55'N 40°18' E 48 2D
Djerba 33°48'N 10°54' E 34 5F
Djerid, Chott 33°42'N 8°30' E 34 5E
Djibouti ■ 12° 0'N 43° 0' E 51 4G
Dnieper → 46°30'N 32°18' E 35 1K
Dniester → 46°18'N 30°17' E 35 2J
Dnipro 48°30'N 35° 0' E 35 2K
Dodecanese 36°35'N 27° 0' E 35 4J
Dodoma 6° 8'S 35°45' E 51 6F
Doha 25°15'N 51°35' E 48 4F
Dolgellau 52°45'N 3°53'W 16 4C
Dominica ■ 15°20'N 61°20'W 63 4M
Dominican Republic ■ 19° 0'N 70°30'W 63 4K
Don →, *England* 53°41'N 0°52'W 16 3E
Don →, *Russia* 47° 4'N 39°18' E 28 6P
Don →, *Scotland* 57°11'N 2° 5'W 18 2F
Doncaster 53°32'N 1° 6'W 16 3E
Donegal 54°39'N 8° 5'W 19 2C
Donegal Bay 54°31'N 8°49'W 19 2C
Donetsk 48° 0'N 37°45' E 35 2L
Dongbei 45° 0'N 125° 0' E 47 2L
Dongting Hu 29°18'N 112°45' E 43 4F
Donostia San Sebastián 43°17'N 1°58'W 33 11H
Doon → 55°27'N 4°39'W 18 4D
Dorchester 50°42'N 2°27'W 17 6D
Dordogne → 45° 2'N 0°36'W 33 10J
Dornoch 57°53'N 4° 2'W 18 2D
Dornoch Firth 57°51'N 4° 4'W 18 2E
Dorset 50°45'N 2°26'W 15 6E
Dortmund 51°30'N 7°28' E 32 7M
Douala 4° 0'N 9°45' E 52 3C
Douglas 54°10'N 4°28'W 16 2B
Douro → 41° 8'N 8°40'W 33 12D
Dove → 52°51'N 1°36'W 16 4E
Dover, *U.K.* 51° 7'N 1°19' E 17 5H
Dover, *U.S.A.* 39°10'N 75°32'W 59 3L
Dover, Strait of 51° 0'N 1°30' E 17 6H
Downpatrick 54°20'N 5°43'W 19 2F
Drake Passage 58° 0'S 68° 0'W 67 17D
Drakensberg 31° 0'S 28° 0' E 50 9E
Drammen 59°42'N 10°12' E 31 4C
Drava → 45°33'N 18°55' E 35 2G
Dresden 51° 3'N 13°44' E 32 7Q
Driffield 54° 0'N 0°26'W 16 2F
Drogheda 53°43'N 6°22'W 19 3E
Dubai 25°18'N 55°20' E 48 4G
Dubbo 32°11'S 148°35' E 54 8J
Dublin 53°21'N 6°15'W 19 3E
Dubrovnik 42°39'N 18° 6' E 35 3G
Dudley 52°31'N 2° 5'W 17 4D
Dumbarton 55°57'N 4°33'W 18 4D
Dumfries 55° 4'N 3°37'W 18 4E
Dumfries and Galloway 55° 9'N 3°58'W 15 4E
Dún Laoghaire 53°17'N 6° 8'W 19 3E
Dunbar 56° 0'N 2°31'W 18 3F
Dunblane 56°11'N 3°58'W 18 3E
Duncansby Head 58°38'N 3° 1'W 13 2E
Dundalk 54° 1'N 6°24'W 19 2E
Dundee 56°28'N 2°59'W 18 3E
Dunedin 45°50'S 170°33' E 55 11P
Dunfermline 56° 5'N 3°27'W 18 3E
Dungannon 54°30'N 6°55'W 19 2E
Dungarvan 52° 5'N 7°37'W 19 4D
Dunkery Beacon 51° 9'N 3°36'W 17 5C
Dunnet Head 58°40'N 3°21'W 18 1E
Dunoon 55°57'N 4°56'W 18 4D
Durango 24° 3'N 104°39'W 62 3D
Durban 29°49'S 31° 1' E 51 8F
Durham 54°42'N 1°45'W 15 4F
Dushanbe 38°33'N 68°48' E 40 6G
Düsseldorf 51°14'N 6°47' E 32 7M
Dyce 57°13'N 2°12'W 18 2F
Dyfi → 52°32'N 4° 3'W 17 4C
Dzungarian Basin 44°30'N 86° 0' E 42 2C

E

Earn → 56°21'N 3°18'W 18 3E
East Antarctica 80° 0'S 90° 0' E 67 7E
East China Sea 30° 0'N 126° 0' E 43 4G
East Indies 0° 0' 120° 0' E 47 7K
East Kilbride 55°47'N 4°11'W 18 4D
East London 33° 0'S 27°55' E 51 9E
East Lothian 55°58'N 2°44'W 15 4E
East Riding of Yorkshire 53°55'N 0°30'W 15 5F
East Sea = Japan, Sea of 40° 0'N 135° 0' E 43 3H
East Siberian Sea 73° 0'N 160° 0' E 41 2R
East Sussex 50°56'N 0°19' E 15 6G
Eastbourne 50°46'N 0°18' E 17 6G
Eastern Ghats 14° 0'N 78°50' E 46 5F
Eastleigh 50°58'N 1°21'W 17 6E
Ebbw Vale 51°46'N 3°12'W 17 5C
Ebinur Hu 44°55'N 82°55' E 42 2C
Ebro → 40°43'N 0°54' E 33 12J
Ecuador ■ 2° 0'S 78° 0'W 65 4D
Eday 59°11'N 2°47'W 18 7F
Eddystone 50°11'N 4°16'W 17 6B
Eden → 54°57'N 3° 1'W 16 2D
Edinburgh 55°57'N 3°13'W 18 4E
Edmonton 53°30'N 113°30'W 57 4H
Égadi Islands 37°55'N 12°16' E 36 6C
Egypt ■ 28° 0'N 31° 0' E 51 3F
Eigg 56°54'N 6°10'W 18 3B
Eilat 29°30'N 34°56' E 48 4B
Eilean Siar 57°30'N 7°10'W 15 3C
El Aaiún 27° 9'N 13°12'W 50 3A
El Paso 31°45'N 106°29'W 62 1C
El Salvador ■ 13°50'N 89° 0'W 62 5G
Elâzığ 38°37'N 39°14' E 48 2C
Elba 42°46'N 10°17' E 36 3C
Elbe → 53°50'N 9° 0' E 32 6P
Elbert, Mount 39° 7'N 106°27'W 58 3E
Elbrus 43°21'N 42°30' E 28 7Q
Elburz Mountains 36° 0'N 52° 0' E 48 2F
Elche 38°15'N 0°42'W 33 13H
Eldoret 0°30'N 35°17' E 53 2B
Elgin 57°39'N 3°19'W 18 2E
Elgon, Mount 1°10'N 34°30' E 53 2A
Ellesmere Island 79°30'N 80° 0'W 56 2M
Ellesmere Port 53°17'N 2°54'W 16 3D
Ellon 57°22'N 2° 4'W 18 2F
Ellsworth Land 76° 0'S 89° 0'W 67 16E
Ellsworth Mountains 78°30'S 85° 0'W 67 16E
Ely 52°24'N 0°16' E 17 4G
Empty Quarter = Rub' al Khālī 19° 0'N 48° 0' E 46 5E
Enderby Land 66° 0'S 53° 0' E 67 5D
England 53° 0'N 2° 0'W 32 6D
English Channel 50° 0'N 2° 0'W 17 6D
Ennis 52°51'N 8°59'W 19 4C
Enniscorthy 52°30'N 6°34'W 19 4E
Enniskillen 54°21'N 7°39'W 19 2D
Enugu 6°30'N 7°30' E 52 2C
Equatorial Guinea ■ 2° 0'N 8° 0' E 51 5C
Erebus, Mount 77°35'S 167° 0' E 67 11E
Erfurt 50°58'N 11° 2' E 32 7P
Eriboll, Loch 58°30'N 4°42'W 18 1D
Erie, Lake 42°15'N 81° 0'W 59 2K
Eritrea ■ 14° 0'N 38°30' E 51 4F
Erne → 54°30'N 8°16'W 19 2C
Erne, Lower Lough 54°28'N 7°47'W 19 2D
Erne, Upper Lough 54°14'N 7°32'W 19 2D
Errigal 55° [illegible]'N 8° 6'W 19 1C
Erzurum 39°57'N 41°15' E 48 2D
Esbjerg 55°29'N 8°29' E 32 5N
Eşfahān 32°39'N 51°43' E 48 3F
Esk →, *England* 54°30'N 0°37'W 16 2F
Esk →, *Scotland* 54°58'N 3° 2'W 18 4E
Eskişehir 39°50'N 30°30' E 35 4K
Esperance 33°45'S 121°55' E 54 8D
Espírito Santo 20° 0'S 40°45'W 66 7G
Espíritu Santo 15°15'S 166°50' E 55 5N
Essen 51°28'N 7° 2' E 32 7M
Essequibo → 6°50'N 58°30'W 63 6N
Essex 51°54'N 0°27' E 15 6G
Estonia ■ 58°30'N 25°30' E 31 4F
Eswatini ■ 26°30'S 31°30' E 51 8F
Ethiopia ■ 8° 0'N 40° 0' E 51 5G
Ethiopian Highlands 10° 0'N 37° 0' E 50 5F
Etna, Mount 37°50'N 14°55' E 36 6E
Etosha Pan 18°40'S 16°30' E 50 7D
Ettrick Water → 55°31'N 2°55'W 18 4F
Euphrates → 31° 0'N 47°25' E 48 3E
Everest, Mount 28° 5'N 86°58' E 46 4G
Everglades, The 25°50'N 81° 0'W 59 5K
Evesham 52° 6'N 1°56'W 17 4E
Exe → 50°41'N 3°29'W 17 6C
Exeter 50°43'N 3°31'W 17 6C
Exmoor 51°12'N 3°45'W 17 5C
Exmouth 50°37'N 3°25'W 17 6C
Eyemouth 55°52'N 2° 5'W 18 4F
Eyre, Lake = Kati Thanda-Lake Eyre 29°30'S 137°26' E 54 7G

F

Fair Isle 59°32'N 1°38'W 13 2F
Fairbanks 64°51'N 147°43'W 57 3E
Faisalabad 31°30'N 73° 5' E 46 3F
Falkirk 56° 0'N 3°47'W 18 4E
Falkland Islands 51°30'S 59° 0'W 64 9F
Falmouth 50° 9'N 5° 5'W 17 6A
Far East 40° 0'N 130° 0' E 38 5Q
Fareham 50°51'N 1°11'W 17 6E
Farewell, Cape 59°48'N 43°55'W 56 4Q
Farne Islands 55°38'N 1°37'W 16 1E
Faroe Islands 62° 0'N 7° 0'W 32 2E
Fastnet Rock 51°22'N 9°37'W 19 5B
Fear, Cape 33°50'N 77°58'W 59 4L
Feira de Santana 12°15'S 38°57'W 66 5H
Felixstowe 51°58'N 1°23' E 17 5H
Fens, The 52°38'N 0° 2'W 16 4F
Fermanagh & Omagh 54°34'N 7°24'W 15 4C
Fermoy 52° 9'N 8°16'W 19 4C
Ferrara 44°50'N 11°35' E 36 2C
Fès 34° 0'N 5° 0'W 51 2B
Fetlar 60°36'N 0°52'W 18 8K
Fife 56°16'N 3° 1'W 15 3E
Fiji ■ 17°20'S 179° 0' E 55 5Q
Findhorn → 57°38'N 3°38'W 18 2E
Finland ■ 63° 0'N 27° 0' E 31 3F
Finland, Gulf of 60° 0'N 26° 0' E 31 4F
Fishguard 52° 0'N 4°58'W 17 5B
Flamborough Head 54° 7'N 0° 5'W 16 2F
Flannan Islands 58° 9'N 7°52'W 18 1A
Flattery, Cape 48°23'N 124°29'W 58 1B
Fleetwood 53°55'N 3° 1'W 16 3C
Flensburg 54°47'N 9°27' E 32 5N
Flinders Island 40° 0'S 148° 0' E 54 9J
Flinders Ranges 31°30'S 138°30' E 54 8G
Florence 43°46'N 11°15' E 36 3C
Flores Sea 6°30'S 120° 0' E 47 7K
Florianópolis 27°30'S 48°30'W 66 8F
Florida 28° 0'N 82° 0'W 59 5K
Florida, Straits of 25° 0'N 80° 0'W 59 5L
Florida Keys 24°40'N 81° 0'W 59 6K
Fóggia 41°27'N 15°34' E 36 4E
Folkestone 51° 5'N 1°12' E 17 5H
Fongafale 8°31'S 179°13' E 55 3Q
Forfar 56°39'N 2°53'W 18 3F
Forres 57°37'N 3°37'W 18 2E
Fort Augustus 57° 9'N 4°42'W 18 2D
Fort-de-France 14°36'N 61° 5'W 63 5M
Fort Lauderdale 26° 7'N 80° 8'W 63 2H
Fort William 56°49'N 5° 7'W 18 3C
Fort Worth 32°43'N 97°19'W 59 4G
Fortaleza 3°45'S 38°35'W 66 3H
Forth → 56° 9'N 3°50'W 18 3E
Forth, Firth of 56° 5'N 2°55'W 18 3F
Foula 60°10'N 2° 5'W 18 8H
Fouta Djallon 11°20'N 12°10'W 50 4A
Foyle, Lough 55° 7'N 7° 4'W 19 1D
Foz do Iguaçu 25°30'S 54°30'W 66 8E
France ■ 47° 0'N 3° 0' E 33 9J
Frankfort 38°12'N 84°52'W 59 3K
Frankfurt 50° 7'N 8°41' E 32 7N
Franz Josef Land 82° 0'N 55° 0' E 67 10A
Fraserburgh 57°42'N 2° 1'W 18 2F
Fredrikstad 59°13'N 10°57' E 31 4C
Freeport 26°30'N 78°47'W 63 2J
Freetown 8°30'N 13°17'W 51 5A
Freiburg 47°59'N 7°51' E 33 8M
French Guiana 4° 0'N 53° 0'W 65 3F
Frisian Islands 53°30'N 6° 0' E 32 6L
Frome 51°14'N 2°19'W 17 5D
Frome → 50°41'N 2° 6'W 17 6D
Fuji-San 35°22'N 138°44' E 45 3C
Fukui 36° 5'N 136°10' E 45 3C
Fukuoka 33°39'N 130°21' E 45 4B
Fukushima 37°44'N 140°28' E 45 3D
Fushun 41°50'N 123°56' E 43 2G
Fuyu 47°49'N 124°27' E 43 2G
Fuzhou 26° 5'N 119°16' E 43 4F
Fyne, Loch 55°59'N 5°23'W 18 4C

G

Gabon ■ 0°10'S 10° 0' E 51 6D
Gaborone 24°45'S 25°57' E 51 8E
Gainsborough 53°24'N 0°46'W 16 3F
Gairdner, Lake 31°30'S 136° 0' E 54 8G
Galápagos Islands 0° 0' 91° 0'W 64 4B
Galashiels 55°37'N 2°49'W 18 4F
Galați 45°27'N 28° 2' E 35 2J
Galdhøpiggen 61°38'N 8°18' E 31 3B
Gällivare 67° 9'N 20°40' E 31 2E
Galloway 55° 1'N 4°29'W 18 4D
Galloway, Mull of 54°39'N 4°52'W 18 5D
Galtymore 52°21'N 8°11'W 19 4C
Galway 53°17'N 9° 3'W 19 3B
Galway Bay 53°13'N 9°10'W 19 3B
Gambia ■ 13°25'N 16° 0'W 51 4A
Gäncä 40°45'N 46°20' E 48 1E
Ganges → 23°20'N 90°30' E 46 4G
Garda, Lake 45°40'N 10°41' E 36 2C
Garissa 0°25'S 39°40' E 53 3B
Garonne → 45° 2'N 0°36'W 33 10H
Garoua 9°19'N 13°21' E 52 2D

Gateshead 54°57′N 1°35′W 16 2E
Gävle 60°40′N 17° 9′ E 31 3D
Gaza Strip 31°29′N 34°25′ E 35 5K
Gaziantep 37° 6′N 37°23′ E 35 4L
Gdańsk 54°22′N 18°40′ E 31 5D
Geneva 46°12′N 6° 9′ E 33 9M
Geneva, Lake 46°26′N 6°30′ E 33 9M
Genoa 44°25′N 8°57′ E 36 2B
Genoa, Gulf of 44° 0′N 9° 0′ E 36 2B
George Town 5°25′N 100°20′ E 47 6J
Georgetown 6°50′N 58°12′W 63 6N
Georgia 32°50′N 83°15′W 59 4K
Georgia ■ 42° 0′N 43° 0′ E 40 5E
Geraldton 28°48′S 114°32′ E 54 7B
Germany ■ 51° 0′N 10° 0′ E 32 7N
Ghana ■ 8° 0′N 1° 0′W 52 2A
Ghent 51° 2′N 3°42′ E 32 7K
Giants Causeway 55°16′N 6°29′W 19 1E
Gibraltar 36° 7′N 5°22′W 33 14F
Gibraltar, Strait of 35°55′N 5°40′W 33 14E
Gibson Desert 24° 0′S 126° 0′ E 54 6E
Gifu 35°30′N 136°45′ E 45 3C
Gijón 43°32′N 5°42′W 33 11F
Gillingham 51°23′N 0°33′ E 17 5G
Gironde → 45°32′N 1° 7′W 33 10H
Girvan 55°14′N 4°51′W 18 4D
Gitega 3°26′S 29°56′ E 51 6F
Gladstone 23°52′S 151°16′ E 54 6K
Glåma → 59°12′N 10°57′ E 31 2P
Glasgow 55°51′N 4°15′W 18 4D
Glen Coe 56°40′N 5° 0′W 18 3D
Glen Mor 57° 9′N 4°37′W 18 2D
Glenrothes 56°12′N 3°10′W 18 3E
Gloucester 51°53′N 2°15′W 17 5D
Gloucestershire 51°46′N 2°15′W 15 6E
Goa 15°33′N 73°59′ E 46 5F
Goat Fell 55°38′N 5°11′W 18 4C
Gobi Desert 44° 0′N 110° 0′ E 43 5B
Godavari → 16°25′N 82°18′ E 46 5F
Goiânia 16°43′S 49°20′W 66 6F
Goiás 12°10′S 48° 0′W 66 5F
Gold Coast 28° 0′S 153°25′ E 54 7K
Golspie 57°58′N 3°59′W 18 2E
Good Hope, Cape of 34°24′S 18°30′ E 50 9D
Goole 53°42′N 0°53′W 16 3F
Gorey 52°41′N 6°18′W 19 4E
Gosport 50°48′N 1° 9′W 17 6E
Götaland 57°30′N 14°30′ E 31 4C
Gothenburg 57°43′N 11°59′ E 31 4C
Gotland 57°30′N 18°33′ E 31 4D
Göttingen 51°31′N 9°55′ E 32 7N
Gqeberha 33°58′S 25°40′ E 51 9E
Grampian Mountains 56°50′N 4° 0′W 18 3D
Gran Chaco 25° 0′S 61° 0′W 64 6E
Granada 37°10′N 3°35′W 33 14G
Grand Bahama Island 26°40′N 78°30′W 63 2J
Grand Canyon 36° 3′N 112° 9′W 58 3D
Grand Teton 43°54′N 110°50′W 58 2D
Grande, Rio → 25°58′N 97° 9′W 62 2E
Grantham 52°55′N 0°38′W 16 4F
Grantown-on-Spey 57°20′N 3°36′W 18 2E
Gravesend 51°26′N 0°22′ E 17 5G
Graz 47° 4′N 15°27′ E 35 2G
Great Australian Bight 33°30′S 130° 0′ E 54 8F
Great Barrier Reef 18° 0′S 146°50′ E 54 5J
Great Basin 40° 0′N 117° 0′W 58 2C
Great Bear Lake 65°30′N 120° 0′W 57 3G
Great Britain 54° 0′N 2°15′W 13 4F
Great Dividing Range 23° 0′S 146° 0′ E 54 6J
Great Khingan Mountains 48° 0′N 121° 0′ E 43 2G
Great Lakes 46° 0′N 84° 0′W 56 5L
Great Malvern 52° 7′N 2°18′W 17 4D
Great Ouse → 52°48′N 0°21′ E 17 4F
Great Plains 47° 0′N 105° 0′W 58 1E
Great Salt Lake 41°15′N 112°40′W 58 2D
Great Salt Lake Desert 40°50′N 113°30′W 58 3D
Great Sandy Desert 21° 0′S 124° 0′ E 54 6D
Great Slave Lake 61°23′N 115°38′W 57 3H
Great Victoria Desert 29°30′S 126°30′ E 54 7E
Great Yarmouth 52°37′N 1°44′ E 16 4H
Greater Antilles 17°40′N 74° 0′W 64 2D
Greater London 51°31′N 0° 6′W 15 6F
Greater Manchester 53°30′N 2°15′W 15 5E
Greece ■ 40° 0′N 23° 0′ E 35 4H
Greenland 66° 0′N 45° 0′W 57 3Q
Greenland Sea 73° 0′N 10° 0′W 67 7B
Greenock 55°57′N 4°46′W 18 4D
Greenwich 51°29′N 0° 1′ E 17 5G
Grenada ■ 12°10′N 61°40′W 63 5M
Grenoble 45°12′N 5°42′ E 33 10L
Gretna Green 55° 1′N 3° 3′W 18 4E
Greystones 53° 9′N 6° 5′W 19 3E
Grimsby 53°34′N 0° 5′W 16 3F
Groningen 53°15′N 6°35′ E 32 6M
Groote Eylandt 14° 0′S 136°40′ E 54 4G
Guadalajara 20°40′N 103°20′W 62 3D
Guadalcanal 9°32′S 160°12′ E 55 3M
Guadalquivir → 36°47′N 6°22′W 33 14E
Guadeloupe 16°15′N 61°40′W 63 4M
Guadiana → 37°14′N 7°22′W 33 14E
Guam 13°27′N 144°45′ E 47 5N
Guangdong 23° 0′N 113° 0′ E 43 4F
Guangzhou 23° 6′N 113°13′ E 43 4F
Guantánamo 20°10′N 75°14′W 63 3J
Guantánamo Bay 19°59′N 75°10′W 63 3J
Guaporé → 11°55′S 65° 4′W 66 5B
Guatemala ■ 15°40′N 90°30′W 62 4F
Guaviare → 4° 3′N 67°44′W 63 7K
Guayaquil 2°15′S 79°52′W 65 4D
Guernsey 49°26′N 2°35′W 17 7D
Guiana Highlands 5°10′N 60°40′W 64 3E
Guildford 51°14′N 0°34′W 17 5F
Guinea ■ 10°20′N 11°30′W 51 4A
Guinea, Gulf of 3° 0′N 2°30′ E 50 5C
Guinea-Bissau ■ 12° 0′N 15° 0′W 51 4A
Guiyang 26°32′N 106°40′ E 42 4E
Gusau 12°12′N 6°40′ E 52 1C
Guyana ■ 5° 0′N 59° 0′W 63 6N
Gwangju 35° 9′N 126°54′ E 43 3G
Gwynedd 52°52′N 4°10′W 15 5D

H

Hadrian's Wall 55° 0′N 2°30′W 16 1D
Hague, Cap de la 49°44′N 1°56′W 33 8G
Hague, The 52° 7′N 4°17′ E 32 6L
Haida Gwaii 53°20′N 132°10′W 56 4F
Haifa 32°46′N 35° 0′ E 48 3B
Ḥā'il 27°28′N 41°45′ E 48 4D
Hailar 49°10′N 119°38′ E 43 2F
Hainan 19° 0′N 110° 0′ E 47 5J
Haiphong 20°47′N 106°41′ E 47 4J
Haiti ■ 19° 0′N 72°30′W 63 4K
Hakodate 41°45′N 140°44′ E 45 2D
Halifax, *Canada* 44°38′N 63°35′W 57 5N
Halifax, *U.K.* 53°43′N 1°52′W 16 3E
Halle 51°30′N 11°56′ E 32 7Q
Halmahera 0°40′N 128° 0′ E 47 6L
Halton 53°22′N 2°45′W 15 5E
Hamadān 34°52′N 48°32′ E 48 3E
Ḥamāh 35° 5′N 36°40′ E 48 2C
Hamamatsu 34°45′N 137°45′ E 45 4C
Hamburg 53°33′N 9°59′ E 32 6P
Hami 42°55′N 93°25′ E 42 2D
Hamilton, *Bermuda* 32°17′N 64°47′W 63 1M
Hamilton, *Canada* 43°15′N 79°50′W 59 2L
Hamilton, *N.Z.* 37°47′S 175°19′ E 55 9Q
Hamilton, *U.K.* 55°46′N 4° 2′W 18 4D
Hammerfest 70°39′N 23°41′ E 31 1E
Hampshire 51° 7′N 1°23′W 15 6F
Handan 36°35′N 114°28′ E 43 3F
Hangzhou 30°18′N 120°11′ E 43 3G
Hangzhou Wan 30°15′N 120°45′ E 43 3G
Hanoi 21° 5′N 105°55′ E 42 4E
Hanover 52°22′N 9°46′ E 32 6N
Har Us Nuur 48° 0′N 92° 0′ E 42 2D
Ḥaraḍ 24°22′N 49° 0′ E 48 5E
Harare 17°43′S 31° 2′ E 51 7F
Harbin 45°48′N 126°40′ E 43 2G
Hardanger Fjord 60° 5′N 6° 0′ E 31 3B
Harlow 51°46′N 0° 8′ E 17 5G
Harris 57°50′N 6°55′W 18 2B
Harrogate 54° 0′N 1°33′W 16 3E
Hartford 41°46′N 72°41′W 59 2M
Hartland Point 51° 1′N 4°32′W 17 5B
Hartlepool 54°42′N 1°13′W 16 2E
Harwich 51°56′N 1°17′ E 17 5H
Hastings 50°51′N 0°35′ E 17 6G
Hatteras, Cape 35°14′N 75°32′W 59 3L
Havana 23° 8′N 82°22′W 63 3H
Havant 50°51′N 0°58′W 17 6F
Haverfordwest 51°48′N 4°58′W 17 5B
Hawaiian Islands 19°30′N 156°30′W 58 8Q
Hawick 55°26′N 2°47′W 18 4F
Hay-on-Wye 52° 5′N 3° 8′W 17 4C
Haywards Heath 51° 0′N 0° 5′W 17 5F
Hebrides 57°30′N 7° 0′W 32 4E
Hebrides, Sea of the 57° 5′N 7° 0′W 18 4B
Hefei 31°52′N 117°18′ E 43 3F
Hegang 47°20′N 130°19′ E 43 8B
Heihe 50°10′N 127°30′ E 43 1G
Helena 46°36′N 112° 2′W 58 1D
Helensburgh 56° 1′N 4°43′W 18 3D
Helmsdale 58° 7′N 3°39′W 18 1E
Helsingborg 56° 3′N 12°42′ E 31 4C
Helsinki 60°10′N 24°55′ E 31 3E
Hemel Hempstead 51°44′N 0°28′W 17 5F
Hengyang 26°59′N 112°22′ E 43 4F
Herāt 34°20′N 62° 7′ E 46 3E
Hereford 52° 4′N 2°43′W 17 4D
Hermosillo 32°27′N 114°56′W 62 2B
Herne Bay 51°21′N 1° 8′ E 17 5H
Hertford 51°48′N 0° 4′W 17 5F
Hertfordshire 51°51′N 0° 5′W 15 6F
Hexham 54°58′N 2° 4′W 16 2D
Heysham 54° 3′N 2°53′W 16 2D
High Willhays 50°40′N 4° 0′W 17 6B
High Wycombe 51°37′N 0°45′W 17 5F
Highland 57°17′N 4°21′W 15 3D
Hiiumaa 58°50′N 22°45′ E 31 4E
Himalayas 29° 0′N 84° 0′ E 46 4G
Himeji 34°50′N 134°40′ E 45 4B
Hinckley 52°33′N 1°22′W 17 4E
Hindu Kush 36° 0′N 71° 0′ E 46 3F
Hiroshima 34°24′N 132°30′ E 45 4B
Hispaniola 19° 0′N 71° 0′W 68 4F
Hitachi 36°36′N 140°39′ E 45 3D
Hitchin 51°58′N 0°16′W 17 5F
Ho Chi Minh City 10°58′N 106°40′ E 47 5J
Hobart 42°50′S 147°21′ E 54 10J
Hoggar 23° 0′N 6°30′ E 50 3C
Hohhot 40°52′N 111°40′ E 43 2F
Hokkaidō 43°30′N 143° 0′ E 45 2D
Holderness 53°45′N 0° 5′W 16 3F
Holguín 20°50′N 76°20′W 63 3J
Holy Island, *England* 55°40′N 1°47′W 16 1E
Holy Island, *Wales* 53°17′N 4°37′W 16 3B
Holyhead 53°18′N 4°38′W 16 3B
Homs 34°40′N 36°45′ E 35 5L
Homyel 52°28′N 31° 0′ E 31 5G
Honduras ■ 14°40′N 86°30′W 62 5G
Honduras, Gulf of 16°50′N 87° 0′W 62 4G
Hong Kong 22°11′N 114°14′ E 43 4F
Honiara 9°27′S 159°57′ E 55 3L
Honiton 50°47′N 3°11′W 17 6C
Honolulu 21°19′N 157°52′W 58 8R
Honshū 36° 0′N 138° 0′ E 45 3C
Hormuz, Strait of 26°30′N 56°30′ E 48 4G
Horn, Cape 55°50′S 67°30′W 64 9E
Horsham 51° 4′N 0°20′W 17 5F
Hotan 37°25′N 79°55′ E 42 3B
Houghton-le-Spring 54°51′N 1°28′W 16 2E
Houston 29°45′N 95°21′W 59 5G
Hove 50°50′N 0°10′W 17 6F
Hövsgöl Nuur 51° 0′N 100°30′ E 42 1E
Howth Head 53°22′N 6° 4′W 19 3E
Hoy 58°50′N 3°15′W 18 6E
Huambo 12°42′S 15°54′ E 51 7D
Huascarán, Nevado 9° 7′S 77°37′W 64 4D
Huddersfield 53°39′N 1°47′W 16 3E
Hudson → 40°42′N 74° 2′W 59 2M
Hudson Bay 60° 0′N 86° 0′W 56 4L
Hudson Strait 62° 0′N 70° 0′W 56 3M
Huelva 37°18′N 6°57′W 33 14E
Hull → 53°44′N 0°20′W 16 3F
Humber → 53°42′N 0°27′W 16 3F
Hungary ■ 47°20′N 19°20′ E 35 2G
Huntingdon 52°20′N 0°11′W 17 7E
Huntly 57°27′N 2°47′W 18 2F
Hurghada 27°15′N 33°50′ E 48 4B
Huron, Lake 44°30′N 82°40′W 59 2K
Hwang Ho → 37°55′N 118°50′ E 43 3F
Hyderabad, *India* 17°22′N 78°29′ E 46 5F
Hyderabad, *Pakistan* 25°23′N 68°24′ E 46 4E

I

Iaşi 47°10′N 27°40′ E 35 2J
Ibadan 7°22′N 3°58′ E 52 2B
Ibagué 4°20′N 75°20′W 63 7J
Iberian Peninsula 40° 0′N 5° 0′W 28 7F
Ibiza 38°54′N 1°26′ E 33 13J
Iça → 2°55′S 67°58′W 66 3B
Iceland ■ 64°45′N 19° 0′W 57 3T
Idaho 45° 0′N 115° 0′W 58 2C
Ifrane 33°33′N 5° 7′W 34 5B
Iguaçu Falls 25°41′S 54°26′W 64 6F
Ilfracombe 51°12′N 4° 8′W 17 5B
Ilkeston 52°58′N 1°19′W 16 4E
Ilkley 53°56′N 1°48′W 16 3E
Illinois 40°15′N 89°30′W 59 3J
Ilorin 8°30′N 4°35′ E 52 2B
Imandra, Lake 67°30′N 33° 0′ E 31 2G
Imperatriz 5°30′S 47°29′W 66 4F
Inari, Lake 69° 0′N 28° 0′ E 31 2F
Incheon 37°27′N 126°40′ E 43 3G
India ■ 20° 0′N 78° 0′ E 46 4F
Indian → 27°59′N 80°34′W 59 5K
Indian Ocean 5° 0′S 75° 0′ E 69 5N
Indiana 40° 0′N 86° 0′W 59 2J
Indianapolis 39°46′N 86° 9′W 59 3J
Indo-China 15° 0′N 102° 0′ E 38 7M
Indonesia ■ 5° 0′S 115° 0′ E 47 7K
Indore 22°42′N 75°53′ E 46 4F
Indus → 24°20′N 67°47′ E 46 4E
Inishbofin 53°37′N 10°13′W 19 3A
Inishmore 53° 8′N 9°45′W 19 3B
Inishowen Peninsula 55°14′N 7°15′W 19 1D
Inishturk 53°42′N 10° 7′W 19 3A
Inner Hebrides 57° 0′N 6°30′W 18 2B
Inner Mongolia 42° 0′N 112° 0′ E 43 2F
Innsbruck 47°16′N 11°23′ E 33 9P
Inveraray 56°14′N 5° 5′W 18 3C
Invercargill 46°24′S 168°24′ E 55 11N
Invergordon 57°41′N 4°10′W 18 2D
Inverness 57°29′N 4°13′W 18 2D
Inverurie 57°17′N 2°23′W 18 2F
Iona 56°20′N 6°25′W 18 3B
Ionian Islands 38°40′N 20° 0′ E 35 4H
Ionian Sea 37°30′N 17°30′ E 35 4G
Iowa 42°18′N 93°30′W 59 2H
Ipswich 52° 4′N 1°10′ E 17 4H
Iqaluit 63°44′N 68°31′W 57 3N
Iquitos 3°45′S 73°10′W 65 4D
Iraklio 35°20′N 25°12′ E 35 4J
Iran ■ 33° 0′N 53° 0′ E 48 3F
Iraq ■ 33° 0′N 44° 0′ E 48 3D
Irbil 36°15′N 44° 5′ E 48 2D
Ireland ■ 53°50′N 7°52′W 19 3D
Ireland's Eye 53°24′N 6° 4′W 19 3E
Irish Sea 53°38′N 4°48′W 32 6F
Irkutsk 52°18′N 104°20′ E 41 4L
Irrawaddy → 15°50′N 95° 6′ E 47 4H
Irtysh → 61° 4′N 68°52′ E 40 3G
Irvine 55°37′N 4°41′W 18 4D
Ischia 40°44′N 13°57′ E 36 4D
Islamabad 33°40′N 73°10′ E 46 3F
Islay 55°46′N 6°10′W 18 4B
Ismail Samani Peak 39° 0′N 72° 2′ E 40 6H
Ismâ'ilîya 30°37′N 32°18′ E 35 5K
Isparta 37°47′N 30°30′ E 35 4K
Israel ■ 32° 0′N 34°50′ E 48 3B
İstanbul 41° 0′N 28°58′ E 35 3J
Itabuna 14°48′S 39°16′W 66 5H
Italy ■ 42° 0′N 13° 0′ E 36 3D
Itchen → 50°55′N 1°22′W 17 5E
Iveragh Peninsula 51°52′N 10°15′W 19 5A
Iwaki 37° 3′N 140°55′ E 45 3D
İzmir 38°25′N 27° 8′ E 35 4J
İzmit 40°45′N 29°50′ E 35 3J

J

Jabalpur 23° 9′N 79°58′ E 46 4F
Jackson 32°18′N 90°12′W 59 4H
Jacksonville 30°20′N 81°39′W 59 4K
Jaffna 9°45′N 80° 2′ E 46 6G
Jahrom 28°30′N 53°31′ E 48 4F
Jaipur 27° 0′N 75°50′ E 46 4F
Jakarta 6° 9′S 106°52′ E 47 7J
Jamaica ■ 18°10′N 77°30′W 63 4J
Jamshedpur 22°44′N 86°12′ E 46 4G
Jan Mayen 71° 0′N 9° 0′W 67 7B
Japan ■ 36° 0′N 136° 0′ E 47 3M
Japan, Sea of 40° 0′N 135° 0′ E 43 3H
Japurá → 3° 8′S 65°46′W 66 3B
Java 7° 0′S 110° 0′ E 47 7K
Java Sea 4°35′S 107°15′ E 38 9M
Jedburgh 55°29′N 2°33′W 18 4F
Jedda 21°29′N 39°10′ E 48 5C
Jeju-do 33°29′N 126°34′ E 43 3G
Jerez de la Frontera 36°41′N 6° 7′W 33 14E
Jersey 49°11′N 2° 7′W 17 7D
Jerusalem 31°47′N 35°10′ E 48 3C
Jiamusi 46°40′N 130°26′ E 43 2H
Jilin 43°44′N 126°30′ E 43 2G
Jimeta 9°17′N 12°28′ E 52 2D
Jinan 36°38′N 117° 1′ E 43 3F
Jingmen 31° 0′N 112°10′ E 43 3F
Jinja 0°25′N 33°12′ E 53 2A
Jinxi 40°52′N 120°50′ E 43 2G
Jixi 45°20′N 130°50′ E 45 1B
João Pessoa 7°10′S 34°52′W 66 4J
Joensuu 62°37′N 29°49′ E 31 3F
Johannesburg 26°11′S 28° 2′ E 51 8E
John o' Groats 58°38′N 3° 4′W 18 1E
Johnstone 55°49′N 4°31′W 18 4D
Jönköping 57°45′N 14° 8′ E 31 4C
Jordan ■ 31° 0′N 36° 0′ E 48 3C
Jos Plateau 9°55′N 9° 0′ E 52 2C
Jotunheimen 61°35′N 8°25′ E 32 2M
Juàzeiro 9°30′S 40°30′W 66 4G
Juàzeiro do Norte 7°10′S 39°18′W 66 4H
Juba 4°50′N 31°35′ E 51 5F
Juiz de Fora 21°43′S 43°19′W 66 7G
Juneau 58°18′N 134°25′W 57 4F
Jura 56° 0′N 5°50′W 18 4C
Jura, Sound of 55°57′N 5°45′W 18 4C
Juruá → 2°37′S 65°44′W 66 3B
Juruena → 7°20′S 58° 3′W 66 4D
Jutland 56°25′N 9°30′ E 32 4N
Jyväskylä 62°14′N 25°50′ E 31 3F

K

K2 35°58′N 76°32′ E 46 3F
Kābul 34°28′N 69°11′ E 46 3E
Kaduna 10°30′N 7°21′ E 52 1C
Kagoshima 31°35′N 130°33′ E 45 4B
Kainji Reservoir 10° 1′N 4°40′ E 52 1B
Kakamega 0°20′N 34°46′ E 53 2A
Kalahari 24° 0′S 21°30′ E 50 8E
Kalgoorlie-Boulder 30°40′S 121°22′ E 54 8D
Kaliningrad 54°42′N 20°32′ E 31 5E
Kamchatka Peninsula 57° 0′N 160° 0′ E 41 4R
Kampala 0°20′N 32°32′ E 51 5F
Kanazawa 36°30′N 136°38′ E 45 3C
Kandahār 31° 0′N 65° 0′ E 46 3E
Kandalaksha 67° 9′N 32°30′ E 31 2G
Kangaroo Island 35°45′S 137° 0′ E 54 9G
Kano 12° 2′N 8°30′ E 52 1C
Kanpur 26°28′N 80°20′ E 46 4G
Kansas 38°30′N 99° 0′W 58 3G
Kansas City 39° 7′N 94°38′W 59 3H
Kansk 56°20′N 95°37′ E 41 4K
Kaohsiung 22°35′N 120°16′ E 43 4G
Kara Kum 39°30′N 60° 0′ E 40 5F
Kara Sea 75° 0′N 70° 0′ E 40 2G
Karachi 24°50′N 67° 0′ E 46 4E
Karaganda 49°50′N 73°10′ E 40 5H
Karakoram 35°30′N 77° 0′ E 46 3F
Karelia 65°30′N 32°30′ E 31 3G
Kariba, Lake 16°40′S 28°25′ E 50 7E
Karlsruhe 49° 0′N 8°23′ E 33 8N
Kasai → 3°30′S 16°10′ E 50 6D
Kāshān 34° 5′N 51°30′ E 48 3F
Kashgar 39°30′N 76° 2′ E 42 3B
Kashmir 34° 0′N 76° 0′ E 46 3F
Kassel 51°18′N 9°26′ E 32 7N
Kati Thanda-Lake Eyre 29°30′S 137°26′ E 54 7G
Katmandu 27°45′N 85°20′ E 46 4G
Katowice 50°17′N 19° 5′ E 35 2G
Katrine, Loch 56°15′N 4°30′W 18 3D
Katsina 13° 0′N 7°32′ E 52 1C
Kattegat 56°40′N 11°20′ E 31 4C
Kaunas 54°54′N 23°54′ E 31 5E
Kawasaki 35°31′N 139°43′ E 45 3C
Kayseri 38°45′N 35°30′ E 35 4L
Kazakhstan ■ 50° 0′N 70° 0′ E 40 5F
Kazan 55°50′N 49°10′ E 38 4E
Kebnekaise 67°53′N 18°33′ E 31 2D
Keighley 53°52′N 1°54′W 16 3E
Keith 57°32′N 2°57′W 18 2F
Kelso 55°36′N 2°26′W 18 4F
Kemi 65°44′N 24°34′ E 31 2E
Kemp Land 69° 0′S 55° 0′ E 67 5D
Kendal 54°20′N 2°44′W 16 2D
Kenmare 51°53′N 9°36′W 19 5B
Kennet → 51°27′N 0°57′W 17 5E
Kent 51°12′N 0°40′ E 15 6G
Kentucky 37° 0′N 84° 0′W 59 3J
Kenya ■ 1° 0′N 38° 0′ E 53 2B
Kenya, Mount 0°10′S 37°18′ E 53 3B
Kerguelen 49°15′S 69°10′ E 69 7N
Kericho 0°22′S 35°15′ E 53 3B
Kermadec Islands 30° 0′S 178°15′W 55 8R
Kermadec Trench 30°30′S 176° 0′W 55 8R
Kermān 30°15′N 57° 1′ E 48 3G
Kermānshāh 34°23′N 47° 0′ E 48 3E
Kerry 52° 7′N 9°35′W 15 5B
Keswick 54°36′N 3° 8′W 16 2C
Kettering 52°24′N 0°43′W 17 4F
Khabarovsk 48°30′N 135° 5′ E 41 5P
Khanka, Lake 45° 0′N 132°24′ E 45 2B
Kharg Island 29°15′N 50°28′ E 48 4F
Kharkiv 49°58′N 36°20′ E 35 2L
Khartoum 15°31′N 32°35′ E 51 4F
Khorramābād 33°30′N 48°25′ E 48 3E
Kidderminster 52°24′N 2°15′W 17 4D
Kiel 54°19′N 10° 8′ E 32 5P
Kiel Canal 54°12′N 9°32′ E 32 5N
Kielder Reservoir 55°10′N 2°29′W 16 1D
Kiev 50°30′N 30°28′ E 31 5G
Kigali 1°59′S 30° 4′ E 51 6F
Kildare 53° 9′N 6°55′W 19 3E
Kilifi 3°40′S 39°48′ E 53 3B
Kilimanjaro 3° 7′S 37°20′ E 53 3B
Kilindini 4° 4′S 39°40′ E 53 3B
Kilkee 52°41′N 9°39′W 19 4B
Kilkenny 52°39′N 7°15′W 19 4D
Killarney 52° 4′N 9°30′W 19 4B
Killiecrankie, Pass of 56°44′N 3°46′W 18 3E
Killybegs 54°38′N 8°26′W 19 2C
Kilmarnock 55°37′N 4°29′W 18 4D
Kilrush 52°38′N 9°29′W 19 4B
Kimberley 16°20′S 127° 0′ E 54 5E
Kimch'aek 40°40′N 129°10′ E 45 2A
King Island 39°50′S 144° 0′ E 54 9H
King's Lynn 52°45′N 0°24′ E 16 4G
Kingston 17°55′N 76°50′W 63 4J
Kingston upon Hull 53°45′N 0°21′W 16 3F
Kingston-upon-Thames 51°24′N 0°17′W 17 5F
Kingstown 13°10′N 61°10′W 63 5M

Kingussie 57° 6′N 4° 2′W 18 2D
Kinross 56°13′N 3°25′W 18 3E
Kinsale 51°42′N 8°31′W 19 5C
Kinshasa 4°20′S 15°15′ E 51 6D
Kintyre 55°30′N 5°35′W 18 4C
Kintyre, Mull of 55°17′N 5°47′W 18 4C
Kiribati ■ 3° 0′S 180° 0′ E 70 5A
Kirkcaldy 56° 7′N 3° 9′W 18 3E
Kirkcudbright 54°50′N 4° 2′W 18 5D
Kirkenes 69°40′N 30° 5′ E 31 2F
Kirkūk 35°30′N 44°21′ E 48 2D
Kirkwall 58°59′N 2°58′W 18 6E
Kirov 54° 3′N 34°20′ E 40 4E
Kiruna 67°52′N 20°15′ E 31 2E
Kisangani 0°35′N 25°15′ E 51 5E
Kisii 0°40′S 34°45′ E 53 3A
Kisumu 0° 3′S 34°45′ E 53 3A
Kitakyūshū 33°50′N 130°50′ E 45 4B
Kitale 1° 0′N 35° 0′ E 53 2A
Klaipėda 55°43′N 21°10′ E 31 4E
Klyuchevskaya 55°50′N 160°30′ E 41 4S
Knock 53°48′N 8°55′W 19 3C
Knockmealdown Mountains 52°14′N 7°56′W 19 4C
Kōbe 34°41′N 135°13′ E 45 4C
Koblenz 50°21′N 7°36′ E 32 7M
Kochi, *India* 9°58′N 76°20′ E 46 6F
Kōchi, *Japan* 33°30′N 133°35′ E 45 4B
Kokopo 4°22′S 152°19′ E 54 2K
Kola Peninsula 67°30′N 38° 0′ E 31 2H
Kolkata 22°34′N 88°21′ E 46 4G
Kolyma Range 63° 0′N 157° 0′ E 41 3R
Kongur Shan 38°34′N 75°18′ E 42 3B
Konya 37°52′N 32°35′ E 35 4K
Korea Strait 34° 0′N 129°30′ E 45 4A
Kos 36°50′N 27°15′ E 35 4J
Kosciuszko, Mount 36°27′S 148°16′ E 54 9J
Košice 48°42′N 21°15′ E 35 2H
Kosovo ■ 42°30′N 21° 0′ E 35 3H
Kota Kinabalu 6° 0′N 116° 4′ E 47 6K
Kotlas 61°17′N 46°43′ E 40 3E
Krakatau 6°10′S 105°20′ E 47 7J
Kraków 50° 4′N 19°57′ E 31 5D
Krasnodar 45° 5′N 39° 0′ E 35 2L
Krasnoyarsk 56° 8′N 93° 0′ E 41 4K
Kristiansand 58° 8′N 8° 1′ E 31 4B
Kristiansund 63° 7′N 7°45′ E 31 3B
Kryvyy Rih 47°51′N 33°20′ E 35 2K
Kuala Lumpur 3° 9′N 101°41′ E 47 6J
Kucing 1°33′N 110°25′ E 47 6K
Kumamoto 32°45′N 130°45′ E 45 4B
Kumasi 6°41′N 1°38′W 52 2A
Kunlun Shan 36° 0′N 86°30′ E 42 3C
Kunming 25° 1′N 102°41′ E 42 4E
Kuopio 62°53′N 27°35′ E 31 3F
Kurdistan 37°20′N 43°30′ E 48 2D
Kure 34°14′N 132°32′ E 45 4B
Kuril Islands 45° 0′N 150° 0′ E 41 5R
Kursk 51°42′N 36°11′ E 35 1L
Kuwait 29°30′N 48° 0′ E 48 4E
Kuwait ■ 29°30′N 47°30′ E 48 4E
Kyle of Lochalsh 57°17′N 5°44′W 18 2C
Kyoga, Lake 1°35′N 33° 0′ E 53 2A
Kyōto 35° 0′N 135°45′ E 45 3C
Kyrgyzstan ■ 42° 0′N 75° 0′ E 40 5H
Kyūshū 33° 0′N 131° 0′ E 45 4B

L

La Coruña 43°20′N 8°25′W 33 11D
La Paz, *Bolivia* 16°20′S 68°10′W 65 5E
La Paz, *Mexico* 24°10′N 110°18′W 62 3B
La Perouse Strait 45°40′N 142° 0′ E 45 1D
La Plata 35° 0′S 57°55′W 65 7F
La Rochelle 46°10′N 1° 9′W 33 9H
La Spézia 44° 7′N 9°50′ E 36 2C
Labrador 53°20′N 61° 0′W 56 4N
Ladoga, Lake 61°15′N 30°30′ E 31 3G
Lae 6°40′S 147° 2′ E 54 3J
Lagan → 54°36′N 5°55′W 19 2F
Lagos 6°25′N 3°27′ E 52 2B
Lahore 31°32′N 74°22′ E 46 3F
Lahti 60°58′N 25°40′ E 31 3F
Lairg 58° 2′N 4°24′W 18 1D
Lake District 54°30′N 3°21′W 16 2C
Lakshadweep Islands 10° 0′N 72°30′ E 46 5F
Lambert Glacier 71° 0′S 70° 0′ E 67 6E
Lamu 2°16′S 40°55′ E 53 3C
Lanark 55°40′N 3°47′W 18 4E
Lancashire 53°50′N 2°48′W 15 5E
Lancaster 54° 3′N 2°48′W 16 2D
Land's End 50° 4′N 5°44′W 17 6A
Lansing 42°44′N 84°33′W 59 2K
Lanzhou 36° 1′N 103°52′ E 42 3E
Laois 52°57′N 7°27′W 15 5C
Laos ■ 17°45′N 105° 0′ E 47 5J
Lapland 68° 7′N 24° 0′ E 31 2F
Laptev Sea 76° 0′N 125° 0′ E 41 2N
Largs 55°47′N 4°52′W 18 4D
Larne 54°55′N 5°55′W 19 2F
Larsen Ice Shelf 67° 0′S 62° 0′W 67 17D
Las Palmas 28° 7′N 15°26′W 51 3A
Las Vegas 36°10′N 115° 8′W 58 3C
Latakia 35°30′N 35°45′ E 35 4L
Latvia ■ 56°50′N 24° 0′ E 31 4F
Launceston 41°24′S 147° 8′ E 54 10J
Lausanne 46°32′N 6°38′ E 33 9M
Le Havre 49°30′N 0° 5′ E 33 8J
Le Mans 48° 0′N 0°10′ E 33 8J
Lea → 51°31′N 0° 1′ E 17 5F
Lebanon ■ 34° 0′N 36° 0′ E 48 3C
Lee → 51°53′N 8°56′W 19 5C
Leeds 53°48′N 1°33′W 16 3E
Leeuwin, Cape 34°20′S 115° 9′ E 54 8C
Leeward Islands 16°30′N 63°30′W 63 4M
Leicester 52°38′N 1° 8′W 17 4E
Leicestershire 52°41′N 1°17′W 15 5F
Leinster 53° 3′N 7° 8′W 19 3D
Leipzig 51°18′N 12°22′ E 32 7Q
Leith Hill 51°11′N 0°22′W 17 5F
Leitrim 54° 8′N 8° 0′W 15 4B
Lena → 72°52′N 126°40′ E 41 2N
León, *Mexico* 21° 6′N 101°41′W 62 3D
León, *Spain* 42°38′N 5°34′W 33 11F
Lérida 41°37′N 0°39′ E 33 12J
Lerwick 60° 9′N 1° 9′W 18 8J
Lesbos 39°10′N 26°20′ E 35 4J
Leshan 29°33′N 103°41′ E 42 4E
Lesotho ■ 29°40′S 28° 0′ E 51 8E
Lesser Antilles 15° 0′N 61° 0′W 64 2E
Letchworth 51°59′N 0°13′W 17 5F
Lethbridge 49°45′N 112°45′W 58 1D
Letterkenny 54°57′N 7°45′W 19 2D
Lewes 50°52′N 0° 1′ E 17 6G
Lewis 58° 9′N 6°40′W 18 1B
Lhasa 29°25′N 90°58′ E 42 4D
Liberia ■ 6°30′N 9°30′W 51 5B
Libreville 0°25′N 9°26′ E 51 5C
Libya ■ 27° 0′N 17° 0′ E 51 3D
Libyan Desert 25° 0′N 25° 0′ E 50 3E
Liechtenstein ■ 47° 8′N 9°35′ E 33 9N
Liepāja 56°30′N 21° 0′ E 31 4E
Liffey → 53°21′N 6°13′W 19 3E
Ligurian Sea 43°20′N 9° 0′ E 36 3B
Lille 50°38′N 3° 3′ E 32 7K
Lillehammer 61° 8′N 10°30′ E 31 3C
Lilongwe 14° 0′S 33°48′ E 51 7F
Lima 12° 3′S 77° 2′W 65 5D
Limassol 34°42′N 33° 1′ E 35 5K
Limerick 52°40′N 8°37′W 19 4C
Limoges 45°50′N 1°15′ E 33 10J
Limpopo → 25° 5′S 33°30′ E 50 8F
Linares 38°10′N 3°40′W 33 13G
Lincoln, *U.K.* 53°14′N 0°32′W 16 3F
Lincoln, *U.S.A.* 40°49′N 96°41′W 59 2G
Lincoln Sea 84° 0′N 55° 0′W 67 5A
Lincolnshire 53°14′N 0°32′W 15 5F
Lincolnshire Wolds 53°26′N 0°13′W 16 3F
Linhai 28°50′N 121° 8′ E 43 4G
Linköping 58°28′N 15°36′ E 31 4D
Linyi 35° 5′N 118°21′ E 43 3F
Linz 48°18′N 14°18′ E 33 8Q
Lipetsk 52°37′N 39°35′ E 40 4D
Lisbon 38°42′N 9° 8′W 33 13D
Lisburn 54°30′N 6° 5′W 19 2E
Lisburn & Castlereagh 54°30′N 6° 4′W 15 4C
Listowel 52°27′N 9°29′W 19 4B
Lithuania ■ 55°30′N 24° 0′ E 31 4E
Little Minch 57°35′N 6°45′W 18 2B
Little Ouse → 52°22′N 1°12′ E 17 4G
Little Rock 34°45′N 92°17′W 59 4H
Littlehampton 50°49′N 0°32′W 17 6F
Liupanshui 26°38′N 104°48′ E 42 4E
Liuzhou 24°22′N 109°22′ E 43 4E
Liverpool 53°25′N 3° 0′W 16 3D
Liverpool Bay 53°30′N 3°20′W 13 5E
Livingston 55°54′N 3°30′W 18 4E
Livorno 43°33′N 10°19′ E 36 3C
Lizard 49°58′N 5°13′W 17 7A
Ljubljana 46° 4′N 14°33′ E 34 2F
Llandovery 51°59′N 3°48′W 17 4C
Llandrindod Wells 52°14′N 3°22′W 17 4C
Llandudno 53°19′N 3°50′W 16 3C
Llanelli 51°41′N 4°10′W 17 5B
Llangollen 52°58′N 3°11′W 16 4C
Lleyn Peninsula 52°51′N 4°36′W 16 4B
Lobamba 26°28′S 31°12′ E 51 8F
Lochgilphead 56° 2′N 5°26′W 18 3C
Lochy, Loch 57° 0′N 4°53′W 18 2D
Lockerbie 55° 7′N 3°21′W 18 4E
Lodwar 3° 7′N 35°36′ E 53 2B
Łódź 51°45′N 19°27′ E 31 5D
Lofoten Islands 68°30′N 13°59′ E 31 2C
Logan, Mount 60°34′N 140°23′W 56 3E
Loire → 47°16′N 2°10′W 33 9G
Lokoja 7°47′N 6°45′ E 52 2C
Lomé 6° 9′N 1°20′ E 52 2B
Lomond, Loch 56° 8′N 4°38′W 18 3D
London 51°30′N 0° 3′W 17 5F
Londonderry 55° 0′N 7°20′W 19 2D
Londrina 23°18′S 51°10′W 66 7E
Long, Loch 56° 4′N 4°50′W 18 3D
Long Eaton 52°53′N 1°15′W 16 4E
Longford 53°43′N 7°49′W 19 3D
Loop Head 52°34′N 9°56′W 19 4B
Lop Nur 40°20′N 90°10′ E 42 2D
Lord Howe Island 31°33′S 159° 6′ E 55 8L
Lorient 47°45′N 3°23′W 33 9G
Lorn, Firth of 56°20′N 5°40′W 18 3C
Los Angeles 34° 4′N 118°15′W 58 4C
Los Mochis 25°45′N 108°57′W 62 2C
Loughborough 52°47′N 1°11′W 16 4E
Loughrea 53°12′N 8°33′W 19 3C
Louisiade Archipelago 11°10′S 153° 0′ E 54 4K
Louisiana 30°50′N 92° 0′W 59 4H
Louisville 38°15′N 85°46′W 59 3J
Louth, *Ireland* 53°56′N 6°34′W 15 5C
Louth, *U.K.* 53°22′N 0° 1′W 16 3F
Lowestoft 52°29′N 1°45′ E 17 4H
Loyalty Islands 20°50′S 166°30′ E 55 6N
Luanda 8°50′S 13°15′ E 51 6D
Lübeck 53°52′N 10°40′ E 32 6P
Lublin 51°12′N 22°38′ E 31 5E
Lubumbashi 11°40′S 27°28′ E 51 7E
Luce Bay 54°45′N 4°48′W 18 5D
Lucknow 26°50′N 81° 0′ E 46 4G
Lugnaquilla 52°58′N 6°28′W 19 4E
Luhansk 48°38′N 39°15′ E 35 2B
Lule → 65°35′N 22°10′ E 31 2E
Luleå 65°35′N 22°10′ E 31 2E
Lundy 51°10′N 4°41′W 17 5B
Lune → 54° 0′N 2°51′W 16 2D
Lurgan 54°27′N 6°20′W 19 2E
Lusaka 15°28′S 28°16′ E 51 7E
Luton 51°53′N 0°24′W 17 5F
Luxembourg ■ 49°45′N 6° 0′ E 33 8M
Luzhou 28°52′N 105°20′ E 42 4E
Luzon 16° 0′N 121° 0′ E 47 5L
Lviv 49°50′N 24° 0′ E 35 2H
Lyme Bay 50°42′N 2°53′W 13 6E
Lyme Regis 50°43′N 2°57′W 17 6D
Lymington 50°45′N 1°32′W 17 6E
Lyons 45°46′N 4°50′ E 33 10L

M

McAllen 26°12′N 98°14′W 58 5G
Macapá 0° 5′N 51° 4′W 66 2E
Macau 22°12′N 113°33′ E 43 4F
Macclesfield 53°15′N 2° 8′W 16 3D
MacDonnell Ranges 23°40′S 133° 0′ E 54 6F
Macduff 57°40′N 2°31′W 18 2F
Maceió 9°40′S 35°41′W 66 4H
Macgillycuddy's Reeks 51°58′N 9°45′W 19 4B
Machakos 1°30′S 37°15′ E 53 3B
Machu Picchu 13° 8′S 72°30′W 65 5D
Mackay 21° 8′S 149°11′ E 54 6J
Mackenzie → 69°10′N 134°20′W 56 3E
McKinley, Mount = Denali 63° 4′N 151° 0′W 56 3D
McKinley Sea 82° 0′N 0° 0′W 67 8A
MacRobertson Land 71° 0′S 64° 0′ E 67 6E
Madagascar ■ 20° 0′S 47° 0′ E 51 8G
Madang 5°12′S 145°49′ E 54 3J
Madeira 32°50′N 17° 0′W 51 2A
Madeira → 3°22′S 58°45′W 66 3C
Madison 43° 4′N 89°24′W 59 2J
Madras = Chennai 13° 8′N 80°19′ E 46 5G
Madre, Laguna 25°15′N 97°30′W 59 5G
Madrid 40°24′N 3°42′W 33 12G
Madurai 9°55′N 78°10′ E 46 6F
Magadan 59°38′N 150°50′ E 41 4R
Magdalena → 11° 6′N 74°51′W 64 2D
Magdeburg 52° 7′N 11°38′ E 32 6P
Magellan, Strait of 52°30′S 75° 0′W 64 9D
Maggiore, Lake 45°57′N 8°39′ E 36 2B
Mahilyow 53°55′N 30°18′ E 31 5G
Maidenhead 51°31′N 0°42′W 17 5F
Maidstone 51°16′N 0°32′ E 17 5G
Maiduguri 12° 0′N 13°20′ E 52 1D
Maine 45°20′N 69° 0′W 59 1N
Mainland, *Orkney* 58°59′N 3° 8′W 18 7E
Mainland, *Shetland* 60°15′N 1°22′W 18 8J
Majorca 39°30′N 3° 0′ E 33 13K
Makassar 5°10′S 119°20′ E 47 7K
Makgadikgadi Salt Pans 20°40′S 25°45′ E 50 8E
Makhachkala 43° 0′N 47°30′ E 40 5E
Makira 10°30′S 161° 0′ E 55 4M
Makurdi 7°43′N 8°35′ E 52 2C
Malacca, Straits of 3° 0′N 101° 0′ E 47 6H
Málaga 36°43′N 4°23′W 33 14F
Malahide 53°26′N 6° 9′W 19 3E
Malaita 9° 0′S 161° 0′ E 55 3M
Malakula 16°15′S 167°30′ E 55 5N
Malatya 38°25′N 38°20′ E 48 2C
Malawi ■ 11°55′S 34° 0′ E 51 7F
Malawi, Lake 12°30′S 34°30′ E 50 7F
Malay Peninsula 7°25′N 100° 0′ E 47 6J
Malaysia ■ 5° 0′N 110° 0′ E 47 6J
Maldives ■ 5° 0′N 73° 0′ E 46 6F
Malé 4°10′N 73°28′ E 46 6F
Mali ■ 17° 0′N 3° 0′W 51 4B
Malin Head 55°23′N 7°23′W 19 1D
Malindi 3°12′S 40° 5′ E 53 3C
Mallaig 57° 0′N 5°50′W 18 2C
Mallow 52° 8′N 8°39′W 19 4C
Malmö 55°36′N 12°59′ E 32 5Q
Malta ■ 35°55′N 14°26′ E 34 4F
Malton 54° 8′N 0°49′W 16 2F
Mamoré → 10°23′S 65°53′W 66 5B
Man, Isle of 54°15′N 4°30′W 16 2B
Managua 12° 6′N 86°20′W 62 5G
Manama 26°10′N 50°30′ E 48 4F
Manaus 3° 0′S 60° 0′W 66 3B
Manchester 53°29′N 2°12′W 16 3D
Manchurian Plain 47° 0′N 124° 0′ E 38 4P
Mandalay 22° 0′N 96° 4′ E 47 4H
Manila 14°35′N 120°58′ E 47 5L
Manisa 38°38′N 27°30′ E 35 4J
Manizales 5° 5′N 75°32′W 63 6J
Mannheim 49°29′N 8°29′ E 33 8N
Mansfield 53° 9′N 1°11′W 16 3E
Manzhouli 49°35′N 117°25′ E 41 5M
Maputo 25°58′S 32°32′ E 51 8F
Mar del Plata 38° 0′S 57°30′W 65 7F
Marabá 5°20′S 49° 5′W 66 4F
Maracaibo 10°40′N 71°37′W 63 5K
Maracaibo, Lake 9°40′N 71°30′W 63 6K
Maracay 10°15′N 67°28′W 63 5L
Maranhão 5° 0′S 46° 0′W 66 4F
Marathon 38°11′N 23°58′ E 35 4H
Marbella 36°30′N 4°57′W 33 14F
March 52°33′N 0° 5′ E 17 4G
Maree, Loch 57°40′N 5°26′W 18 2C
Margate 51°23′N 1°23′ E 17 5H
Mariana Trench 13° 0′N 145° 0′ E 69 4S
Marie Byrd Land 79°30′S 125° 0′W 67 14E
Mariupol 47° 5′N 37°31′ E 35 2L
Markham, Mount 83° 0′S 164° 0′ E 67 11F
Maroua 10°40′N 14°20′ E 52 1D
Marrakesh 31° 9′N 8° 0′W 51 2B
Marree 29°39′S 138° 1′ E 54 7G
Marsabit 2°18′N 38° 0′ E 53 2B
Marseilles 43°18′N 5°23′ E 33 11L
Marshall Islands ■ 9° 0′N 171° 0′ E 71 4T
Martinique 14°40′N 61° 0′W 63 5M
Maryland 39° 0′N 76°30′W 59 3L
Maryport 54°44′N 3°28′W 16 2C
Masai Steppe 4°30′S 36°30′ E 53 3B
Maseru 29°18′S 27°30′ E 51 8E
Mashhad 36°20′N 59° 0′ E 48 7G
Mask, Lough 53°36′N 9°22′W 19 3B
Massachusetts 42°30′N 72° 0′W 59 2M
Massif Central 44°55′N 3° 0′ E 33 10K
Matamoros 25°53′N 97°30′W 62 2E
Matanzas 23° 0′N 81°40′W 63 3H
Matlock 53° 9′N 1°33′W 16 3E
Mato Grosso 14° 0′S 55° 0′W 66 5D
Mato Grosso, Plateau of 15° 0′S 55° 0′W 64 5F
Mato Grosso do Sul 18° 0′S 55° 0′W 66 6D
Matsumoto 36°15′N 138° 0′ E 45 3C
Matsuyama 33°45′N 132°45′ E 45 4B
Maturín 9°45′N 63°11′W 63 6M
Mauna Kea 19°50′N 155°28′W 58 9S
Mauna Loa 19°30′N 155°35′W 58 9S
Mauritania ■ 20°50′N 10° 0′W 51 3B
Mauritius ■ 20° 0′S 57° 0′ E 71 6M
Mawsynram 25°15′N 91°30′ E 46 4H
Maynooth 53°23′N 6°34′W 19 3E
Mayo 53°53′N 9° 3′W 15 5B
Mayotte 12°50′S 45°10′ E 51 7G
Mazatlán 23°13′N 106°25′W 62 3C
Mbabane 26°18′S 31° 6′ E 51 8F
Mbale 1° 8′N 34°12′ E 53 2A
Mbuji-Mayi 6° 9′S 23°40′ E 51 6E
Mead, Lake 36° 0′N 114°44′W 58 3D
Meath 53°40′N 6°57′W 15 5C
Mecca 21°30′N 39°54′ E 48 5C
Medan 3°40′N 98°38′ E 47 6H
Medellín 6°15′N 75°35′W 63 6J
Medina 24°35′N 39°52′ E 48 5C
Mediterranean Sea 35° 0′N 15° 0′ E 34 4F
Medway 51°25′N 0°32′ E 15 6G
Medway → 51°27′N 0°46′ E 17 5G
Meekatharra 26°32′S 118°29′ E 54 7C
Mekong → 9°30′N 106°15′ E 47 5J
Melanesia 4° 0′S 155° 0′ E 55 2L
Melbourne 37°48′S 144°58′ E 54 9J
Melekeok 7°27′N 134°38′ E 47 6M
Melilla 35°21′N 2°57′W 34 4C
Melrhir, Chott 34°13′N 6°30′ E 34 5E
Melton Mowbray 52°47′N 0°54′W 16 4F
Melville Island 11°30′S 131° 0′ E 54 4F
Memphis 35° 8′N 90° 2′W 59 3J
Mendip Hills 51°17′N 2°40′W 17 5D
Mendocino, Cape 40°26′N 124°25′W 58 2B
Mendoza 32°50′S 68°52′W 65 7E
Mérida 20°58′N 89°37′W 62 3G
Mérida, Cordillera de 9° 0′N 71° 0′W 63 6K
Merrick 55° 8′N 4°28′W 18 4D
Mersey → 53°25′N 3° 1′W 16 3D
Merseyside 53°31′N 3° 2′W 15 5E
Mersin 36°51′N 34°36′ E 35 4K
Merthyr Tydfil 51°45′N 3°22′W 17 5C
Mesopotamia 33°30′N 44° 0′ E 48 3D
Messina 38°11′N 15°34′ E 36 5E
Messina, Strait of 38°15′N 15°35′ E 35 4G
Metz 49° 8′N 6°10′ E 33 8M
Meuse → 50°45′N 5°41′ E 33 8L
Mexicali 32°40′N 115°30′W 62 1B
Mexico 19°24′N 99° 9′W 52 4E
Mexico ■ 25° 0′N 105° 0′W 62 3D
Mexico, Gulf of 25° 0′N 90° 0′W 62 2E
Miami 25°46′N 80°11′W 59 5K
Mianyang 31°22′N 104°47′ E 42 3E
Michigan 44° 0′N 85° 0′W 59 2J
Michigan, Lake 44° 0′N 87° 0′W 59 2J
Micronesia, Federated States of ■ 9° 0′N 150° 0′ E 71 4S
Mid & East Antrim 54°52′N 6°14′W 15 4C
Mid Ulster 54°36′N 6°45′W 15 4C
Middle East 35° 0′N 40° 0′ E 38 5F
Middlesbrough 54°35′N 1°13′W 16 2E
Midlothian 55°51′N 3° 5′W 15 4E
Midwest 42° 0′N 90° 0′W 59 2J
Milan 45°28′N 9°10′ E 36 2B
Mildura 34°13′S 142° 9′ E 54 8H
Milford Haven 51°42′N 5° 7′W 17 5A
Milltown Malbay 52°52′N 9°24′W 19 4B
Milton Keynes 52° 1′N 0°44′W 17 4F
Milwaukee 43° 2′N 87°54′W 59 2J
Milwaukee Deep 19°50′N 68° 0′W 63 4L
Minas Gerais 18°50′S 46° 0′W 66 6F
Mindanao 8° 0′N 125° 0′ E 47 6L
Minehead 51°12′N 3°29′W 17 5C
Minna 9°37′N 6°30′ E 52 2C
Minneapolis 44°57′N 93°16′W 59 2H
Minnesota 46° 0′N 94°15′W 59 1H
Minorca 40° 0′N 4° 0′ E 33 12L
Minsk 53°52′N 27°30′ E 31 5F
Mississippi 33° 0′N 90° 0′W 59 4J
Mississippi → 29° 9′N 89°15′W 59 5J
Mississippi River Delta 29°10′N 89°15′W 59 5J
Missouri 38°25′N 92°30′W 59 3H
Missouri → 38°49′N 90° 7′W 59 3H
Missouri, Coteau du 47° 0′N 100° 0′W 58 1F
Mitchell → 15°12′S 141°35′ E 54 5H
Miyakonojō 31°40′N 131° 5′ E 45 4B
Miyazaki 31°56′N 131°30′ E 45 4B
Mjøsa, Lake 60°40′N 11° 0′ E 32 2N
Módena 44°40′N 10°55′ E 36 2C
Mogadishu 2° 2′N 45°25′ E 51 5G
Moher, Cliffs of 52°58′N 9°27′W 19 4B
Mojave Desert 35° 0′N 116°30′W 58 3C
Mold 53° 9′N 3° 8′W 16 3C
Moldova ■ 47° 0′N 28° 0′ E 35 2J
Moluccas 1° 0′S 127° 0′ E 47 7L
Mombasa 4° 3′S 39°40′ E 53 3B
Monaco ■ 43°46′N 7°23′ E 33 11M
Monaghan 54°15′N 6°57′W 19 2E
Mongolia ■ 47° 0′N 103° 0′ E 42 5B
Mongolia, Plateau of 45° 0′N 105° 0′ E 47 2J
Monmouth 51°48′N 2°42′W 17 5D
Monrovia 6°18′N 10°47′W 51 5A
Montana 47° 0′N 110° 0′W 58 1D
Montego Bay 18°28′N 77°55′W 63 4J
Montenegro ■ 42°40′N 19°20′ E 35 3G
Montería 8°46′N 75°53′W 63 6J
Monterrey 25°40′N 100°19′W 62 2D
Montes Claros 16°30′S 43°50′W 66 6G
Montevideo 34°50′S 56°11′W 65 7F
Montgomery 32°23′N 86°19′W 59 4J
Montpelier 44°16′N 72°35′W 59 2M
Montpellier 43°37′N 3°52′ E 33 11K
Montréal 45°30′N 73°33′W 59 1M
Montrose 56°44′N 2°27′W 18 3F
Montserrat 16°40′N 62°10′W 63 4M
Morar, Loch 56°57′N 5°40′W 18 3C
Morava → 44°36′N 21° 4′ E 35 3H
Moray Firth 57°40′N 3°52′W 18 2E
Morecambe 54° 5′N 2°52′W 16 2D
Morecambe Bay 54° 7′N 3° 0′W 16 2C
Morena, Sierra 38°20′N 4° 0′W 33 13F
Morocco ■ 32° 0′N 5°50′W 51 2B
Morpeth 55°10′N 1°41′W 16 1E
Moscow 55°45′N 37°37′ E 31 4H
Moselle → 50°22′N 7°36′ E 33 8M
Moshi 3°22′S 37°18′ E 53 3B

Mossoró 5°10'S 37°15'W 66 4H
Mostaganem 35°54'N 0° 5'E 34 4D
Mosul 36°15'N 43° 5'E 48 2D
Motherwell 55°47'N 3°58'W 18 4E
Moulmein 16°30'N 97°40'E 47 5H
Mount Gambier 37°50'S 140°46'E 54 9H
Mount Isa 20°42'S 139°26'E 54 6G
Mourne → 54°52'N 7°26'W 19 2D
Mourne Mountains 54°10'N 6° 0'W 19 2E
Moville 55°11'N 7° 3'W 19 1D
Mozambique ■ 19° 0'S 35° 0'E 51 7F
Mozambique Channel 17°30'S 42°30'E 50 7G
Mudanjiang 44°38'N 129°30'E 45 2A
Mulhacén 37° 4'N 3°20'W 33 14G
Mull 56°25'N 5°56'W 18 3C
Mullet Peninsula 54°13'N 10° 2'W 19 2A
Mullingar 53°31'N 7°21'W 19 3D
Multan 30°15'N 71°36'E 46 3F
Mumbai 18°56'N 72°50'E 46 5F
Munich 48° 8'N 11°34'E 33 8P
Münster, *Germany* 51°58'N 7°37'E 32 7M
Munster, *Ireland* 52°18'N 8°44'W 19 4B
Murcia 38° 5'N 1°10'W 33 13H
Murmansk 68°57'N 33°10'E 31 2G
Murray → 35°20'S 139°22'E 54 9G
Murrumbidgee → 34°43'S 143°12'E 54 8H
Muscat 23°37'N 58°36'E 48 5G
Musgrave Ranges 26° 0'S 132° 0'E 54 7F
Musselburgh 55°57'N 3° 2'W 18 4E
Muz Tag 36°25'N 87°25'E 42 3C
Mwanza 2°30'S 32°58'E 53 3A
Mweru, Lake 9° 0'S 28°40'E 53 6D
Myanmar ■ 21° 0'N 96°30'E 47 4H
Mykolayiv 46°58'N 32° 0'E 35 2K

N

Naas 53°12'N 6°40'W 19 3E
Nafud Desert 28°15'N 41° 0'E 48 4D
Nagano 36°40'N 138°10'E 45 3C
Nagasaki 32°47'N 129°50'E 45 4A
Nagoya 35°10'N 136°50'E 45 3C
Nagpur 21° 8'N 79°10'E 46 4F
Naha 26°13'N 127°42'E 43 4G
Nairn 57°35'N 3°53'W 18 2E
Nairobi 1°17'S 36°48'E 53 3B
Naivasha 0°40'S 36°30'E 53 3B
Nakuru 0°15'S 36° 4'E 53 3B
Namangan 41° 0'N 71°40'E 40 5H
Namib Desert 22°30'S 15° 0'E 50 8D
Namibia ■ 22° 0'S 18° 9'E 51 8D
Namp'o 38°52'N 125°10'E 43 3G
Nanchang 28°42'N 115°55'E 43 4F
Nanchong 30°43'N 106° 2'E 42 3E
Nancy 48°42'N 6°12'E 33 8M
Nanjing 32° 2'N 118°47'E 43 3F
Nanning 22°48'N 108°20'E 42 4E
Nantes 47°12'N 1°33'W 33 9H
Nanyang 33°11'N 112°30'E 43 3F
Naples 40°50'N 14°15'E 36 4D
Narvik 68°28'N 17°26'E 31 2D
Nashville 36°10'N 86°47'W 59 3J
Nassau 25° 5'N 77°20'W 63 2J
Nasser, Lake 23° 0'N 32°30'E 48 5B
Natal 5°47'S 35°13'W 66 4H
Natron, Lake 2°20'S 36° 0'E 53 3B
Nauru ■ 1° 0'S 166° 0'E 71 5T
Navan 53°39'N 6°41'W 19 3E
Naxçıvan 39°12'N 45°15'E 48 2E
Naypyidaw 19°44'N 96°12'E 47 5H
Ndjamena 12°10'N 15° 0'E 51 4D
Neagh, Lough 54°37'N 6°25'W 19 2E
Neath 51°39'N 3°48'W 17 5C
Neblina, Pico da 0°48'N 66° 0'W 66 2B
Nebraska 41°30'N 99°30'W 58 2F
Nefteyugansk 61° 5'N 72°42'E 40 3H
Negro → 3° 0'S 60° 0'W 66 3C
Neisse → 52° 4'N 14°46'E 32 7R
Nelson, *N.Z.* 41°18'S 173°16'E 55 10P
Nelson, *U.K.* 53°50'N 2°13'W 16 3D
Nene → 52°49'N 0°11'E 16 4G
Nepal ■ 28° 0'N 84°30'E 46 4G
Ness, Loch 57°15'N 4°32'W 18 2D
Netherlands ■ 52° 0'N 5°30'E 32 6L
Neuquén 38°55'S 68° 0'W 65 7E
Nevada 39° 0'N 117° 0'W 58 3C
New Britain 5°50'S 150°20'E 54 3K
New Caledonia 21° 0'S 165° 0'E 55 6N
New Delhi 28°36'N 77°11'E 46 4F
New England 43° 0'N 71° 0'W 59 2M
New Forest 50°53'N 1°34'W 17 6E
New Georgia Islands 8°15'S 157°30'E 55 3L
New Guinea 4° 0'S 136° 0'E 54 3H
New Hampshire 44° 0'N 71°30'W 59 2M
New Ireland 3°20'S 151°50'E 54 2K
New Jersey 40° 0'N 74°30'W 59 2M
New Mexico 34°30'N 106° 0'W 58 4E
New Orleans 29°57'N 90° 4'W 59 5J
New Siberian Islands 75° 0'N 142° 0'E 41 2P
New South Wales 33° 0'S 146° 0'E 54 8J
New York 43° 0'N 75° 0'W 59 2L
New Zealand ■ 40° 0'S 176° 0'E 55 10Q
Newark-on-Trent 53° 5'N 0°48'W 16 3F
Newbridge 53°11'N 6°48'W 19 3E
Newbury 51°24'N 1°20'W 17 5E
Newcastle, *Australia* 33° 0'S 151°46'E 54 8K
Newcastle, *Ireland* 52°27'N 9° 3'W 19 4B
Newcastle-under-Lyme 53° 1'N 2°14'W 16 3D
Newcastle-upon-Tyne 54°58'N 1°36'W 16 2E
Newfoundland 49° 0'N 55° 0'W 56 5P
Newhaven 50°47'N 0° 3'E 17 6G
Newman 23°18'S 119°45'E 54 6C
Newmarket 52°15'N 0°25'E 17 4G
Newport, *England* 50°42'N 1°17'W 17 6E
Newport, *Wales* 51°35'N 3° 0'W 17 5D
Newquay 50°25'N 5° 6'W 17 6A
Newry 54°11'N 6°21'W 19 2E
Newry, Mourne & Down 54° 8'N 6° 3'W 15 4C
Newton Abbot 50°32'N 3°37'W 17 6C
Newton Aycliffe 54°37'N 1°34'W 16 2E
Newton Stewart 54°57'N 4°30'W 18 5D
Newtown 52°31'N 3°19'W 17 4C
Newtownabbey 54°40'N 5°56'W 19 2F
Newtownards 54°36'N 5°42'W 19 2F
Neyshābūr 36°10'N 58°50'E 48 2G
Niagara Falls 43° 7'N 79° 5'W 56 5M
Niamey 13°27'N 2° 6'E 52 1B
Nicaragua ■ 11°40'N 85°30'W 62 5G
Nicaragua, Lake 12° 0'N 85°30'W 62 5G
Nice 43°42'N 7°14'E 33 11M
Nicobar Islands 8° 0'N 93°30'E 46 6H
Nicosia 35°10'N 33°25'E 35 4K
Nidd → 53°59'N 1°23'W 16 2E
Niemen → 55°25'N 21°10'E 31 5E
Niger ■ 17°30'N 10° 0'E 51 4D
Niger → 5°33'N 6°33'E 52 2C
Niger Delta 5° 0'N 6° 0'E 52 3C
Nigeria ■ 8°30'N 8° 0'E 52 2C
Nile → 30°10'N 31° 6'E 50 2F
Nîmes 43°50'N 4°23'E 33 11L
Ningbo 29°51'N 121°28'E 43 4G
Nith → 55°14'N 3°33'W 18 4E
Niue 19° 2'S 169°54'W 55 5T
Nizhniy Novgorod 56°20'N 44° 0'E 40 4E
Nogales 31°19'N 110°56'W 62 1B
Nore → 52°25'N 6°58'W 19 4D
Norfolk, *U.K.* 52°39'N 0°54'E 15 5G
Norfolk, *U.S.A.* 36°50'N 76°17'W 59 3L
Norfolk Island 28°58'S 168° 3'E 55 7N
Norilsk 69°20'N 88° 6'E 41 3J
Normandy 48°45'N 0°10'E 33 8H
Norrköping 58°37'N 16°11'E 31 4D
Norrland 62°15'N 15°45'E 31 3D
North America 40° 0'N 100° 0'W 56 6K
North Berwick 56° 4'N 2°42'W 18 3F
North Cape 71°10'N 25°50'E 31 1F
North Carolina 35°30'N 80° 0'W 59 3K
North Dakota 47°30'N 100°15'W 58 1F
North Downs 51°19'N 0°21'E 17 5G
North Esk → 56°46'N 2°24'W 18 3F
North Foreland 51°22'N 1°28'E 13 6G
North Island 38° 0'S 175° 0'E 55 9Q
North Korea ■ 40° 0'N 127° 0'E 43 3G
North Macedonia ■ 41°53'N 21°40'E 35 3H
North Magnetic Pole 86°25'N 157°41'W 67 17A
North Minch 58° 5'N 5°55'W 18 1C
North Northamptonshire 52°24'N 0°43'W 15 5F
North Pole 90° 0'N 0° 0'W 67 8A
North Rona 59° 7'N 5°49'W 13 2D
North Ronaldsay 59°22'N 2°26'W 18 7F
North Sea 56° 0'N 4° 0'E 32 4K
North Tyne → 55° 0'N 2° 8'W 16 1D
North Uist 57°40'N 7°15'W 18 2A
North West Cape 21°45'S 114° 9'E 54 6B
North West Highlands 57°33'N 4°58'W 18 2C
North York Moors 54°23'N 0°53'W 16 2F
North Yorkshire 54°15'N 1°25'W 15 4E
Northallerton 54°20'N 1°26'W 16 2E
Northampton 52°15'N 0°53'W 17 4F
Northern Dvina → 64°32'N 40°30'E 28 3Q
Northern Ireland 54°45'N 7° 0'W 19 2E
Northern Marianas 17° 0'N 145° 0'E 47 5N
Northern Territory 20° 0'S 133° 0'E 54 6F
Northumberland 55°12'N 2° 0'W 15 4E
Norway ■ 63° 0'N 11° 0'E 31 3C
Norwegian Sea 66° 0'N 1° 0'E 28 2F
Norwich 52°38'N 1°18'E 16 4H
Noss Head 58°28'N 3° 3'W 18 1E
Nottingham 52°58'N 1°10'W 16 4E
Nottinghamshire 53°10'N 1° 3'W 15 5F
Nouakchott 18° 9'N 15°58'W 51 4A
Nouméa 22°17'S 166°30'E 55 6N
Nova Iguaçu 22°45'S 43°28'W 66 7G
Nova Scotia 45°10'N 63° 0'W 56 5N
Novara 45°28'N 8°38'E 36 2B
Novaya Zemlya 75° 0'N 56° 0'E 40 2F
Novgorod 58°30'N 31°25'E 31 4G
Novokuznetsk 53°45'N 87°10'E 40 4J
Novosibirsk 55° 0'N 83° 5'E 40 4J
Nubian Desert 21°30'N 33°30'E 50 3F
Nuevo Laredo 27°30'N 99°31'W 62 2E
Nuku'alofa 21°10'S 175°12'W 55 6R
Nukus 42°27'N 59°41'E 40 5F
Nullarbor Plain 31°10'S 129° 0'E 54 8E
Nuneaton 52°32'N 1°27'W 17 4E
Nur-Sultan 51°10'N 71°30'E 40 4H
Nuremberg 49°27'N 11° 3'E 33 8P
Nuuk 64°10'N 51°35'W 57 3P

O

Oates Land 69° 0'S 160° 0'E 67 11D
Oaxaca 17° 3'N 96°43'W 62 4E
Ob → 66°45'N 69°30'E 40 3G
Ob, Gulf of 69° 0'N 73° 0'E 40 3H
Oban 56°25'N 5°29'W 18 3C
Odense 55°22'N 10°23'E 32 5P
Oder → 53°33'N 14°38'E 32 6R
Odesa 46°30'N 30°45'E 35 2K
Offaly 53°15'N 7°30'W 15 5C
Ogbomosho 8° 1'N 4°11'E 52 2B
Ogooué → 1° 0'S 9° 0'E 50 5D
Ohio 40°15'N 82°45'W 59 2K
Ohio → 36°59'N 89° 8'W 59 3J
Ōita 33°14'N 131°36'E 45 4B
Ojos del Salado, Cerro 27° 0'S 68°40'W 64 6E
Okavango Delta 18°45'S 22°45'E 50 7E
Okayama 34°40'N 133°54'E 45 4B
Okhotsk 59°20'N 143°10'E 41 4Q
Okhotsk, Sea of 55° 0'N 145° 0'E 41 4Q
Oklahoma 35°20'N 97°30'W 58 3G
Oklahoma City 35°30'N 97°30'W 58 3G
Öland 56°45'N 16°38'E 31 4D
Ólbia 40°55'N 9°31'E 36 4B
Oldenburg 53° 9'N 8°13'E 32 6N
Oldham 53°33'N 2° 7'W 16 3D
Olympia, *Greece* 37°39'N 21°39'E 35 4H
Olympia, *U.S.A.* 47° 3'N 122°53'W 58 1B
Olympus, Mount 40° 6'N 22°23'E 35 3H
Omagh 54°35'N 7°15'W 19 2D
Omaha 41°17'N 95°58'W 59 2G
Oman ■ 23° 0'N 58° 0'E 46 4D
Oman, Gulf of 24°30'N 58°30'E 48 5G
Omdurmân 15°40'N 32°28'E 51 4F
Omsk 55° 0'N 73°12'E 40 4H
Onega → 63°58'N 38° 2'E 31 3H
Onega, Lake 61°44'N 35°22'E 31 3H
Onitsha 6° 6'N 6°42'E 52 2C
Ontario, Lake 43°20'N 78° 0'W 59 2L
Oporto 41° 8'N 8°40'W 33 12D
Oran 35°45'N 0°39'W 34 4C
Orange → 28°41'S 16°28'E 50 8D
Örebro 59°20'N 15°18'E 31 4D
Oregon 44° 0'N 121° 0'W 58 2B
Orense 42°19'N 7°55'W 33 11E
Orinoco → 9°15'N 61°30'W 63 6M
Orizaba, Pico de 18°58'N 97°15'W 62 4E
Orkney Islands 59° 0'N 3° 0'W 18 7E
Orlando 28°32'N 81°22'W 59 5K
Orléans 47°54'N 1°52'E 33 9J
Ormskirk 53°35'N 2°54'W 16 3D
Ōsaka 34°42'N 135°30'E 45 4C
Osh 40°37'N 72°49'E 40 5H
Oshogbo 7°48'N 4°37'E 52 2B
Oslo 59°54'N 10°43'E 31 4C
Osnabrück 52°17'N 8° 3'E 32 6N
Östersund 63°10'N 14°38'E 31 3C
Oswestry 52°52'N 3° 3'W 16 4C
Otranto, Strait of 40°15'N 18°40'E 36 4G
Ottawa 45°26'N 75°42'W 59 1L
Ouagadougou 12°25'N 1°30'W 51 4B
Oubangi → 0°30'S 17°50'E 50 6D
Oujda 34°41'N 1°55'W 34 5C
Oulu 65° 1'N 25°29'E 31 3F
Oulu, Lake 64°25'N 27°15'E 31 3F
Ouse →, *East Sussex* 50°47'N 0° 4'E 17 5G
Ouse →, *North Yorkshire* 53°44'N 0°55'W 16 3E
Outer Hebrides 57°30'N 7°15'W 18 2A
Oxford 51°46'N 1°15'W 17 5E
Oxfordshire 51°48'N 1°16'W 15 6F
Oyo 7°46'N 3°56'E 52 2B
Ozark Plateau 37°20'N 91°40'W 59 3H
Ozarks, Lake of the 38°12'N 92°38'W 59 3H

P

Pacaraima, Sierra 4° 0'N 62°30'W 63 7M
Pacific Ocean 10° 0'N 140° 0'W 68 4B
Padang 1° 0'S 100°20'E 47 7J
Pádova 45°25'N 11°53'E 36 2C
Pago Pago 14°16'S 170°43'W 55 4S
Paignton 50°26'N 3°35'W 17 6C
Paisley 55°50'N 4°25'W 18 4D
Pakistan ■ 30° 0'N 70° 0'E 46 4E
Palau ■ 7°30'N 134°30'E 47 6M
Palawan 9°30'N 118°30'E 47 6K
Palembang 3° 0'S 104°50'E 47 7J
Palermo 38° 7'N 13°22'E 36 5D
Palma de Mallorca 39°35'N 2°39'E 33 13K
Palmas 10°13'S 48°16'W 66 5F
Palmer Land 73° 0'S 63° 0'W 67 17E
Palmerston North 40°21'S 175°39'E 55 10Q
Palmira 3°32'N 76°16'W 63 7J
Pamir 37°40'N 73° 0'E 46 3F
Pampas 35° 0'S 63° 0'W 64 7E
Panama ■ 8°48'N 79°55'W 63 6H
Panama, Gulf of 8° 4'N 79°20'W 63 6J
Panama, Isthmus of 9° 0'N 79° 0'W 63 6J
Panama Canal 9°10'N 79°37'W 64 3D
Pantelleria 36°50'N 11°57'E 36 6D
Panzhihua 26°33'N 101°44'E 42 4E
Papua New Guinea ■ 8° 0'S 145° 0'E 54 3J
Pará 3°20'S 52° 0'W 66 3E
Paraguay ■ 23° 0'S 57° 0'W 65 6F
Paraguay → 27°18'S 58°38'W 64 6F
Paraíba 7° 0'S 36° 0'W 66 4H
Parakou 9°25'N 2°40'E 52 2B
Paramaribo 5°50'N 55°10'W 65 3F
Paraná 24°30'S 51° 0'W 66 7E
Paraná → 33°43'S 59°15'W 64 7F
Paris 48°53'N 2°20'E 33 8K
Parma 44°48'N 10°20'E 36 2C
Parnaíba → 3° 0'S 41°50'W 66 3G
Parrett → 51°12'N 3° 1'W 17 5D
Passage West 51°52'N 8°21'W 19 5C
Patagonia 45° 0'S 69° 0'W 64 8E
Patna 25°35'N 85°12'E 46 4G
Patra 38°14'N 21°47'E 35 4H
Pau 43°19'N 0°25'W 33 11H
Peak, The 53°24'N 1°52'W 16 3E
Pearl → 30°11'N 89°32'W 43 4F
Pecos → 29°42'N 101°22'W 62 2D
Peebles 55°40'N 3°11'W 18 4E
Peloponnese 37°10'N 22° 0'E 35 4H
Pelotas 31°42'S 52°23'W 66 9E
Pembroke 51°41'N 4°55'W 17 5B
Pennines 54°45'N 2°27'W 16 2D
Pennsylvania 40°45'N 77°30'W 59 2L
Penrith 54°40'N 2°45'W 16 2D
Pentland Firth 58°43'N 3°10'W 18 1E
Penza 53°15'N 45° 5'E 40 4E
Penzance 50° 7'N 5°33'W 17 6A
Pereira 4°49'N 75°43'W 63 7J
Perm 58° 0'N 56°10'E 38 4F
Pernambuco 8° 0'S 37° 0'W 66 4H
Perpignan 42°42'N 2°53'E 33 11K
Persepolis 29°55'N 52°50'E 48 4F
Persian Gulf 27° 0'N 50° 0'E 48 4F
Perth, *Australia* 31°57'S 115°52'E 54 8C
Perth, *U.K.* 56°24'N 3°26'W 18 3E
Peru ■ 4° 0'S 75° 0'W 65 4D
Perúgia 43° 7'N 12°23'E 36 3D
Pescara 42°28'N 14°13'E 36 3D
Peterborough 52°35'N 0°15'W 17 4F
Peterhead 57°31'N 1°48'W 18 2G
Peterlee 54°47'N 1°20'W 16 2E
Petrozavodsk 61°41'N 34°20'E 31 3G
Philadelphia 39°57'N 75° 9'W 59 2L
Philippines ■ 12° 0'N 123° 0'E 47 5L
Phnom Penh 11°33'N 104°55'E 47 5J
Phoenix 33°26'N 112° 4'W 58 4D
Phoenix Islands 3°30'S 172° 0'W 55 2S
Phuket 7°53'N 98°24'E 47 5H
Piacenza 45° 1'N 9°40'E 36 2B
Piauí 7° 0'S 43° 0'W 66 4G
Pierre 44°22'N 100°21'W 58 2F
Pindus Mountains 40° 0'N 21° 0'E 35 4H
Pingxiang 27°43'N 113°48'E 43 4F
Pisa 43°43'N 10°23'E 36 3C
Pitlochry 56°42'N 3°44'W 18 3E
Pittsburgh 40°26'N 79°58'W 59 2K
Plata, Río de la → 34°45'S 57°30'W 64 7F
Ploieşti 44°57'N 26° 5'E 35 3J
Plovdiv 42° 8'N 24°44'E 35 3H
Plymouth 50°22'N 4°10'W 17 6B
Plzeň 49°45'N 13°22'E 32 8Q
Po → 44°57'N 12° 4'E 36 2C
Pobedy Peak 42° 0'N 79°58'E 40 5H
Podgorica 42°30'N 19°19'E 35 3G
Pointe-à-Pitre 16°15'N 61°32'W 63 4M
Pointe-Noire 4°48'S 11°53'E 51 6D
Poitiers 46°35'N 0°20'E 33 9J
Poland ■ 52° 0'N 20° 0'E 31 5D
Polynesia 10° 0'S 162° 0'W 68 5B
Pompeii 40°45'N 14°30'E 36 4E
Ponta Grossa 25° 7'S 50°10'W 66 8E
Pontchartrain, Lake 30° 5'N 90° 5'W 59 4J
Pontianak 0° 3'S 109°15'E 47 7J
Pontine Mountains 41° 0'N 36°45'E 35 3L
Pontypool 51°42'N 3° 2'W 17 5C
Pontypridd 51°36'N 3°20'W 17 5C
Poole 50°43'N 1°59'W 17 6D
Poopó, Lake 18°30'S 67°35'W 64 5E
Popocatépetl, Volcán 19° 2'N 98°38'W 62 4E
Pori 61°29'N 21°48'E 31 3E
Port-au-Prince 18°40'N 72°20'W 63 4K
Port Augusta 32°30'S 137°50'E 54 8G
Port Harcourt 4°40'N 7°10'E 52 3C
Port Hedland 20°25'S 118°35'E 54 6C
Port Lincoln 34°42'S 135°52'E 54 8G
Port Moresby 9°24'S 147° 8'E 54 3J
Port of Spain 10°40'N 61°31'W 63 5M
Port Pirie 33°10'S 138° 1'E 54 8G
Port Said 31°16'N 32°18'E 35 5K
Port Talbot 51°35'N 3°47'W 17 5C
Port Vila 17°45'S 168°18'E 55 5N
Portadown 54°25'N 6°27'W 19 2E
Porthmadog 52°55'N 4° 8'W 16 4B
Portland, *Maine* 43°39'N 70°16'W 59 2M
Portland, *Oregon* 45°32'N 122°37'W 58 1B
Portland Bill 50°31'N 2°28'W 17 6D
Portlaoise 53° 2'N 7°18'W 19 3D
Pôrto Alegre 30° 5'S 51°10'W 66 9E
Porto-Novo 6°23'N 2°42'E 52 2B
Pôrto Velho 8°46'S 63°54'W 66 4C
Portree 57°25'N 6°12'W 18 2B
Portsmouth 50°48'N 1° 6'W 17 6E
Portugal ■ 40° 0'N 8° 0'W 33 13E
Potomac → 38° 0'N 76°23'W 59 3L
Potsdam 52°23'N 13° 3'E 32 6Q
Poulaphouca Reservoir 53° 8'N 6°30'W 19 3E
Powys 52°20'N 3°20'W 15 5E
Poznań 52°25'N 16°55'E 31 5D
Prague 50° 4'N 14°25'E 32 7R
Prayagraj 25°25'N 81°58'E 46 4G
Preston 53°46'N 2°42'W 16 3D
Pretoria 25°44'S 28°12'E 51 8E
Prince Charles Mountains 72° 0'S 67° 0'E 67 6E
Pripet → 51°20'N 30°15'E 35 1J
Prishtinë 42°40'N 21°13'E 35 3H
Provence 43°40'N 5°46'E 33 11L
Providence 41°49'N 71°24'W 59 2M
Prydz Bay 69° 0'S 74° 0'E 67 6D
Pskov 57°50'N 28°25'E 31 4F
Puebla 19° 3'N 98°12'W 62 4E
Puerto Barrios 15°40'N 88°32'W 62 4G
Puerto Rico 18°15'N 66°45'W 63 4L
Pumlumon Fawr 52°28'N 3°46'W 17 4C
Pune 18°29'N 73°57'E 46 5F
Punjab 31° 0'N 76° 0'E 46 3F
Punta Arenas 53°10'S 71° 0'W 65 9D
Purus → 3°42'S 61°28'W 66 3C
Putrajaya 2°55'N 101°40'E 47 6J
Putumayo → 3° 7'S 67°58'W 66 3B
Pwllheli 52°53'N 4°25'W 16 4B
P'yŏngyang 39° 0'N 125°30'E 43 3G
Pyramids 29°58'N 31° 9'E 48 4B
Pyrenees 42°45'N 0°18'E 33 11J

Q

Qaidam Basin 37° 0'N 95° 0'E 42 3D
Qatar ■ 25°30'N 51°15'E 48 4F
Qazvīn 36°15'N 50° 0'E 48 2E
Qilian Shan 38°30'N 96° 0'E 42 3D
Qingdao 36° 5'N 120°20'E 43 3G
Qiqihar 47°26'N 124° 0'E 43 2G
Qom 34°40'N 51° 0'E 48 3F
Quanzhou 24°55'N 118°34'E 43 4F
Québec 46°52'N 71°13'W 59 1M
Queen Elizabeth Islands 76° 0'N 95° 0'W 56 1H
Queen Elizabeth Land 84° 0'S 42° 0'W 67 18F
Queen Mary Land 70° 0'S 95° 0'E 67 7E
Queen Maud Land 72°30'S 12° 0'E 67 3E
Queensland 22° 0'S 142° 0'E 54 6H
Querétaro 20°36'N 100°23'W 62 3D
Quetta 30°15'N 66°55'E 46 3E
Quibdó 5°42'N 76°40'W 63 6J
Quilpie 26°35'S 144°11'E 54 7H
Quimper 48° 0'N 4° 9'W 33 9F
Quito 0°15'S 78°35'W 65 4D

R

Rabat 34° 2'N 6°48'W 51 2B
Race, Cape 46°40'N 53° 5'W 56 5P
Rainier, Mount 46°52'N 121°46'W 58 1B
Rajkot 22°15'N 70°56'E 46 4F

Raleigh 35°47'N 78°39'W 59 3L
Ramsey 54°20'N 4°22'W 16 2B
Rangoon = Yangôn 16°45'N 96°20' E 47 5H
Rannoch, Loch 56°41'N 4°20'W 18 3D
Ra's al Khaymah 25°50'N 55°59' E 48 4G
Rathlin Island 55°18'N 6°14'W 19 1E
Ravenna 44°25'N 12°12' E 36 2D
Reading 51°27'N 0°58'W 17 5F
Recife 8° 0'S 35° 0'W 66 4H
Red →, *U.S.A.* 31° 1'N 91°45'W 59 4H
Red →, *Vietnam* 20°16'N 106°34' E 42 4E
Red Sea 25° 0'N 36° 0' E 48 5C
Redcar 54°37'N 1° 4'W 16 2E
Redditch 52°18'N 1°55'W 17 4E
Redruth 50°14'N 5°14'W 17 6A
Ree, Lough 53°35'N 8° 0'W 19 3D
Regensburg 49° 1'N 12° 6' E 33 8Q
Réggio di Calábria 38° 6'N 15°39' E 36 5E
Réggio nell'Emília 44°43'N 10°36' E 36 2C
Reigate 51°14'N 0°12'W 17 5F
Reims 49°15'N 4° 1' E 33 8L
Rennell 11°40'S 160°10' E 55 4M
Rennes 48° 7'N 1°41'W 33 8H
Réunion 21° 0'S 56° 0' E 71 6M
Revilla Gigedo Islands 18°40'N 112° 0'W 62 4B
Rey Malabo 3°45'N 8°50' E 52 3C
Reykjavík 64°10'N 21°57'W 57 3S
Reynosa 26° 7'N 98°18'W 62 2E
Rhine → 51°52'N 6° 2' E 32 7M
Rhode Island 41°40'N 71°30'W 59 2M
Rhodes 36°15'N 28°10' E 35 4J
Rhodope Mountains 41°40'N 24°20' E 35 3H
Rhondda 51°39'N 3°31'W 17 5C
Rhône → 43°28'N 4°42' E 33 11L
Rhyl 53°20'N 3°29'W 16 3C
Ribble → 53°52'N 2°25'W 16 3D
Ribeirão Prêto 21°10'S 47°50'W 66 7F
Richmond, *U.K.* 54°25'N 1°43'W 16 2E
Richmond, *U.S.A.* 37°33'N 77°27'W 59 3L
Rift Valley 7° 0'N 30° 0' E 50 5F
Riga 56°53'N 24° 8' E 31 4E
Riga, Gulf of 57°40'N 23°45' E 31 4D
Riiser-Larsen Sea 67°30'S 22° 0' E 67 4D
Rimini 44° 3'N 12°33' E 36 2D
Rio Branco 9°58'S 67°49'W 66 4B
Rio de Janeiro 22°54'S 43°12'W 66 7G
Rio Grande do Norte 5°40'S 36° 0'W 66 3H
Rio Grande do Sul 30° 0'S 53° 0'W 66 9E
Ripon 54° 9'N 1°31'W 16 2E
Riviera 44° 0'N 8°30' E 36 2B
Riyadh 24°41'N 46°42' E 48 5E
Rochdale 53°38'N 2° 9'W 16 3D
Rochester, *U.K.* 51°23'N 0°31' E 17 5G
Rochester, *U.S.A.* 43°10'N 77°37'W 59 2L
Rockhampton 23°22'S 150°32' E 54 6K
Rocky Mountains 49° 0'N 115° 0'W 58 2E
Roma 41°54'N 12°28' E 36 4D
Romania ■ 46° 0'N 25° 0' E 35 2H
Romney Marsh 51° 2'N 0°54' E 17 5G
Romsey 51° 0'N 1°29'W 17 5E
Rondônia 11° 0'S 63° 0'W 66 5C
Ronne Ice Shelf 77°30'S 60° 0'W 67 18E
Roraima 2° 0'N 61°30'W 66 2C
Roraima, Mount 5°10'N 60°40'W 63 6M
Rosario 33° 0'S 60°40'W 65 7E
Roscommon 53°38'N 8°11'W 19 3C
Roscrea 52°57'N 7°49'W 19 4D
Roseau 15°17'N 61°24'W 63 4M
Ross Ice Shelf 80° 0'S 180° 0' E 67 12F
Ross-on-Wye 51°54'N 2°34'W 17 5D
Ross Sea 74° 0'S 178° 0' E 67 11E
Rosslare Harbour 52°15'N 6°20'W 19 4E
Rostock 54° 5'N 12° 8' E 32 5Q
Rostov 47°15'N 39°45' E 35 2L
Rother → 50°59'N 0°45' E 17 5G
Rotherham 53°26'N 1°20'W 16 3E
Rothesay 55°50'N 5° 3'W 18 4C
Rotorua 38° 9'S 176°16' E 55 9Q
Rotterdam 51°55'N 4°30' E 32 7L
Rouen 49°27'N 1° 4' E 33 8J
Rousay 59°10'N 3° 2'W 18 7E
Rovaniemi 66°29'N 25°41' E 31 2F
Royal Leamington Spa 52°18'N 1°31'W 17 4E
Royal Tunbridge Wells 51° 7'N 0°16' E 17 5G
Rub' al Khālī 19° 0'N 48° 0' E 46 5E
Rugby 52°23'N 1°16'W 17 4E
Rùm 57° 0'N 6°20'W 18 3B
Runcorn 53°21'N 2°44'W 16 3D
Rushden 52°18'N 0°35'W 17 4F
Russia ■ 62° 0'N 105° 0' E 40 3F
Rutland 52°38'N 0°40'W 15 5F
Rwanda ■ 2° 0'S 30° 0' E 51 6F
Ryan, Loch 55° 0'N 5° 2'W 18 5C
Rybinsk Reservoir 58°30'N 38°25' E 31 4H
Ryde 50°43'N 1° 9'W 17 6E
Rye → 54°11'N 0°44'W 16 2F
Ryukyu Islands 26° 0'N 126° 0' E 43 4G

S

Saarbrücken 49°14'N 6°59' E 33 8M
Saaremaa 58°30'N 22°30' E 31 4E
Sabah 6° 0'N 117° 0' E 47 6K
Sabine → 29°59'N 93°47'W 59 5H
Sacramento 38°35'N 121°29'W 58 3B
Sacramento Mountains 32°30'N 105°30'W 58 4E
Sacramento Valley 39°30'N 122° 0'W 58 3B
Sado 38° 0'N 138°25' E 45 3C
Sahara 23° 0'N 5° 0' E 50 3C
Sahel 16° 0'N 5° 0' E 50 4C
Saimaa, Lake 61°15'N 28°15' E 31 3F
St. Albans 51°45'N 0°19'W 17 5F
St. Andrews 56°20'N 2°47'W 18 3F
St. Austell 50°20'N 4°47'W 17 6B
St. David's Head 51°54'N 5°19'W 17 5A
St-Étienne 45°27'N 4°22' E 33 10L
St. George's 12° 5'N 61°43'W 63 5M
St. George's Channel 52° 0'N 6° 0'W 19 5E
St. Helena 15°58'S 5°42'W 51 7B
St. Helens 53°27'N 2°44'W 16 3D
St. Helens, Mount 46°12'N 122°12'W 58 1B
St. Helier 49°10'N 2° 7'W 17 7D
St. Ives 50°12'N 5°30'W 17 6A
St. John's, *Antigua* 17° 6'N 61°51'W 63 4M
St. John's, *Canada* 47°35'N 52°40'W 57 5P
St. Kilda 57°49'N 8°34'W 32 4D
St. Kitts & Nevis ■ 17°20'N 62°40'W 63 4M
St. Lawrence → 49°30'N 66° 0'W 59 1M
St. Louis 38°37'N 90°11'W 59 3H
St. Lucia ■ 14° 0'N 60°57'W 63 5M
St-Malo 48°39'N 2° 1'W 33 8H
St. Mary's 49°55'N 6°18'W 17 8J
St-Nazaire 47°17'N 2°12'W 33 9G
St. Neots 52°14'N 0°15'W 17 7E
St. Paul 44°56'N 93° 5'W 59 2H
St. Peter Port 49°26'N 2°33'W 17 7D
St. Petersburg, *Russia* 59°55'N 30°20' E 31 4G
St. Petersburg, *U.S.A.* 27°46'N 82°40'W 59 5K
St. Vincent & the Grenadines ■ 13° 0'N 61°10'W 63 5M
Saitama 35°54'N 139°38' E 45 3C
Sakai 34°34'N 135°27' E 45 4C
Sakhalin 51° 0'N 143° 0' E 41 4Q
Salamanca 40°58'N 5°39'W 33 12F
Sale 53°26'N 2°19'W 16 3D
Salerno 40°41'N 14°47' E 36 4E
Salford 53°30'N 2°18'W 16 3D
Salisbury 51° 4'N 1°47'W 17 5E
Salisbury Plain 51°14'N 1°55'W 17 5E
Salt Lake City 40°45'N 111°53'W 58 2D
Saltash 50°24'N 4°14'W 17 6B
Salton Sea 33°15'N 115°45'W 58 4C
Salvador 13° 0'S 38°30'W 66 5H
Salween → 16°31'N 97°37' E 47 5H
Salzburg 47°48'N 13° 2' E 33 9Q
Samara 53° 8'N 50° 6' E 40 4F
Samarkand 39°40'N 66°55' E 40 6G
Samoa ■ 14° 0'S 172° 0'W 55 4S
Samos 37°45'N 26°50' E 35 4J
Samsun 41°15'N 36°22' E 35 3L
San Andreas Fault 36° 0'N 121° 0'W 58 3B
San Antonio 29°25'N 98°29'W 58 5G
San Bernardino 34° 7'N 117°19'W 58 4C
San Blas, Cape 29°40'N 85°21'W 59 5J
San Cristóbal 7°46'N 72°14'W 63 6K
San Diego 32°42'N 117° 9'W 58 4C
San Francisco 37°46'N 122°23'W 58 3B
San Joaquin Valley 37°20'N 121° 0'W 58 3B
San José, *Costa Rica* 9°55'N 84° 2'W 63 6H
San Jose, *U.S.A.* 37°20'N 121°53'W 58 3B
San Juan, *Argentina* 31°30'S 68°30'W 65 7E
San Juan, *Puerto Rico* 18°28'N 66° 7'W 63 4L
San Lucas, Cabo 22°52'N 109°53'W 62 3B
San Luis Potosí 22° 9'N 100°59'W 62 3D
San Marino ■ 43°56'N 12°25' E 36 3C
San Miguel de Tucumán 26°50'S 65°20'W 65 6E
San Pedro Sula 15°30'N 88° 0'W 62 4G
San Salvador 13°40'N 89°10'W 62 4G
Sana 15°27'N 44°12' E 46 5C
Sanaga → 3°35'N 9°38' E 52 2C
Sanandaj 35°18'N 47° 1' E 48 2E
Sanday 59°16'N 2°31'W 18 7F
Sanliurfa 37°12'N 38°50' E 48 2C
Sanquhar 55°22'N 3°54'W 18 4E
Santa Catarina 27°25'S 48°30'W 66 8F
Santa Clara 22°20'N 80° 0'W 63 3H
Santa Cruz 17°43'S 63°10'W 65 5E
Santa Cruz Islands 10°30'S 166° 0' E 55 4N
Santa Fé, *Argentina* 31°35'S 60°41'W 65 7E
Santa Fe, *U.S.A.* 35°41'N 105°57'W 58 3E
Santander 43°27'N 3°51'W 33 11G
Santarém 2°25'S 54°42'W 66 3E
Santiago 33°26'S 70°40'W 65 7D
Santiago de Compostela 42°52'N 8°37'W 33 11D
Santiago de Cuba 20° 0'N 75°49'W 63 3J
Santiago de los Caballeros 19°30'N 70°40'W 63 4K
Santo Domingo 18°30'N 69°59'W 63 4L
Santos 24° 0'S 46°20'W 66 7F
Sanya 18°14'N 109°29' E 43 5E
São Francisco → 10°30'S 36°24'W 66 5H
São Luís 2°39'S 44°15'W 66 3G
São Paulo 23°32'S 46°38'W 66 7F
São Tomé & Príncipe ■ 0°12'N 6°39' E 51 5C
Saône → 45°44'N 4°50' E 33 10L
Sapporo 43° 0'N 141°21' E 45 2D
Sarajevo 43°52'N 18°26' E 35 3G
Sarasota 27°20'N 82°32'W 59 5K
Saratov 51°30'N 46° 2' E 38 4E
Sarawak 2° 0'N 113° 0' E 47 6K
Sardinia 40° 0'N 9° 0' E 36 4B
Sargasso Sea 27° 0'N 72° 0'W 63 2K
Sark 49°25'N 2°22'W 17 7D
Sasebo 33°10'N 129°43' E 45 4A
Sássari 40°43'N 8°34' E 36 4B
Saudi Arabia ■ 26° 0'N 44° 0' E 48 4D
Savannah 32° 5'N 81° 6'W 59 4K
Savannah → 32° 2'N 80°53'W 59 4K
Scafell Pike 54°27'N 3°14'W 16 2C
Scandinavia 64° 0'N 12° 0' E 28 3J
Scarborough 54°17'N 0°24'W 16 2F
Scilly, Isles of 49°56'N 6°22'W 17 8J
Scotland 57° 0'N 4° 0'W 18 3D
Scottish Borders 55°35'N 2°50'W 15 4E
Scunthorpe 53°36'N 0°39'W 16 3F
Seaham 54°50'N 1°20'W 16 2E
Seattle 47°36'N 122°19'W 58 1B
Seine → 49°26'N 0°26' E 33 8J
Sekondi-Takoradi 4°58'N 1°45'W 52 3A
Selkirk 55°33'N 2°50'W 18 4F
Sellafield 54°25'N 3°29'W 16 2C
Selsey Bill 50°43'N 0°47'W 17 6F
Selvas 6°30'S 67° 0'W 66 4C
Semarang 7° 0'S 110°26' E 47 7K
Sendai 38°15'N 140°53' E 45 3D
Senegal ■ 14°30'N 14°30'W 51 4A
Sénégal → 15°48'N 16°32'W 50 4A
Senkaku Islands 25°45'N 123°30' E 43 4G
Seoul 37°31'N 126°58' E 43 3G
Seram 3°10'S 129° 0' E 47 7L
Serbia ■ 43°20'N 20° 0' E 35 3H
Serengeti Plain 2°40'S 35° 0' E 53 3A
Sergipe 10°30'S 37°30'W 66 5H
Serov 59°29'N 60°35' E 40 4G
Sevastopol 44°35'N 33°30' E 35 3K
Severn → 51°35'N 2°40'W 17 5D
Severnaya Zemlya 79° 0'N 100° 0' E 41 2K
Seville 37°23'N 5°58'W 33 14F
Seychelles ■ 5° 0'S 56° 0' E 38 9G
Sfax 34°49'N 10°48' E 34 5F
Shackleton Ice Shelf 66° 0'S 100° 0' E 67 8D
Shanghai 31°15'N 121°26' E 43 3G
Shangqiu 34°26'N 115°36' E 43 3F
Shannon → 52°35'N 9°30'W 19 3C
Shantou 23°18'N 116°40' E 43 4F
Shapinsay 59° 3'N 2°51'W 18 7F
Sharjah 25°23'N 55°26' E 48 4G
Sharm el Sheikh 27°53'N 34°18' E 48 4B
Shebele → 2° 0'N 44° 0' E 50 5G
Sheerness 51°26'N 0°47' E 17 5G
Sheffield 53°23'N 1°28'W 16 3E
Shenyang 41°48'N 123°27' E 43 2G
Shenzhen 22°32'N 114° 5' E 43 4F
Shetland Islands 60°30'N 1°30'W 18 8J
Shihezi 44°15'N 86° 2' E 42 2C
Shijiazhuang 38° 2'N 114°28' E 43 3F
Shikoku 33°30'N 133°30' E 45 4B
Shimonoseki 33°58'N 130°55' E 45 4B
Shīrāz 29°42'N 52°30' E 48 4F
Shizuoka 34°57'N 138°24' E 45 4C
Shrewsbury 52°43'N 2°45'W 16 4D
Shropshire 52°36'N 2°45'W 15 5E
Shymkent 42°18'N 69°36' E 40 5G
Si Kiang → 22°20'N 113°20' E 43 4F
Siberia 60° 0'N 100° 0' E 40 4J
Sichuan 30°30'N 103° 0' E 42 3E
Sicily 37°30'N 14°30' E 36 6D
Sidmouth 50°40'N 3°15'W 17 6C
Sidra, Gulf of 31°40'N 18°30' E 50 2D
Siena 43°19'N 11°21' E 36 3C
Sierra Blanca Peak 33°23'N 105°49'W 58 4E
Sierra Leone ■ 9° 0'N 12° 0'W 51 5A
Sierra Madre 16° 0'N 93° 0'W 62 2C
Sierra Nevada, *Spain* 37° 3'N 3°15'W 33 14F
Sierra Nevada, *U.S.A.* 39° 0'N 120°30'W 58 3B
Sikhote Alin Range 45° 0'N 136° 0' E 45 2B
Simpson Desert 25° 0'S 137° 0' E 54 7G
Sinai 29° 0'N 34° 0' E 48 4B
Singapore ■ 1°17'N 103°51' E 47 6J
Sinkiang 42° 0'N 86° 0' E 42 3C
Siracusa 37° 4'N 15°17' E 36 6E
Sivas 39°43'N 36°58' E 35 4L
Sjælland 55°30'N 11°30' E 31 5D
Skagen 57°43'N 10°35' E 31 4C
Skagerrak 57°30'N 9° 0' E 31 4B
Skegness 53° 9'N 0°20' E 16 3G
Skellefteå 64°45'N 20°50' E 31 3E
Skipton 53°58'N 2° 3'W 16 3D
Skopje 42° 1'N 21°26' E 35 3H
Skye 57°15'N 6°10'W 18 2B
Slaney → 52°26'N 6°33'W 19 4E
Slea Head 52° 6'N 10°27'W 19 4A
Slieve Donard 54°11'N 5°55'W 19 2F
Sligo 54°16'N 8°28'W 19 2C
Sligo Bay 54°18'N 8°40'W 19 2C
Slough 51°30'N 0°36'W 17 5F
Slovakia ■ 48°30'N 20° 0' E 35 2G
Slovenia ■ 45°58'N 14°30' E 34 2F
Smolensk 54°45'N 32° 5' E 31 5G
Snaefell 54°16'N 4°27'W 16 2B
Snake → 46°12'N 119° 2'W 58 2C
Snowdon 53° 4'N 4° 5'W 16 3B
Snowy Mountains 36°30'S 148°20' E 54 9J
Sobradinho Reservoir 9°30'S 42° 0'W 66 4G
Sochi 43°35'N 39°40' E 35 3L
Socotra 12°30'N 54° 0' E 50 4H
Sofiya 42°45'N 23°20' E 35 3H
Sogne Fjord 61°10'N 5°50' E 31 3B
Sokoto 13° 2'N 5°16' E 52 1C
Solapur 17°43'N 75°56' E 46 5F
Solihull 52°26'N 1°47'W 17 4E
Solomon Islands ■ 6° 0'S 155° 0' E 55 3L
Solomon Sea 7° 0'S 150° 0' E 54 3K
Solway Firth 54°49'N 3°35'W 16 2C
Somalia ■ 7° 0'N 47° 0' E 51 5G
Somerset 51° 9'N 3° 0'W 15 6E
Songkhla 7°13'N 100°37' E 47 6J
Sonora 29°20'N 110°40'W 58 5D
Sousse 35°50'N 10°38' E 34 4F
South Africa ■ 32° 0'S 23° 0' E 51 9E
South America 10° 0'S 60° 0'W 64 5F
South Australia 32° 0'S 139° 0' E 54 8G
South Carolina 34° 0'N 81° 0'W 59 4K
South China Sea 10° 0'N 113° 0' E 47 5K
South Dakota 44°15'N 100° 0'W 58 2F
South Downs 50°52'N 0°25'W 17 6F
South East Cape 43°40'S 146°50' E 54 10J
South Esk → 56°43'N 2°31'W 18 3F
South Georgia 54°30'S 37° 0'W 64 9H
South Island 44° 0'S 170° 0' E 55 10P
South Korea ■ 36° 0'N 128° 0' E 43 3G
South Magnetic Pole 64° 2'S 135°43' E 67 9D
South Orkney Islands 63° 0'S 45° 0'W 67 18D
South Pole 90° 0'S 0° 0'W 67 3F
South Ronaldsay 58°40'N 2°58'W 18 6F
South Shetland Islands 62° 0'S 59° 0'W 67 18D
South Shields 55° 0'N 1°25'W 16 2E
South Sudan ■ 8° 0'N 30° 0' E 51 5E
South Uist 57°20'N 7°15'W 18 2A
South Yorkshire 53°27'N 1°36'W 15 5F
Southampton 50°54'N 1°23'W 17 6E
Southend-on-Sea 51°32'N 0°44' E 17 5G
Southern Alps 43°41'S 170°11' E 55 10P
Southern Ocean 62° 0'S 60° 0' E 69 8N
Southern Uplands 55°28'N 3°52'W 18 4E
Southport 53°39'N 3° 0'W 16 3D
Spain ■ 39° 0'N 4° 0'W 33 12G
Spalding 52°48'N 0° 9'W 16 4F
Sparta 37° 5'N 22°25' E 35 4H
Spencer Gulf 34° 0'S 137°20' E 54 8G
Sperrin Mountains 54°50'N 7° 0'W 19 2D
Spey → 57°40'N 3° 6'W 18 2E
Sporades 39° 0'N 24°30' E 35 4H
Springfield 39°48'N 89°39'W 59 3J
Spurn Head 53°35'N 0° 8' E 16 3G
Sredinnyy Range 57° 0'N 160° 0' E 41 4R
Sri Jayewardenepura Kotte 6°56'N 79°58' E 46 6G
Sri Lanka ■ 7°30'N 80°50' E 46 6G
Srinagar 34° 5'N 74°50' E 46 3F
Staffa 56°27'N 6°21'W 18 3B
Stafford 52°49'N 2° 7'W 16 4D
Staffordshire 52°53'N 2°10'W 15 5E
Staines-upon-Thames 51°26'N 0°29'W 17 5F
Stamford 52°39'N 0°29'W 17 4F
Stanley 51°40'S 59°51'W 65 9F
Stanovoy Range 55° 0'N 130° 0' E 41 4N
Start Point 50°13'N 3°39'W 17 6C
Stavanger 58°57'N 5°40' E 31 4B
Stavropol 45° 5'N 42° 0' E 35 2M
Stevenage 51°55'N 0°13'W 17 5F
Stewart Island 46°58'S 167°54' E 55 11N
Stirling 56° 8'N 3°57'W 18 3E
Stockholm 59°19'N 18° 4' E 31 4D
Stockport 53°25'N 2° 9'W 16 3D
Stockton-on-Tees 54°35'N 1°19'W 16 2E
Stoke-on-Trent 53° 1'N 2°11'W 16 3D
Stonehaven 56°59'N 2°12'W 18 3F
Stonehenge 51° 9'N 1°45'W 17 5E
Stornoway 58°13'N 6°23'W 18 1B
Storsjön 63° 9'N 14°30' E 31 3C
Stour →, *Dorset* 50°43'N 1°47'W 17 6D
Stour →, *Suffolk* 51°57'N 1° 4' E 17 5H
Stourbridge 52°28'N 2° 8'W 17 4D
Stowmarket 52°12'N 1° 0' E 17 4G
Strabane 54°45'N 7°25'W 19 2D
Stranraer 54°54'N 5° 1'W 18 5C
Strasbourg 48°35'N 7°42' E 33 8M
Stratford-upon-Avon 52°12'N 1°42'W 17 4E
Strath Spey 57° 9'N 3°49'W 18 2E
Strathmore 56°37'N 3° 7'W 18 3E
Strómboli 38°47'N 15°13' E 36 5E
Stromeferry 57°21'N 5°33'W 18 2C
Stronsay 59° 7'N 2°35'W 18 7F
Stroud 51°45'N 2°13'W 17 5D
Sturt Stony Desert 28°30'S 141° 0' E 54 7G
Stuttgart 48°48'N 9°11' E 33 8N
Sucre 19° 0'S 65°15'W 65 5E
Sudan ■ 15° 0'N 30° 0' E 51 4F
Suez 29°58'N 32°31' E 48 4B
Suez Canal 31° 0'N 32°20' E 48 3B
Suffolk 52°16'N 1° 0' E 15 5G
Şuḩār 24°20'N 56°40' E 48 5G
Suining 30°26'N 105°35' E 42 3E
Sukhumi 43° 0'N 41° 0' E 35 3M
Sullom Voe 60°27'N 1°20'W 18 8J
Sulu Archipelago 6° 0'N 121° 0' E 47 6L
Sulu Sea 8° 0'N 120° 0' E 47 6K
Sumatra 0°40'N 100°20' E 47 6J
Sumba 9°45'S 119°35' E 47 7L
Sumbawa 8°26'S 117°30' E 47 7K
Sumburgh Head 59°52'N 1°17'W 18 7J
Sumy 50°57'N 34°50' E 35 1K
Sunda Islands 5° 0'S 105° 0' E 47 7K
Sunderland 54°55'N 1°23'W 16 2E
Sundsvall 62°23'N 17°17' E 31 3D
Sungari → 47°45'N 132°30' E 43 2H
Superior, Lake 47° 0'N 87° 0'W 59 1J
Surabaya 7°17'S 112°45' E 47 7K
Surat 21°12'N 72°55' E 46 4F
Surgut 61°14'N 73°20' E 40 3H
Suriname ■ 4° 0'N 56° 0'W 65 3F
Surrey 51°15'N 0°31'W 15 6F
Sutherland 58°12'N 4°50'W 18 1D
Sutton Coldfield 52°35'N 1°49'W 17 4E
Sutton in Ashfield 53° 8'N 1°16'W 16 3E
Suva 18° 6'S 178°30' E 55 5Q
Suzhou 31°19'N 120°38' E 43 3G
Svalbard 78° 0'N 17° 0' E 67 8B
Svealand 60°20'N 15° 0' E 31 3C
Swale → 54° 5'N 1°20'W 16 2E
Swanage 50°36'N 1°58'W 17 6D
Swansea 51°37'N 3°57'W 17 5C
Sweden ■ 57° 0'N 15° 0' E 31 3D
Swilly, Lough 55°12'N 7°33'W 19 1D
Swindon 51°34'N 1°46'W 17 5E
Switzerland ■ 46°30'N 8° 0' E 33 9M
Swords 53°28'N 6°13'W 19 3E
Sydney 33°52'S 151°12' E 54 8K
Syktyvkar 61°45'N 50°40' E 40 3F
Syrdarya → 46° 3'N 61° 0' E 40 5G
Syria ■ 35° 0'N 38° 0' E 48 3C
Syrian Desert 32° 0'N 40° 0' E 48 3C
Szczecin 53°27'N 14°27' E 31 5C

T

Tabrīz 38° 7'N 46°20' E 48 2E
Tabūk 28°23'N 36°36' E 48 4C
Tacheng 46°40'N 82°58' E 42 2C
Taff → 51°28'N 3°11'W 17 5C
Tagus → 38°40'N 9°24'W 33 13D
Tahiti 17°37'S 149°27'W 68 5C
Taichung 24° 9'N 120°37' E 43 4G
Taimyr Peninsula 75° 0'N 100° 0' E 41 2K
Tain 57°49'N 4° 4'W 18 2D
Taipei 25° 4'N 121°29' E 43 4G
Taiwan ■ 23°30'N 121° 0' E 43 4G
Taiyuan 37°52'N 112°33' E 43 3F
Taizhou 28°40'N 121°24' E 43 4G
Tajikistan ■ 38°30'N 70° 0' E 40 6G
Takamatsu 34°20'N 134° 5' E 45 4B
Taklamakan Desert 38° 0'N 83° 0' E 42 3C
Tallahassee 30°27'N 84°17'W 59 4K
Tallinn 59°22'N 24°48' E 31 4E
Tamale 9°22'N 0°50'W 52 2A
Tamar → 50°27'N 4°15'W 17 6B
Tampa 27°56'N 82°27'W 59 5K
Tampere 61°30'N 23°50' E 31 3E
Tampico 22°13'N 97°51'W 62 3E

Tamworth 31° 7′S 150°58′E 54 8K
Tana →, *Kenya* 2°32′S 40°31′E 53 3C
Tana →, *Norway* 70°30′N 28°14′E 31 2F
Tana, Lake 13° 5′N 37°30′E 50 4F
Tanami Desert 18°50′S 132° 0′E 54 5F
Tanganyika, Lake 6°40′S 30° 0′E 50 6F
Tangier 35°50′N 5°49′W 34 4B
Tangshan 39°38′N 118°10′E 43 3F
Tanimbar Islands 7°30′S 131°30′E 47 7M
Tanzania ■ 6° 0′S 34° 0′E 51 6F
Tapajós → 2°24′S 54°41′W 66 3E
Táranto 40°28′N 17°14′E 36 4F
Táranto, Gulf of 40° 8′N 17°20′E 36 4F
Taraz 42°54′N 71°22′E 40 5H
Tarim Basin 40° 0′N 84° 0′E 42 2C
Tarragona 41° 5′N 1°17′E 33 12J
Tashkent 41°20′N 69°10′E 40 5G
Tasman Sea 36° 0′S 160° 0′E 55 9L
Tasmania 42° 0′S 146°30′E 54 10J
Taunton 51° 1′N 3° 5′W 17 5C
Taurus Mountains 37° 0′N 32°30′E 35 4K
Taw → 51° 4′N 4° 4′W 17 6C
Tay → 56°37′N 3°38′W 18 3E
Tay, Firth of 56°25′N 3° 8′W 18 3F
Tbilisi 41°43′N 44°50′E 48 1D
Tees → 54°37′N 1°10′W 16 2E
Tegucigalpa 14° 5′N 87°14′W 62 5G
Tehrān 35°41′N 51°25′E 48 2F
Tehuantepec, Gulf of 15°50′N 95°12′W 62 4F
Tehuantepec, Isthmus of 17°15′N 94°30′W 62 4F
Teifi → 52° 5′N 4°41′W 17 4B
Teign → 50°32′N 3°32′W 17 6C
Teignmouth 50°33′N 3°31′W 17 6C
Tel Aviv-Jaffa 32° 4′N 34°48′E 48 3B
Teles Pires → 7°21′S 58° 3′W 66 4D
Telford 52°40′N 2°27′W 16 4D
Tema 5°41′N 0° 0′W 52 2B
Teme → 52°11′N 2°13′W 17 4D
Temuco 38°45′S 72°40′W 65 7D
Tennant Creek 19°30′S 134°15′E 54 5F
Tennessee 36° 0′N 86°30′W 59 3J
Tennessee → 37° 4′N 88°34′W 59 3J
Teófilo Otoni 17°50′S 41°30′W 66 6G
Teresina 5° 9′S 42°45′W 66 4G
Terni 42°34′N 12°37′E 36 3D
Test → 50°56′N 1°29′W 17 5E
Tétouan 35°35′N 5°21′W 34 4B
Teviot → 55°29′N 2°38′W 18 4F
Tewkesbury 51°59′N 2° 9′W 17 4D
Texas 31°40′N 98°30′W 58 4F
Thailand ■ 16° 0′N 102° 0′E 47 5J
Thailand, Gulf of 11°30′N 101° 0′E 47 5J
Thame → 51°39′N 1° 9′W 17 5E
Thames → 51°29′N 0°34′E 17 5G
Thames Estuary 51°29′N 0°52′E 17 5H
Thar Desert 28° 0′N 72° 0′E 46 4F
Thessaloniki 40°38′N 22°58′E 35 3H
Thetford 52°25′N 0°45′E 17 4G
Thika 1° 1′S 37° 5′E 53 3B
Thimphu 27°31′N 89°45′E 46 4G
Thirsk 54°14′N 1°19′W 16 2E
Three Gorges Dam 30°45′N 111°15′E 43 3F
Thurrock 51°31′N 0°23′E 15 6G
Thurso 58°36′N 3°32′W 18 1E
Thurston Island 72° 0′S 100° 0′W 67 16E
Tian Shan 40°30′N 76° 0′E 42 2C
Tianjin 39° 7′N 117°12′E 43 3F
Tianshui 34°32′N 105°40′E 42 3E
Tiber → 41°44′N 12°14′E 36 3D
Tibesti 21° 0′N 17°30′E 50 3D
Tibet 32° 0′N 88° 0′E 42 3C
Tibet, Plateau of 32° 0′N 86° 0′E 46 3G
Tierra del Fuego 54° 0′S 67°45′W 64 9E
Tigris → 31° 0′N 47°25′E 48 3E
Tijuana 32°32′N 117° 1′W 62 1A
Timbuktu 16°50′N 3° 0′W 51 4B
Timişoara 45°43′N 21°15′E 35 2H
Timor 9° 0′S 125° 0′E 38 9P
Timor-Leste ■ 8°50′S 126° 0′E 47 7L
Tipperary 52°28′N 8°10′W 19 4C
Tirana 41°18′N 19°49′E 35 3G
Tiree 56°31′N 6°55′W 18 3B
Tiruchchirappalli 10°45′N 78°45′E 46 5F
Titicaca, Lake 15°30′S 69°30′W 64 5E
Tiverton 50°54′N 3°29′W 17 6C
Tobermory 56°38′N 6° 5′W 18 3B
Tocantins 10° 0′S 48° 0′W 66 5F
Tocantins → 1°45′S 49°10′W 66 3F
Togliatti 53°32′N 49°24′E 40 4E
Togo ■ 8°30′N 1°35′E 52 2B
Tokelau Islands 9° 0′S 171°45′W 55 3S
Tōkyō 35°43′N 139°45′E 45 3C
Toledo, *Spain* 39°50′N 4° 2′W 33 13G
Toledo, *U.S.A.* 41°39′N 83°33′W 59 2K
Tombigbee → 31° 8′N 87°57′W 59 4J
Tomsk 56°30′N 85° 5′E 40 4H
Tonbridge 51°11′N 0°17′E 17 5G
Tonga ■ 19°50′S 174°30′W 55 5S
Tonga Trench 18° 0′S 173° 0′W 55 5S
Tonkin, Gulf of 20° 0′N 108° 0′E 47 5J
Toowoomba 27°32′S 151°56′E 54 7K
Topeka 39° 3′N 95°40′W 59 3G
Torbay 50°26′N 3°31′W 17 6C
Torfaen 51°43′N 3° 3′W 15 6E
Toronto 43°39′N 79°20′W 59 2L
Torquay 50°27′N 3°32′W 17 6C
Torrens, Lake 31° 0′S 137°50′E 54 8G
Torreón 25°33′N 103°26′W 62 2D
Torres Strait 9°50′S 142°20′E 54 4H
Torridge → 51° 0′N 4°13′W 17 6B
Torridon, Loch 57°35′N 5°50′W 18 2C
Tórshavn 62° 5′N 6°56′W 32 1E
Tory Island 55°16′N 8°14′W 19 1C
Tottori 35°30′N 134°15′E 45 3B
Toubkal, Djebel 31° 0′N 8° 0′W 50 2B
Toulon 43°10′N 5°55′E 33 11L
Toulouse 43°37′N 1°27′E 33 11J
Tours 47°22′N 0°40′E 33 9J
Townsville 19°15′S 146°45′E 54 5J
Toyama 36°40′N 137°15′E 45 3C
Trabzon 41° 0′N 39°45′E 35 3L
Tralee 52°16′N 9°42′W 19 4B
Tramore 52°10′N 7°10′W 19 4D
Transantarctic Mountains 85° 0′S 170° 0′W 67 12F
Transylvanian Alps 45°30′N 25° 0′E 35 2H
Trent → 53°41′N 0°42′W 16 3F
Trento 46° 4′N 11° 8′E 36 1C
Trenton 40°14′N 74°46′W 59 2M
Trieste 45°40′N 13°46′E 36 2D
Trinidad & Tobago ■ 10°30′N 61°20′W 63 5M
Trinity → 29°45′N 94°43′W 59 5H
Tripoli, *Lebanon* 34°31′N 35°50′E 48 3C
Tripoli, *Libya* 32°49′N 13° 7′E 51 2D
Tristan da Cunha 37° 6′S 12°20′W 68 6J
Tromsø 69°40′N 18°56′E 31 2D
Trondheim 63°36′N 10°25′E 31 3C
Troon 55°33′N 4°39′W 18 4D
Trowbridge 51°18′N 2°12′W 17 5D
Troy 39°57′N 26°12′E 35 4J
Troyes 48°19′N 4° 3′E 33 8L
Trujillo 8° 6′S 79° 0′W 65 4D
Truro 50°16′N 5° 4′W 17 6A
Tsavo 2°59′S 38°28′E 53 3B
Tucson 32°13′N 110°58′W 58 4D
Tula 54°13′N 37°38′E 40 4D
Tullamore 53°16′N 7°31′W 19 3D
Tulsa 36°10′N 95°55′W 59 3G
Tunis 36°50′N 10°11′E 51 2D
Tunisia ■ 33°30′N 9°10′E 51 2C
Turfan 43°58′N 89°10′E 42 2C
Turfan Basin 42°40′N 89°25′E 42 2C
Turin 45° 3′N 7°40′E 36 2A
Turkana, Lake 3°30′N 36° 5′E 53 2B
Turkey ■ 39° 0′N 36° 0′E 35 4K
Türkmenbashi 40° 5′N 53° 5′E 40 5F
Turkmenistan ■ 39° 0′N 59° 0′E 40 6F
Turks & Caicos Islands 21°20′N 71°20′W 63 3K
Turku 60°30′N 22°19′E 31 3E
Turriff 57°32′N 2°27′W 18 2F
Tuvalu ■ 8° 0′S 178° 0′E 55 3Q
Tuxtla Gutiérrez 16°45′N 93° 7′W 62 4F
Tuz Gölü 38°42′N 33°18′E 35 4K
Tver 56°55′N 35°59′E 31 4H
Tweed → 55°45′N 2° 0′W 18 4F
Tyne → 54°59′N 1°32′W 16 2E
Tyne & Wear 55° 6′N 1°17′W 15 4F
Tynemouth 55° 1′N 1°26′W 16 1E
Tyrrhenian Sea 40° 0′N 12°30′E 36 4D
Tyumen 57°11′N 65°29′E 40 4G
Tywi → 51°48′N 4°21′W 17 5B

U

Uaupés → 0° 2′N 67°16′W 66 3B
Uberlândia 19° 0′S 48°20′W 66 6F
Ucayali → 4°30′S 73°30′W 64 4D
Udine 46° 3′N 13°14′E 36 1D
Uganda ■ 2° 0′N 32° 0′E 51 5F
Ukhta 63°34′N 53°41′E 40 3F
Ukraine ■ 49° 0′N 32° 0′E 35 2K
Ulan Bator 47°55′N 106°53′E 42 5B
Ulan Ude 51°45′N 107°40′E 41 4L
Ullapool 57°54′N 5° 9′W 18 2C
Ullswater 54°34′N 2°52′W 16 2D
Ulm 48°23′N 9°58′E 33 8N
Ulster 54°35′N 6°30′W 19 2E
Uluru 25°23′S 131° 5′E 54 7F
Ulverston 54°13′N 3° 5′W 16 2C
Ulyanovsk 54°20′N 48°25′E 40 4E
Umeå 63°45′N 20°20′E 31 3E
United Arab Emirates ■ 23°50′N 54° 0′E 48 5F
United Kingdom ■ 53° 0′N 2° 0′W 32 5H
United States of America ■ 37° 0′N 96° 0′W 57 6K
Unst 60°44′N 0°53′W 18 8K
Uppsala 59°53′N 17°38′E 31 4D
Ural → 47° 0′N 51°48′E 40 5F
Ural Mountains 60° 0′N 59° 0′E 38 4F
Ure → 54° 5′N 1°20′W 16 2E
Urmia 37°40′N 45° 0′E 48 2D
Urmia, Lake 37°50′N 45°30′E 48 2E
Uruguaiana 29°50′S 57° 0′W 66 8D
Uruguay ■ 32°30′S 56°30′W 65 7F
Uruguay → 34°12′S 58°18′W 64 7F
Ürümqi 43°45′N 87°45′E 42 2C
Usk → 51°33′N 2°58′W 17 5C
Ussuri → 48°27′N 135° 0′E 43 2H
Ust-Ilimsk 58° 3′N 102°39′E 41 4L
Ust Shchugor 64°16′N 57°36′E 40 3F
Ustyurt Plateau 44° 0′N 55° 0′E 38 4G
Utah 39°20′N 111°30′W 58 3D
Utrecht 52° 5′N 5° 8′E 32 6L
Utsunomiya 36°30′N 139°50′E 45 3C
Uvs Nuur 50°20′N 92°30′E 42 1D
Uyo 5° 1′S 7°53′E 52 2C
Uzbekistan ■ 41°30′N 65° 0′E 40 5G

V

Vaasa 63° 6′N 21°38′E 31 3E
Vadodara 22°20′N 73°10′E 46 4F
Vadsø 70° 3′N 29°50′E 31 1F
Vaduz 47° 8′N 9°31′E 33 9N
Valence 44°57′N 4°54′E 33 10L
Valencia, *Spain* 39°27′N 0°23′W 33 13H
Valencia, *Venezuela* 10°11′N 68° 0′W 63 5L
Valencia Island 51°54′N 10°22′W 19 5A
Valladolid 41°38′N 4°43′W 33 12F
Valledupar 10°29′N 73°15′W 63 5K
Valletta 35°54′N 14°31′E 34 4F
Valparaíso 33° 2′S 71°40′W 65 7D
Van 38°30′N 43°20′E 48 2D
Van, Lake 38°30′N 43° 0′E 48 2D
Vancouver 49°15′N 123° 7′W 58 1B
Väner, Lake 58°47′N 13°30′E 31 4C
Vanuatu ■ 15° 0′S 168° 0′E 55 5N
Varanasi 25°22′N 83° 0′E 46 4G
Vardø 70°23′N 31° 5′E 31 1G
Varna 43°13′N 27°56′E 35 3J
Västerås 59°37′N 16°38′E 31 4D
Vatican City ■ 41°54′N 12°27′E 36 4C
Vätter, Lake 58°25′N 14°30′E 31 4C
Venezuela ■ 8° 0′N 66° 0′W 63 6L
Venice 45°27′N 12°21′E 36 2D
Veracruz 19°11′N 96° 8′W 62 4E
Verkhoyansk 67°35′N 133°25′E 41 3P
Verkhoyansk Range 66° 0′N 129° 0′E 41 3N
Vermont 44° 0′N 73° 0′W 59 2M
Verona 45°27′N 10°59′E 36 2C
Vesterålen 68°45′N 15° 0′E 31 2C
Vesuvius, Mount 40°49′N 14°26′E 36 4E
Vicenza 45°33′N 11°33′E 36 2C
Victoria, *Australia* 37° 0′S 144° 0′E 54 9H
Victoria, *Canada* 48°30′N 123°25′W 58 1B
Victoria, *Seychelles* 4°38′S 55°28′E 46 7D
Victoria, Lake 1° 0′S 33° 0′E 50 6F
Victoria Falls 17°58′S 25°52′E 50 7E
Victoria Island 71° 0′N 111° 0′W 56 2H
Victoria Land 75° 0′S 160° 0′E 67 11E
Vienna 48°12′N 16°22′E 35 2G
Vientiane 17°58′N 102°36′E 47 5J
Vietnam ■ 19° 0′N 106° 0′E 47 5J
Vigo 42°12′N 8°41′W 33 11D
Villahermosa 17°59′N 92°55′W 62 4F
Vilnius 54°38′N 25°19′E 31 5F
Vinnytsya 49°15′N 28°30′E 35 2J
Vinson Massif 78°35′S 85°25′W 67 16E
Virgin Islands 18°30′N 64°30′W 63 4M
Virginia 37°30′N 78°45′W 59 3L
Vishakhapatnam 17°45′N 83°20′E 46 5G
Vistula → 54°22′N 18°55′E 31 5D
Viti Levu 17°30′S 177°30′E 55 5Q
Vitória 20°20′S 40°22′W 66 7G
Vitória da Conquista 14°51′S 40°51′W 66 5G
Vitsyebsk 55°10′N 30°15′E 31 4G
Vladivostok 43°10′N 131°53′E 41 5P
Voi 3°25′S 38°32′E 53 3B
Volga → 46° 0′N 48°30′E 38 5E
Volgograd 48°40′N 44°25′E 38 5E
Volta → 5°46′N 0°41′E 52 2B
Volta, Lake 7°30′N 0° 0′W 52 2B
Vorkuta 67°48′N 64°20′E 41 3G
Voronezh 51°47′N 33°28′E 40 4D
Vyborg 60°43′N 28°47′E 31 3F
Vyrnwy, Lake 52°48′N 3°31′W 16 4C

W

Wagga Wagga 35° 7′S 147°24′E 54 9J
Wakayama 34°15′N 135°15′E 45 4C
Wakefield 53°41′N 1°29′W 16 3E
Wales 52°19′N 4°43′W 17 4C
Wallasey 53°25′N 3° 2′W 16 3C
Wallis & Futuna 13°18′S 176°10′W 55 4R
Walney, Isle of 54° 6′N 3°15′W 16 2C
Walsall 52°35′N 1°58′W 17 4E
Wanxian 30°42′N 108°20′E 42 3E
Warrego → 30°24′S 145°21′E 54 8J
Warrenpoint 54° 6′N 6°15′W 19 2E
Warri 5°30′N 5°41′E 52 2C
Warrington 53°24′N 2°35′W 16 3D
Warsaw 52°14′N 21° 0′E 31 5E
Warwick 52°18′N 1°35′W 17 4E
Warwickshire 52°14′N 1°38′W 15 5F
Wash, The 52°58′N 0°20′E 16 3G
Washington, *U.K.* 54°55′N 1°30′W 16 2E
Washington, *U.S.A.* 47°30′N 120°30′W 58 1B
Washington, *D.C., U.S.A.* 38°53′N 77° 2′W 59 3L
Washington, Mount 44°16′N 71°18′W 59 2M
Waterford 52°15′N 7° 8′W 19 4D
Watford 51°40′N 0°24′W 17 5F
Waveney → 52°35′N 1°39′E 17 4H
Wear → 54°55′N 1°23′W 16 2D
Weddell Sea 72°30′S 40° 0′W 67 1E
Welland → 52°51′N 0° 5′W 17 4F
Wellingborough 52°19′N 0°41′W 17 4F
Wellington, *N.Z.* 41°19′S 174°46′E 55 10P
Wellington, *U.K.* 50°58′N 3°13′W 17 6C
Wells-next-the-Sea 52°57′N 0°51′E 16 4G
Welshpool 52°39′N 3° 8′W 17 4C
Welwyn Garden City 51°48′N 0°12′W 17 5F
Wensleydale 54°17′N 2° 0′W 16 2E
Wenzhou 28° 0′N 120°38′E 43 4G
Weser → 53°36′N 8°28′E 32 6N
West Antarctica 80° 0′S 90° 0′W 67 16F
West Bank 32° 6′N 35°13′E 35 5L
West Bromwich 52°32′N 1°59′W 17 4D
West Lothian 55°54′N 3°36′W 15 4E
West Midlands 52°26′N 2° 0′W 15 5E
West Northamptonshire 52° 8′N 0°59′W 15 5F
West Siberian Plain 62° 0′N 75° 0′E 40 3H
West Sussex 50°55′N 0°30′W 15 6F
West Virginia 38°45′N 80°30′W 59 3K
West Yorkshire 53°45′N 1°40′W 15 5F
Western Australia 25° 0′S 118° 0′E 54 7C
Western Dvina → 57° 4′N 24° 3′E 31 4F
Western Ghats 14° 0′N 75° 0′E 46 5F
Western Sahara 25° 0′N 13° 0′W 51 3A
Westhill 57° 9′N 2°19′W 18 2F
Westmeath 53°33′N 7°34′W 15 5C
Weston-super-Mare 51°21′N 2°58′W 17 5D
Westport 53°48′N 9°31′W 19 3B
Westray 59°18′N 3° 0′W 18 7F
Wewak 3°38′S 143°41′E 54 2H
Wexford 52°20′N 6°25′W 19 4E
Wey → 51°22′N 0°27′W 17 5F
Weymouth 50°37′N 2°28′W 17 6D
Whalsay 60°22′N 0°59′W 18 8K
Wharfe → 53°51′N 1° 9′W 16 3E
Wharfedale 54° 6′N 2° 1′W 16 2D
Whernside 54°14′N 2°24′W 16 2D
Whitby 54°29′N 0°37′W 16 2F
White Nile → 15°38′N 32°31′E 50 4F
White Sea 66°30′N 38° 0′E 31 2H
White Volta → 9°10′N 1°15′W 52 2A
Whitehaven 54°33′N 3°35′W 16 2C
Whitley Bay 55° 3′N 1°27′W 16 1E
Whitney, Mount 36°35′N 118°18′W 58 3C
Wichita 37°42′N 97°20′W 59 3G
Wick 58°26′N 3° 5′W 18 1E
Wicklow 52°59′N 6° 3′W 19 4E
Wicklow Mountains 52°58′N 6°26′W 19 4E
Widnes 53°23′N 2°45′W 16 3D
Wiesbaden 50° 4′N 8°14′E 32 7N
Wigan 53°33′N 2°38′W 16 3D
Wight, Isle of 50°41′N 1°17′W 17 6E
Wigtown 54°53′N 4°27′W 18 5D
Wilkes Land 69° 0′S 120° 0′E 67 9D
Willemstad 12° 5′N 68°55′W 63 5L
Wiltshire 51°18′N 1°53′W 15 6F
Winchester 51° 4′N 1°18′W 17 5E
Windermere 54°23′N 2°55′W 16 2D
Windhoek 22°35′S 17° 4′E 51 8D
Windrush → 51°43′N 1°24′W 17 5E
Windsor 51°29′N 0°36′W 17 5F
Windward Islands 13° 0′N 61° 0′W 63 5M
Winnipeg 49°54′N 97° 9′W 57 5R
Winnipeg, Lake 52° 0′N 97° 0′W 56 4K
Winsford 53°12′N 2°31′W 16 3D
Wisbech 52°41′N 0° 9′E 16 4G
Wisconsin 44°45′N 89°30′W 59 2J
Witham → 52°59′N 0° 2′W 16 3F
Withernsea 53°44′N 0° 1′E 16 3G
Woking 51°19′N 0°34′W 17 5F
Wokingham 51°25′N 0°51′W 15 6F
Wollongong 34°25′S 150°54′E 54 8K
Wolverhampton 52°35′N 2° 7′W 17 4D
Worcester 52°11′N 2°12′W 17 4D
Workington 54°39′N 3°33′W 16 2C
Worksop 53°18′N 1° 7′W 16 3E
Worthing 50°49′N 0°21′W 17 6F
Wrangel Island 71° 0′N 180° 0′E 67 17B
Wrath, Cape 58°38′N 5° 1′W 18 1C
Wrexham 53° 3′N 3° 0′W 16 3C
Wrocław 51° 5′N 17° 5′E 31 5D
Wuhan 30°31′N 114°18′E 43 3F
Würzburg 49°46′N 9°55′E 32 8P
Wuwei 37°57′N 102°34′E 42 3E
Wye → 51°38′N 2°40′W 17 5D
Wyndham 15°33′S 128° 3′E 54 5E
Wyoming 43° 0′N 107°30′W 58 2E

X

Xiamen 24°25′N 118° 4′E 43 4F
Xi'an 34°15′N 109° 0′E 43 3E
Xiangfan 32° 2′N 112° 8′E 43 3F
Xingu → 1°30′S 51°53′W 66 3E
Xining 36°34′N 101°40′E 42 3E
Xuzhou 34°18′N 117°10′E 43 3F

Y

Yablonovyy Range 53° 0′N 114° 0′E 41 4M
Yakutsk 62° 5′N 129°50′E 41 3N
Yalta 44°30′N 34°10′E 35 3K
Yamoussoukro 6°49′N 5°17′W 51 5B
Yanbu 'al Baḩr 24° 0′N 38° 5′E 48 5C
Yancheng 33°23′N 120° 8′E 43 3G
Yangôn 16°45′N 96°20′E 47 5H
Yangtse → 31°48′N 121°10′E 43 3G
Yanji 42°59′N 129°30′E 45 2A
Yantai 37°34′N 121°22′E 43 3G
Yaoundé 3°50′N 11°35′E 52 3D
Yaqui → 27°37′N 110°39′W 62 2B
Yare → 52°35′N 1°38′E 17 4H
Yaroslavl 57°35′N 39°55′E 40 4D
Yazd 31°55′N 54°27′E 48 3F
Yekaterinburg 56°50′N 60°30′E 40 4G
Yell 60°35′N 1° 5′W 18 8J
Yellow Sea 35° 0′N 123° 0′E 43 3G
Yellowknife 62°27′N 114°29′W 57 3H
Yellowstone National Park 44°40′N 110°30′W 58 2D
Yemen ■ 15° 0′N 44° 0′E 46 5C
Yenisey → 71°50′N 82°40′E 40 3H
Yeovil 50°57′N 2°38′W 17 6D
Yerevan 40°10′N 44°31′E 48 1D
Yinchuan 38°30′N 106°15′E 42 3E
Yokkaichi 34°55′N 136°38′E 45 4C
Yokohama 35°27′N 139°28′E 45 3C
Yongzhou 26°17′N 111°37′E 43 4F
York 53°58′N 1° 6′W 16 3E
York, Cape 10°42′S 142°31′E 54 4H
Yorkshire Wolds 54° 8′N 0°31′W 16 2F
Youghal 51°56′N 7°52′W 19 5D
Yü Shan 23°25′N 120°52′E 43 4G
Yucatán 20°50′N 89° 0′W 62 4G
Yucatán Channel 22° 0′N 86°30′W 62 3G
Yukon → 62°32′N 163°54′W 56 3C
Yulin 38°20′N 109°30′E 43 3E
Yumen 39°50′N 97°30′E 42 3D
Yuzhno-Sakhalinsk 46°58′N 142°45′E 41 5Q

Z

Zagreb 45°50′N 15°58′E 35 2G
Zagros Mountains 33°45′N 48° 5′E 48 3E
Zambezi → 18°35′S 36°20′E 50 7F
Zambia ■ 15° 0′S 28° 0′E 51 7E
Zamboanga 6°59′N 122° 3′E 47 6L
Zanjān 36°40′N 48°35′E 48 2E
Zanzibar 6°12′S 39°12′E 50 6F
Zaporizhzhye 47°50′N 35°10′E 35 2L
Zaragoza 41°39′N 0°53′W 33 12H
Zaria 11° 0′N 7°40′E 52 1C
Zaysan, Lake 48° 0′N 83° 0′E 40 5J
Zhangjiakou 40°48′N 114°55′E 43 2F
Zhangye 38°50′N 100°23′E 42 3E
Zhaotong 27°20′N 103°44′E 42 4E
Zhengzhou 34°45′N 113°34′E 43 3F
Zhezqazghan 47°44′N 67°40′E 40 5G
Zhytomyr 50°20′N 28°40′E 31 5F
Zibo 36°47′N 118° 3′E 43 3F
Zimbabwe ■ 19° 0′S 30° 0′E 51 7F
Zonguldak 41°28′N 31°50′E 35 3K
Zürich 47°22′N 8°32′E 33 9N